LONDON MIDLAND
&
SCOTTISH

Britain's Greatest Railway

by

Bill Horsfall

authorHOUSE®

AuthorHouse™ UK
1663 Liberty Drive
Bloomington, IN 47403 USA
www.authorhouse.co.uk
Phone: 0800.197.4150

© 2014 Bill Horsfall. All rights reserved.

No part of this book may be reproduced, stored in a retrieval system, or transmitted by any means without the written permission of the author.

Published by AuthorHouse 12/17/2014

ISBN: 978-1-4969-8178-3 (sc)
ISBN: 978-1-4969-8179-0 (hc)
ISBN: 978-1-4969-8185-1 (e)

Any people depicted in stock imagery provided by Thinkstock are models, and such images are being used for illustrative purposes only. Certain stock imagery © Thinkstock.

This book is printed on acid-free paper.

Because of the dynamic nature of the Internet, any web addresses or links contained in this book may have changed since publication and may no longer be valid. The views expressed in this work are solely those of the author and do not necessarily reflect the views of the publisher, and the publisher hereby disclaims any responsibility for them.

LONDON MIDLAND
& SCOTTISH

CONTENTS

Abbreviations vii
Select Bibliography ix
Foreword xi
Preface xiii
Introduction xix

PART I: The LMS: its formation and operation 1

Chapter 1: The Glory Days...3
Chapter 2: 1923: the Birth of the Empire 5
Chapter 3: 1932-39, The Stanier Years 32
Chapter 4: World War 2, 1939-45, And its Aftermath.................89
Chapter 5: LMS Achievements: Organization, Steam and
    Diesel Traction...100

PART II: A selection of LMS operations (1) 141

Chapter 6: The Leeds to Skipton line at Apperley Bridge.............143
Chapter 7: Leeds—Skipton (2): Skipton in the 1940s...................167
Chapter 8: The LMS In Halifax 202

PART III: Nationalization 1948 243

Chapter 9: The LMS and BR. Personalities and Influences 245
Chapter 10: 1958-62 292
Chapter 11: Steam Withdraws to its Last Redoubt:
    The LMS Triangle... 318
Chapter 12: What Might Have Been 363

ABBREVIATIONS

AEC	Associated Equipment Co., the London Transport bus-manufacturer
Atlantic	A locomotive having wheels arranged as 4-4-2; the middle four are driving-wheels
ASLOA	Association of Steam Locomotive Operators
Baltic	A locomotive having wheels arranged as 4-6-4; the six are driving-wheels
BEF	British Expeditionary Forces
BR	British Railways (the nationalized corporation wef. 1 January 1948)
CME	Chief Mechanical Engineer
CR	Caledonian Railway (constituent of the LMS wef 1 Jan 1923)
DB	Deutsche Bundesbahn (German Railways)
dbhp	Drawbar horsepower
down	The track leading from London, or the local HQ, e.g. the LYR from Manchester
ecml	East Coast Main Line (the LNER wef 1 January 1923)
EE	English Electric Co. Ltd.
FR	Furness Railways (constituent of the LMS wef 1 Jan 1923)
GCR	Great Central Railway (constituent of the LNER wef 1 Jan 1923)
GER	Great Eastern Railway (" ")
GNR	Great Northern Railway (" ")
GNSR	Great North of Scotland Railway (" ")
GSWR	Glasgow & South Western Railway (constituent of the LMS wef 1 Jan 1923)
GWR	Great Western Railway (on 1 Jan 1923 it absorbed minor Welsh railways)
HR	Highland Railway (constituent of the LMS wef 1 Jan 1923)
HST	High-Speed Train
IB	Intermediate-block signals, controlled from a neighbouring signal-box

LBSCR	London Brighton & South Coast Railway (constituent of the SR wef 1 Jan 1923)
LMS	London Midland & Scottish Railway, LMS (1 January 1923-31 December 1947)
LNER	London & North Eastern Railway, LNER (" ")
LNWR	London & North Western Railway (constituent of the LMS wef 1 Jan 1923)
LSWR	London & South Western Railway (constituent of the SR wef 1 Jan 1923)
LT	London Transport (formed in 1933 by merging bus-companies & Underground)
LYR	Lancashire & Yorkshire Railway (constituent of the LMS wef 1 Jan 1923)
M&GNR	Midland & Great Northern Railway, a joint Co. running from E Midlands-Norfolk
MPD	Motive-Power Depot
MR	Midland Railway (constituent of the LMS wef 1 Jan 1923)
NBR	North British Railway (constituent of the LNER wef 1 Jan 1923)
NCC	Northern Counties Committee, the ex-MR subsidiary operating out of Belfast, N.I.
NER	North Eastern Railway (constituent of the LNER wef 1 Jan 1923)
NSR	North Staffordshire Railway (constituent of the LMS wef 1 Jan 1923)
Pacific	A locomotive with wheels arranged as 4-6-2; the six are driving-wheels
S&DJR	Somerset & Dorset Joint Railway (operated jointly by LSWR/MR, later by SR/LMS)
SECR	South Eastern & Chatham Railway (constituent of the SR wef 1 Jan 1923)
SNCF	Société Nationale des Chemins de Fer Français (French Railways)
SO	Trains timetabled on Saturdays only
SR	Southern Railway (1 Jan 1923-31 Dec 1947); Southern Region of BR wef 1 Jan 1948
up	The track leading towards London, or the local HQ, e.g. the LYR towards Manchester
wcml	LNWR West Coast Main Line (LMS wef 1 Jan 1923)
WR	Western Region of British Railways from 1 January 1948 (mostly the former GWR)
WYPTE	West Yorkshire Public Transport Executive

SELECT BIBLIOGRAPHY

Allen, C.J., *Salute to the LMS* (Ian Allan, 1972)
Binns, D. *The Skipton-Colne Railway, the Barnoldswick Branch* (Trackside Publications, Skipton 1995).
Bellwood, J. & Jenkinson, D. *Gresley and Stanier* (HMSO, 1976)
Bloom, A., *Locomotives of the London Midland and Scottish Railway* (Jarrold Colour Publications, 1979)
Bulleid, H.A.V., *Master Builders of Steam* (Ian Allan 1963). [Stanier's LMS work]
Clay, J. F. *Jubilees of the LMS* (Ian Allan, 1971, 2nd impr 1974)
Dorman, C.C., *LMS Album* (Ian Allan, 1967), Vol.1. [Vols 2 & 3 below]
Ellis, C.H. *London Midland & Scottish* (Ian Allan, 1970)
Essery, R. & Jenkinson, D., *An Illustrated History of LMS Locomotives* Vol. One 'General Review & Loco Liveries' (Oxford Pub Co., 1981)
Ferneyhough, F., *The History of Railways in Britain* (Alban/Osprey Books, 1975)
Marshall, J. *The Lancashire & Yorkshire Railway*, vol.3 (David & Charles, 1972)
Nock, O.S. *A History of the LMS. 1. The First Years, 1923-30* (Allen & Unwin)
" " 2. *The Record-Breaking 'Thirties, 1931-39* "
" " 3. *The War Years and Nationalisation, 1939-48* " *The Royal Scots and Patriots of the LMS* (David & Charles, 1978)
" *The Railways of Britain* (Batsford, 1947)
" *William Stanier* (Ian Allan, 1964) [a biography]
Powell, A.J., *Stanier Locomotive Classes* (Ian Allan, 1991)
Rowledge, P., *Engines of the LMS built 1923-1951* (Oxford Publishing Co., 1975)
Stephenson, B., *LMS Album* No.2 (Ian Allan 1971) [See Vol 1 above]
" *LMS Album* No.3 (" 1973)
" *LMS Steam Portrait* (" 1985)
Tuffnell, R.M., *The British Railcar: AEC to HST* (David & Charles, 1984)
Whitehouse, P. & Thomas, D. St J., *LMS 150* (David & Charles, 1987)

FOREWORD

The LMS was a behemoth, by some margin the largest of the Big Four. In the mid-1930s it was the most highly capitalized joint-stock company in Britain, as well as being the country's second largest employer. The LMS was much more than a railway though, even if running trains—or more accurately, selling and providing train *services*—was always at the core of its business. Hotels, short-sea shipping, buses, road-freight and even air services, all brought the LMS into the lives of travellers and traders across much of the country. And then there were the huge engineering and manufacturing activities that provided jobs for tens of thousands and supplied many of the LMS's needs; the company's workshops alone made it one of the largest manufacturing enterprises in inter-war Britain. The LMS was a big player on a global scale too: some overseas railways could beat it hands down in terms of route mileage, but only a few, such as the USA's 'Standard Railroad', the mighty Pennsylvania, could match it in terms of the reach and complexity of its businesses and operations. It was no accident that Sir Josiah Stamp, brought in shortly after grouping as general manager, quickly adopted the American title of President along with a whole host of US management techniques as part of his long struggle to forge one railway out of the LMS's squabbling constituents. In this he was largely successful, and it is possible that, had the Second World War not put paid to the Square Deal, the LMS might have moved decisively to becoming a transport provider in the round, utilizing whatever mode best suited its customers' circumstances.

In any case, the LMS's very size, reach and complexity makes it a hard company to write about. We have C. Hamilton Ellis's useful overview, but that is over 40 years old now, and O.S. Nock's three brief volumes published in the early 1980s, although these are rather biased towards engineering and operational matters. Nothing wrong with that, but it does mean that we still lack a comprehensive understanding of what made the LMS tick as a business. No historian has been brave—or perhaps foolish—enough to attempt to evaluate the company's effectiveness across the whole range of its activities. The LMS Society does an excellent job casting light onto many facets, and various academics (myself included) have looked at others. Perhaps these articles are the building blocks that might one day be brought together into a systematic analysis.

Understandably, Bill Horsfall doesn't set himself this task. So why read this book? Because as well as reminding us of the range of LMS achievements, as a witness Bill brings so many facets of the company to life. He takes us back to the 1940s when he observed and travelled on a railway that, given the circumstances of war and immediate post-war austerity was certainly not at its best but which was still doing the job the grouping had intended for it. In short, we get a real sense of what the LMS was like from the point of view of its users—not only its "customers" (a description that the LMS used more and more frequently from the 1920s) but also from that of its younger admirers. The LMS well understood the value of encouraging this sort of thing. 'It is, of course, extremely important that the "young mind" should be taught to be "railway minded"' wrote one LMS man in the company's in-house magazine in 1933, noting that the 'boy of today is the traveller of tomorrow . . .' As Bill's fascinating and illuminating account shows, in his case the LMS publicity department certainly did a thorough job.

Professor Colin Divall
Institute of Railway Studies & Transport History, University of York

PREFACE

This work is my considered appreciation of the company sixty years or so after it was nationalized and attempts to answer the question, "Why another book on the LMS?"

The LMS was not a glamorous railway—in fact it was often seen as a lumbering giant—and therefore I am bringing it into the limelight to accord the credit it deserves for its achievements. I believe that my lifelong interest in railways, particularly in the LMS, equips me to offer the discerning reader a comprehensive story distinct from the huge range of book, art and magazine literature where the details are inevitably dispersed. Here, I bring them together, blending in my own experiences and analyses of the company's last decade before nationalization in 1948, a significant era that needs more focus. I present the available information from my own perspective to reveal the big picture. My analyses of LMS locomotive-stock and classes are unique, published here for the first time. Fascinating anecdotes, geographical notes and social comments add a special flavour. My viewpoint as an observer and traveller, plus archival research, represent an endeavour to share my passion for the LMS. However, this does not deflect me from objectivity in reaching my conclusions on its achievements. Among the many writers I have to thank for information, I must single out my acquaintance the late Mr O.S. Nock, whose books and articles still fascinate me. Further acknowledgements appear in the text. A select bibliography lists others, and the occasional footnote provides information on specific points. The technical details I give are comfortably within the ambit of the average railway *aficionado*, who is conversant with boiler-pressures, valve-gears, wheel-arrangements and so on.

Part I of the book addresses the question, 'What was the LMS?'
Part II describes 'The LMS in action', and finally its influence on the nationalized British Railways.

Part III, 'Nationalization and after', covers the post-1948 period, with visits to all the regions as steam-operations shrink to their last redoubt, 'The LMS Triangle'.

Part I begins with Sir Guy Granet's early reorganization of the management by appointing Sir Josiah Stamp (from 1928, Baron Stamp of Shortlands), shows the interplay of staff appointments and the design-work of the successive Chief Mechanical Engineers (CMEs). Since a railway's business is to haul trains, motive-power is vital, thus I focus upon the LMS locomotive fleet. However, the rolling-stock, managerial appointments, publicity, and the company's hotels and ships, are described in context. My observations, beginning during schooldays, are broadened with analyses of locomotive-classes, working-arrangements and numbering; they lead to discussions of LMS policy, the company's requirements and how they were met. This broad approach will, I believe, interest both long-time, informed, devotees, as well as younger enthusiasts, who of course did not have an opportunity of seeing the LMS at work. Observing a preserved locomotive in a yard, or even working on a restored branch-line—rather like a caged animal—is quite a different experience from watching the engines and trains during their working days. To ride an excursion hauled by a preserved LMS locomotive is the closest approach one can make now to its working life.

I have drawn on fascinating accounts of LMS events occurring before my time, or on distant parts of the network, and also through older friends' reminiscences of the company during its early, uncertain years. In this way I have learned about the 1920s, when the pre-grouping engines were running alongside the new locomotives by Hughes and Fowler, before William Stanier arrived to revitalize the company and bring it up to date. These observations extend the time-scale of the work to give my readers a similar pleasure.

Stanier's remit was to intensify Stamp's policy of 'build-and-scrap' by introducing a range of modern, standardized, efficient locomotives. Stamp, an administrator holding honours-degrees from British and American universities and an author in his own right, had been recruited from outside the railway-industry, a radical move, with a brief to reorganize the LMS out of its difficulties, principally the rivalry between its two largest constituents. In order to avoid continuing the strife by favouring one or the other, to appoint a locomotive engineer from outside the company was clearly the appropriate remedy. Following earlier examples, Stamp turned to the mature Great Western Railway, unique among the 'big four' companies in having been largely unaffected by the Grouping of 1923, and advanced in its technology, to bring in W.A. (later Sir William A.) Stanier, Principal Assistant to the CME at Swindon. With little chance of taking over the GWR driving-seat, it was Stanier's big opportunity, though not one he was seeking. Like his father, he was a Great Western man through and through. His selection by the LMS Executive makes fascinating reading. I outline Stanier's individual approach to design in order to demonstrate that, in the new field of diesel haulage as well as steam, he made the LMS the leader of Britain's railway-companies. In his biography *William Stanier,* Nock stresses Stanier's enthusiasm for machinery, his love of making things, and his high standards of workmanship. In the steam and diesel traction fields as well as others, I spotlight the LMS as a pioneer, which it owed to the work of earlier CMEs such as George Hughes, and then to Stanier, his assistants and successors. From his first day as CME of the LMS on 1 January 1932, Stanier concerned himself with the comfort of the footplate-crews. Another key facet of his character was his genial way of encouraging his staff to give of their best, to put old animosities behind them and to work positively for their company's future.

In this way, Stanier demonstrated leadership qualities, including his ability to pick the right men to create a cohesive team with a new loyalty, and the corporate image the company sorely needed. These dedicated men would continue his work of producing efficient and easily-maintained locomotives and rolling-stock long-term, rather than risk the usual policy-change after his retirement, perhaps only ten years ahead. The LNER, the principal competitor to the LMS, owed its success largely to the long service of H.N (later Sir Nigel) Gresley, the established locomotive-engineer of its constituent, the Great Northern Railway, who continued in that post for much of the LNER's existence. Stanier's lieutenants Ivatt and Riddles went on to design the last generation of steam engines built in Great Britain; I consider that Ivatt's diesel-electric express-locomotive of 1947 represented the company's crowning achievement. The BR diesel-electrics, from the humble 0-6-0 standard shunter to the stud of express-machines, stemmed from the pioneer-work carried out by the LMS during the 1930s.

Four distinct eras of the company can be identified:

1) the uncertain decade of the 1920s;
2) recovery under Stanier from 1932;
3) the further difficulties of the 1939-45 war-years;
4) and finally, determined progress recommencing even before the war ended, progress which intensified into the company's last days before nationalization in 1948.

Thus the company's life-span of a mere quarter-century ended—unlike its contemporaries—on a positive and powerful upward trajectory, fitting it to take the lead in the new BR. Its designer Robin Riddles became its CME, assisted by several former LMS men, deriving his standard classes from Stanier designs. LMS influence within BR was therefore dominant from the outset.

The photographs, from my collection and others acknowledged below, have been selected to reflect developments and the extent of the LMS network, and are mostly unpublished. Particularly in Parts I and II, they portray locomotives in their LMS liveries, a contrast with with other publications. Since at the end of its life, the LMS locomotive stock comprised as many as 144 classes of (many of them veterans retained on account of the 1939 war), pressure on space precludes a photograph of every type; however, the selection is representative. Further pictures depict rolling-stock and other LMS operations, the ships, hotels and stations in its huge empire. Concerning my own photographs, I must thank Mr David Nunn, photographer, for his efforts in upgrading some of my pictures taken of necessity in unfavourable conditions. Acknowledgements for other photographs are made to NRM, York; R.K. Blencowe in Somerset; ColourRail; Mortons Publishers; Getty Images and especially to Mr Richard Casserley for offering advice along with many photographs from his and his father's H.C. Casserley collections. For information, acknowledgements are made to Ordnance Survey, National Archive, Midland Railway Trust, Halifax Guardian, Halifax Courier & Guardian, Craven Herald & Pioneer, Yorkshire Post,

The Wyvern, Meccano Magazine and Railways. My grateful thanks also go to Professor Colin Divall of the University of York/The National Railway Museum for writing the Foreword.

Copyright is acknowledged where known and every effort has been made to trace all copyright holders. Concerning any oversights, they are invited to contact the author through the publishers to enable any errors to be corrected in future editions.

MR 2F 0-6-0 of 1878, 3477, passes ex-MR 1F 0-6-0 shunter 1855 of a similar vintage in the up Skipton exchange-sidings. The other three railways of Britain had also retained many machines of this age, due to several factors, such as the 1930s Trade Depression and WW2. The private-owner coal-wagons are notable (author).

Sir Josiah Stamp (afterwards Baron Stamp of Shortlands), President of the LMS from 1926 (National Rail Museum).

INTRODUCTION

AN OUTLINE OF BRITAIN'S RAILWAYS AND THE BIRTH OF THE LMS

The early difficulties of the LMS had their origin in the growth of Britain's railway system.

During the first world war, 1914-18, the government controlled the railways through its Railway Executive Committee. Its work quickly convinced chairman Sir Eric (later Lord) Geddes, a former General Manager of the North Eastern Railway, that a thorough reorganization was needed to fit the railways for the post-war era. Geddes became the first Minister of Transport.

During the industrial revolution, that great metamorphosis of the character of Britain through the development of steam-driven machinery in factories, scores of railway companies had grown up across the land, forming an important element that serviced trade and increased the momentum of industrialization. The Victorians idolized their railways and could not foresee anything to replace them. The reason was simple: the steam-locomotive was the first *machine* to move people and goods on land. Hitherto, throughout the history of mankind, all land transportation had been dependent upon muscle-power, such as a mule, a horse or a human. This is reflected in the words of Fanny Kemble, a music-hall artist and one of the celebrities carried on the Liverpool & Manchester Railway on its opening-day in 1830. Her words encapsulate the marvel of the age. "We were progressing without visible means, pulled along by the *magical machine* at the front. I felt perfectly secure with no fear at thirty miles per hour, and when I closed my eyes, the sensation was delightful, a feeling of flying." My italics emphasize the wonder she felt at the new, intangible, power transporting her.

Much later, during the Edwardian decade, between the Victorians and the 1914 war, significant changes were stirring in Britain, both sociological and technical. A technical transport advance particularly destined to affect the future of the railways was the pioneering work and commercial development of the internal combustion engine from the 1870s on the Continent of Europe. Whereas the steam engine was an *external* combustion machine, using fuel to boil water to make steam to drive the machine through cylinders and wheels, the new *internal* combustion engine's power came from liquid fuel, benzene (petrol), burned directly in its cylinders. This method reduced the stages and complications involved in converting fuel to power. During the Edwardian decade, the internal combustion engine in road-vehicles made a quantum leap from the temperamental contraptions of the nineteenth century to a dependable means of transport. By 1910, the number of motor-buses in London equalled horse-buses. In particular, the petrol-engined buses built for the London General Omnibus Company by its subsidiary The Associated Equipment Company (AEC) at Walthamstow, north-east London, were well-established on London's streets.

The second model of the AEC bus was even better, the 'B' class, introduced in 1910; these were the buses ferried over to Flanders to transport the troops of the British Expeditionary Force, seen in early cinema newsreels. They acquitted themselves well and paved the way for even better models. Wars accelerate technological advance, and so it was during 1914-18: thousands of motor-vehicles of different types were manufactured for the Ministry of Munitions. After the Armistice, most were sold on the open market as war surplus, bargains snapped up by men who now possessed capital—their gratuity—enabling them to start up a transport business. These men were among the thousands who had learned to drive motor vehicles and to maintain them in the army; they represented the seeds of future road competition against the railway monopoly.

From 1916, in the midst of the war, parliament had been considering the post-war role of the railways, recognizing that in those few wartime years the world was changing radically. The new situation had reduced the fear of monopoly power and revealed a fresh objective: to provide a better service, both for passengers and freight—and one provided by viable companies. Even speeches by King George V and by Lloyd

George, the wartime premier, sent out this message, promising 'no return to the old ways', a reference to unbridled capitalism and poor working-conditions. George Jackson Churchward, the long-serving Chief Mechanical Engineer of the Great Western Railway, encountered this sentiment during a speech outlining future developments he made to the workers at Swindon in 1920. They responded by telling him they now wanted representation, that is, a say in making decisions, rather than to have them handed down by management. Churchward, approaching his retirement anyway, bowed out.

The railways had been largely profitable, but the ending of the war in 1918 released the pent-up changes, which then swept through Britain, threatening railway profitability. Furthermore, maintenance of railways during the war had been reduced to a minimum, and the huge amounts of extra traffic had exacerbated the wear and tear. Capital expenditure was needed to restore their efficiency. With his practical experience, the dynamic Geddes had foreseen all this and that a thorough reorganization was needed. It would take time. Therefore Parliament temporarily retained control through its Railway Executive Committee. Any reorganization represented a radical swing of government policy towards control of industry, away from the nineteenth-century *laissez-faire*, or free-market, policy. Such a step was rational, not only in the economic context but also to eliminate harmful rivalries and overlapping interests. These had been allowed to develop with the aim of encouraging competition, since the rationale of nineteenth-century British governments had been to avoid monopoly at all costs. The result was that some towns had two- or even more—separate stations belonging to different companies, competing for a limited or fixed volume of traffic.

A White Paper by Sir Eric proposed gathering the 123 principal railways into seven groups. Their traditional monopoly, that of being the sole long-distance general carrier, faced a challenge from the road vehicle. The small railways, often in rural areas, were the most vulnerable to road competition, and faced declining profits, if not losses and outright bankruptcy. Partly to protect these small concerns, and partly to avoid nationalization, Parliament adopted Geddes' concept, to collect all the railways, save some minor lines, into a few large, geographical, units. Several schemes were put forward, ranging from amalgamations to outright nationalization, a scheme favoured by the trade unions. A group controlling Scotland's railways was dismissed as economically unviable, but another scheme proposed 'North West' and 'North East' groupings. This led to the idea of four large companies, called 'groups' of railways, straddling the boundaries of England, Wales and Scotland as the most likely to be commercially viable. It was a halfway stage, a typically-British compromise—to avoid too radical a change. It was adopted in the Act of 1921.

Merger-arrangements were to be completed on or before 1 January 1923 (though a few were later), which explains the amalgamation of the London & North Western (LNWR) and the Lancashire & Yorkshire (LYR) a year earlier. Actually, a hint of this merger had been the appointment of Sir Arthur Watson, General Manager of the LYR, to be GM of both companies from 1 January 1921. The Great Western Railway, GWR, a natural geographical entity (the triangle bounded by London-Penzance-Birkenhead), was left largely untouched, merely having to absorb small Welsh railways; it does however play an important part in our story. The smallest group, the Southern Railway, (SR), was formed by amalgamating the South Eastern & Chatham Railway with the London Brighton & South Coast Railway and the London & South Western Railway. The second-biggest concern was the 'North East' group, which took the name 'London & North Eastern Railway' (LNER), a combination of the North Eastern, Great Central, Great Eastern, Great Northern, North British and Great North of Scotland Railways plus a few minor lines. Uncertain over the presentation of its insignia—perhaps through the influence of the powerful North Eastern Railway—the initials 'NE' appeared on wagons and on some engines, but 'LNER' on most passenger-engines.

The largest amalgamation was the 'North-West, Midland and West Scottish' group, which adopted the title 'London Midland & Scottish Railway.' It comprised the London & North Western and the Lancashire & Yorkshire (already amalgamated in 1922), the Midland, Furness, North Staffordshire, Caledonian, Glasgow & South Western and Highland, plus a number of smaller concerns, the LMSR. After brief periods of showing simply the company-motif and then 'LM&SR' on locomotives, it adopted the initials LMS as its company insignia; its dismissal of the

'R' as superfluous can be seen as an early sign of the company's matter-of-fact approach. It was the very size of this conglomerate that proved to be a disadvantageous factor, at least at first. Added to this was the historic rivalry between the two largest constituents, the LNWR and MR, expressed through management policy, locomotive design and livery. These strands run through the story.

Standard 4F 0-6-0 goods-engine 4245 shunting the daily pick-up goods at Apperley Bridge, Leeds-Carlisle line, (author).

Sir W. Guy Granet, first Chairman of the LMS, 1923 (National Rail Museum).

Ex-LYR radial tank-engine 10793 on carriage-pilot duty at Preston, Lancashire in 1947. (author).

Mr W.A. Stanier (later Sir William A. Stanier, FRS), the CME of the LMS from 1 January 1932 (National Rail Museum).

Stanier 2-8-0 heavy-freight locomotive 8652 entering Skipton on through Carlisle freight in 1947, carrying an under-bufferbeam snow-plough, normal on this mountain line (author).

PART I

THE LMS: ITS FORMATION AND OPERATION

Derby-designed 2-6-2 3P tank-engine 21 at Hellifield is crossing to the south bay platform to haul a train to Blackburn. Withdrawal took place in 1959 in the first batch of this class to go (author).

Ex-MR 4-4-0 express locomotive 999, the last of a class of ten built specially for the Settle-Carlisle line (H.C. Casserley collection).

Ex-MR 3F 0-6-0 3351, a regular at Apperley Bridge, shunts the yard in 1947, when over 300 of these handy goods-engines were in operation.

Chapter 1

THE GLORY DAYS

The misery of the First World War sowed the seeds of creativity, in art, music and architecture, as people appreciated the value of life. An explosion of fun in the 1920s resulted. Speed was paramount, and new records were created on land, on water and in the air; the railways too wanted faster trains. Despite being disadvantaged by its hilly and curvy West Coast line, the LMS felt forced to compete with its rival for Scottish traffic the LNER, whose *Flying Scotsman*—a name deriving from stage-coach days—had created a non-stop record from Kings Cross to Edinburgh. The company had built prestige carriages for the service and its express-speeds were continually rising.

The LMS, once over its uncertain first decade and with Mr W.A. Stanier as Chief Mechanical Engineer, began to regain ground. His *Princess Elizabeth* pacific-locomotive broke records in 1936 with non-stop runs from London to Glasgow and back. The hiatus that year over the Edward VIII-Mrs Simpson affair ended with the coronation in 1937 of his brother King George VI, celebrated by the LMS with the Stanier 'super-pacific' train, *Coronation Scot (Duchess)*—also a response to the LNER *Silver Jubilee* train of 1935. The smooth curves of the art-deco movement were symbolized in new architecture: of houses, cinemas and factories—and in the Supermarine *Spitfire* fighter-plane, cars, motor-coaches and streamlined locomotives. On 5 July 1937, the inaugural run of *Coronation Scot* was extremely successful in maintaining a sustained high speed, though still short of the LNER's recent record of 113 mph.

It led to a press-run on 29 July from Euston to Crewe. From the start, high speeds were attained, but it was the final, thrilling, part of the journey that created a record. In an all-or-nothing throw, the LMS achieved 114 mph approaching Crewe, wresting the record from its arch-rival, the LNER. In fact, considerable potential remained, for *Coronation Scot* was still accelerating when he had to be braked on approaching Crewe. In a headline-grabbing speed-attempt, the LMS had been forced to demonstrate its mastery over the LNER, which had built a few prestigious trains concentrating on speed and luxury, making it iconic and fashionable. The LMS objective however, was to accelerate and modernize its services across the board. In its final years, after WW2, it was unique in completing this programme.

The LMS was robbed!

Compared with contemporary speed-records, these railway records are puzzling. First, they were gained on a single run, without a return trip; second, they were measured by themselves. In contrast, the cars, boats and aeroplanes had to make a return run within a short time over a measured mile, both runs timed by impartial observers. Furthermore, to render the competition fair, the two rivals should have had an equal chance by running over the same stretch of line. Nevertheless, the LMS indeed gained a record, revealed only much later, when its Duchess pacific was scientifically proved to be the most powerful express-passenger steam-locomotive in the country.

Stanier 2-6-2 3P 183 'the hoodoo engine' awaits duty at Hellifield, Leeds-Carlisle line (author).

Chapter 2

1923: THE BIRTH OF THE EMPIRE

The Introduction has described the reorganization of Britain's railways following the first world war ending in 1918, outlining the early difficulties of the LMS. Amalgamations of large-scale businesses are rarely consummated without undercurrents—a huge understatement in the case of the LMS group, and aggravated by the very size of the conglomerate. Underlying this was the historic rivalry between the two largest constituents, the London & North Western Railway (LNWR) and the Midland Railway (MR), expressed through management policy and locomotive design. As well as the LMS locomotive fleet, its rolling-stock, managerial-appointments, the company's hotels and steamships, and its pioneering-work in different fields, will be described in context. Strangely, the LMS had no coat of arms registered with the College of Heralds. Soon after its formation, the daughter of one of its officers designed a circular motif comprising the rose of England, a dragon's wing from the City of London's coat of arms and the Scottish thistle. It adorned posters, its locomotives in the early years and the panels of many carriages.

Chronologically, the history of the LMS falls naturally into four slots: the first decade, when the company failed to produce a corporate image and practical, long-term, policies; the halcyon years of 1932-9 cut short by WW2; the six years of war when once again all the railways fell under government control; and the final few, but triumphant, years preceding nationalization on 1 January 1948. These eras will now be described in turn.

The uncertain first decade, 1923-31

What was the LMS? It was a system of enormous size and complexity and with paradoxes: its crack Euston-Glasgow premier route (the wcml) contrasts with branch-lines up Pennine valleys to mills and mines, some greatly underused. It was the world's largest transport undertaking, the Empire's largest commercial conglomerate, and easily the biggest of Britain's four railways from 1923 to nationalization in 1948. It also possessed the Empire's largest hotel-chain, and was involved in every kind of industry, from engineering and land-development to shipping, bus—and air-services. As the most important railway, its activity reflected national activity. Concerned over the value of the pound in 1930, Prime Minister James Ramsay MacDonald quoted LMS traffic-receipts as a barometer of Britain's economic activity.

The first chairman of the board of directors was General The Rt Hon Charles Napier Lawrence, later, Lord Lawrence of Kingsgate (Broadstairs, Kent), with deputies Mr E.B. Fielden, from the Lancashire and Yorkshire Railway, (LYR), and Sir W. Guy Granet, Midland Railway, (MR). Granet had enjoyed a remarkable career. A barrister, he had succeeded Sir Henry Oakley as secretary of the Railway Companies Association in 1900 and, from Assistant General Manager of the MR in 1905, he rose to Chairman in 1922. After a year, Lawrence and Fielden resigned from office, Lawrence however remaining on the board, and Granet became chairman. The constituent-companies were represented by directors in proportion to their profitability in 1913, the last complete year of trading before the Great War; for example, the MR and the LNWR each had eight, but each constituent had at least one. This demonstrates that the MR had achieved equality with the mighty LNWR, 'The Premier Line', through its relentless expansion, explored in detail later. Sir Arthur Watson (LYR), the former GM of the combined LNWR and LYR, took the same position in the new Group. R.C. Irwin, Company Secretary of the LYR, and George Hughes, its CME, were appointed to the same posts in the new Group. The Chief General Superintendent, J.H. Follows, Deputy CME, Sir Henry Fowler and Carriage & Wagon Superintendent R.W. Reid came from the MR.

The first two years of the LMS were blighted by the rivalry of Granet's old company, the MR, with the LNWR. But Granet's loyalty was to his new company so, to set it on a sound commercial footing, he brought in Sir Josiah Stamp, a Director and Secretary of Nobel Industries, to reorganize the management. His arrival in 1926 from the world of business rather than railways astonished observers—but Stamp would follow this example by bringing in other 'outside' recruits, a mark of the new company. An economist by training, and with experience gained in the Civil Service and the Inland Revenue, Stamp had proved his management-skills by expanding the production of explosives during the 1914-18 war. A director of the Bank of England, a member of a Royal Commission and the author of several books, he held twenty-three honorary degrees in Britain, North America and elsewhere, was respected for his honesty and simplicity and was a devout Christian. His father managed the railway bookstall at Wigan. From Stamp's arrival, organization and standardization became the LMS watchwords, with company-policies based on statistics. Yet, these did not prevent the LMS from retaining many loss-making rural lines, with only minor closures—as if some unwritten law dictated that all lines be kept open; they were felt to be valuable as feeders. Stamp's big picture was to integrate the disparate constituents into one modern, standardized company, with centralized management, rather than devolution through geographical divisions, as undertaken by the GWR, the LNER and the SR, all more suited to this form of organization. The LMS changes were made largely in two spheres: management; locomotives and rolling-stock.

Stamp introduced systematic costing, eliminated inefficient processes, plant and equipment, set up the Executive Research Office to reduce administration-costs, and—another surprise—reorganized the board of directors as an Executive on the American model with himself as President. In 1927, he succeeded Granet as chairman, skilfully combining these duties with president. On the Executive, he was assisted by three vice-presidents each supervising a specific activity: traffic, commercial-operations and finance. Following tradition, they were professional railwaymen, but in 1930, following his chief's example, Stamp head-hunted Sir Harold Hartley, a renowned Oxford scientist. He was appointed the fourth vice-president, to take charge of works and ancillary undertakings except hotels; he established a research laboratory at Derby to test all products. When Railway Air Services was formed in 1934, Sir Harold became its chairman. RAS began with flights from London to Glasgow via Birmingham, Stoke-on-Trent and Liverpool, and Liverpool-Belfast-Glasgow. From its Western Division, the LMS notably promoted two ex-LYR men, Ashton Davies as general superintendent and T.W. Royle as his assistant, both destined to become vice-presidents of the LMS, and typical of the down-to-earth leaders the company produced.

Stamp had immediately identified an urgent need: the sprawling LMS company, formed from a hotch-potch of constituents, needed a locomotive-policy to produce a stud of standard-locomotives, certainly for the express passenger-trains, following the example of the Great Western Railway. Trains were becoming heavier, making this issue pressing. The LMS had inherited some 10,300 locomotives in hundreds of different classes, mostly obsolescent—and fewer than 2,000 were superheated; clearly the policy had to be 'build-and-scrap.' What the company needed were four types of locomotive: a powerful machine to haul the heavy Anglo-Scottish expresses, a mixed-traffic of wide availability, a large general-purpose passenger-tank and a heavy-freight engine, all of them more powerful, modern in concept, and therefore cheaper and easier to maintain, reducing the total number required. Instead, the company was continuing construction of obsolescent designs favoured by CMEs appointed through seniority. The four large locomotive-works also continued independently. In this way, the first eight years passed uncertainly.

The LMS was not glamorous: it was a workaday railway. It had neither the long tradition of the GWR, the panache of the Gresley-inspired LNER, nor the smooth continuity of Sir Herbert Walker's SR. Its problems, of disparate standards and of rivalry between the two largest constituents, took time to resolve. The appearance of the 'Royal Scot' locomotives in 1927 for the heavy haul on the west-coast line was the first symbol of unification; William Stanier, the CME from 1932, completed it. The Derby-style of the Scot marked Stamp's rationalization of the 1920s, whereas Stanier's 'converted Scot' exemplified the following period; the class therefore uniquely represented both periods. The provenance of the Scot is a fascinating story in itself, told later.

In 1923, the buzz-word on the railways was main-line electrification, already proven on suburban—lines. Before the 1923 Grouping, the North Eastern Railway had drawn up detailed plans to electrify its section of the East Coast main-line, and had even built two locomotives, but the LNER, which included the NER after 1923, did not proceed with this plan. The LMS Electrical Engineer, J. O'Brien, also produced an electrification scheme, for the west-coast route from Crewe to Carlisle, the section with the steepest gradients. A locomotive of the 2-D-2 wheel-arrangement ('D' = the middle six driving-wheels) was drafted out, based on the latest Swiss practice. In 1924, O'Brien presented a paper on his scheme to the Institution of Electrical Engineers, a move that alienated him from the Euston management. They dropped his scheme and disbanded his team, so he retired to Ireland. Though high in capital-cost, this scheme would have been so very advantageous in providing the power finally to conquer the slow and arduous slog over the northern hills of Grayrigg, Shap and Beattock, thereby obviating the costly banking-arrangements for almost every train over each incline. The LMS felt it was too ambitious and costly so early in its existence and resorted instead to using its four large locomotive-works to construct bigger and bigger locomotives, a policy which failed to hit the nub of the problem. The LMS had the resources and expertise in steam-construction in its engineering-works: the LNWR at Crewe, the MR at Derby, the LYR at Horwich (near Bolton) and the Caledonian at St Rollox in Glasgow. They continued to operate more or less independently, inhibiting integration programmes and modernization, so it was a case of 'continue as before.' Further examples of this approach to construction will be described. From 1948, BR followed the same retrogressive policy.

On the locomotive-engineering side, George Hughes, the former CME of the LYR, then of the combined LNWR and LYR in 1922, had been appointed CME of the LMS, again through seniority, *de facto* making Horwich its design-centre. H.A.V. Bulleid, in *Master Builders of Steam, A Mighty Re-stocking,* identifies this traditional approach to promotion, accession through seniority, as disadvantageous. It constituted a prime causal factor of the early difficulties of the LMS, a misguided sense of loyalty, preventing a logical solution to the problem of locomotive-stock. The answer was to detail the work required and appoint the best man to carry it out, whatever his origins. Eventually, the company grasped the nettle in this way: the Stanier era is explored in the next chapter.

Hughes was unpopular with the senior Midland men, in particular J.E. Anderson, who was appointed to the post of Motive Power Superintendent in 1924. He set up the Midland model of management, which significantly separated the Running Department from that of the CME. Thus 'Midlandization' of the company was begun, made visible to observers by painting passenger-engines and carriages in the Midland crimson-lake, arguably the most attractive of the pre-grouping companies' liveries—and different from the other three groups, which were in shades of green. The red was especially popular in Scotland. Simultaneously, locomotives had to be renumbered to avoid duplication. Midland classes had blocks of numbers and so kept them as the LMS adopted this system. It allocated numbers to the LNW engines beginning at 5000, the LYR at 10000 (this number allocated to Hughes' inspection-car), the Caledonian at 14000 and the Highland at 17000. At first, Crewe repainted its passenger-engines quite happily, but suddenly they began to return them to service from the works in Crewe's former 'blackberry-black' even with their LNW number-plates. This has been attributed to a workshop reorganization in 1927 which was unpopular at Crewe. In 1928, the LMS management resolved the impasse by simply repainting its locomotives in (LMS) black, unpopular on the Highland, only the Claughtons receiving the hated Midland-red. The cast-iron smokebox number-plates too were unpopular at Crewe, which refused to fit them to many engines. Even in the BR era decades later, their remaining engines were still running without them. One system not inherited from the Midland however was a power-classification of locomotives. The LMS introduced this, giving a range of power from 0-7, suffixed 'P' or 'F' according to their design for freight or passenger haulage, for example classifying small dock-tank shunters 0F, the MR/LMS 4-4-0 'compound' 4P and the Claughton and Dreadnought 4-6-0s 5P.

Instead of the large express-locomotives required, the LMS built further small MR-type engines, a policy that further damaged relations with Crewe and St Rollox. MR goods-trains were hauled by nothing larger than an 0-6-0—often in pairs—while its passenger-trains were light, frequent, and pulled by smallish four-coupled engines, 2-4-0s and 4-4-0s, the latter including forty-five compounds; even their older 4-2-2 'Spinners' were still in service. The LNWR's engines, however, had to run hard on heavy trains: the dichotomy between the Derby and Crewe managements.

An anecdote on the early days of the LMS was told to me by my chief Arthur Kinder, at the David Brown tractor-works at Meltham, West Yorkshire, mentioned elsewhere as the greatest fan of the LMS I have ever known. During the autumn around 1928, he took a day-trip to Blackpool to visit an elderly aunt, the fare probably 2/6d (12½p), quite a bite out of a wage of a pound or two. He crossed the valley from his home at Honley (near 'Last of the Summer Wine' town of Holmfirth) to Netherton on the Meltham branch-line to board the train, hauled by an ex-L&Y radial tank-engine. Shortly, at Lockwood on the Penistone line, the tank-engine was exchanged for ex-LNW 'George The Fifth' 4-4-0 *Boar Hound*. The two branches had been built by the L&Y but, down the line at Springwood Junction outside Huddersfield, the Penistone branch joined the ex-LNW Leeds-Manchester line, hence the interesting variety of motive-power—and showing pre-grouping locomotives still in charge. Returning in the darkness, he recalled hearing the change of engines at Lockwood, in particular the two distinctive whistles, a shriek by the 'George', which, too heavy for the branch, was changed for a radial-tank, with a deeper-toned whistle, to run up to Meltham.

Hughes took an early initiative by organizing running-trials of the several types of 4-4-0 inherited from the constituents in order to select the most efficient for mass-production. It must have been thrilling for enthusiasts to watch the LNW, CR, GSW and MR engines battling it out over the heavy gradients between Settle and Carlisle. The MR '990' 4-4-0, of compound dimensions, but with two simple-expansion inside-cylinders, a class built especially for this line, was allotted more runs than its rivals and acquitted itself well, but as a class of only ten was at a disadvantage. The results were loaded: the MR-dominated running-department had already decided policy, their bias showing in the use of five MR 4-4-0 compounds. The compound 1008 scored best—both in coal-consumption and maintenance. The outcome was that a batch of a hundred, now with left-hand drive, but otherwise only slightly updated, was immediately put into production, following the forty built at Derby in 1924. To be fair, they were very good performers for their size, sometimes hauling twelve-coach trains, and formed a stop-gap until a large express-locomotive appeared, although they had to run in pairs on the heaviest West Coast expresses, countering Stamp's rigid economy-drive.

Hughes was a logical thinker and keen to incorporate the latest ideas into locomotive-designs. He had been directed by the Executive in 1923 to design and produce an outside cylinder 2-6-0 mixed-traffic engine, a type already in service with other companies. Following the Grouping, he assembled the CMEs of all the constituent companies at Euston with the aim of utilizing the latest thinking in the design of the new mixed-traffic locomotive. It was an impossible discussion, with no compromise possible. How can one, for example, reconcile the features of a long, narrow firebox with a wide one? After the last meeting, H.G. Ivatt asked the Horwich chief draughtsman, Billington, what he intended to do. He answered simply that he was 'returning to Horwich to design the engine'. The result, the 'Land-Crab' 2-6-0, was an efficient machine that steamed well, and it was popular everywhere, from the Scottish Highlands to the south coast. Its valve-gear was Walschaerts, a type coming into vogue. Apart from its long-lap, long-lead characteristic, a further benefit was that this outside valve-gear avoided disadvantages of the Stephenson gear, where four eccentrics mounted inside on the crank-axle weakened it and placed undue strain on the bearings; the Stephenson gear also needed an inspection-pit for maintenance. The LMS had considered several pre-grouping locomotive-designs it had inherited, in particular an attractive one from St Rollox, derived partly from two 4-6-0s, the CR '60' and the HR 'River'. However, its large cylinders gave insufficient clearance on English lines. In fact, from the earliest days of the LMS, many schemes were drawn up at Horwich, some of them compounds—including a 4-6-2 passenger-engine, with a sister 2-8-2 to haul freight. The Horwich mogul mixed-traffic locomotive (*not* a Crab, nor a Land-Crab to the staff) used the standard Midland G8AS 180lb/sq.in boiler, as fitted to its 3P 'Belpaire' 4-4-0 of 1901. Cox, trained at Horwich, says that Hughes was determined to stay with 180lb-pressure. Was it a 'make-do' design, a characteristic of the British temperament? Furthermore, Horwich traditionally ran its design-office on a shoestring. However, the boiler steamed well and the machinery ran efficiently, the outcome an excellent mixed-traffic engine, built in small lots from 1926. By 1932 it totalled 245 examples, a large class for the time. Numbered 13000-13245 following the L&Y 0-8-0 coal-engines, they were renumbered 2700-2945 under the 1933-4 scheme to have all standard engines numbered under 10000. Ten engines, 2900-9, were allocated to the Highland Division to assist the struggling 'Clans', and performed well there till largely displaced by the Stanier 5P5F Mixed-traffic 4-6-0 locomotives (Black Fives) of 1934. In 1931, five engines, 13118/22/24/25/29 were fitted with Lentz rotary poppet-vale gear. In 1953, the Lentz gear was replaced with a Reidinger version. The last Horwich mogul noted by the author was 42777 hauling a Leeds-Manchester parcels-train at Mirfield, West Yorkshire, in 1964. The LMS classified the Horwich mogul as 4, then 5P4F, later 5P5F. Later still they became 6P5F and eventually plain 5.

A word on the history of the steam-locomotive is necessary here to explain why the Horwich mogul was such a ground-breaking design. Following the dawn of railways around 1830, Stephenson had established the basic locomotive: his 'Planet' 2-2-0 design had the Stephenson tubed-boiler plus other features, and inside cylinders: it remained dominant for almost a century. The reason was partly because the 'invisible' drive was felt in some circles to be neater and more refined than outside cylinders and valve-gear, a visibleness frowned upon in that prudish age. Commenting upon higher thermal efficiency, Mr Stanier, in his address to the Institution of Mechanical Engineers in 1941, dealt with the question of high superheat and increased valve and cylinder efficiency. Churchward's development of the last two produced results at least as good as the superheated engines of other railways and therefore he applied only a low degree of superheat. Thus, these two, high superheat plus improved valve-gear design, were not combined. Although Maunsell's 2-6-0 for the South Eastern & Chatham Railway in 1917 did so to some extent, *the Horwich mogul with outside cylinders and Walschaerts valve-gear with large valve-ports, plus a high degree of superheating* (600° or so) fully combined these features, making it a very efficient engine. This is a point of great significance, and one that signalled a new departure in design and efficiency. Marshall remarks, in *The Lancashire & Yorkshire Railway*, p.197: "The Hughes 2-6-0, despite depredations made on it by Fowler after Hughes' premature retirement, became, and remained, one of the best locomotives on the LMS." Indeed, the whole class of 245 engines lasted intact into the 1960s, that is. almost to the end of steam-haulage. Its design had paved the way for *every* Stanier standard class.

The first one to arrive at Derby made a huge impression on the MR staff, accustomed to the Midland tradition of inside-cylinder 4-2-2s, 2-4-0s, 4-4-0s and 0-6-0s. The Horwich mogul paved the way for *every standard-class on the LMS* (and many on the other railways)—and also on its successor BR, decades away in the future. It represented a significant milestone in design and efficiency.

Now here is an anecdote on one of these locomotives, again from my chief, at David Brown Tractors in Meltham, West Yorkshire, Arthur Kinder. The time was around 1928, when Arthur, aged 17, was a choirboy at nearby Honley Methodist church. A choir day-excursion was organized from his local station, Honley, to, incredibly, The Kyles of Bute, Scotland, no less. He took his friend, Thelma, with whom he was 'walking-out'. The engine was one of the new Horwich 2-6-0s, based at Low Moor MPD (25F), beyond Halifax. First, it had to bring the empty stock through to Clayton West, then return via other stations to Honley to pick up the chapel-party at 5am, a very early start for the footplate-crew. From there, the complicated journey involved a circuitous route across West Yorkshire and Lancashire to reach the West Coast line at Farington Junction south of Preston, then a climb over the Grayrigg and Shap banks to Carlisle, followed by a further hundred miles to Glasgow over the Beattock bank. The last leg was to Dunoon, where the excursionists embarked on a steamer for the trip around the Kyles of Bute, with lunch served on board. The locomotive-crew rested during their stopover, once having turned their engine, raked the fire and prepared for the long journey home.

Arthur recalled the excellent trip they had enjoyed behind that 2-6-0— but that it developed a squeak as they passed through Blackburn station on the way home—small wonder! But it had not finished at Honley, for then it had to continue down the branch to drop passengers for Clayton West and other stations at 5.30am and finally return with the empty stock to Low Moor. Day-excursions were certainly ambitious in those days; the details of the fare are unavailable now, but probably 5/- or 7/6d (25p/37½p), a considerable sum then, when £2-3 was a decent wage. The sequel was that Arthur, of course agog for every detail of this, his first trip over Shap, almost ignored his lady-friend, who took umbrage at his preoccupation with the railway. She announced, in the forthright Yorkshire way, that the future was to be either her or trains. You can guess Arthur's response—and that was the end of their relationship. She married a widower, but Arthur remained a bachelor, becoming a local preacher and Chairman of the West Riding branch of the Railway Correspondence & Travel Society (RCTS), through which he continued to follow his interest in railways across the breadth of the country until his death in 1996 aged 85.

The Horwich mogul, painted red as a passenger-engine, was immediately so successful in traffic and popular with the enginemen, that a tank-engine version was proposed to fulfil the urgent need for a large machine of this type, unfulfilled by the Hughes 'Baltic' tank. So was born the so-called Fowler 2-6-4—the modifier here because Fowler admitted he had never designed an engine in his life; he was a workshop-man. The drawing-office carried out the designs, which however were always accredited to the CME. Fowler's engineering reputation was founded largely upon ancillary activities, in particular his work for the Ministry of Munitions during the 1914 war, and at the International Railway Congress. The 2-6-4 design included new cylinders with straight ports and large valves with Walschaerts long-lap valve-gear—the long-lap setting a last-minute modification proposed by H.G Ivatt, when Fowler had admitted he did not understand the Walschaerts. Fowler had settled on this valve-gear after hearing a paper read by one of his junior staff at the Institution of Locomotive Engineers, although Derby had included it on a few 2-8-0s in 1914 for its joint-line, the Somerset & Dorset. And so, the Horwich 2-6-0 influenced the design of the 2-6-4, including its long-lap Walschaerts valve-setting. This was the key to the 2-6-4's speed, acceleration and free-running characteristics. Nock recorded them hauling his seven-coach Euston to Bushey suburban-train attaining 83mph at Wembley, faster than the Liverpool express, departing simultaneously—and double-headed. Other observers have timed these 2-6-4s at 90mph-plus. The successors to the Fowlers were the equally-successful Stanier 2-6-4Ts, described later. The tank-engines too remained in service almost to the end of steam-haulage in 1968.

Hughes had several initiatives, if not outright inventions, to his credit, some of which were taken up by later CMEs of the LMS, notably in the realm of superheating. Hughes' initiatives further underline the disproportionate influence of the smallish LYR company on LMS policy, referred to already, and explored later. Now two of the urgent needs had been met, but a powerful locomotive for the west-coast expresses was still required, and a heavy freight-engine, also to avoid double-heading—with consequent expense—especially on the heavy coal-haul from the Toton collection-sidings near Nottingham to London. Frustrated by the Midland faction at Derby, Hughes retired in August 1925, allowing his former pupil and assistant at Horwich, Sir Henry Fowler, to take over, again through seniority.

Fowler intensified 'Midlandization' immediately. Following the tests of the various 4-4-0s already described, the Midland 4P 4-4-0 compound had become a company standard. Now joining it were Fowler's weak 2P simple 4-4-0, with front-end somewhat modified but still unsatisfactory, and his 2-6-2 tank, a very poor performer. Some two hundred of these two designs were constructed from 1925-32. Details of the 4-4-0 developments appear in Chapter 6. Most of the other companies' 4-4-0s were scrapped, particularly those of the G&SWR; its Glasgow-Kilmarnock-Carlisle line was re-equipped with new 4-4-0s of both types. St Rollox, the former Caledonian Railway's headquarters, was now the Scottish HQ of the LMS, and tended quietly to ignore instructions from distant Euston felt to be unfavourable. Thus they made sure to scrap GSW engines while keeping their own, of which the large majority lasted through the LMS period into the BR-regime from 1948. However, the CR engines were superior to the GSW designs. St Rollox even fitted CR boilers to some ex-HR engines. The LMS also constructed hundreds of Midland 0-6-0 shunting-tanks deriving from a design of 1899. Thus some rationalization, if not modernization, was achieved, the first stage of Stamp's 'build-and-scrap' policy, which was to assume a greater significance later. The 4-4-0-story leads us to look at three distant limbs of the LMS, two of which employed them.

The Somerset & Dorset Joint Railway, a historical portrait

Midland 4-4-0s also penetrated the West of England, following the company's absorption of the Birmingham & Gloucester Railway and its leasing of the two Gloucester companies, allowing through-services to Bristol. From here, it built a branch in 1869 to Bath (later named Bath Green Park). The Somerset & Dorset Railway, an amalgamation of the Somerset Central and Dorset Central Railways, ran from Wimborne, Dorset, to Burnham-on-Sea, Somerset, with branches, and exercised running-powers over the L&SWR from Wimborne to Poole, later to Bournemouth. Passengers were brought from Cardiff on the railway's own boats to Burnham and thence to Bournemouth, a flourishing and fashionable seaside-resort. On the arrival of the MR at Bath, the S&DJR recognized an opportunity to gain a through-route from the North; its link from Evercreech to Bath was welcomed by the MR as an opportunity for further expansion. The extension was costly, with considerable civil-engineering works to surmount the Mendip Hills, entailing numerous steep gradients, cuttings, tunnels and viaducts.

Opening in 1874, the new line met the Midland close to Bath station. After two years, financial constraints compelled the S&D to accept leasing by the MR and L&SWR as equal partners in a Joint Committee, and the line became the S&D Joint Railway, with the L&SWR responsible for civil-engineering and rolling-stock, the MR for locomotives, largely 1P 0-4-4 tanks, 2P 4-4-0s, plus 3F and 4F 0-6-0 goods-engines (using the later LMS power-classifications). In 1914, Derby constructed six 7F 2-8-0s to cope with the heavier freight trains; later, they hauled passengers as well. Five further locomotives followed with larger boilers, but were later rebuilt with the original boilers. In this way, Midland trains from Birmingham arrived in Bournemouth. Coal-mines in the belt from Midsomer Norton to Radstock provided freight-traffic to add to the clay from Carter's mine near Corfe Mullen. The Grouping of 1923 ended the leasing by the MR and the L&SWR; their successors, the SR and the LMS, became the legal owners of the line. In 1926, the LMS moved its Birmingham departure-point back to Manchester, naming this train *The Pines Express* in 1927. Some northern towns, such as Leeds and Derby, had through-trains to Bournemouth, others through-carriages, while another train ran from Cleethorpes to Exmouth. The latter was another example of the use of running-powers over other companies' metals, in this case the LNER, to extend the reach of the LMS. During 1928-30, the LMS absorbed the S&DJ locomotives into its own stock-list, its red paint banishing the local blue livery to history; the carriages went to the SR, which soon scrapped them in favour of its green vehicles. In a rationalization during 1930, Highbridge Works was closed, with a loss of some 300 jobs. One of the line's attractive features was the sight of black LMS engines hauling green SR carriages, but through-expresses wore the LMS red.

A shortage of capital when building the line had left a considerable mileage as single track, so that operating-skill and punctuality were essential to avoid delaying traffic. The heavy expresses needed two 4-4-0s to climb out of Bath and over the Mendip Hills—often with bankers—but during the 1930s the LMS strengthened bridges from Mangotsfield to Bath, and then on the S&DJ as well, to allow its new 5P5F (Black Five) 4-6-0s over the line. Examples were 5194 (Bath, 22C) and 5440, based for years at 22A, Bristol Barrow Road. However, new regional boundaries under BR transferred the S&DJR to the Western Region, which progressively diverted traffic to its other routes; for example, the *Pines Express* now came through Oxford. Owing to this and to the general decline of rail traffic, the whole network was closed in 1966. Short stretches are operated by preservationists, notably at Midford and Shillingstone, while the S&DJ trust aims to reopen the whole line, a daunting task with many bridges removed and cuttings filled in.

The ex-Highland Railway's Far North line

At the other end of the huge network, new 5P5F 4-6-0s were sent up to the Scottish Highlands to assist the Horwich moguls to replace obsolete HR types, such as 'small' and 'large' 4-4-0 'Bens' and 4-6-0 'Castles'; some standard 4F 0-6-0s replaced small goods-engines. The Black Fives headed expresses to Aberdeen, largely avoiding the former double-heading, and also hauled long-distance stopping-trains from Inverness to Wick and Thurso on the Far North line. Despite these inroads and the Scottish directors' bias towards CR engines, a few of the old HR types outlasted the LMS era, for example 14385 *Loch Tay*—the last of its class—to be withdrawn from Forres by BR in 1950, as well as several Bens. The last of these, 14398 *Ben Alder*, was placed in store for preservation but was eventually scrapped as late as the 1960s.

The Northern Counties Committee

The NCC operated lines out of Belfast, Northern Ireland. At the Grouping, the LMS took over this MR subsidiary—an overseas-operation unique among the big four railways—and continued at first to run its trains with Derby 2-4-0s and 4-4-0s. However, its distant location in no way disadvantaged it, for it received capital upgrading to match the mainland. Some second-hand petrol-engined railcars were purchased and, especially in their later years when fitted with diesel-engines, prolonged the viability of branches, particularly some narrow-gauge lines in the west. The company introduced a fine express-engine, the class 5 2-6-0 of 1933, based on the Horwich 2-6-0, providing extra power over the obsolete ex-MR 4-4-0s. In 1931, an infrastructure investment to accelerate traffic was the reconstruction of the Bleach Green Junction out of Belfast York Road. One aim was to provide employment to Belfast's heavy-industry, depressed during the Great Slump of the early-1930s, and made possible with a low-interest government loan. The new layout comprised two notable concrete Greenisland Viaducts over Valentine's Glen, one straddling the other to allow uninterrupted running on all lines, to Coleraine, Portrush and Londonderry, and to Larne Harbour for the steamers to Stranraer and Heysham. The works were completed in 1934 at the huge cost of £200,000. The seaside-resort of Portrush was served daily by three fast expresses from Belfast. In its final years, the LMS placed Stanier/Fairburn 2-6-4 tank-engines in service. It was one of these that I saw leaving Leeds on the daily Heysham freight around 1946-7 in 'ckd' form, its parts set out on a series of flat—and tube-wagons, painted red with the NCC insignia, ready for assembly at NCC's Belfast works.

However, the Midland-inspired small-engine practice on the LMS was not meeting the company's urgent need for a large express-locomotive to serve the steeply-graded trunk-route from Euston to Glasgow. The new compounds performed extremely well for their size, sometimes hauling twelve-coach trains, but double-heading was still required on the heaviest west-coast expresses, frustrating Stamp's strict economy-drive.

Four-coupled engines had been giving way to Atlantics, even to 4-6-0s, well before the 1914 war.

The LMS had inherited four 4-6-0 designs from its constituents: the LNWR 'Prince of Wales' inside-cylinder engine and its four-cylinder 'Claughton', the rather similar LYR 4-6-0 Class 18/ N.1 'Dreadnought', and an outside-cylinder 4-6-0 from the Caledonian Railway. The latter comprised six locomotives built in 1916 by Pickersgill, plus twenty almost identical machines built by the LMS at St Rollox in 1925 after the grouping, but too wide for the English loading-gauge. In fact, none was ideal. The Prince of Wales was the superheated version of George Whale's 'Experiment' class of 1906 and as such was essentially an old design, though a good performer. The LMS gave them a chance in 1924 by building an experimental example, 5845, with outside Walschaerts valve-gear, aiming to improve performance, and nineteen of the earlier locomotives were similarly modified. Little improvement resulted, therefore they were placed on the reserve list by adding the prefix 2 to their numbers. Now here is an anecdote about these engines. The Walschaerts locos' valve-gear in motion presented a peculiar action, reminding observers of 'Tishy', a contemporary racehorse which habitually crossed its legs. This became the engines' unofficial tag. As CME, Hughes naturally favoured his Dreadnoughts and therefore pitted them against the LNW Claughtons on the West Coast route. His rebuild of these 4-6-0s in 1920 had improved their performance to the extent that it almost equalled that of the Claughtons, though their coal-consumption remained high. He had many more of the modified Dreadnoughts built, and they figured in LMS publicity for a few years as their newest express-engine. One of the new engines, 10456, was rebuilt as a compound, to run as a test-bed. On the freight side however, both the LNWR and the LYR had some excellent 0-8-0 coal-engines (described later), which could be relied upon for the time being, like the 0-6-0 goods-engines from all constituents. It was the prestigious West-Coast expresses that were increasingly suffering from a shortage of power, spotlighted by competition.

Their main rival for Scottish traffic, the LNER, with its fast and level East Coast route, had as CME H.N. Gresley, the former Locomotive Superintendent of its GNR constituent since 1911, with O.V.S.

Bulleid as his Chief Assistant. Since the other constituents' CMEs were approaching retirement at the 1923 grouping, these two had been largely acceptable to them, allowing a seamless transition to be made, increasing efficiency and setting Gresley's design-policy for the LNER's greatest years. The Southern Railway had similarly contrived its amalgamation fairly smoothly. Maunsell from the South Eastern & Chatham Railway, supported by the Sou'west's Pearson and other recruits from Swindon, was the unquestioned leader of the three amalgamated companies. The Great Western however, little affected by the grouping, was pressing ahead with the standardization policy initiated by Churchward two decades earlier, led by his protégé, the well-established CME Collett and his Principal Assistant, William Stanier. These three grouping-companies had new express engines on their heaviest trains and the LMS Executive was aware they needed one as well. As no new design had appeared to haul the heavy West Coast expresses since the Claughton of 1913, one was certainly due.

Fowler at first proposed a 4-6-0 version of the Compound, his favourite engine, then enlarged it into a four-cylinder compound Pacific, which was drafted out. However, the four railways were not hermetically sealed off from each other: their staffs interacted at different levels, including at meetings of the Institutions. One of these interactions was the post-1923 GWR/LNER relationship, which now appears as a factor in this story. It was a fascinating era, when large engines were just appearing, but the LNER, competing with the LMS for Scottish traffic, had also encountered motive-power difficulties, in particular with its new pacific. At this time, the prestige of the Great Western stood at an all-time high. Hardly affected by the turmoil of the grouping and therefore unique among the 'big four' railways, it had continued its policies and therefore was in a position to seize the initiative. It did so immediately by accelerating its schedules, leaving rivals far behind. Its 'Cheltenham Spa Express' of 1923, dubbed 'The Cheltenham Flyer', was a prime example, the world's fastest regular train for several years, with an average speed of 80mph-plus. The GW had standardized its locomotive-construction by designing parts, especially boilers and cylinders, common to different classes of engine. Perceiving that the boiler represented the heart of the machine, Churchward had adopted an American idea, the taper-boiler, as the basis of his own. Its shape concentrates a relatively-large volume of water close to the firebox tube-plate, the hottest part. Contemporary cinema-goers were familiar with the American 4-4-0s ('The General'), designed for the restricted axle-loading needed on the lightly-laid tracks of the USA. Another foreign idea adopted by Churchward was the rectangular flat-topped firebox invented by the Belgian designer Alfred Belpaire. This high-pitched firebox formed a circulating space for the water, allowing a cushion over the firebox crown, as well as steam-space. His final borrowing was the French 'de Glehn bogey', to stabilize the front of the engine. Churchward was seeking the perfect steam-locomotive.

The GWR/LNER relationship began on the stands of the British Empire Exhibition, the biggest-ever trade-exposition, held in 1924-5 in the new Empire Stadium at Wembley. Gresley's new pacific, 4472, *Flying Scotsman,* was on the LNER stand close to the GWR engine, the latest product of Swindon, the 4-6-0 *Caerphilly Castle,* that had created such a huge impression at its launch in the previous year. A notice announced it as the most powerful locomotive in the British Isles. Comments were circulating about this claim for the smaller engine. Puzzled and nettled at this, Gresley arranged to borrow a Castle to compare its efficiency with his pacifics. Parochialism prevailed in those days: apart from the principal dimensions of their new 4-6-0, Swindon's affairs were a closed book. Thus Gresley relished the prospect of having a Castle at Doncaster for that week in 1925. It was effectively a locomotive-exchange—not the first in railway history, but one that would have widespread repercussions. The engines actually exchanged were *Pendennis Castle* and the Gresley pacific 1474. This, as a Great Northern locomotive, was afterwards renumbered 4474, and named *Victor Wild.* The Castle typically hauled its King's Cross-Doncaster expresses with quiet efficiency, but 1474 had some difficulty in maintaining the tight 'Cornish Riviera' schedules. Gresley learned lessons from the exchange: better front-end design giving economy of coal, and a long-lap, long-travel, valve-gear. These adjustments he immediately made to good effect on his pacifics, allowing him in turn to creep further ahead of the LMS.

The agreement to end racing (to Aberdeen) made after 1895 between the East Coast and West Coast companies was still in force, but slack trade during the 1920s had reduced passenger-numbers—and 4472 *Flying Scotsman* was deliberately derailed, at Cramlington, Northumberland, during the 1926 General Strike. The LNER needed the publicity that would be generated by a non-stop run and so broke the agreement. This set the stage for a publicity coup: the exchange of a locomotive of the *Flying Scotsman* type with a GW 'Castle' in 1925 had, among other important details, indicated to Gresley how to reduce 4472's coal-consumption, so that it could now run through from London to Edinburgh on nine tons, that is, without refuelling. To enable crews to change over without stopping, in 1927 Gresley had designed a new type of tender incorporating a side-corridor. On 1 May 1928, the widely-advertized new service was waved off at King's Cross by the Lord Mayor of London, and the fortunate passengers settled down to enjoy the new facilities on board, such as the barber, the female retiring-room and meals cooked in the 'all-electric' kitchen. However, on the West Coast, the rival LMS upstaged the LNER's non-stop run by running one of its own on the previous day, described shortly. Such was the competition between the two group-companies for Scottish traffic—intensified by the LNER high-profile publicity-machine. Interestingly, this LNER initiative would have been difficult, if not impossible, had it taken up its constituent NER's plan to electrify its section of the East Coast route in 1923, since changes of locomotive would normally have been necessary. It is thought that Gresley had the electrification project quashed in favour of his new pacific locomotives to enable him to compete with the LMS head-to-head, thus altering the course of history.

Simultaneously, Fowler was designing his huge four-cylinder compound Pacific for the West Coast, although Dreadnought 10456, rebuilt as a compound by his predecessor, Hughes, had been unspec-tacular. Actually, Derby, the old Midland headquarters and now the centre of LMS design, had never built anything larger than a 4-4-0—apart from Paget's experimental eight-cylinder double-framed 2-6-2, and 'Big Bertha', the 0-10-0 banking-engine for the Lickey Incline, plus the 2-8-0s for the Somerset & Dorset Joint Railway—both of the latter essentially enlarged 0-6-0 freight-engines—and some of Fowler's colleagues were apprehensive about his new design, particularly the ex-LNW faction, recalling the unfortunate Webb compounds. The new compound Pacific would take time to settle down and iron out the inevitable teething-troubles inherent in such a complex design, quite apart from training crews to operate it. As noted, Fowler was not a locomotive-designer; his interests lay in metallurgy and workshop practices. In the design field, he had contented himself with modifications to the various 4-4-0 designs dating from 1882. Detailed design-work was carried out by the Derby drawing-office, whose deeply-ingrained Midland practices inhibited the adoption of new ideas. The 2-6-6-2 Beyer-Garratts of 1927 represented a prime example, an excellent design by Beyer-Peacock of Manchester, but Anderson at Derby foisted obsolete details onto them, short-travel valves and especially undersized axle-boxes, vitiating the efficiency of the design. The long-travel Walschaerts valve-gear of the Horwich 2-6-0s, currently being incorporated into the design of the 2-6-4 tank-engine, was ignored for the sake of continuing with hallowed Midland practices. However, during this period the 'battle of the valves' was finally won—though not preventing the production of the weak 2P 4-4-0s and 2-6-2 tanks.

For an anecdote on these tank-engines, the author is indebted to Chris Banks *British Railways Locomotives 1948*, p.199 (Foulis-OPC/Haynes 1990), for information on their unpopularity. The ex-LNE (CLC/GC) shed at Lower Ince, Wigan, having been incorporated into the London Midland region of BR after 1948, was closed on 24 March 1952, when its entire allocation of engines, J.10 ex-CLC/GC 0-6-0s dating from 1892, was sent to nearby ex-LMS Springs Branch shed. Eight were transferred to ex-LNE Darlington shed in mid-December 1956, running up to Carnforth and Tebay, turning there up the branch to Kirkby Stephen and over the Stainmore summit. Darlington had received eight Derby 2-6-2Ts which its staff heartily disliked, so it rid itself by exchanging them for the J.10s. These Darlington withdrew immediately, but it is unclear whether Springs Branch divested itself of the unpopular 2-6-2Ts on their arrival. Certainly, heavy scrapping reduced their number to the extent that, a decade later, only twenty of the original seventy remained.

To underline a significant point made earlier, the new 2-6-0 of 1926 and its derivative, the 2-6-4 tank-engine of 1927, with their outside cylinders and Walschaert's valve-gear represented a departure from the traditional inside-cylinder locomotive. The significance is that the 2-6-4 tank, acknowledged as 'Fowler's best design', was not only a powerful engine but above all remarkably free-running, owing to the long-lap, long-travel valve-gear that Ivatt had incorporated. It formed the basis for improvements made by successive CMEs, Stanier, Fairburn, Ivatt and Riddles, over three decades. This then, was the LMS background as the construction of Fowler's Compound Pacific locomotive was beginning in 1926. However, some of the management—thought to be Anderson, Motive-Power Superintendent, and Follows, Chief General Superintendent—recalling the success of the GWR 4-6-0 Castle on LNER metals during their locomotive exchange only the previous year—felt that a 4-6-0 might well do the work required and that now they really had to take an initiative. Circumventing their CME, they communicated their disquiet over the new design to their chairman Granet. Although Midland by tradition, his objective was now the success of his larger group and, importantly, he was a close personal friend of Sir Felix Pole, the general manager of the Great Western Railway. It is likely that Granet confided—or confirmed—to Sir Felix something of the internal dissensions besetting his LMS group. Now Pole was a confident, forthright man, and proud of GWR traditions. Back in 1903, on the departure of Pearson to the South Eastern & Chatham Railway, the GWR's CME Churchward had remarked, "If another railway wants a good man, they come to Swindon." Pole's attitude was similar, characteristically replying to a request for locomotive-help with, "Why not try one of ours?" The upshot was that on a September evening in 1926, 5000 *Launceston Castle* ran quietly up the North and South-Western Junction line to Willesden to appear on shed at Camden.

On LMS metals for the first time, the Castle hauled expresses competently from Euston to Crewe, then to Carlisle, and from Carlisle to Leeds. Its efficiency revealed that Bowen-Cooke's 1913 Claughton had not incorporated the improved valve-events and front-end design suggested in the GW-LNW locomotive-exchange of 1910. The Castle's dynamometer-car report demonstrated to the LMS management seven features of the design that led to its success, in particular a machine that used the steam efficiently to give a low fuel-consumption. It was enough. With Fowler's 4-6-2 fully designed and two sets of frames actually cut at Derby, the LMS Executive decided that what they needed was a simple (i.e. non-compound) 4-6-0 locomotive, the so-called 'improved Castle'. Fowler had already been instructed to stop work on his Pacific and was now told to approach the GWR for fifty Castles. Swindon refused. Apart from its unwillingness in principle, it lacked the manufacturing capacity to deliver such an order within the short time-scale demanded by the LMS, a matter of months. Swindon also refused to supply drawings. In desperation now, Fowler turned to the Southern Railway, which had just launched its 6ft 7in 'Lord Nelson' four-cylinder 4-6-0, the most powerful locomotive in the country, built by The North British Locomotive Company. Maunsell supplied a full set of drawings, enabling some features to be copied, in particular the boiler and firebox, these deriving from GWR-practice, brought to Ashford from Swindon. An interesting sidelight here is that Lord Nelson with *Belpaire* firebox followed the *round*-topped firebox King Arthur 4-6-0, launched only the previous year. Apparently the SR, perhaps influenced by its recruits from Swindon, considered the GWR Belpaire the better option. It is plausible that the SR helped the LMS out of its difficulty because the SR, unlike the GWR, felt no competitive threat from the LMS, since they were a completely different kind of railway and also were geographically separated. Photographs of the two 4-6-0s reveal the strong family likeness. Thus, after efforts lasting over four years, was born the powerful express-locomotive that the LMS urgently needed.

Derby rapidly schemed out the basic 4-6-0—to be built by North British, the constructors of 'Lord Nelson'—for which the credit is due to Herbert Chambers, the Chief Draughtsman. Anderson persuaded North British to adopt three cylinders, and handed over the project to them for final design-work and production of fifty of these 4-6-0s. Utilizing the capacity of its two extensive Glasgow locomotive works, Hyde Park and Queen's Park, NB Loco manufactured fifty engines and the LMS introduced its accelerated summer schedules on the West Coast in 1927. The first engine was named *Royal Scot* after the time-honoured morning express in each direction. Its name also indicated the old Scottish regiment, giving the new LMS publicity chief at Euston the idea of naming all the engines after regiments of the British Army: the LMS now realized the publicity to be gained from named engines. At first, however, some Royal Scots bore names inherited from LNW locomotives, such as *Vesta* and *Lion*. The running of the Scots raised LMS locomotive-work into a different league, even before later modifications, described below. As 'The Pride of the LMS', they featured in company publicity for some years. The large boiler, now feeding three cylinders instead of four, was fully competent to maintain pressure over long and steeply-inclined routes. The cylinders were derived from the 2-6-4 tank, its valve-gear too—this originating on the Horwich mogul—plus Midland practice. Horwich thus considerably influenced the final design, which was of course credited to Fowler, as CME. The Royal Scots were graded as power-class 6. However, after a few years, their efficiency deteriorated considerably, because wear on the Midland Schmidt-type single stiff piston-ring was allowing steam to leak past into the exhaust-area, particularly as the Scots were fitted with 250lb/sq.in boilers. When Stanier fitted solid valve-heads with narrower, flexible, rings (as on a car), larger cylinder-ports and GW-type axleboxes, the locomotives ran even more efficiently, to cover over 30,000 miles between repairs.

With the aim of accelerating schedules—and as a 'prequel' to the rival LNER's publicized non-stop run from London to Edinburgh on the following day described earlier, a special non-stop run of The Royal Scot was made on 30 April 1928 from Euston to Glasgow, utilizing a Royal Scot locomotive that was nicely run-in, 6113 *Cameronian,* to take the first portion, to Glasgow. Remarkably, 1054, a 4-4-0-compound of the 1924 batch, hauled the other portion through to Edinburgh, easily the longest non-stop run ever achieved by this class of locomotive. Both set records for their distances. The success of the Royal Scots encouraged the LMS to build twenty more, but this time they could be constructed in-house, and they were built at Derby in 1930. Concurrently, the above modifications were being made, enabling them to be incorporated on the last four engines, 6166-69, from new. They brought the class-total to seventy.

One of Stamp's early objectives was the streamlining of repair-schedules, partly on economic grounds, and partly to return engines to the road more speedily, thereby reducing the total locomotive requirement. Ex-LNW H.P.M. Beames, Assistant CME and charged with implementing this directive in the Crewe works, did a brilliant job, while in 1928, H.G. Ivatt, the Derby works-manager, with assistant Robert Riddles, reorganized this works too, reducing the percentage of down-time considerably, thus achieving Stamp's objective. They identified boilers as the factor delaying the completion of repairs, and so now they were lifted from the locomotives on entering the shops, to be repaired separately, allowing a spare boiler to be mounted when the general maintenance was finished. This accelerated the repair-process: it simply required the construction of a few spare boilers for each class of engine. The incoming boilers were repaired and added to the stock of spares. Horwich, a newer works built on a greenfield-site and therefore having a logical layout of facilities, needed less reorganization compared with the older works, which had grown *ad hoc*.

With the urgent problem of locomotive-power for the West Coast solved, at least for the time being, the Executive felt the company needed a 'second-eleven', a less-powerful 4-6-0, to haul lighter expresses to an equivalent schedule, but one that could deputize for a Royal Scot without losing too much time. Of the inherited 4-6-0s, the best two, the Claughton and the Dreadnought, lacked consistent performance, and additionally were expensive to maintain. Furthermore, the Dreadnoughts never produced an individual epic of haulage equal to the best of pre-war Claughton performance, especially that achieved by 1159 *Sir Ralph Brocklebank* in 1913. The long runs over the west-coast line, compared with the shorter stretches of the LYR, caused overheated bearings on the Dreadnoughts; moreover their smaller grates, 27sq ft against the 30.5 of the Claughton, limited their ultimate power-output and development-potential. The Executive therefore concentrated on improving the Claughton and, in all fairness, the ex-Midland men at Derby tried to make the best of this Crewe design. They retubed the boiler and redesigned the front-end for better steaming. The improvements recorded stimulated further upgrading, namely replacing the Claughton's 175lb-boiler with one of a larger diameter pressed to 200lbs. It was fitted to twenty engines, upgraded to power-5X, midway between 5 and 6. The Claughton had been designed down to a boiler really too small for it, mainly to utilize the biggest flanging-plates at Crewe—another example of the British way of 'making-do' and reminiscent of the Horwich 2-6-0's boiler. Such a policy almost invariably represents false economy in the long term. The new boiler gave a bigger reserve of steam and thus a greater ability to keep schedules. In seeking better valve-events to accompany it, ten of the reboiled engines were fitted with Beardmore/Caprotti poppet-valve gear and the other ten with Walschaert's gear. The two Claughton redesigns were monitored with the dynamometer-car, a slight advantage being noted for the Walschaert's engines. Following an accident to a Royal Scot attributed to drifting smoke, deflector-plates, pioneered in Germany and used by the SR, were fitted. However, Claughton maintenance remained expensive and, with a directive from the Executive to cut costs, another solution had to be found.

The larger boiler needed to be paired with a more-efficient machine. It was mated with the successful Royal Scot chassis, providing the lower axle-loading required, essentially a 'light Royal Scot'. The first engine was a rebuild of Claughton 5971 *Croxteth*, standing damaged in the works after an accident at Waste Bank, Culgaith, between Appleby and Carlisle. This prototype was followed by 5902 *Sir Frank Ree*. Their success led to the construction of fifty more from 1932, twenty of them officially rebuilds of large-boilered Claughtons—to satisfy the accountants. They were renumbered in the 1934 scheme to 5500-51, the last ten numbered 5542-51 from new in 1933. Because of their origin, the Claughton-rebuilds were dubbed 'Baby Scots', a name frowned upon by management, who felt the new class needed a more prestigious name. With their former work done by Royal Scots and the 5X 4-6-0s, the unrebuilt Claughtons were all withdrawn by 1935. One was *Patriot*, the engine commemorating company staff killed in the 1914-18 war, and on its withdrawal, 5971, by now renumbered to 5500, took its name at the suggestion of a *Railway Magazine* correspondent. The company announced that this would be the name of the new class, and gradually the nickname fell out of use. In fact, I knew the engines as Patriots, because of their listing as such in Ian Allan's *ABC of LMS Locomotives*, and because I knew no railwaymen.

The majority of the Patriots received names, several inherited from their predecessors. Some commemorated heroes of the Great War, others famous people, some connected with the company. Examples were 5534 *E. Tootal Broadhurst*, 5536 *Private W. Wood, VC, Private E. Sykes, VC* and 5538 *Giggleswick*. The name *Home Guard* was given to 5543 during WW2 in 1941 in a ceremony at Euston, while several others bore names of seaside-resorts served by the LMS, including 5520

Llandudno, 5524 *Blackpool,* and 5526 *Morecambe and Heysham,* some stabled at 20A (Leeds, Holbeck) which I saw at Apperley Bridge in the 1940s. The 5XP classification was continued on account of the enlarged Claughton-boiler. The Patriots came fully up to expectations, in their haulage-capacity, their top speed and free-running characteristics—and, most importantly, when compared with their Claughton predecessors, significantly lower repair-costs, vindicating the design in the eyes of management. Their performance was exemplary on the two-hour Birmingham expresses, which were mostly accelerated to 1hr 55min. From the publicity viewpoint, this was an important LMS service, for, quite apart from linking England's two largest cities, it represented the sole main-line competition the LMS could mount against the prestigious Great Western Railway, with its Paddington-Birmingham expresses. It was therefore the shop-window of the LMS facing the GWR. These developments took place during the period 1927-33, a time of flux in LMS locomotive-engineering.

In 1930, affairs in the locomotive department of the LMS remained uncertain, with the partisanship of the constituents prevailing. While some rationalization of types had been achieved, no stud of modern, standard locomotives had appeared. Clearly, the Executive policy had to be 'build-and-scrap', but Stamp had no engineer to carry out this plan. To escape from the continuing rivalry, a fresh face from outside the company was clearly the remedy. As detailed earlier, the CME, Fowler, was not a locomotive-designer, but an improver: workshop-organization was his *forte*; however, as CME, he was credited with the designs produced by the drawing-office. He had rather fallen from grace over having been ordered by the Executive to stop work on his compound Pacific locomotive for the heavy haul on the wcml, and then to approach the GWR for drawings as the basis for an LMS 'improved Castle-class 4-6-0'. 'Royal Scot' resulted, largely a combination of elements of the new SR 'King Arthur' 4-6-0—itself incorporating GWR know-how—and the North British design-office.

In October 1930, Fowler was moved 'sideways' to be Assistant to the Vice-President for Works, and E.J.H. Lemon, Carriage and Wagon Engineer, appointed CME. These moves surprised observers, but they became aware of LMS strategy when Lemon's term of office ended only a year or so later. He was promoted to Vice-President on the retirement of J.H. Follows at the end of 1931, leaving the post of CME vacant. Lemon's short term in post could now be seen as an interim measure while arrangements were made for a substantive successor. He was to be William Stanier from the Great Western Railway, and we will now look at the arrangements to appoint him.

Horwich-designed 'Dreadnought' 4-6-0 10456, rebuilt experimentally as a compound, running down into Oxenholme, Cumbria, wcml (H.C. Casserley collection)

Standard 3F shunter 7562 pauses between tasks on Skipton down exchange-sidings.

Chapter 3

1932-39, THE STANIER YEARS

The concentrated activity during the early Stanier era renders adherence to strict chronology difficult, but the events are described sequentially as far as possible. This chapter outlines Stanier's designs, but the fine detail can be found in Rowledge, Nock, Cox, Bond and Bulleid, including their references to proceedings of the Institutions.

Stanier himself told Nock the story of his appointment to the LMS, a fascinating account of the Stanier 'head-hunting' episode that you may not be aware of. Stanier was approached in a roundabout way, in fact twice. In October 1931, he received an invitation to luncheon at the Athenaeum Club, London, from the CME of the LMS, E.J.H. Lemon, to discuss aspects of water-softening, of which the GWR had great experience. On arrival, Stanier was taken aback to see also present Sir Harold Hartley, the LMS Vice-President in charge of research. Although water-softening was certainly discussed, Stanier felt puzzled. His contribution was mainly to say that the LMS experience in Glasgow of using untreated water from Loch Katrine in The Trossachs, Scottish Highlands, (including, significantly, in the batteries of electric vehicles) must have indicated how eminently suitable it was. Shortly afterwards, Stanier was again asked to luncheon, appropriately at the Travellers' Club, this time by Hartley. He was well acquainted with Great Western affairs and moreover, his position as a Vice-President of the LMS Executive gave the meeting official recognition. Stanier reported to his chief, Collett, the CME of the GWR, this second, discreet, invitation. Now Collett was only some five years older than Stanier, who could therefore hope for only a brief period of tenure, if indeed the post were offered to him at all. In the context of the GWR tradition outlined earlier, and very likely aware of LMS difficulties, Collett probably divined what was afoot. He gave Stanier his blessing. At the lunch, Hartley told Stanier frankly what he needed: a modern stud of standard locomotives that would haul his trains to all parts; he then offered Stanier outright the position of CME of the LMS Railway. This dumbfounded Stanier. He had served the GWR for forty years and expected to continue to his retirement; like his father, he was a Great Western man through and through. He expressed surprise to Hartley that no approach by Sir Josiah Stamp to the GWR General Manager, Sir James Milne, had been made, but this omission of protocol was quickly rectified. Stanier told Collett of Hartley's offer to him and suggested that Sir James be told straightaway. Collett went up to Paddington to report to him but, as he was speaking, the GWR chairman, Viscount Churchill, walked into the room. "Yes, Stamp has told me" he intervened. "Well, Collett, we want you to run your full term, so there's no chance for you to become our CME, Stanier." In fact, Collett continued in post up to the age of 70. Stamp confirmed his offer to Churchill, thereby clearing the way for Stanier, and he was appointed CME of the LMS from New Year's Day 1932. The short time-scale indicates the urgency but, in the context of Lemon's interim appointment as CME, no doubt Hartley had been discreetly planning to meet Stanier for some time and hoping to appoint him quickly. Actually, during Lemon's short reign as CME, the LMS had tried to recruit Gresley from the LNER, but when this proved impossible, had immediately turned to Stanier. His potential for updating the LMS soon showed it was a wise move. These events indicate the anxiety of the LMS over its motive-power situation and its desperation to appoint at last a CME to carry out the Executive's policy. From Stanier's point of view, his appointment was a huge transition: from simply assisting his CME at Swindon to becoming the CME himself—and of a very much bigger railway, in fact by far the largest in Britain.

But what had Stanier to offer and what had he brought with him? After an active sporting youth, at 55 he was still healthy and energetic, offering at least ten active years, with his experience in managerial posts in the works and on the running-side, plus a lifetime's experience of the GWR and its superior technology. Another advantage was a box of vital papers he had brought, engineering-drawings that he handed out to his team at Euston, E.S. Cox, in charge of design and development and R.A. Riddles, locomotive-assistant. They formed the nucleus of his team and would prove his judgement in choosing the right people. Furthermore, he had an agreeable personality that motivated them to work enthusiastically towards a clear objective. He also fostered the career of Tom Coleman at Horwich, later promoting him to chief draughtsman at Derby. Roland Bond too benefited from the new CME's influence. The Deputy CME of the LMS, H.P.M. Beames, the former CME of the LNWR, already bypassed at the grouping in 1923 through seniority, felt during the changes happening in 1930-1 that his moment had finally come (even though he was only two years short of retirement). However, writing to Stanier of his disappointment, he expressed full support for him as the new CME. Stanier, fully realizing that changes would have to be gradual, moved ineffective staff to more-suitable posts in order to remove the conflicts that were inhibiting the company's policies, and put in people who would assist him to fulfil his remit. His new staff quickly realized that he was big in mind as well as stature and was no doctrinaire; he adopted Swindon principles where they suited the much-larger LMS company, often adapting them to its needs—and he was quick to recognize and correct any mistake. Other changes were coming. Within a year, J.E. Anderson retired, appointed from the MR in 1924 as Motive Power Superintendent, and to fill the vacancy, D.C. Urie was moved from Divisional Mechanical Engineer in Glasgow. H.G. Ivatt went from Works Superintendent at Derby to replace him, a position that came to be regarded as a stepping-stone to senior office.

Stanier set himself resolutely to the task that Stamp had given him: to design and produce standardized engines to haul the various kinds and weights of trains on the large network. This followed the GWR policy, the reason why Hartley had chosen Stanier for the job. But the huge LMS company was a world away from the GWR, therefore Stanier needed time to become acquainted with its organization. For one thing, the four large locomotive-works of the LMS continued to operate more or less independently, contrasting sharply with the GWR system, centralized on Swindon. Stanier therefore spent some time evaluating the existing arrangements, visiting the four main works and the ancillaries to see what was being done, how it was done, and observing the performances of the various classes of engine in traffic. In view of the magnitude of this task, he did well to bring out his first designs in the year following his appointment. However, it was not a large, prestigious, locomotive that appeared as the first credited to Stanier, but a shunting-tank, followed by ten 0-4-4 tanks to replace similar Midland types. They too had a Derby appearance— and stovepipe chimneys as well. "Were they the new standard?" asked observers. No, these two classes were in the pipeline already, and Stanier, as CME, was credited with their design.

When Stanier arrived on the LMS in 1932, five further Compounds were under construction (935-9), a 1905-design, reflecting the last throw of Midland influence on the company. Also scheduled for the building-programme were a further thirty Derby 2-6-4 tanks launched in 1927, but Stanier took the opportunity of modifying the design, including fitting side-window cabs for the comfort of the enginemen, to act as a halfway-stage before his taper-boiler could be produced. The rebuilding of the large-boilered 5X Claughtons into Patriots was also under way, but here too Stanier took a hand, delaying their reconstruction in order to fit some of his specialities, principally improved axleboxes, wheels, tyres and bogeys. Since his brief was to produce a stud of modern engines having low maintenance costs and wide availability, Stanier looked at all classes with a view to upgrading. Of the 9,000-plus locomotives in stock, only four classes had potential: the mixed-traffic Horwich mogul, the 5X Patriot 4-6-0, the 2-6-4 tank and the 2-6-2 tank. Additionally, a heavy freight-engine would shortly be required. Stanier's policy was to fit a taper-boiler with low superheat, Swindon-style Belpaire firebox, top-feed, circular smokebox cast integral with its saddle, cylinders with large piston-valves, large, straight, steam-ports with direct exhaust-passages to a jumper blastpipe, generous axle-journals with Swindon-style horn-block axleboxes, bogeys and pony-trucks with side-bolsters, and a comfortable cab with a handy grouping of controls. A determined effort by the three main design-offices produced Stanier versions of the 2-6-0 and the 5X 4-6-0 (Jubilee) as well as the three-cylinder 2-6-4 tank designed specifically for the Tilbury-network, and the mixed-traffic 5P5F 4-6-0. They came into service during 1933-4. The following year saw the appearance of two further tank-engines, a two-cylinder general-purpose 2-6-4 and a 2-6-2. This was the upgrading, but Stanier's powerful express-locomotive for the west coast was on the stocks.

In 1933, the commentators saw Stanier's first designs, the pacific and the mixed-traffic 2-6-0 tender-engine. The Horwich standard 2-6-0 designed by Hughes, turned out in 1926 after his retirement—the first new design produced by the LMS—had proved to be extremely efficient and well-received, and 245 were in service. On his arrival at the LMS, Stanier found a further forty authorized. He seized the opportunity to alter the specification in order to introduce the Swindon taper-boiler to his LMS design-team and the works. Its 225lbs-boiler allowed smaller cylinders, which could therefore be set lower, allowing level, rather than stepped, footplating, giving the locos a better, perhaps a rather Great Western, appearance. Three Horwich moguls were fitted with lead fingers at platform-level to simulate the profile of the new engine's cylinders and sent to 314 places in England and Wales where clearances were considered tight. Fortunately, very few alterations had to be made to lineside structures. In this way, Stanier introduced the 'new look' of a taper-boiler. However, this was less apparent on later, larger, locomotives such as the Princess Coronation (Duchess) of 1937, because her huge taper-boiler had been designed up to the limit of the loading-gauge. The Walschaerts valve-gear was in vogue and already fitted to the Horwich 2-6-0s, the Derby 2-6-4 tank-engines and the Royal Scots; Stanier considered this the way forward, rather than the inside valve-gear of his Great Western role-models; as observed, the four eccentrics of the Stephenson gear placed undue strain on the bearings and furthermore needed a pit for maintenance. Stanier's 1933 taper-boiler moguls lasted into the 1960s, approaching the end of the steam era. He ended their construction with that 'lot' of forty engines, since his Mixed-Traffic 4-6-0 design (the Black Five) was ready, described below. The taper-boilered mogul served its purpose well however, so that, when Stanier's substantive programme began in the following year, the men were becoming accustomed to seeing the narrower front-end of his taper-boiler moguls, and the two pacifics on the daily Royal Scot train, compared with the heavy front-ends of the traditional Midland parallel-boilers and the Royal Scots. These strong 4-6-0s were masters of their duties, hauling the heavy West Coast expresses, but, now, five years on, even more power was needed. Trains were becoming longer, often with restaurant—and kitchen-cars, not to mention the prestigious sleeping-car expresses, and a more-powerful express-locomotive was urgently needed.

During 1933, the word spread that Crewe was constructing a Pacific. The first of Stanier's standard-classes, it was schemed out in alternative three- and four-cylindered form, the latter being decided on, since Stanier's guideline was the four-cylinder King 4-6-0, the GWR's largest standard engine, along with a look at the same company's 'Great Bear' pacific. He decided straightaway that the long through-turns envisaged dictated a wider and longer firebox, implying a Pacific design to allow a wide grate set behind the rear driving-axle and therefore a two-wheeled truck to carry it. This apart, the engine's main dimensions were the same as the GWR King, but the extended chassis had allowed a much longer boiler, giving quite a different appearance. Its nominal tractive-effort too was also the same as the King, 40,000lb. Because the pacific locomotive represented such a radical departure from previous LMS practice, only two were constructed, 6200 and 6201, later named *The Princess Royal* and *Princess Elizabeth* respectively. A third set of frames was reserved for an experimental locomotive, described shortly. With only two pacifics in service, any teething-troubles could be rapidly and cheaply rectified. Actually, they were few. The Princesses rode well from the beginning, exhibiting no hint of pitching nor oscillation, a testimony to Stanier's careful chassis design, in particular his use of the Churchward-de Glehn bogie as the leading-wheels.

With the Royal Scots holding the fort on the West Coast, a breathing-space was available for testing these very large engines in order to iron out any faults. After evaluation trips from Euston to Liverpool and Manchester, the two pacifics were rostered in 1934 to work the *Royal Scot,* the London-Glasgow prestige-train, each day one working down to Glasgow, the other up to London. Their crews appreciated especially their smooth riding and Stanier's carefully-conceived cab-layout. These workings soon revealed however that an improved boiler would increase efficiency, including the small GWR-style superheater, which needed enlarging. With only two engines involved, this was straightforward. Over a few years, several different boilers were tried. Nock, in *William Stanier*, gives the details of them, including the modified boiler fitted to 6200 early in 1935 with an improved tube-layout and the number of superheater elements almost doubled over the original boiler, but it was still domeless. Ten more of the class were built with this boiler in 1935.

Although the LMS schedules of that era were moderate, for example 89min allowed for the 82.6 miles from Euston to Rugby, even this timing proved an exacting test of the new engines, and a demanding task for the men who had to discover the best methods of operating them. The large 45 sq ft grate was overwhelming for the firemen at first, and the coal did not trim forward well in the Derby-type tender. Stanier's bigger tender came later. But, well handled, the work of 6200 and 6201 was of a quality denoting an excellent design. The Churchward-type boiler and high Belpaire firebox allowed ample space for the upward circulation of water at the firebox tube-plate, the hottest part, and, although more expensive to construct, these boilers required much less maintenance than the traditional parallel boiler with Belpaire firebox. The modifications to the boiler and superheater were made so as to equip the engines for the long diagrams that were being contemplated to utilize them effectively, including short fill-in express-turns after arrival in Glasgow. First, Stanier had the steam-circuit of *The Princess Royal* analyzed; the figures obtained showed that the cross-sectional area through the superheater headers was restricting the steam-flow. Since the superheater was closely based upon Great Western practice, he found to his surprise that the Kings were similarly constricted.

The modifications solved the restricted steaming, giving the margin required for operation over the northern hills and in the varying conditions of common-user service, including the variety of fuels supplied at different sheds, whether Welsh coal at Crewe, Scottish soft coal at Polmadie in Glasgow or Yorkshire 'Silkstone Hards'/Notts Blidworth supplied to Camden. To the author, the Princess looked an enormous machine. The author's first close-up view and haulage by one was as a schoolboy returning home to Halifax with mother after visiting our Scots relatives in 1945: a glimpse of 6211 *Queen Maud* sweeping into the up-platform at Motherwell. The engine's size and smooth lines impressed me, and then her fast run over Beattock summit to Carlisle, detailed in the chapter describing two Leeds-Glasgow return-trips. Nock mentions this locomotive specifically as a sprinter, judged by his fastest-ever journey from Euston to Mossley Hill (a Liverpool suburb) in 1936—and hauling the heaviest load. For exciting reading, look up back numbers of *The Railway Magazine* or *Trains Illustrated* for the his detailed logs and those compiled by the late Cecil J. Allen. Nock's accounts in his *William Stanier* bring out vividly the thrilling Stanier era on the LMS. All make splendid reading. After arrival at Carlisle and while awaiting the connection to Leeds, the author walked up the platform to study the huge machine in close-up before she hooted and departed for Birmingham. The hooter represented another pioneering project. Following tests of different whistles, for its standard engines the LMS Executive had adopted the Caledonian hooter, derived from the siren on the Clyde steamers of its subsidiary company, the Caledonian Steam Packet Co. Ltd., now part of the LMS group. It distinguished the company from the high-pitched whistles on the other railways and, particularly in the darkness, it unmistakeably announced LMS territory. The pacifics were coupled at first to tenders of MR design, then to 9-ton tenders and finally to the curved-top 10-ton type, aesthetically suited to the engines, continuing their cab roof-line to the carriages perfectly.

It was in 1933 with the Princess pacifics launched that a chain of important personnel-changes were made in the CME's department. Riddles, Assistant Works Superintendent at Crewe, was appointed Locomotive Assistant to the CME and, after Beames' retirement in 1934, was promoted, in August 1935, to Principal Assistant to the CME, and Herbert Chambers was appointed Locomotive and Personal Assistant to the CME in March 1935. Tom Coleman, Chief Draughtsman at Horwich, but originally from the North Staffordshire Railway at Stoke-on-Trent, went to succeed him as Chief Draughtsman at Derby. Bond, who had been encouraged to return from the commercial locomotive-industry, succeeded Riddles as Assistant Works Superintendent at Crewe. However, with Chambers' health uncertain, the burden of the next stage of Stanier's programme fell on his assistants, Riddles, Bond and Coleman.

First however, Stanier had to take on another project personally. Early in the summer of 1933, the Executive decided to send a locomotive and train on a goodwill-mission to the USA to represent Great Britain at the 'Century of Progress Exposition' in Chicago. Stanier, a driver, two firemen and a fitter accompanied the train. The new pacific was not ready, so a Royal Scot was sent, actually 6152 *The King's Dragoon Guardsman* masquerading as 6100 *Royal Scot*, since it was of the later series and relatively new. The number 6152 stamped on the motion was spotted by an alert observer during the engine's tour, but other details betrayed its origin as one of the last twenty locomotives built at Derby in 1930. The front of its smokebox carried an oblong plate *The Royal Scot* to denote the train. To prepare the engine for the tour, Stanier designed a special tender—one of three, the other two coupled to the two Princesses—and had the engine's running-gear completely rebuilt with his wheels, steel axleboxes and side-bearing bogey, plus the requisite headlamp—before being dismantled and shipped with eight carriages from Tilbury Docks on the Canadian Pacific Railway *SS Beaverdale* to Montreal, Canada, where Royal Scot was re-assembled and fitted with a cowcatcher in the CPR workshops. From there, the train embarked on a circuitous tour to allow as many people as possible to see this ambassador of British trains. It included an 'all-electric kitchen-car' to show that Britain was up to date. After crossing over to the USA at Detroit, the train traversed different systems to reach New York, including the Burlington, the Pennsylvania and the New York Central Railroads. The thousands of visitors who passed through the train and over the engine proved their popularity as an attraction to such an extent that the tour was extended—to the west coast of the United States, no less. From San Francisco, Royal Scot crossed back into Canada, returning to Montreal on the Canadian Pacific RR, after climbing unassisted over a 5,600ft summit through the Rocky Mountains. The testament to the improved Royal Scot locomotive was its faultless running throughout, an arduous six-month tour covering over 11,000 miles; its finish and workmanship too were admired by the North Americans. It returned, again on the CPR ship *Beaverdale,* late in November 1933, and on arrival back at Euston, gold watches were presented to the men who had operated *Royal Scot*. Instructed by the Executive, the publicity-department designed a curved plate outlining the North American tour, which was mounted below the name-plate. To gain maximum publicity, a commemorative booklet was produced, *The Triumph of The Royal Scot,* and its own label, 'Royal Scot Whisky'. This is the wording of the special nameplate.

THIS LOCOMOTIVE WITH THE ROYAL SCOT TRAIN WAS EXHIBITED AT THE CENTURY OF PROGRESS EXPOSITION, CHICAGO, 1933, AND MADE A TOUR OF THE DOMINION OF CANADA AND THE UNITED STATES OF AMERICA. THE ENGINE AND TRAIN COVERED 11,194 MILES OVER THE RAILROADS OF THE NORTH AMERICAN CONTINENT AND WAS INSPECTED BY 3,021,601 PEOPLE.

W. GILBERTSON.—DRIVER.   T. BLACKETT.—FIREMAN.
J. JACKSON.—FIREMAN.   W.C. WOODS.—FITTER.

The locomotive and train, the engine complete with its special name-plates and bell, were displayed to the public at different places around the LMS system. Public-relations had become important and this successful tour thus generated further valuable publicity for the LMS. When returned to traffic, the engine retained its identity and bell, though not its special tender. After withdrawal from service, the engine, now in converted form and LMS red, was placed on display at Bressingham, Norfolk, complete with its name-plates and bell, later moving to Southall, where its restoration was begun in 2004. During 2009, the owning trust moved the engine to LNWR Heritage at Crewe for the completion of its restoration to running-order. For the information on restoration, acknowledgement is made to Keith Langston *British Steam, Past & Present.* Stanier modified the rest of the class with the new axleboxes and bogey, bringing an immediate reduction in the number of hot boxes, and giving improved reliability of the Scots along with reduced maintenance-costs, thereby ensuring the engines remained top-class performers.

The missing number in the Pacific series, 6202, was the set of frames reserved for Stanier's experimental turbine-locomotive, an idea he had been considering as a way of improving the low thermal-efficiency of the steam-locomotive by producing a higher power-output from the same chassis and boiler. Since the decade before the first world war, interest had been high in turbines, particularly to drive ships. Parsons' revolutionary *Turbinia* of 1909, a prototype steam-turbine-driven torpedo-boat, apparently offered advantages over the conventional reciprocating-engine. The pace-setting Pennsylvania RR in America had built an experimental turbine-locomotive and the LMS Executive, interested in the concept of turbine-drive, had already tried out the Reid-Ramsay turbine-electric machine. The company went on to test the Ljungström prototype, a condensing-machine, built under licence in 1926 by Beyer-Peacock Ltd, Gorton, Manchester, to conform to the British loading-gauge. After tests at the maker's works, the engine was sent to the LMS at Derby and illustrated in *The Railway Gazette* of 29 October 1926. On 20 May 1927, it left Manchester with an eight-coach train on the Midland main-line to St Pancras, a steeply-graded route through the Derbyshire High Peak. From Nottingham to London, 123 miles, it ran non-stop averaging 54.8 mph, with a maximum of 67. During 1928, the turbine-machine ran trials on freight-trains from Leeds and Derby to London to compare it with the new standard Horwich 2-6-0 according to a correspondent in *The Railway Magazine* of May 1978, which also pictures the engine at Beyer-Peacock's Gorton works. The initial interest of the LMS in purchasing the locomotive came to nothing, for it languished at the works until the 1950s. Acknowledgements are made to *The Railway Magazine* for some of this information.

The explanation for this inaction seems to be that the three advantages of turbine-drive with rotary motion replacing cylinders and valve-gear, the elimination of reciprocating parts and of dirt and grit, and an enclosed oil-bath gear-drive, were largely outweighed by the maintenance of the complex condenser-equipment with the associated downtime of the locomotive. At the time, three different designs of turbine-locomotive were running in Sweden; one of them a Ljungström non-condensing turbine-locomotive, which was hauling heavy iron-ore trains on the Grangesberg-Oxelösund line, in the south-west. In 1934, having brought his new pacifics to the standard required for haulage of the crack west-coast expresses, Stanier judged it was a propitious moment to leave his staff to manage them, while he slipped off quietly to observe this turbine-engine. He went off to Sweden at the behest of Dr H. (later Sir Henry) Guy, Chief Turbine Engineer of Metropolitan-Vickers Electrical Co in Manchester (now part of GEC-Alsthom), to observe the non-condensing locomotive at work. Favourably impressed, the two men returned with an outline of what the LMS required, Guy to Manchester to draw up a suitable specification of turbine, and Stanier to instruct his design-team. Guy quickly came up with a turbine already designed for Egypt, but some details had to be worked out, including how to reverse the engine. This was accomplished by fitting a smaller turbine on the offside footplating. The locomotive appeared on the rails in June 1935.

For a prototype, it performed well with few troubles, considering that it was a ground-breaking design, and demonstrated a haulage capacity well above that of the Princesses. Maintenance-costs proved to be lower too, with less hammer-blow on the track, and in the important sphere of boiler and firebox. Here, the smooth operation of the turbine-drive gave less wear, obviating the grooving that occurred on conventional reciprocating engines. But its smooth operation also produced a soft blast from the double-chimney that allowed the smoke to drift down and cling to the top of the boiler, tending to obscure the driver's view, just as it had previously on the Royal Scots. The crews also complained that the smoke entered the cab—but they also acknowledged the engine was an advance on the traditional design. As on the Scots, the LMS fitted smoke-deflector plates—eventually. The locomotive ran with three different types of boiler, the first with 32 superheater-elements, the second with 40 and the third with 40 having triple-flow elements. Observers soon dubbed the unnamed engine 'Turbomotive'. After running to Glasgow and back with the dynamometer-car, the engine spent the majority of its time hauling *The Merseyside Express*—and so, living in the West Riding of Yorkshire, the author never saw it. At that time, schoolboys could not travel around the country to spot engines. On the outbreak of the 1939 war, the engine was stored in Crewe works, but later in the conflict, when every available engine was needed, Turbomotive was brought out to run again. However, as a prototype, it needed adjustments and repairs, difficult during wartime, since they were of a specialist nature. If a stud of turbine-locomotives had been built, the workshops would have been equipped to handle their requirements efficiently and quickly. As it was, Turbomotive often had to wait for a time-slot to be found in the busy repair schedule, as well as having to stand idle awaiting the manufacture of specialist parts when the majority of Metropolitan-Vickers' capacity was devoted to war-production. This explains why the records show the locomotive with a statistically-low availability compared with her sisters; it was a reflection not on the design, simply on its uniqueness. It is the view of steam experts that 'Turbomotive' was outstandingly the most successful venture into the unorthodox. In this respect, it represents another 'first' for the LMS Railway.

Post-war, some engineers considered further development-work would pay off, but costs—principally those of procuring a new forward turbine—ruled this out and Riddles had the engine rebuilt in August 1952 as a conventional pacific named *Princess Anne*, essentially a hybrid, with a Princess boiler and Duchess cylinders. Extreme bad luck gave her the shortest of lives, only a matter of weeks, for she was involved in the second of the tragic collisions at Harrow & Wealdstone in October 1952, leaving it, along with its pilot, Jubilee *Windward Islands*, too damaged to be repaired, and both engines were scrapped. The potential performance of *Princess Anne* therefore remains unknown.

Stanier had planned a series of locomotive-types which were to be the new standard classes of the LMS: a Pacific for the heaviest trains, a 4-6-0 for lighter expresses, and which could deputize for a pacific without losing too much time, a mixed-traffic 4-6-0, tank engines for cross-country or suburban-work, and shunting locomotives.

Upgrading the 5XP locomotives

Routine-testing on the LMS went on continuously, from the early trials of constituents' express-engines, of high-pressure locomotives and turbine machines, along with trying various engines on the heavy Toton-Brent mineral-haul. Efficiency and economy were the aim, and Stanier's designs with high superheat achieved these objectives. His priority now was to upgrade the 5X Patriot 4-6-0s. Although the Patriots were performing well in 1933, Stanier felt that a taper-boiler would give greater efficiency. The next batch, 5552-6, was re-programmed with a taper-boiler. The taper-boiler three-cylinder 5X 4-6-0 appeared along with the two-cylinder 4-6-0, the 'Black Five', classified '5P5F mixed-traffic'. As passenger locomotives, the 5Xs were painted red, the mixed-traffics black, and were therefore called by many drivers 'goods engines'. Late in 1934, the new regime on the LMS was well under way, and everyone was eagerly anticipating the performance of the new 4-6-0s. Unfortunately, all was not well. Footplate-crews reported that the black engines ran well, but the red ones were shy of steam. Experienced footplate-inspectors confirmed their reports. Something was seriously wrong, but what?

Stanier set his staff to tackle the difficulty. It was not a single aspect of design however; typically, there were a number a factors. The GWR practice of low superheat and jumper-top blastpipe represented two. This type of blastpipe increases the effective aperture-diameter to reduce the blast while the engine is being worked in full gear. It was Riddles, Principal Assistant to Stanier, who spotted that its effect was the exact opposite of what was needed: the 5Xs needed *more* blast, not less, to stimulate the lack-lustre fire. Accordingly, the jumper-top was removed and, in stages, the orifice-diameter was reduced and the blast-pipe lowered with a smaller chimney-petticoat diameter. Alterations were made to the grate as well, resulting in a marked improvement in steaming. Double-chimneys and blastpipes were also tried on a few engines. Detailed superheater-tests were conducted at Derby and, although Stanier felt the men in charge were rather young, he accepted their findings and stepped up the elements from 14 to 24. The dimensions and layout of the boiler-tubes were not ideal either for a three-cylinder engine. For one thing, insufficient free space was provided around the tubes for upward circulation of the water. Stanier's experience had been confined to locomotives with two or four cylinders, so his 5X-essay led him to conclude that three-cylinder engines were temperamental. Yet the three-cylinder Royal Scots had steamed well from the outset, however designed largely by NB Loco. Their progeny, the Patriots, similarly configured, had also performed well from the beginning. The fact was that the Swindon blastpipe/chimney-dimensions were designed for two- or four-cylinder engines and were unsuitable for one with three-cylinders and a six-beat exhaust, the audible signature of these engines. When the modifications had been tested step-by-step on the road, the red 5X 4-6-0s, the *Jubilees*, as they were named later after the first of the class, became strong, reliable engines, fully competent to slog up gradients and to run very fast on the level or downhill. They fully vindicated Stanier's design as an improvement on the Patriots.

E.D. Bruton's photograph, taken in the BR-era of the 1950s, says it all: the appropriately-named 45706 *Express* speeding through Tebay hauling a Liverpool-Glasgow express of amazingly, thirteen carriages—around 450 tons gross—for *an unassisted climb to Shap summit*. The author's own experiences with many Jubilees on the Leeds-Carlisle road—including on the footplate—bear this out: a steady haul from Settle Junction up to Blea Moor or from Kirkby Stephen up to Ais Gill was usually followed by a very fast run down to Appleby or descending Ribblesdale to the stop at Hellifield. Some Jubilees were timed at well over 90mph. It was just unfortunate that they were built in volume straight from the drawing-board—in fact, a hundred and thirteen, (5552-5664), evidencing the urgency of Stanier's restocking programme—and his confidence in his design. If a few had been built for trials, like the Princesses, the resulting modifications would have been easier, more straightforward, and of course cheaper to carry out. But this is the wisdom of hindsight. As it was, modifications were incorporated on successive batches from engine 5665 and further improvements from 5702 to the end of the class at 5742. Larger superheaters than the two-row, seven-element type of the early locomotives were fitted: three-row—and each of eight elements now—even a four-row to one engine, both to improve steaming and to economize on coal. The improvements they gave were more significant than when carried out on the 5P5F, described shortly. Earlier locomotives were gradually updated, but five domeless boilers remained to be carried by different engines after repairs. As well as a few double-chimneys, three different types and heights of single-chimney were fitted to various engines, and four different types of tender: Derby 3,500-gallon—with and without coal-rails—a high-sided version without rails, and the Stanier 4,000-gallon type. Aesthetically, the latter with its high curved top suited the locomotive, continuing the cab roof-line to carriages perfectly. Low superheat and the jumper blastpipe were the only Swindon precepts that Stanier abandoned, demonstrating that he did not slavishly follow Swindon traditions; he adopted them where practicable, adapting them with his own experience. 'Adopt and adapt' is a proven maxim. However, even after the modifications, the Jubilee remained more sensitive and delicate to operate, compared with the Black Five, which performed easily from the start. With the Jubilees now performing satisfactorily, faster than the compounds on the Midland-line, the accelerated schedules could be instituted: they gave thirty-four runs averaging over a-mile-a-minute. These illustrate the LMS policy of improvements across the board, rather than a headline-grabbing speed on one premier train.

In preparation for the accelerated schedules, three Jubilees were run on test during 1937 with the dynamometer-car, 5740 *Munster*, 5614 *Leeward Islands* and 5660 *Rooke* with just over 300 tons including dynamometer-car. *Leeward Islands* was run from St Pancras to Leeds giving excellent uphill climbing with high maxima downhill. *Munster*, one of the final improved batch, ran from Crewe to Carlisle, and then from Wolverhampton to Euston. The intermediate modifications mentioned above had brought down coal-consumption considerably, but *Munster* reduced this further, giving a reduction of 30% over Patriots on the same trains, and fully comparable with the performance of a GWR Castle 4-6-0, a trail-blazer in this field. The significance of the *Munster* test was that the LMS London-Birmingham/Wolverhampton schedule represented, as remarked, the only express shop-window that the LMS could present to the GWR; it showed the LMS was now a serious competitor. Later in the year, from 12-15 October, a final, four-day test was carried out, and it produced remarkable results. It was the turn of 5660 *Rooke*. The locomotive was run non-stop from Bristol-Leeds-Glasgow via Kilmarnock and back, 869 miles with a train of similar weight, just over 300 tons including dynamometer-car. Two crews ran return-trips, Bristol-Leeds and Leeds-Glasgow. The locomotive was worked very hard throughout, reflected in a higher coal-consumption. At several points on the journey, indicated horsepower figures in excess of 1,800 were recorded, an outstanding achievement for an engine of moderate size; it completely vindicated the design. In fact, *Rooke*'s performance on 'The Long Drag' (Settle-Blea Moor) compared very favourably with later ascents by A.4 and Duchess pacifics. Full technical details of the Jubilee tests are contained in J.F. Clay's splendid *Jubilees of the LMS* (Ian Allan, 1971), which is acknowledged for some of the above information. Late in the steam era, in 1965, the author was fortunate to be hauled by *Rooke* up 'The Long Drag', described in a later chapter. Photographs and preserved locomotives illustrate the 4-6-0 developments: from the Claughton, through its 5XP large-boiler rebuild, to this boiler mounted upon a Royal Scot chassis (the Baby Scot/Patriot), then the taper-boiler on this chassis (the Jubilee), a locomotive fully competent to deputize for a pacific without losing too much time. But one final development was to come, which would transform the Jubilee from a competent into a brilliant performer, described under the Royal Scots.

The 5P5F mixed-traffic locomotive (Black Five)

Of Stanier's six classes, the two-cylinder 4-6-0/2-8-0 designs represented the heart of the new standard programme, at the end of the LMS era representing 60% of the total Stanier output. The mixed-traffic 4-6-0 needs little introduction, whether you know it as 'Class 5', '5MT', 'Black Stanier' or 'Black Five'; my aim here is simply to place the locomotive in the LMS scheme of operations.

Stanier specified a straightforward design using the principal dimensions of the successful GWR 'Hall' mixed-traffic 4-6-0, plus proven LMS technology. Initially, it was schemed out with the Royal Scot's three cylinders as an alternative. However, unconvinced that the extra weight gave corresponding additional power—possibly suspecting this of his 2-6-4 tank, (specially designed with three-cylinders to operate the Tilbury lines as explained later)—Stanier chose the two-cylinder layout, entrusting the detailed design to Coleman. He gave it his own individuality, producing a balanced layout and an attractive 'Stanier' look. The engine ran well from the start without teething-troubles, in fact exceeding expectations. It possessed such potential for development that it received a host of modifications stretching over seventeen years, essentially in three stages, further enhancing its performance. Following experience with the early pacific boilers, the boiler/firebox design was altered in 1935 to improve water-circulation and an increased cross-sectional area to improve steam-flow through the superheater from locomotives 5070-4 built at Crewe as a pilot batch. Also, the degree of superheat was increased from 14 to 24 elements (in three rows of eight), following that on the Jubilees. No fewer than 377 engines were then built by contractors, 5075-5124 by Vulcan Foundry, and 5125-5451 by Armstrong Whitworth. From 5452 in 1938, the superheating-elements were further augmented to 28—even a four-row of 32 elements on some engines—along with an increased tube heating-area. Like Stanier's other designs, the Black Five was built at first with a boiler having only a top-feed and no dome. However, from 5225, domed boilers were fitted, with regulator in the dome. Early engines also had taller chimneys.

Apart from the early war-years, the Black Five was built continuously from 1934, by the LMS itself, by outside contractors, and by BR up to 1951, that is, well into the nationalized era. The five-hundred number-slot reserved for the class had almost been filled by 1939, but the last batch, 5472-5499, had to await a slight easing of wartime steel-requirements and was built at Derby in 1943. Thus, when the author started observing the LMS in 1941, the Black Fives totalled 472, a considerable class to have in traffic at that time, but noted, deliciously, in my *ABC of LMS Locomotives* (Ian Allan, 1943), as 'still being delivered'. Although 5452-5471 were constructed at Crewe—with the larger superheaters—the preceding batches had been built either by Armstrong-Whitworth or Vulcan Foundry, except 5000-19 and 5070-4, built at Crewe. Many of the last hundred or so were allocated to depots in Carlisle or Scotland, allowing the author to see them working on fitted-freights and superseding the compounds on Edinburgh expresses. Examples appearing at Apperley Bridge were: 5384/9/92; 5401-4/7, 5418/20-9/31, 5440/3/4/6/48/ 51, 5455/7/61, 5467/72/3/82/4/7/9/91/4/7.

The wartime steel-requirements were easing more once the 'D-Day' operations scheduled for 5 June 1944 had been prepared, the planned assault on Hitler's 'Atlantic Wall', much of it with American equipment. The wartime Railway Executive therefore allowed the construction of mixed-traffic types, and so the LMS plan for two hundred identical locomotives went ahead immediately, numbered 4800-4999, preceding the original series. They came into service from January 1944 as part of Lot 153, bringing the class-total to 700. This indicates the unrelenting determination of the LMS to press ahead with its programme of standardization. The two hundred engines were completed early in 1947, of which we saw the majority in the Leeds area. I noted 4813/4 on the daily Saltley Goods bearing that depot's shed-plate, 21A. Locomotives 4837-59 all ran around Leeds for a time when new in 1945, for example 4828/9 that I saw at Hellifield in 1945 while out cycling with father, 4829 one of four converted for oil-burning. Post-war, coal-supplies became a problem—one only exacerbated by hard winters and this alternative was the government's response. The emergency lasted only a short time however, allowing the railways to revert to coal before oil-facilities had been fully implemented. Surprisingly, the Black Five apparently possessed exactly the right characteristics for any kind of work. On a trip to Scotland, with surprise, the author even saw one shunting, in the Viaduct Yard, north of Carlisle Citadel station. They hauled heavy expresses, fast freights, weighty loose-coupled mineral-trains, stopping-trains and the Royal train, leading to their description as 'maids-of-all-work'. All this was an eye-opener, as previously engines had been designed for specific types of work, often on specific routes. This was Gresley's policy on the LNER: 'horses for courses', that is, locomotives designed for certain traffic and routes according to their power and axle-weights. Their cabs consequently bore the instruction 'RA' (route-allocation) followed by a number, painted below the side-window. The LMS 'go-anywhere' locomotives put it ahead of its rival's policy. After Gresley's early death in 1941, his successor, Thompson, followed the LMS with his B.1 *Springbok* (the first of the class) mixed-traffic 4-6-0, and on the Southern Railway Bulleid designed his Merchant Navy and West Country/Battle of Britain 4-6-2s, also for mixed-traffic work. The LMS Class Five could be driven with wide-open regulator and 10-15% cut-off or one-port regulator and 30% cut-off, real 'drivers' engines'.

In a delightful small collection, *Titans of the Track, 1947: LMS*, by the then-Canon E. Treacy, one of his photographs impressed itself on the author's memory: his super picture of the Royal Train standby-engine in the Citadel Station, Carlisle, 4883, of course bright as a new pin. The monochrome photograph shows up the gleaming lined-out black paint with its flame-coloured insignia. This relatively-new machine was probably based at Carlisle Kingmoor (12A) at the time, as it used to pass the school. A footnote is that the famous Canon the lived near the author's home, when Archdeacon of Halifax, before his elevation, first to Suffragan Bishop of Pontefract, then to Bishop of Wakefield.

Before Lot 153 was completed early in 1947, the Executive had authorized a further hundred, to be numbered 4700-99, but built in batches in reverse order, since nationalization was approaching. These appeared in the 1946 post-war livery of black, with cream lining outlined in red, the number and initials in 'straw' block style with an inset red line, inferior, many felt, to the earlier livery of gold/gilt insignia, countershaded in red. Many of these last hundred were based for a time at Leeds (Holbeck) and the author noted 4772/5/95 passing his school, possibly on running-in diagrams. To continue this topic to its conclusion, the authorized construction of the Black Fives was completed by BR from 1948, back to 4658 (numbered by BR

44658). Many of these locomotives included significant modifications introduced by H.G. Ivatt, the last CME of the LMS: the 'SC' devices described elsewhere, steel fireboxes, Timken roller-bearings, Ivatt/Caprotti valve-gear or double-chimneys. The steel firebox—and the associated welding—had been pioneered by Hughes on the LYR back in 1910, developed by Bulleid on the LNER and later on the SR but especially in the USA, evidenced in their welded ships of WW2. America had also pioneered the roller-bearing, while various designs of double-chimneys had been tried on the Continent.

The 700-plus LMS Black Fives were now to be seen everywhere on the LMS, from Bournemouth (south coast) to Thurso (north of Scotland), the extent of the system from the Somerset & Dorset Joint Railway to the extremity of the old Highland Railway's Far North line. The recognition of this adaptability to almost all conditions and routes sang a paean of praise for the Black Five design. The LMS Executive's plans for 500 of these machines, evidenced by the original block of numbers reserved for them, underlines the measure by which their success had exceeded all expectations: already 40% more had been built, and potential still remained. This success and availability made the class ever more popular with the crews too, with only a moderate-sized firebox to fire. The final batches were overtaken by time, which was running out for the LMS as a corporate entity: the Transport Act 1947 was on the statute book with vesting-day coming soon on 1 January 1948. However, in its last months during 1947, the company managed to put further Black Fives into traffic numbered back to 4758. Because they were built at both Horwich and Crewe, the different lots appeared out of numerical sequence. Under Ivatt as the CME, the fresh options mentioned above were tried out and these late models of course bore the SC plate too on their smoke-boxes, further evidence of the unceasing search by the LMS for ever-greater efficiency, reliability and availability. One of the last engines built by the company was one of these modified 'Fives', the unique 4767 with Stephenson's Link motion—both return-cranks mounted outside too, a radical idea. It sounded cumbersome, but apparently worked well and appeared aesthetically acceptable to the author. His last sighting occurred in the summer of 1967, near the end of the steam-era, as 44767 (its BR number) slogged unassisted up the Shap incline past me in Scout Green signal-box with a Blackpool-Glasgow football-special. It is indeed fortunate that this singleton has been preserved, and can be seen on the North York Moors Railway. The modifications of the final batches are now considered.

On his appointment, Ivatt decided straightaway to try Caprotti poppet-valve gear on a Black Five. This gear had been tried on different classes of engine earlier, but Ivatt felt that the previous attempts had lacked enthusiasm and he now wanted to make a serious attempt to prove his hunch that the Caprotti gear would show greater efficiency. It was authorized for twenty of the later engines, 4738-57. In order to eliminate driving-box difficulties found during the earlier trials, Ivatt designed his own version, easily accommodated between the frames, since this was a two-cylinder engine. The result was a rather ugly creature; the first one not quite making it in LMS livery: 4748 appeared from the Crewe shops over the BR-divide early in 1948 coupled to a tender with no insignia. The twenty locomotives of this sub-class were allocated equally to four sheds: Manchester Longsight, Llandudno Junction, Bristol Barrow Road and Leeds Holbeck. Consequently we saw the Leeds engines often. In the author's opinion, the double-chimneys on locomotives 44755-7 detracted from their appearance. The author noted 44753 (M4753 at first), 44754-7 on the usual trains, the Leeds-Morecambe 'resi' at tea-time, on express—and stopping-trains between Bradford and Leeds, as well as on freights. Some observers felt they lacked the lusty pull of the piston-valve version, and it is on record that the enginemen too felt they were less powerful than their Walschaerts counterparts; a contention that Ivatt doubted; he countered by simply relabelling the reverse-gear quadrant, from 40% to 30%, quelling complaints. However, these engines remained unpopular with the maintenance staff, partly on account of the valve-gear and partly through the need for specialist spares. The very-last Black Fives, 44686/7 built at Horwich in 1951, also looked strange with their high footplating, needed to accommodate their now-external Caprotti-gear, but they proved outstandingly successful. Their modified camboxes gave variable expansion of the steam, making them very strong indeed. Their crews rated them as 'one coach better' than the standard Five, even equivalent to a power-class 6. Afterwards, they could be seen rather as prototypes for the BR Standard Five

73000s—but with Walschaerts gear instead of Caprotti—their high footplating rendering maintenance easier.

These last two Black 5s, 44686/7, brought to an end the construction of the largest class ever built and operated by a railway in Britain, such is the evidence of an outstandingly-successful design. Its numbers ran from 44658 to 45499, an amazing total of 842 locomotives. Although boilers were usually exchanged during heavy repairs, some Fives, like the few Jubilees mentioned, retained their domeless boilers throughout their lives, notably the first, 5000, which can be seen in the NRM, York. Seventeen others are preserved in running order. This testifies to the investment the LMS made in taper-boilers. Powell details the range of modifications carried out. Concerning the power-classification, the '5P5F' was changed on the wartime and post-war engines to a plain '5'. However, the riding-qualities of 4-6-0 locomotives were always less than ideal. Nock (*Steam Railways*), after many footplate-trips on various 4-6-0s, considered the LNER B.1 rough and uncomfortable in comparison with the LMS Black Five. One of his anecdotes is amusing here. Travelling on his normal train from Euston-Rugby during the early Stanier years, he observed the train was running faster than usual, and stepping off the train at Rugby, he saw with surprise that the taper-boilered engine at the front was not a 5X Jubilee but a Class Five. Nock congratulated the driver on his performance. "Yes", he replied, "We haven't done badly, with a goods engine!"

A design of light 4-6-0 for Scotland was not built however. Two classes of twenty-one 4-6-0s, Caledonian 'Callander-and-Oban' and Highland 'Jones goods', were due for re-boilering, a counter-productive step on such outmoded engines, so a lighter version of the Class 5P5F 4-6-0 was schemed out with an axle-load limited to about 15 tons, ten to be built in 1934, followed by a further eleven in 1935. However, some bridge-strengthening allowed the 'Clans' and later, 5P5Fs, to reach Oban, thus rendering the light 4-6-0 unnecessary. Interestingly however, it was indeed built, though much later, by Riddles as a BR standard-class, discussed in the chapter describing nationalization. The various 1933-designs are reproduced by Cox in his *Locomotive Panorama*. Stanier now turned to the 2-6-4 tank-engine, the third class suitable for improvement.

The 2-6-4 tank-engine

Later in 1934, with the steaming difficulties of the 5X 4-6-0s on the way to being cured, Stanier again looked at other recent classes worthy of improvement, even considering fitting taper-boilers to existing locomotives. But it was not merely a case of updating designs; he evaluated the tasks the various classes were called upon to perform. One outstanding need was to accelerate residential-trains (later called commuter-trains), particularly those on the London Tilbury & Southend network. The trains from Fenchurch Street to Southend-on-Sea were hauled by eighteen Derby-designed saturated 4-4-2 tank-engines of 1900-vintage, plus a batch of fifty-one to a similar specification built by the LMS in 1925 during the Derby-dominated period, and they were becoming unable to cope with the increasing weight of these trains. The LMS already had the excellent 2-6-4 tank-engine of 1927, already noted as very fast and free-running, but the hammer-blow of this engine on the track was considered too severe for the three-mile stretch from Fenchurch Street Station to Campbell Street Junction, Bow. Stanier therefore designed his taper-boiler version with three cylinders, to gain a smoother, more-balanced, rotation of the machinery. In this, he may have been influenced by Gresley on the LNER, who claimed the three-cylinder design gave quicker acceleration, among other advantages. The class was an instant success and thirty-seven were constructed, 2500-36. The majority went to LT&S sheds, but two were based at 20E, Manningham (Bradford) for many years, 2522 and 2524, for the haulage of Bradford-Leeds business-expresses past the school, superseding obsolete Midland 4-4-0s. These non-stop trains were easier tasks than the constant stopping and starting on the Tilbury lines. From Bradford, the morning trains ran bunker-first, returning from Leeds chimney-first. The scalloped bunker-top gave excellent visibility for running in reverse, and I think improved the appearance of the engine.

A BBC television programme in the 1990s reported a study of the new Stanier 3-cylinder 2-6-4 tank-engines made by a resident living alongside the London-Southend-line during the 1930s. Over a period, he took detailed notes on the workings of this intensive service—and, interestingly, ciné-film. They reveal the great improvements achieved by the new Staniers. The many intermediate stops demanded hard acceleration and, in dry conditions, these 2-6-4 tank engines hauling twelve-coach trains could be driven out of a station in full gear with wide regulator for half-a-minute without slipping, that is, 'all out', completely outclassing the Derby 4-4-2Ts. The observer related that the LMS had intended to electrify the network, but instead, with the aim of mollifying complainants, had provided an engine 'of the pacific wheel-arrangement' (2-6-4 in reverse) and 'three cylinders' (an express-type), to demonstrate that this was 'an express-line'. Rowledge gives the real reason, explained above. A retired driver, featured on the programme sitting in the cab of 2500 preserved in the NRM, the first Stanier 2-6-4, commented that the riding-quality of the 2500-class was definitely superior to the two-cylinder engines. Ideally, the network should have been electrified, following the Weir Committee's 1929 report favouring electrification, 1500v dc from overhead line. Later, the LNER began to electrify its rival line to Southend (Victoria) via Shenfield on this system, but the 1939-war delayed its completion. It seems that the LMS considered the cost too great at a time of financial stringency—and they had the resources of four locomotive-works to construct the alternative steam-engines. This recalls the cancelled project for the west-coast route electrification in 1924 and the make-do boiler on the Horwich 2-6-0 of 1926, detailed earlier: it was another case of 'continue as before'. But the LMS did electrify other suburban-lines, described under multiple-unit trains.

Once the particular Southend requirements had been met, Stanier continued constructing the 2-6-4s. However, comparisons made between the Derby 2-6-4s, well entrenched on northern suburban lines, and the three-cylinder engines, showed none of the advantages claimed by Gresley for the latter, neither in acceleration, steaming, coal-consumption nor any other claim for three cylinders. Stanier quickly recognized this, that an inside cylinder was not cost-effective for general use, and had a two-cylinder version drawn out at Derby. Altogether, 206 were produced from 1935, at first continuing numerically, 2537-2672, then a further seventy, 2425-94, following the Derby engines. A gap of five followed here: 2495-9 were not built. The first batch of eight, 2537-2544, was originally scheduled with three cylinders, but Stanier amended this construction-lot to the two-cylinder design, while retaining their domeless boilers. The 206 two-cylinder models, plus the 37 with three cylinders and the original Derby class of 125, totalled

368, a substantial number of one type for that era. The two-cylinder 2433 and 2634 also came flying past the school on the Bradford-Leeds non-stops and the up morning *Torbay Express* (Bradford-Bristol in winter), always travelling bunker-first up to Leeds for the reversal there and provision of an express-engine, usually a Jubilee. Many more did appear from time to time in the early 1940s. The author's notes show 2545/51/70/81/95, 2619/44/6/8/52-4. They displaced pre-grouping types of tank-engine, notably the LNW and L&Y 2-4-2s, the LNW 'Prince of Wales' tanks and 'Watford' tanks; around Leeds, various 4-4-0s of Midland vintage.

It was in 1945 that the final development of these excellent locomotives occurred, the short-wheelbase version. Following Stanier's secondment to the War Department, C.E. Fairburn became Acting-CME of the LMS in 1943, and later was confirmed in the post. An electrical engineer by training, he delegated the design to Coleman, who amended the two-cylinder 2-6-4-design only in minor respects. He discarded the Midland's sacrosanct 8ft 0in + 8ft 6in coupled-wheelbase for a shorter one to enable the engines to negotiate 5-chain instead of 6-chain-radius curves in sidings and depots for increased availability. (A chain equals 66 feet.) In order to avoid increasing the axle-loading, he economized in weight, the explanation for the altered appearance, as discussed in the contemporary railway press. Visually this showed in the loss of the vertical footplating (or fall-plate) in front of the cylinders, the substitution of welded tanks for the riveted variety, and ladder-type footsteps, detracting somewhat from the engine's attractiveness. The footplating may have been chosen for omission after experience with 'defrocked' ex-streamlined locomotives had given easier access to pistons and valves for maintenance. The other details can be seen on Rowledge's drawings. Further refinements by Fairburn to the 2-6-4s were his self-cleaning smoke-box, rocking-grate and hopper-ashpan, introduced from locomotive 2229, the devices denoted by the 'SC' plate below the shed-plate on the smokebox. The modified 2-6-4 was fully the equal of its forerunner, to the extent that the astonishing number of 277 were built. First, the odd twenty-seven 2673-99 were constructed from pre-war parts held in stock, then a further hundred, 2200-2299. Many of these later examples were drafted on to the former L&Y lines, displacing long-lived radial tanks to the scrapyard, while substantial numbers also went to the Glasgow suburban lines of the former CR, superseding that company's McIntosh 4-6-2 and 0-4-4 tanks.

But now 1947 was well advanced, the last year of the LMSR company, as construction continued on the batch numbered 2180-99. The author's contemporaneous notes show that 2193 was the last example to carry the LMS insignia. The next engine built was drafted onto the Leeds-Ilkley branch to begin replacing the obsolete Derby 1900-class 0-4-4 tanks of 1932 and was the first locomotive observed passing the school bearing the title of the new owners, lettered in off-white on the tank, and numbered M2194. Actually, this occurred on Friday 13 February 1948, which seemed significant for, as a fan of the LMS, the author disliked the repainting and renumbering. After trials, the type was found ideal for the Southern Railway (now the Southern Region) suburban lines, therefore BR built forty-one engines at its Brighton works for this purpose, numbered 42066-42106 in two lots, as well as continuing the construction of the batches already authorised. When BR ended construction of the 2-6-4s in 1951, the numbers reached back from the original Derby class (LMS 2300, BR 42300) to 42050 and forward to 42699 (with the gap of five), giving a class-total of 645. The total on the take-over of the LMS by BR was 502, another very considerable class, in fact the company's fourth largest.

Many more of the new engines were sent to the ex-Caledonian lines, where they rapidly replaced the remaining ex-CR 4-6-2Ts and 0-4-4Ts, including both types stationed at Beattock, Dumfries-shire (12F), for banking duties. Indeed, it was here, almost twenty years later, that the author enjoyed a splendid ride on one of them, his favourite tank-engine, 42200 slogging up to Summit, described under footplate-trips in chapter 12. The Fairburn short-wheelbase 2-6-4 tanks formed the basis for the BR Standard-2-6-4, the Riddles 80000s; crews have commented that they prefer the LMS design. Unfortunately, many of the newer engines had a short working-life: their duties were taken over by electrification, by the fleets of diesel multiple-units or by the closure of cross-country services from the 1950s. In addition to the first taper-boiler 2-6-4, the 3-cylinder 2500, held by the National Railway Museum, Stanier/Fairburn 42073 and 42085 are preserved by The Lakeside & Haverthwaite Railway in Cumbria.

The 2-6-2 tank-engine

This was the fourth class with potential for improvement by Stanier, the parallel-boiler 2-6-2, introduced only recently, in 1930, under Fowler. Stanier produced a taper-boiler version in 1935, apparently a rather hurried re-vamp of the unsatisfactory Derby engine. Even with its taper-boiler and new cylinders, it had the same characteristics as its predecessor, namely indifferent steaming, a poor front-end, and a small boiler due to weight-restrictions. Many changes were made, including fitting a larger grate and a new version of the Adams 'Vortex' blastpipe. On the local trio, 74, 90 and 96 (Manningham, 20E), it produced a distinctive humming under enforced-draught as the engines were coasting into Apperley Bridge station. A larger boiler was tried on four engines, 148, 163, 169 and 203, with little measurable improvement. BR repeated the exercise in 1956 on (40)142 and (40)167, but again the results were inconclusive. It is recorded as Stanier's worst engine; it should have been completely re-designed. The 2-6-4 clearly augured well, but no doubt Stanier and the LMS Executive felt the need for a smaller, lighter machine, suitable to operate certain routes of the extensive network. But, were further 2-6-2Ts necessary? The Executive's objective was to minimize maintenance, improve availability, and reduce the number of classes of locomotive by scrapping pre-grouping tank engines. But hundreds of these were still running as late as 1950, for example ex-LNW 2-4-2Ts, 0-6-2 coal-tanks (and 'Cauliflowers', often used for the same work) so the 2-6-2Ts represented a further class created unnecessarily, it is thought, defeating the Executive's objective.

The 2-8-0 Heavy Freight locomotive

It is this 8F-design, essentially the freight-version of the Black Five, that holds the record of the largest number *constructed* of any class of British locomotive. It was again an immediate success and another Stanier locomotive of aesthetically-pleasing appearance.

Through necessity, Stanier's passenger-locomotives took preference over freight, and so the Class 8F 2-8-0 was introduced only in 1935, once the pacifics, the Class 5P5F, the 5XP Jubilee and the 2-6-4 tanks were properly launched. Partly on account of this low priority, and partly over construction-commitments to the mixed-traffic and passenger-engines, the building of the 8F proceeded slowly, Crewe constructing only fifteen in 1935-6 and another twelve in 1937. Certainly, the need for them was far less pressing, since the majority of the goods-haulage remained in the capable hands of the 0-8-0s originating on the L&Y and the LNW Railways, and of all constituents' pre-grouping classes of 0-6-0. These sturdy guys continued their work almost exactly as before the Grouping, while 175 replacement 0-8-0s had been constructed under Fowler from 1929-32, the 7F 'Austin Sevens', and were still new.

However during 1936-7, construction of the 2-8-0s by Vulcan Foundry (lot 132) of 69 machines brought the class-total to 96, and 30 further engines came out of Crewe in 1938-9, both evidently a preparation for war, particularly following the Munich crisis of 1938. They brought the total to 126, numbered 8000 to 8125. This clearly reveals the precedence of passenger-engines, since by this date the 5P5Fs alone amounted to 472—although designated 'mixed-traffic'—the Pacifics totalled 41, the Royal Scots 71, the Patriots 52 and the Jubilees 191. On the outbreak of war in September 1939 therefore, the LMS possessed only 126 of Stanier's modern heavy-freight locomotives. The sequel to this construction is detailed under 'World War 2 and its aftermath'.

Pacific Test-Runs

At this time, speeds of trains were increasing across the 'big four' railways, and so in 1935, the LMS Executive decided to accelerate some expresses, to compete partly with the LNER to Scotland, and partly with the new air-services. Riddles was put in charge and rode on the footplate during these tests. Locomotive 6200 *The Princess Royal,* with her redesigned boiler of 1935, ran three tests in June that year. Hauling an up *Merseyside Express w*ith weight specially increased to 453 tons tare, 6200 performed brilliantly, running from Crewe to Willesden in 129 min 33 sec start to stop, an everage speed of 70.7 mph—and on less than 20% cut-off. The run lifted the LMS into a different league. Nock, delayed in London that evening by urgent design-work on signalling and now on his way home to Bushey, saw 6200 arriving in Euston. It was when Riddles stepped off the footplate that he realized something unusual had happened. It was reported in *The Railway Gazette*. The other two runs are also notable. That from Crewe to Glasgow and back showed remarkable hill-climbing ability over the West Coast banks and a steady speed, achieving the aim of running at 90mph maximum with strict observance of the various speed-restrictions. The second run recorded an average speed from Crewe to Euston of 77+ mph over 67 miles, with a maximum of 86mph. These runs demonstrated that a six-hour schedule from London to Glasgow was now achievable but, as a final test before the introduction of the planned *Coronation Scot*, a special high-speed return-run to Glasgow was made over the West Coast route in 1936.

Locomotive 6201 *Princess Elizabeth* was chosen, largely because Stanier had re-fitted the engine with a boiler further modified—and a speedometer. Unlike the shortened boiler of 6200, that of 6201 was of the original length, but with larger-diameter small tubes, a 32-element superheater and a steam-dome. Nock gives a splendid account of this run—complete with the episode of the leaking steam-pipe on shed at Willesden for which a sealing-ring had to be found in the pitch-black Crewe stores with only minutes to spare, and no time to fit a replacement Princess with a speedometer and other details—and then of another night's work by Riddles after the company's celebratory dinner-party in Glasgow, to re-metal a slide-bar in St Rollox works ready for the return-trip. This brilliant run achieved 95 mph approaching Crewe. The average speed down was 68.2mph, and up to London, 70mph, both averages exceeding that required for a six-hour schedule. At the informal afternoon-tea in the Central Station Hotel, Glasgow—where a toast was drunk to 'Driver Tom Clarke and his mates'—Vice-President E.J.H. Lemon calmly announced that records had been broken for speed and distance. He emphasized that the runs involved a scientific analysis of the operating and maintenance conditions to discover if they had met those required for a six-hour schedule between London and Glasgow. They had, and it made quite a story.

In the following year, 1937, Herbert Chambers, Personal and Technical Assistant to the CME, died suddenly, triggering important staff-changes. Cox was sent to replace him at Euston, Riddles was moved to Glasgow as Mechanical and Electrical Engineer for Scotland, replacing Ivatt, who was promoted to Principal Assistant to Stanier at Euston.

A high-speed express from Euston to Glasgow was now possible but, with the coronation of King George VI approaching in 1937, an appropriate gesture was indicated—and a response to the rival LNER's streamlined *Silver Jubilee* train of 1935. Stanier therefore made plans for a 'super-pacific'. This is indeed just what the locomotive turned out to be. While he was in India as a member of a committee investigating the riding-qualities of express pacific-locomotives which had suffered derailments, Stanier's team, led by the redoubtable Coleman, designed the *Princess Coronation* 4-6-2s. Interestingly, its frames and valve arrangements closely followed those of the rebuilt Hughes Dreadnought 4-6-0s of the LYR—possibly reflecting Coleman's training at Horwich. The first locomotive, *Coronation,* appeared from the Crewe works in 1937. Its number 6220, closely following the Princess Royal class, testifies to an improvement of the Princess pacific, resulting in a locomotive capable of continuous high-speed steaming. In addition to improvements in the boiler-firebox design, measures were taken to reduce side-movement on the bogey and Bissel-truck in order to reduce wear on the track caused by such oscillations. The disaster at Bihta in India, recently investigated by Stanier as a member of the visiting committee, was his object-lesson. The result was a fast, free-running engine completely free from oscillation or hunting. Departing from the four sets of valve-gear as used on the Princess Royals, two sets only were provided on the Duchess to operate the four cylinders, a reversion to Great Western practice, but an inversion of the GW-design in that the valve-gear was outside, Walschaerts, as fitted to all the standard Stanier locomotives. This used rocking-levers to operate the valves of the inside cylinders, leaving more space inside the frames, thereby easing maintenance. Here again, Stanier was seeking reduced down-time and therefore greater availability. The various improvements over the Princess pacifics, including a large increase in heating-surface and grate-area, had been made so ingeniously that the new engine weighed in at only about a ton heavier.

The fashionable *art-décoratif* style virtually dictated a streamlined-form ('streaks' to the spotters) similar to that initiated by the LNER on its 'hush-hush' 2-8-2 high-pressure locomotive and then used on its A.4 pacific. Design-circle opinion held that the Duchess-shape probably caused less drag at 75 mph-plus than the LNER A.4. The first six LMS streamlined locomotives were painted to reproduce the Caledonian prussian-blue, with silver stripes added along the sides of the locomotive and tender—and continuing the length of the train as well. This spectacular novelty, combined with the unusual streamlined shape, excited much comment. The last four of the ten streamliners, in LMS red with gold stripes, were followed by a batch of five non-streamlined engines, 6230-6234. On 5 July 1937, the inaugural run of the *Coronation Scot* train was successful in maintaining a higher, sustained, speed, though still outside the six-hour objective. It fulfilled the LMS aim of a general acceleration, rather than going for high speed on one service. However, it disappointed the many who had hoped for speeds of 100 mph plus, since the LNER now held the record with 113 mph, but it was a start.

The sequel was a press-run from Euston to Crewe and back on 29 July. Before departure, it was learned that this locomotive, 6220, had recently attained 95 mph on the level between Blisworth and Weedon with a load of over 300 tons, suggesting that an attempt on the speed-record might now be made. High speeds were indeed attained, including passing Tring summit at 79 mph, but after a maximum of 89 below Cheddington, the engine was eased and the various speed-restrictions rigorously observed. But the disappointment of the passengers turned to exhilaration as the locomotive was opened out on the ascent to Whitmore summit, which it passed at no less than 85mph, followed by very rapid acceleration to an amazing 114 mph shortly before Crewe. Nock was an invited journalist on this run and excitedly relates the details of his observations of the mileposts flying past the window while his companion read the stop-watch. The LMS had done it. It had wrested the record from its arch-rival, the LNER. In fact, considerable potential remained, for the locomotive was still accelerating when it had to be sharply braked in the approaches to Crewe. A railway historian contributing to a BBC tv documentary on the LNER and LMS streamlined trains commented that the LMS—with Riddles on the footplate—had nearly gone too far in their zeal to beat the LNER, for, with sparks flying from the brake-blocks, the Duchess hit the turnout to the platform at 57 mph, holding the rails by probably only a hairsbreadth. LMS supporters were left wishing for a stretch of line similar to the LNER's speed-record stretch down Stoke Bank between

Grantham and Peterborough, where the engine could really have been given her head.

The inter-war years of the 1920s-30s were noted for their addiction to speed, with constant attempts on existing records. On the Continent of Europe, Hitler wanted to demonstrate that his Third Reich, rapidly rearming to challenge Great Britain as a world-power, was also in the forefront with its railways. His speed-attempts culminated in a world record for steam on the Deutsche Reichbahn, the German State Railways. Its streamlined 4-6-4 locomotive 05.002 achieved 124.5 mph on 11 May 1936 between Berlin and Hamburg (*der fliegende Hamburger*) and retained the record for two years. The LNER directors at first considered purchasing a similar machine, but then asked Gresley to design a luxury train to run from London to Newcastle in four hours. The work included a visit to the French locomotive test-rig at Vitry and a test-run with *Flying Scotsman* on which Driver William Sparshatt (a noted speed-merchant) later raised the stakes in Britain by achieving 100mph. Gresley's friend on the SNCF, its CME André Chapelon, also contributed some details. The combined information resulted in the streamlined A.4 pacific and the Silver Link train, and in 1938 one member of the class, 4468 *Mallard,* managed to break the German record with 126 mph down Stoke Bank, ecml—though at the cost of a failed bearing.

However, these railway speed records demand comment. Cars, boats and aeroplanes making similar attempts were timed twice over a measured mile, the return-run made shortly after the outward. The railway records were however gained on a single run, and both the LMS and LNER runs were made downhill. Also, they were 'unofficial' in that the companies themselves did the measuring, with their own instruments. Finally, why did BR not run both engines over the same length of track—presumably the East Coast line? Perhaps they did not wish to upstage *Mallard*. The LMS was disadvantaged with its hilly and curvy west coast line compared with the straighter, level, east coast—two, very different, playing-fields. Actually, the LMS was not really interested in speed-records, preferring to upgrade its services across the board. But its high-speed burst lifted the average for the press-run to 80 mph. Stanier had built an astonishingly free-running machine—and one with adequate bearings, unlike *Mallard*. In terms of power-output too, measured scientifically, *Coronation* proved to be the most powerful express-passenger design in the country. This was the record the LMS gained, but many years would pass before it would be proved.

Soon after the Duchess pacifics appeared, Stanier conceived a further development. A design was worked out for a larger version, a 4-6-4, with a bigger boiler and higher pressure, 300lb, and a large grate with mechanical stoker. The aim was to compete with the developing air-aervices by accelerating the west-coast expresses and increasing haulage-capacity from 300 to 500 tons—and to run non-stop from London to Glasgow in 6 hours, rather than the current 6½. The mechanical-stoking could have caused problems, and a very capacious ashpan would have been needed to be to contain the ash from burning ten or twelve tons of coal. A plan to build two more Duchesses in 1940 with 300lb boilers and improvements to the steam-circuit as a halfway-stage was shelved along with other projects on account of the imminent threat of war. Instead, resources were concentrated on the drive to reduce total coal-consumption. However, preparations for the American tour went ahead.

The author is indebted to Nock's *The Railways of Britain* for details of runs by two Duchesses, 6234 *Duchess of Abercorn* in 1939 and 6244 *King George VI* during WW2. The latter, hauling a fifteen-coach train, was stopped by signals on the Grayrigg bank. After re-starting his heavy train on the 1:106 gradient, the engine accelerated quickly in six miles to pass the summit at 55mph, a feat probably more significant than the very high speeds over short distances by comparable engines. However, despite splendid runs by the Princess pacifics, the northern gradients were stretching them on the demanding Midday Scot schedule, and so for comparison a Duchess headed a test-train on this route on Sunday, 26 February 1939. Perhaps the LMS executive felt that this might be the last chance to prove their pacific, in view of the uncertain international situation. Britain had escaped war at the Munich crisis of the previous summer, but matters on the Continent of Europe remained decidedly threatening. The non-streamlined 6234 *Duchess of Abercorn,* recently fitted with double-blastpipe and chimney, was chosen to haul twenty coaches unaided, 604 tons tare, a huge load, on the West Coast both ways. The Duchess surmounted the inclines supremely—and with a low coal-consumption; the water though had to be replenished with a special stop at Symington. Nock calls the performance 'phenomenal'. It seemed as if the LMS was determined to show that the three notorious inclines of Grayrigg, Shap and Beattock, bugbears to the operators for a century, had finally been mastered. They had—and final proof of the Duchess' power would come later.

Production of small batches of non-streamlined engines (called by fans 'semi-streaks') took the class to 6255, the few wartime-builds finished in black, bearing the insignia in gilt countershaded in red. The author noted 6250 *City of Lichfield* and 6251 *City of Nottingham* at Preston when brand-new, and later 6249 *City of Sheffield* and 6252 *City of Leicester,* completing the quartet of locomotives built at this time. The final two were 6256 *Sir William A. Stanier, FRS* and 6257 *City of Salford,* the latter completed by BR in 1948. They formed part of an Executive decision in 1947 to build four express-locomotives; the other two, the first diesel-electrics, 10000/1, considered later, for comparison purposes. These two pacifics carried Ivatt's latest improvements of a still-larger superheater, roller-bearings, the self-cleaning devices, redesigned Bissel-truck and other details, bringing the class-total to thirty-eight. It seems that Stanier had reverted to the 6ft 9in driving-wheels after the 6ft 6" of the Princess Royals with a higher maximum-speed in mind, possibly something like 130mph—and the 5X/6P 4-6-0s were running successfully with 6ft 9in driving-wheels. These last two pacifics were widely considered to be Britain's finest express-locomotives.

On 18 December 1947, in the closing days of the LMS railway, an impressive ceremony took place on Euston Station. The newest Duchess, 6256, and the new diesel-electric locomotive 10000, were standing on exhibition. Before it was opened, Sir Robert Burrows, who had succeeded Sir William Wood as chairman of the company, officially named the Duchess *Sir William A. Stanier, FRS*. After hosting many such naming-ceremonies, Sir Robert remarked that this was his first one named after an individual and that the LMSR had never had a better engine, nor a better name connected with it. "This class contributed not a little to the success with which the LMSR surmounted the difficulties of wartime, and it is to Sir William Stanier that we owe it." He concluded his tribute with "Sir William Stanier has reached the highest spheres of scientific achievement and recognition. The debt which the LMSR owes him is difficult to assess. He has reduced the number of locomotive-types, simplified their design, and increased their availability. With all his distinctions, he has remained a railwayman, and his first love—the locomotive—has remained his last love." This demonstrates Stanier's standing in the world of railways. Now we must revert to the immediate pre-war period, 1939.

The New York World's Fair ran from 30 April to 1 October that year and, as mentioned, to this event the LMS sent 6220 *Coronation* with some of the new, lightweight, articulated carriages, a complete *Coronation Scot* train. Nock (*A History of the LMS*, Volume 2, p.93) pictures the locomotive being lifted on board at Southampton docks. Actually, since she was almost new, locomotive 6229 *Duchess of Hamilton* was sent, one of the group finished in LMS crimson-lake rather than the original blue, to masquerade as 6220 *Coronation*. An observant American friend of Nock's wrote to him after the tour, asking why the motion of 6220 was stamped 6229! To match the locomotive, the whole train was finished in LMS red, carrying the silver stripes throughout. This greatly impressed the huge crowds. Where Stanier had accompanied *The Royal Scot* on its tour six years earlier, now it was the turn of Riddles. The train toured the eastern United States, at first running from Washington up the coast through Baltimore to Philadelphia and back. Retracing its steps from Washington up to Philadelphia, the train then embarked on its tour of American cities in the Eastern states. Turning west, the train visited Altoona, Pittsburgh, Columbus, Dayton, Cincinnati, Louisville, Indianapolis and St Louis, its furthest point west. Here, it turned north to Chicago, then east through Kalamazoo, Detroit, Cleveland, Youngstown, Buffalo, Rochester, Albany and Boston, turning south to terminate in New York City for exhibition at the World's Fair. The train had traversed several railroads: the Baltimore & Ohio, Pennsylvania, B & G Four, Louisville & Nashville, Alton, Michigan Central, New York Central, Boston & Albany and New York, New Haven & Hartford. Unfortunately the second world war had begun in Europe on 3 September. The consequent uncertainty curtailed further touring to repeat *The Royal Scot*'s extensive trip, and stranded the train in America. However, British wartime motive-power requirements in 1942 brought the locomotive back, to Cardiff, running the gauntlet of the German U-boats. The carriages though, remained stateside for the duration of the war, used as an officers' club. They were brought back afterwards, but the era of the glamorous streamlined train had vanished, replaced by dreary post-war austerity, and *Coronation Scot* was not reinstated into the schedule. This engine, restored to her real *persona* of 6229 *Duchess of Hamilton* is preserved in the NRM and has operated many main-line specials. With her streamlining restored in 2012 and painted in LMS crimson-lake with the stripes, she is a splendid example of the LMS at its height.

Rebuilding the Royal Scots: 'converted' Scots

Having launched his standard-classes and improved the steaming of the Jubilees, Stanier gained permission in 1935 to begin a project comprising several stages. His taper-boilers, particularly successful regarding maintenance, suggested an upgrading of the Royal Scots, and the experimental locomotive 6399 *Fury,* constructed on a Royal Scot chassis, was his starting-point. It was standing 'awaiting instructions' in the Derby paint-shop after the fatal failure of its Schmidt-Henschel high-pressure boiler at Carstairs, which had led to little further use. It had been built in 1929 by North British Locomotive Co Ltd., the builders of the Royal Scots two years earlier, in collaboration with The Superheater Co Ltd., at a time when high pressure was in vogue as a means of improving the low thermal-efficiency of the steam-locomotive. The LNER had also tried high pressure, with its 2-8-2 P.2 10000 *Cock o' the North* 'hush-hush' express-locomotive, but had rebuilt the engine into a conventional pacific. The LMS too felt the way forward was to use a traditional boiler. Prompted by his chief draughtsman Coleman, Stanier took the frames of *Fury* as the basis for his project. On its engineering-drawings, *Fury* is described as 'Royal Scot Class' and upon this Royal Scot chassis Stanier mounted his number 2 taper-boiler, pressed to 250lb. It made the engine look rather nose-heavy. Numbered 6170 at the end of the Royal Scot class, and later named *British Legion,* the locomotive was felt by its crews to be 'fully one coach better' than the Royal Scots, though its boiler-tube ratios were not ideal. The experience of running in traffic for two years revealed potential for improvement, and accordingly larger ports and valves were fitted, making 6170 a fine engine. The launch of the Duchesses, the preparations for the American tour and the 1939-war halted progress to the next stage of Stanier's plan, a similar upgrade of the Royal Scots. They had rendered sterling service for over a decade on west-coast expresses and would need re-boilering when conditions allowed. However, following wartime experiences of further bad steaming by Jubilees lacking the boiler-modifications described earlier—plus the delicate handling they still required—a determined step was taken in May 1942 to solve the problem logically by making a fresh start with a re-designed boiler. This was the final modification to the Jubilee alluded to earlier. Wartime constraints allowed only two engines to be treated—as an experiment: 5736 *Phoenix* and 5735 *Comet* were chosen to be fitted with a shortened number 2 boiler, notwithstanding its imperfect tube-ratios. An alternative was available however in the shape of boiler 2A, already schemed out for a two-cylinder version of the 5X Jubilee in 1937 to save weight. The removal of certain civil-engineering restrictions had rendered the two-cylinder version unnecessary, but its 2A boiler-design was now taken and modified for the rebuild of *Phoenix* and *Comet*, with ports enlarged further over 6170 and valve-gear lead increased. They steamed perfectly and were a great success. With a boiler 15in shorter than 6170, they now 'looked right' too— and again they exceeded a Royal Scot in haulage-capacity. Following bridge-strengthening on the Leeds-Carlisle line during 1941, these two were allocated to Leeds Holbeck shed on test to haul the over-weight Leeds-Glasgow expresses. These tasks confirmed their success, and incidentally brought them past the school. They were reclassified 6P and transferred to the Western Division. No more Jubilees were rebuilt, but these two formed the blueprint for the eventual rebuilding of the Royal Scots, as well as some Patriots. The positive results obtained with double blastpipes on the Duchesses provided a further detail. A trial of short, curved smoke-deflectors on 6115 *Scots Guardsman* was deemed satisfactory and gave the final modification. They were fitted new to rebuilds from 1949 as well as to the earlier converted engines. In addition to requiring reboilering, the built-up smokeboxes of the Scots were leaking air, weakening the draught and, but for the war, rebuilding would have begun earlier. In 1943, however, the wartime requirements for steel were easing a little, allowing some rebuilding. Since Stanier had been seconded to the Ministry of Production, and his deputy, C.E.

Fairburn, was primarily an electrical man, the responsibility for steam-locomotive work fell on H.G. Ivatt.

In view of the outstanding success of the rebuilt engines, salient details are given here. Five Stanier features were incorporated deriving from his Swindon experience: a taper-boiler, bolster-bogeys of the 'de Glehn' type; cast-steel coupled axleboxes with pressed-in brasses and a large-capacity underkeep with pad-lubrication; coupled-wheel springs with adjustable links and tension-hangers; and abandonment of the flat-bottomed smokebox in favour of a circular type, cast integral with its saddle and the inside-cylinder. The first rebuild was 6103 *Royal Scots Fusilier* in April 1943, finished in wartime black with gilt insignia countershaded red. Again, it was allocated to Holbeck (20A), this time permanently, to haul the overloaded trains to Carlisle and Glasgow. Three more rebuilds soon followed, 6109 *Royal Engineer*, 6108 *Seaforth Highlander* and 6117 *Welsh Guardsman* in this order, later joined by others including 6133 *The Green Howards* (a Yorkshire regiment), all joyfully noted when passing the school. The author and his mother travelled behind them many times on visits to her sisters at Motherwell-Wishaw in Lanarkshire, Scotland. The term 'converted' was adopted by the LMS for the rebuilding, and gradually more engines were converted. Aong others, 6132 *The King's Regiment Liverpool* appeared on this line and, appropriately, 6145 *The Duke of Wellington's Regiment (West Riding)*, its long title requiring a two-line nameplate. To conclude this subject, ahead now to the final conversions by British Railways of the remainder of the class from 1948 onwards. The last Scot converted was 46137 *The Prince of Wales' Volunteers (South Lancashire)*, in 1954. The LMS Executive had calculated that after the war ninety-one engines of this power would be needed (a figure that far undershot the eventual needs): the seventy-one Royal Scots, the two converted Jubilees, and eighteen converted Patriots, which, it is recalled, had Royal Scot chassis. Rather than rebuilding further Jubilees, Patriots were chosen for a full rebuild, since their frames were prone to fracture. However, the first twelve Patriots were rejected on account of the many Claughton parts retained in their construction, so the eighteen were drawn from later members of the class. Late in the BR steam-era, the author observed the converted 45526 *Morecambe and Heysham* and 45531 *Sir Frederick Harrison* still performing powerfully over Shap. However, the unrebuilt

Patriots continued to give sterling service too, often hauling parcels or freight, in particular 45502 *Royal Naval Division*, noted breasting Grayrigg Bank manfully on a parcels in 1960.

Although somewhat prone to rough-riding, the converted engines proved to be the most effective and efficient 4-6-0s of any group-company. They represented the culmination of the development, from the Claughton of 1913, through its reboilering, then to matching this boiler with a Royal Scot chassis (the Patriot), to the taper-boiler version (the Jubilee) and finally the succesful rebuild of the Jubilee with 2A taper-boiler, leading to the converted Scot. This protracted development demonstrates the empirical method of design before scientific testing became available in the Locomotive Testing Station at Rugby. It is recalled that the Royal Scots of 1927 were planned as 'improved Castles' following the test of *Pendennis Castle* by the LMS in 1926. The converted 4-6-0s would prove themselves conclusively in the BR locomotive-exchanges of 1948, in particular those running out of Waterloo and Paddington, described later. Notably, the final improvements to the GWR Castles and Kings were carried out around this time, that is, after nationalization. Stanier's LMS engines demonstrate his integration of the best features of the earlier GWR designs with his own ideas. The refined, modern, appearance of his LMS engines contrasts with the heavier look of their GWR ancestors, in particular, the shaped buffer-beam and the neat, flat-sided cylinders of the LMS engines. A photograph of a Jubilee in BR Brunswick-green recalls the Great Western, symbolizing the engine's ancestry and Stanier's career.

Improved Carriage-stock and its use

The LMS had naturally inherited a miscellany of carriages, from humble Caledonian four-wheelers, through many types of third-class to the splendid LNW twelve-wheelers built as West Coast Joint stock, so it took time for a settled policy to produce results. It was achieved by Robert Whyte Reid, the capable MR Carriage Superintendent, who continued in post on the LMS. The 'races to the north' of 1888 and 1895, with their implications of safety coming second to speed, had brought about an enduring time-table agreement to prevent racing by the two sets of rivals, the east-coast and west-coast companies. This was still in place after the 1923 Grouping, so that their successors, the LNER and the LMS, had to resort to other ways of competing with each other—in services, just as rivals do nowadays. The LNER led the way with their streamlined trains, including on-board hairdressing-salons, cinemas and telephone/secretarial facilities, but these trains formed only a fraction of their operations; as for their much-vaunted bucket-seats, one commentator remarked that they made you feel as though you were sitting in a bucket!

LMS policy however—just as in the realm of speed—lay in the introduction of modern, comfortable carriages—not on a few prestigious trains, but across the whole range of their services. The Midland Railway had built the most comfortable carriages, and ex-Midland man Reid lifted the general standard of comfort on the LMS to this level. His 60ft carriages gave more leg-room but, imporantly, he updated construction-methods, where the timber body had largely continued unchanged from the earliest railway-carriages—and even from the stage-coaches before them. The parts were roughly machined, then finished to a precise fit by the craftsmen for assembly. For this traditional hand-construction, Reid substituted machine mass-production on jigs so that on assembly the sections fitted perfectly. This streamlining shortened the construction of a carriage from six weeks to six days—and enabled all the work to be carried out at Derby and Wolverton—allowing smaller, older works to be closed, a further economy. Later, Reid introduced steel-panels on timber frames, and after 1932 Stanier added steel ends and roofs as well, leading to his all-steel flush-sided carriage with end-doors, the mass-produced saloon, or 'vestibule-coach', in LMS terminology. They were often marshalled next to a kitchen—or restaurant-car for dining-purposes. The modern carriage is their successor. The use of steel helped to preserve jobs in the steel-industry, suffering during the 1930s depression. Outside contractors were employed too, since the works' capacity was insufficient to meet the Executive's orders. Stanier's carriage had a neat appearance, and without the earlier panelling was easier to clean. It was built in configurations of first-class, third, and composite, restaurant-cars and the shorter kitchen-cars. These carriages also led the Big Four railways in design with the main windows of the late-1920s enlarged into the attractive 'picture' windows, with opening air-vents along the top, each window aligned with a table-bay of four seats, of course upholstered in the company's red-and-black moquette. Again in the forefront of Britain's railways, the LMS introduced three-a-side seating for third-class passengers with intermediate arm-rests and reading-lights. Seat-designs were tested to destruction in the new Technical Department at Derby, enabling it to design a shape that uniquely fitted the human frame, making its carriages probably the most comfortable in Britain. Later builds had internal panelling of Empire timbers, labelled to show their origin.

Once Reid's carriage mass-production facilities were up and running at Derby, some facilities could be closed, for example the smaller ex-LYR plant at Newton Heath, Manchester, further exemplifying rationalization and efficiency. This depot's football-club had joined with others to create the Manchester United FC in 1903. A bright spot among the routine construction and repair of carriages was the role of Wolverton, the former LNW carriage-plant in Buckinghamshire which prided itself on the maintenance of the royal train and on the construction of its new vehicles. In 2011, work was transferred to Derby as a prelude to the closure of the Wolverton works.

LMS resources were enormous, with for example over 20,000 carriages and 2,500 stations. Advantageous ticketing meant that few paid the full fare on regular trains. As well as its headline expresses, the company exerted itself to run a huge number of excursions to places of interest, for which carriages were stored between week-ends, despite the protestations of the accountants. This practice enabled the company to run through summer-services, such as from Derby and points north over its Somerset & Dorset joint-line to Bournemouth, supplementing *The Pines Express* from Manchester. Other specials were run at times of exceptional demand, to the Cup Finals at Wembley for Association Football and Rugby League clubs, and to cater for the Wakes holidays of the Yorkshire and Lancashire industrial towns. Often, over a thousand specials ran at these times to various seaside-resorts. The Blackpool traffic was the largest such concentration on the LMS but, after a special section was set up in 1929, the excursion-traffic generally expanded hugely. More restaurant-cars were also provided. Each autumn, numerous excursions were run to the famous Blackpool Illuminations. Locomotive maintenance was postponed as engines were urgently pressed into service, even smallish goods-engines, while passed-cleaners became firemen and passed-firemen became drivers. My father remarked that corridor-coaches were used on the excursions to Morecambe and Southport, but non-corridor stock (without lavatories) to Blackpool, considered 'good enough'—a comment on the class-structure of the country at that time. Many were the tales of how the calls of nature were answered in the non-corridor stock: 'desperate situations require desperate remedies.' In addition to the long-distance trains, through-carriages were run to many places, including over lines of other companies through running-power agreements.

Combined train-and-boat excursions were available as well, to Lakes, Lochs and the Isle of Man. Through-services were operated for a while to Dunkirk, France, by running LMS boat-trains from St Pancras to Tilbury, there continuing on the French line Alsace-Lorraine-Angleterre (ALA). The travelling post-office trains (TPOs) formed a service that ran for well over a century. The Down Special TPO ran from Euston to Carstairs, where it divided, one portion running to Glasgow and the other continuing north to Inverness. The nets and arms fitted to carriages allowed mail to be picked up and deposited at important towns on the way, the incoming mail being sorted immediately on the train. A stop was made at Crewe to exchange mail from the Midlands, Chester and Wales, including the Irish mail to and from Holyhead. In 1936, the Crown Film Unit made a documentary-film *Night Mail*, which, although GPO-sponsored, remains a classic record of the LMS in the Stanier era. W.H. Auden's eponymous poem expresses the drama better than the prose here. It recalls *Brief Encounter*, a classic, nostalgic film, made at Carnforth and Watford Junction stations, showing Royal Scots speeding through on expresses and Stanier 2-6-4 tank-engines heading local-trains, governed by the famous clock at Carnforth, now conserved. The author used to see TPO stock on the back-road of Carlisle's Citadel station in 1950/1, ready to be marshalled and loaded for the re-named 'North Western TPO Night Up'. From the early days, charter-business was important too for such events as football cup-finals played in the new Empire Stadium at Wembley. Quicker and more-efficient servicing allowed a reduction in the amount of coaching-stock. By 1947, two-thirds of LMS passenger—and goods-vehicles had been built since 1923. In 1939, the continual modernization and efficiency would pay dividends during the war that was looming.

Specialist Trains

This account describes a specialist military-operation and also a train chartered by a family, for both of which the author is indebted to his friend Mr Charles Hibberd, a retired Chartered Engineer, originally from Glasgow. The Admiralty maintains large stores on a branch-line near Kilmarnock, utilized to supply Royal Navy ships at the various dockyards, such as Rosyth, Chatham, Portsmouth or Plymouth. When a ship docks and needs fresh supplies, an order is sent to Kilmarnock, where the food, ammunition and other stores are loaded onto a special train of parcel-vans, vacuum-braked (later air-braked), and run as an express-parcels to the port. In steam-days, the locomotive would usually be a Black Five, which hauled its train northwards along the old Sou'west line, partly because the branch turnout faced that way, and partly to confuse German reconnaissance-aircraft during WW2. Approaching Glasgow, the train is diverted along the link to the Carlisle main-line. From there, it follows the London (St Pancras) sleeper, departing from Glasgow at 4pm, and terminates at the appropriate port. It has always been imperative to run the train non-stop and therefore it is accorded priority at the various stations and junctions en route.

One of Charles' friends, a Mr Leake, had a senior position at the stores and had 'married well'; in Charles' words, 'his wife paid the bills and he wore the medals!' They resided at Holybrook House near Ayr, an estate run with the usual staff of servants. The Leakes also had a flat in Grosvenor House, Park Lane, London, which they would visit once or twice a year. Transporting the family and servants there was a considerable exercise, accomplished by train. The LMS hired them one of its special saloon-carriages used for such charters, with separate accommodation for the servants. As no kitchen was incorporated, the family took along a picnic-lunch. A goods-engine eased the train along the branch to Kilmarnock, where they were attached to *The Thames-Clyde Express* for a through journey to St Pancras. The detritus of the picnic was taken off at Leeds (City) Station on the reversal there, before the journey continued to London. But it all ended in 1939.

Royal Trains

In 1923, the LMS inherited the LNWR royal train, which it continued to use, but here is an interesting note. On the Grouping of the railways in 1923 with the consequent repainting of trains into new liveries, King George V requested the LMS to keep this train in its original colours which he liked, and so the train uniquely retained its LNWR livery. All four railways had inherited royal trains, composed of a miscellany of vehicles, each presenting a varied appearance with different styles of carriage of varied lengths and heights, such as clerestories and six-wheelers. During the 1930s, the GWR abandoned its antiquated stock and borrowed royal saloons from the LMS when required. None of the railways built new stock except the LMS, which in 1941 constructed three armour-plated carriages for King George VI's journeys during WW2. With special equipment such as air-conditioning, a diesel generating-set and telephones for overnight stabling, they were the heaviest passenger-vehicles in Britain, weighing in at 56 tons. To maintain secrecy during wartime, telegraphic names were employed, such as 'Grove' (the train with the king on board) or, more rarely, 'Deepdene' (either the train without the king, or a service-train with a royal saloon attached). This description became commoner post-war. Grove was the name of the mansion near Watford, the LMS headquarters for the duration of the war.

The other companies retained their Edwardian stock—especially the Southern Railway, whose train, originating on the SE&CR, was used to bring foreign dignitaries from the ferry at Dover to London Victoria. It represented the peak of British luxury-carriage construction. Luckily, some survive in preservation. After the war, the GWR restored its royal train, in reality special saloons provided for its directors and important guests, but the SR had finally discarded its ancient train, employing Pullman-cars where necessary. In the early years of her reign with the railways nationalized, Queen Elizabeth II therefore had three royal trains at her disposal, from the GWR, the LNER and the LMS. In the 1950s, British Railways built two saloons for the royal children, Prince

Charles and Princess Anne, the last such vehicles to be constructed in steam days. Since the ending of steam-traction in 1968, preserved steam-engines have been used occasionally to haul the royal train.

Containers

In 1926, the LMS pioneered containers and the other three railways followed suit. The concept is well-understood now, with much of the world's freight carried in this way—though the boxes are larger. The container allowed house-removals to be carried out smoothly, banishing the householder's worries, as the LMS staff took care of everything, delivering the empty container on an LMS lorry and packing his effects. The service was also available to businesses. Insulated and refrigerated designs were introduced later. A lorry took the packed container to the local goods-depot, where the crane lifted it on to a flat-wagon. The pick-up goods-train hauled it to a main yard, where it was attached to the appropriate long-distance express-freight train; at the destination, the reverse procedure was followed. Understandably, the service was marketed as a 'House-to-House Container Service.' Speed was another advantage, with an overnight delivery frequently offered. Gauge 'O' models of these LMS containers and wagons were marketed by Hornby Railways, the container in an appropriate shade of maroon.

Freight traffic

In 1909, a centralized control-system of freight-train movements had been pioneered by Sir Cecil Paget, the Midland Railway General Manager, which was soon copied by other railways. The system was set up by his Chief General Superintendent, J.H Follows, at Masborough, Rotherham. It comprised a central control-room linked by telephone to area-depots and signal-boxes, allowing the progress of every freight-train to be followed on an illuminated diagram, a precursor of the signal-box line-diagrams actuated by track-circuits. He succeeded in reducing costs and accelerating services considerably, so that the MR went on to extend the system across its network. Follows continued in post on the LMS after 1923, when he expanded the system to its entire network too, and models of it were proudly displayed by the LMS at the British Empire Exhibition at Wembley in 1924. The publicity-department produced a booklet for sale to the public. Later, Follows was promoted again, this time to a Vice-Chairman of the Executive. The system was another pioneering-effort by the LMS—or at least by one of its constituents—and it was adopted by the nationalized BR in 1948 for all Britain's railways. However, the spread of power signal-boxes gradually diminished the importance and role of the centralized control to dealing with general matters of freight, including area-arrangements to cope with accidents and diversions. The signalman in a power-box, controlling many miles of line, became better placed to anticipate movements and delays than a controller in a distant office with only telephone-reports and a control-board to guide him.

As noted, Stamp aimed to reduce the amount of time taken in shunting. In the layout of small yards, gravity had traditionally been used where practicable, enabling wagons to roll down into the sidings. While the LNW had been first to use this concept in a large yard, Edge Hill, Liverpool, early in the twentieth century, in 1929 the LNER developed it with their huge Whitemoor yard, near March in Cambridgeshire. This was a new type of yard, pioneered in the USA, where wagons were rapidly marshalled by being pushed up a hump by a shunting-engine (a 'switcher' in America), from where they ran down by gravity into a fan of sidings selected electrically by a controller in a tower on the hump. He could also activate electro-mechanical retarders fitted to the rails to control the speed of the wagons entering the sidings. March lay at the hub of six routes, including a heavy mineral-flow from the Yorkshire and East Midlands coalfields to east London. Despite a visit by Vice-President Lemon to observe this new yard, the LMS took no action immediately, belatedly beginning construction of their huge yard at Toton, north of Nottingham—again largely to assemble mineral-trains—so that it was only partially operational on the outbreak of the 1939 war. The LNER therefore beat the LMS on this score by more than a decade. It replicated Whitemoor too, including another two-hump yard at Hessle, approaching Hull, again largely for marshalling coal-trains.

Much earlier however, the LMS Executive had set up a study-group under Lemon to analyse freight-flow in their depots. It reduced the amount of walking by staff, introduced mechanical handing where feasible, including capstans to release shunting-locomotives; the result was to reduce the number required and to release wagons more quickly. Later, similar principles were applied to parcels-traffic, and conveyor-belts were installed to handle luggage, for example at the ferry-ports of Holyhead and Stranraer.

Through-freight trains

The new LMS company of 1923 had gained the advantage of two routes from the Midlands to Carlisle and Scotland, over Shap and over Ais Gill. The MR had enjoyed running-powers over the LYR from Hellifield to Manchester, establishing its own goods-depot at Ancoats, and through to Liverpool. The choice of two routes northwards allowed the LMS to relieve the pressure on Shap by taking up some slack on the Settle-Carlisle line to run through-freights direct from the Midlands, and from Manchester via Hellifield. The LNW had even considered providing extra capacity over Shap, a diversionary line including a tunnel at the summit to reduce the gradient. This was now unnecessary. With the new Horwich standard 2-6-0s available, the LMS ran some thirty-five through-freights daily between Hellifield and Carlisle, as well as shorter workings. Including the Heysham, Barrow and West Cumbria services, the stretch between Hellifield and Settle Junction, some three-and-a-half miles, funnelled these trains through what now became one of the busiest sections on the Midland Division. Electrically-operated intermediate-block (IB) signals—of MR-design—were installed at several places to shorten the sections. Stanier 4-6-0s and 2-8-0s later, plus 2-10-0s in the BR-era, headed many trains. However, as late as 1964, 44044, a 4F 0-6-0 built c.1923-4, was noted trundling the daily Stourton-Carlisle freight down through Kirkby Stephen. Evidently no larger engine was available on that day. These 4Fs had shared through-freights with the moguls before the arrival of the Stanier engines, both on the main line and via Settle Junction to the branches, including the daily Heysham tanker-train. This 4F had successfully slogged up the 'Long Drag' from Settle Junction to Blea Moor with his long freight-train.

Freight (or 'goods'; the LMS was ambivalent, using both terms synonymously) accounted for about 60% of traffic-receipts, of which a high proportion was coal. In the early-1930s, the LMS was moving 85 million tons of the stuff, 9 millions carried to the company's own coal-loading jetties for export or bunker-coal, as well as supplying its own depots with 'loco-coal'. London grates burnt it too, by courtesy of the LMS Toton-Brent mass-mineral flow, drawn from scores of collieries in South Yorkshire, Nottinghamshire and Derbyshire. Coke too, was hauled from hundreds of coke-ovens, much destined for the private sidings of factories or municipal gas—and electricity-works. From the Toton gathering-ground, the minerals were taken forward via the Silkstream Junction flyover between Hendon and Cricklewood, on trip-workings to the GWR at Acton, to the SR at Feltham and Hither Green, and to LMS depots at such arcane destinations as Clapham Wharf, West India Dock, Walworth Road and even High Street, Kensington. The procession of mineral-trains from the Midlands, mostly sidelined in permissive-block workings, averaged less than 30 mph, but its huge tonnage made it profitable. The Clean Air Act of 1957 gradually phased out this traffic, a loss of revenue to the railways, and was also a factor in the closure of many secondary lines.

Fast-freight services were also important. Express perishable-trains were run overnight, carrying meat to Smithfield Market, fish from Fleetwood to Broad Street for Billingsgate market; at Leeds the LMS took over from the LNER the evening fish-train from Grimsby to Manchester and places west. Milk for London was carried in glass-lined or stainless-steel tank-wagons. One example was the concentration at Carlisle of wagons from all over Galloway, south-west Scotland, with a final pick-up from the Express Dairy sidings at Appleby, controlled by a ground-frame south of the station. While at school, the author used to see this train running up to Leeds on the way to London as an express-parcels, described in Chapter 6. On arrival at Cricklewood, the tankers were tripped around London to depots on the other three railways.

Locomotive-Depots

The many main-works and subsidiary facilities inherited by the LMS largely kept their individual character and were naturally reluctant to change. The reorganizations made a start in welding them effectively into one entity and in developing the existing loyalties into one for the new, composite, company. Again, it was the LNW that was a pioneer, in its introduction of mechanical means of coaling—and ash-disposal plants at five large depots. The remainder of the sheds inherited by the LMS, like the other railways, remained antediluvian workplaces, where little progress had been made since the mid-nineteenth century, leaving them dark, draughty and uncomfortable, with few amenities for the men. The Executive recognized this, but change crept in only slowly, such as the twin-bunker steel coaling-tower with wagon-hoist in 1925 at Polmadie, Glasgow, the principal Scottish depot serving west-coast trains. Following analyses of shed-operations that revealed a low availability of locomotives, a three-pronged programme was decided upon: the installation of mechanical coaling-towers and ash-disposal plants at large depots; rationalizing their yard-layouts for a quicker throughput of engines; rationalization of the shed-network itself by closing some sheds. An example was the former LYR shed at Hellifield (situated in the V of the junction), closed in 1927, since the larger ex-Midland shed alongside the main line north of the station had accommodation. This shed was ideal for platform-spotters, who could now see ex-L&Y engines there from Blackburn and Manchester. In 1931, the modernization programmers issued orders for coalers and ash-plants, some from private manufacturers, for depots where the layout was viable, continuing until halted by World War 2. The different models revealed the search for an optimum design. Steady progress saw the re-organization of the motive-power depots into twenty-nine districts in 1935. In 1943, some scattered Scottish districts were sub-divided bringing the total to thirty-two. Each district comprised a head, or 'concentration-depot', carrying the suffix 'A' to its number. An example was Leeds Holbeck, 20A, with seven subsidiaries, Stourton 20B, up to Lancaster 20H. The head-depot was equipped with lifting—or wheel-drop facilities, and machine-tools to handle heavy repairs (e.g. cylinders, boilers and axle-boxes), leaving minor work and adjustments to the subsidiary, or 'garage', depots. Steel shortages in the post-war period (after 1945) caused some replacement-roofs to be made of unsatisfactory and unsightly pre-cast concrete-sections. However, the modernizations made the servicing of locomotives a quicker, more efficient, and attractive task, especially important after the war, when recruitment had to compete with cleaner, easier, jobs available at a time of full employment. An example of a concrete coaling-tower and ash-plant built by the LMS in 1944 can be seen at the preserved depot of Carnforth in north Lancashire, the only depot to receive a complete shed-makeover. Preserved as 'Steamtown', it is now home to many locomotives, also preserved, and to West Coast Railways, preservation specialists.

Locomotive Works

Crewe works had grown *ad hoc* from its birth in 1843, with no less than nine different shops, but a new erecting-shop, sanctioned by the LNW in 1920, was begun by the LMS, to a modified plan, in 1925. It allowed shops 1-4 to be converted into a new plant to construct all boilers for the LMS. It made sound economic sense and turned out to be highly successful, though it provoked resentment at Derby, Horwich and St Rollox, now relegated simply to repairing boilers. As observed, St Rollox, the Scottish HQ of the LMS, used its isolation from Euston and Derby to ignore instructions felt to be unfavourable; for example, they fitted Caledonian boilers to ex-Highland engines. As they were unsuitable for ex-G&SW locomotives, these were quietly scrapped—but they had come off badly in the early comparative-tests. However, as mentioned in the chapter describing Stanier's appointment in 1932, Crewe lost its steelworks in that year, a victim of pressure from outside steelmasters, the depression and re-investment needs. Henceforth, Horwich concentrated on enhancing its workshop-techniques, an investment for the future. The new repair-schedules of 1927 cut engine down-time in half. Once Crewe's new capacity was proved, the closure of the smaller works went ahead, first Barrow (FR) in 1927, then Stoke-on-Trent (NSR) and Highbridge (S&DJR) in 1930. The LMS policy of advancement on all fronts was possible through its immense resources. As an example, the main works were always kept at the cutting-edge of technology, notably in the surface-finish of parts (to minimize fatigue-cracking) and in electric-welding (for fabrication and the repair of contact-surfaces), especially at Crewe. In this technique, the company was something of a pioneer.

Ports and Steamer-services

It was inevitable that such a large conglomerate as the LMS would inherit a range of activities from its constituents, and that some overlapped. So it was in the realm of harbours and the ships that plied from them, comprising some seventy steamers, from five ports on the west coast and one on the east. The LYR had contributed Liverpool, the LNW Fleetwood, both serving ports in Ireland and Douglas, Isle of Man, while the LNW's Holyhead Harbour at the tip of the island of Anglesey, North Wales, was its main port serving the Irish Republic, later taking the mail-contract from the B & I Line. The smaller LYR had nevertheless brought a considerable fleet of steamers based on both the west and east coasts. Goole, a busy inland-port on the River Ouse in the then West Riding of Yorkshire, operated several services across the North Sea. The MR had brought Bristol (Avonside and Kings Wharf), which specialized in handling banana imports. In south-west Scotland, the G&SW port of Stranraer served Larne, for Belfast, with connections via the LMS (formerly the MR) subsidiary, the Northern Counties Committee, to all parts of Northern Ireland, and to Dublin through Belfast. The short crossing of the North Channel was popular with travellers who disliked sea-voyages, making it the busiest Irish crossing. By the 21st century though, Cairnryan, further down the loch, had largely taken Stranraer's trade. The G&SW had other piers, at Ayr, Troon, Fairlie, Largs and Renfrew. Also from the LNW, the LMS inherited a small Irish network: the Dundalk, Newry & Greenore Railway with port-facilities at Greenore, and the Dublin North Wall steamer-berths, warehouses and a hotel, along with a short branch-line. The MR's Heysham, south of Morecambe in Lancashire, represented another harbour serving Ireland and the Isle of Man. The duplication of Irish Sea services made some rationalization necessary. The Belfast (via Larne) services from Fleetwood were switched to Heysham in 1928, but succumbed to Northern Irish political difficulties in 1975. The Londonderry sailings had been withdrawn many years earlier. Liverpool operated ships to Dublin, more convenient for travellers coming from London, but Fleetwood continued to serve Douglas, Isle of Man. Additionally, by dint of running-powers over the LNER, LMS trains ran to Grimsby, north Lincolnshire, whose ex-GC out-port of Immingham provided other North Sea services. Services to Hull ran similarly, but the LMS withdrew its staff (to York) around 1930.

Hotels & Tourism

In 1938, the LMS owned 30 hotels, 73 steamers, with a staff of 8,000, including an entertainments-manager. The hotels were nationwide, some offering specialized facilities, such as golf at the ex-GSW Turnberry Hotel, reached from Ayr on a light railway, and the Gleneagles Hotel in Perthshire. Two others had been developed by the former Highland Railway, Dornoch and Strathpeffer. Visitors used a further light railway from The Mound to reach Dornoch, where the railway had built a resort-hotel; however, the five-mile branch from Dingwall to the tiny Strathpeffer spa (usually called a 'hydro' in Scotland) was an ordinary line—and considered important enough to warrant through-carriages from the south.

The LMS converted a historic mansion near Stratford-upon-Avon, Warwickshire, into their Welcombe Hotel, opening it on 1 July 1931. Part of the estate once belonged to William Shakespeare. The company even ran a door-to-door service for a time, using a bus-on-rails, the 'Ro-railer', a Karrier single-deck bus, fitted with two sets of wheels, the road-wheels swivelling down for the last stage of the journey at Stratford. It collected West-coast route passengers at Blisworth, Northanptonshire, then ran on a section of the former Stratford & Midland Junction Railway to the station at Stratford and along the road to the hotel. An experiment, it was not a success and was soon withdrawn. It is described in the section on railcars. The Welcombe's telegraphic-address 'Bestotel', was a convenience shared by many of the LMS hotels. A picture of this hotel graced many a carriage compartment, allowing passengers to share in the experience, if only vicariously. The refreshments-business comprised over 200 dining—and kitchen-cars, catering for 'meals-on-wheels' to passengers; these were also provided on the steamers. After the Grouping, the LMS built new cars for the principal trains, allowing pre-grouping vehicles to be cascaded to other trains. Following the successful tour of The Royal Scot in North America, the LMS launched their 'Royal Scot Whisky' as a publicity exercise.

Improvements came gradually. One was the splendid 1935 Queen's Hotel, Leeds, designed in the contemporary art-deco style, ideally placed for the shopping—and business-hub of the West Riding of Yorkshire. It stands over a spacious new concourse containing shops and ticket-offices, and originally had a News Theatre. A new loud-speaker system was installed and electric-trolleys transported luggage. The LMS crest is carved into the facade. The amalgamation of the Central and City in the 1960s allowed Central to be closed, with its London traffic re-routed into City—a huge convenience to transfer-passengers that was long overdue. The combined station is named simply 'Leeds', leaving the former Midland terminus as a parcels-depot. Lovers of art-deco design will also know the Midland Hotel at Morecambe, built by the LMS in 1933 to replace the Midland Railway's earlier structure, if only through watching Agatha Christie's Belgian detective Hercule Poirot on ITV.

Although the LMS served only small portions of the English and Welsh coastlines, it did have the jewel in the crown, Blackpool, Britain's largest resort, where it had three stations. It continued the offer by the LYR in 1895 to run a prestigious 'Club Train' for businessmen commuting from Manchester, similar to that from Southport—and that operated by the LNWR from Llandudno. Passengers had to guarantee regularly to buy a certain number of tickets at a premium rate for the extra facilities of bar and armchairs in their two special saloons. At holiday-times, the company carried huge crowds of people, especially during the 'Wakes Week', the annual summer block-exodus from the Lancashire and Yorkshire textile-towns. The Blackpool Central station had eight platforms dedicated to this business, including excursion-trains at other times of the year, offered at affordable tariffs to entice people who lived on a limited budget. However, holidays-with-pay from 1938 helped. The Talbot Road (now North) and South stations catered for other destinations.

The company also popularized the north coast of Wales, Rhyl, Prestatyn and Colwyn Bay, and the largest resort, Llandudno, all situated on its Irish mail-route to the port of Holyhead on the Isle of Anglesey. Day-trippers could sail from Liverpool to Llandudno on the yellow-funnelled *St Seriol* or *St Tudno,* returning by train, or vice-versa. The LMS branch from Bangor met the GWR on the Cambrian Coast line at Afon Wen, helping to develop its Welsh seaside-resorts.

In Scotland, the LMS served the Ayrshire coast, running services from Glasgow to Wemyss Bay and Ardrossan for steamers (ferries) to Arran and the Kyles of Bute. This area also benefited from the steamers operated by the LMS subsidiary, the Caledonian Steam Packet Co. Ltd., which plied from Glasgow to Dunoon, Rothesay, the Kyles of Bute and Arran. Many is the time when our Scots relatives took us out from Glasgow on a day-trip to one of these places, but for the local people, the steamers acted as a bus-service, for shopping or entertainment in Glasgow. The author's mother's parents went this way from Glasgow to spend their honeymoon at Rothesay in 1890. The LMS steamers crossing from Helensburgh to Gourock competed with those of the LNER at neighbouring Craigendoran, serving Greenock pier. Up in the Highlands, a daily train over the lengthy branch to the Kyle of Lochalsh—complete with restaurant-car—served the Isle of Skye, reached from Kyle on a very short ferry before the present bridge was built. In Northern Ireland, the LMS owned hotels at Larne and Portrush. Finally, "The company has 108 'caravans' (carriages converted into camping-coaches), 70 in England and Wales (7 at the seaside), 30 in Scotland, and 8 in Northern Ireland (6 by the sea), placed at 32 stations close to beauty-spots and places of interest. Caravans are on view at various stations up and down the line during January for inspection by prospective visitors. They will see that the caravans are well appointed, delightfully comfortable, with equipment complete in every detail." This was the message written by Ashton Davies, chief commercial manager, in the March 1935 issue of *LMS Magazine*.

Publicity

The LMS appointed a Midland man, T.C. Jeffrey, as its advertising and publicity officer, at first at Derby, later quartered at Euston. Apart from advertising holiday-resorts, his office produced a range of attractive coloured posters painted by Royal Academicians, collectors' pieces now, publicizing the company's activities, the places it served. and most aspects of the company's business. The posters can be seen at the NRM, York. On Jeffrey's retirement in 1934, his deputy G.H. Loftus Allen took over. He had joined the LNWR as a probationer in 1913, had had a good war-record, was well connected and had a leaning towards the arts, which favourably influenced the quality of the posters. Coloured booklets and pictures of the company's locomotives and trains were published when appropriate to commemorate special events. Posters on the Square Deal (a joint-campaign by 'the big four' railways for equality with the road-hauliers on tariffs) and other campaigns, staff at their work, technical innovations in passenger-comfort and in freight-wagons, the company's centenary in 1938. 'Your Friends on the LMS' portrayed a steelworks at night, a station-scene, the company's ships, a driver's cab at night, porters and restaurant-car staff. Views of the countryside were more examples, showing the LMS serving a varied, attractive, country, and many passengers counted the journey as an important aspect of their holiday. Though on a rather smaller scale than GWR publicity, large numbers of guides and leaflets complemented the posters. The LMS shilling (5p) stamps and ten-shilling (50p) vouchers offered generous terms of interest. The epic 114 mph speed-record in 1937 appeared in special editions of newspapers. The author's father bought *The Times*, which showed pictures (monochrome in those days) of *Coronation Scot* in full cry and the crew being congratulated on arrival at Crewe by the top-hatted station-master. Press-releases became an important facet of the business.

Concerning book-publicity, the LMS usually employed outside authors. An early effort was made in 1924 for the British Empire Exhibition at Wembley, opening on 23 April, with 'The Magic Wand of Transport', a 15-page booklet describing the train-control system. It was produced for the company by the *Railway Gazette* and sold at 6d. The celebrations to commemorate the centenary of the Liverpool & Manchester Railway in 1830 were organized jointly by the City of Liverpool and the LMS. They included a big exhibition in St George's Hall, a railway fair and a nightly pageant in Wavertree Park. The noted railway historian C.F. Dendy Marshall was commissioned to write a 62-page booklet *One Hundred Years of Railways*, published by the company at a shilling. By 1929, the LMS was issuing a million and a quarter guide-books, covering holidays-resorts served by the company, in particular *Holidays by LMS*, selling at 6d, comprising 700 pages with hundreds of illustrations.

In 1932, a great expansion of activity occurred, with ex-LNW E.J.H. Lemon as vice-president taking charge of the commercial and operating sides of traffic, with Ashton Davies, ex-LYR, as assistant. The hard times of the Great Depression made it urgent to become pro-active to drum up business. D.S.M. Barrie, an experienced Fleet Street journalist, was appointed to strengthen the team. A series of guide-books describing the principal routes mile-by-mile was issued. 'The Track of the Royal Scot' was a prime example, while the last one appearing pre-war, 'The Track of the Coronation Scot', detailed the train-equipment and up and down passing-times at principal places to cater for the growing interest in railways.

The Executive felt that its house-journal, *The LMS Magazine*, was inappropriate for propaganda, and therefore introduced two free staff-newspapers, for the operating and commercial departments, *On Time* and *Quota News* respectively. The April-1935 edition of *On Time* featured details of the handling of the huge freight-traffic through Crewe—to inform the staff, as well as the general public. *Quota News* gave details of targets set by Ashton Davies for every station and district, with the aim of encouraging a competitive spirit to enhance the company's standing and staff-morale. Slogans advertised the company. LMS: 'This is Your Way Sir, Travel by LMS, *The Best Way* (the slogan of the old MR), The Finest Permanent-Way in the World (borrowed from the LNW); Year-in, Year-out, Day-in, Day-out, LMS Express Trains provide a superb service of communication to all parts of Great Britain'; and many more. 'Stay at LMS Hotels' exhorted a notice superimposed on a map of the company's extensive system. An outstanding poster of 1947 was a picture painted by the celebrated artist Terence Cuneo, titled 'The Day Begins', showing a Duchess pacific locomotive—almost certainly the newest, 6256 *Sir William Stanier*—in steam on the Willesden roundhouse turntable (although a pacific would normally be found at Camden), in company with a Royal Scot, a Horwich mogul, a Compound and other engines, an evocative picture of the LMS at its peak.

A series of ciné-films largely replaced lantern-slides, covering training and general matters to interest the public. Two ex-LNW carriages were converted into mobile-cinemas to show them to staff, their families and to the general public around the country. The Crown Film Unit's epic documentary *Night Mail* of 1936 has already been mentioned. The war beginning in September 1939 greatly reduced the activity, with nearly half of the staff leaving for active service, causing the suspension of both staff journals and *The LMS Magazine*. They were replaced with the news-sheet *Carry On*, giving non-restricted information to staff 'for the duration' which now carried advertisements on behalf of the wartime Railway Executive Committee. All this publicity was an undoubted success towards building a corporate identity and encouraging pride in the LMS to replace loyalties to the constituent companies.

The GWR and the LMS were unique among the Big Four companies in sending a locomotive and train to North America. However, while the GWR 'King' visited the Baltimore & Ohio RR for 'The Festival of the Iron Horse' in 1927 to celebrate the B & O centenary, the LMS not only sent a train on two occasions, but *The Royal Scot* in 1933 made an extensive tour of Canada and the USA, a trip lasting six months with faultless running throughout. The final flourish by the LMS was to send its streamlined *Coronation Scot* train for a tour of the Eastern States before being exhibited at the New York World's Fair in 1939.

A LYR 4-4-2 'High-Flyer' races through Copley, Halifax, on a Leeds express c.1910 (H. Horsfall, the author's father).

Ex-CR 0-4-4 tank-engine 15234 awaits further banking-duty at Beattock wcml in 1947 (author).

Chapter 4

WORLD WAR 2, 1939-45, AND ITS AFTERMATH

Long before the declaration of war on 3 September 1939, the LMS, in common with the other three railways, had played its full part when asked by the War Department to reorganize its works for munitions. The design and mass-production of Covenanter tanks at Crewe and Matildas at Horwich, and of aircraft at Derby, were but a part of it. This vital wartime task of the LMS was made much easier through Stamp's persevering reorganizations of the 1920s and 1930s. Since the LMS was not only the largest railway, but by now the most mechanized and scientific of the big four, it played a leading part in the war-effort. It was just a crowning misfortune that President Stamp was killed in his home, Shortlands, Beckenham, Kent, by a German bomb in 1941, as he would no doubt have brought a different perspective to post-war activities and to the nationalized era that followed. Sir William Wood, originally from the NCC in Northern Ireland, took over as President of the Executive. The extreme shortages during and after the war—including coal—inhibited the restoration of pre-war standards; consequently engines and rolling-stock were often dirty, and even large stations remained run down. All this prompted the catch-phrase 'the LMS—a hell of a mess', a back-handed compliment really, contrasting the company's current state with its high pre-war standards of comfort. But, as the largest railway, its difficulties were more apparent. Trains ran late, connections were missed, and there was tremendous overcrowding. The author often stood in the corridor from Carlisle to Leeds—but luckily, his journeys avoided Crewe, that butt of music-hall comedians—in the limelight because of the long delays encountered there, since the BBC's Variety

Department had been removed to Bangor 'for the duration'. Crewe, like other great stations such as St Pancras, Manchester Victoria/Central, and Birmingham New Street, had a palpable aura, a grandeur, despite the dirt and peeling paint. An occasional pre-war holiday poster, surviving alongside those issued by the wartime Railway Executive, reminded the observer of happier times and of better days to come. They did come from 1945, with the LMS still determinedly improving its service and raising standards across its system.

In 1942, Stanier was seconded as one of three scientific advisers to the Ministry of Production and set up an office at The Grove, Watford, a mansion where most management had been evacuated for safety, to liaise with the other railways, with the Railway Executive and government departments. Mechanical engineering matters were now handled by Fairburn who remained at Derby, with Principal Assistants Ivatt (locomotive), Harper (electrical) and Pugson (carriage & wagon). The proposals for five standard-classes to haul all traffic post-war and development of the pacifics were suspended 'for the duration', together with plans to construct: a replacement for the 0-6-0 freight-engine; the Mobile Test Units; the Flange-Force Testing equipment; the Rugby Testing-Station; and a new dynamometer-car. Its equipment arrived from the makers, Amsler in Switzerland, on the very eve of the war and was put into store.

The first priority at Derby was to turn the workshops over to munitions. The great achievement of the LMS was that, by the autumn of 1940, it was utilizing as many weekly man-hours on direct government-contracts as the other three railways put together. It had gained a flying-start through Ivatt's work on tank-design and construction in 1937-8, and through a concentrated effort by Fairburn and Pugson to bring aircraft-work into the carriage-shops. 'Operation Dynamo' came in 1940, the great evacuation of the British Expeditionary Force from Dunkirk, necessitating many specials from Dover and Ramsgate to distant destinations. In this exercise, LMS trains and some of its ships, now requisitioned by the government, played a big part. It lost the SS *Scotia* (ex-Holyhead—Dublin route) to enemy-bombing at Dunkirk.

The second priority in the workshops was to fit locomotive repair and maintenance into this busy schedule to enable the maximum number of engines to be returned to traffic quickly. Materials and finish were therefore modified to B.S. (British Standard) limits from the higher LMS specifications. By saving condemned engines from the breakers, an additional 500 were restored to traffic by mid-1941. Despite this, by 1942 a severe locomotive-shortage appeared, owing to the enormous extra traffic caused by the war. Ironically, the remedy now was to modify the earlier efforts to bring government-work into the railway-workshops, to make space for building locomotives.

Only mixed-traffic and freight-engines were allowed. Candidates for a standard heavy-freight locomotive were reviewed by the War Department. The Great Western '28xx' had restricted route-availability, the conjugated valve-gear of the Gresley three-cylinder 'O2' had proved difficult to maintain in wartime-conditions, and the other 2-8-0, the ex-GCR of WW1, was now felt to be out-dated. The Stanier 2-8-0 was the only one suitable for general service and was adopted as a standard for all the railways by the Railway Executive. Initially, following the practice of the previous war, some were destined for the Continent, but Hitler's *blitzkrieg* (lightning war) overran Belgium and France too quickly for this plan. Therefore batches of the 2-8-0 were adapted for oil-burning for the only theatre of war free of German occupation, the Middle East. In knocked-down form (CKD), twenty-two were despatched via the Cape of Good Hope and the Red Sea to Suez, but four were lost to enemy action. The remaining eighteen engines ran on the Egyptian State Railway's extension into the Western Desert (useful to supply Montgomery's Eighth Army via El Alamein) and over the new line across the Suez Canal at El Kantara to connect with Palestinian Railways running to Tel Aviv, to help the British run their mandate— and also useful to connect with Turkish railways for a 'back-door' supply-route to the USSR. In 1941-2, a further 24 locomotives joined them, some partially armour-plated. Then, another batch of 2-8-0s arrived CKD at Suez for Turkey via the Cape, though they languished in pieces on islands near Suez for a time. They replaced an order placed with Britain in 1939 for German-designed 2-10-0s, but unfulfilled owing to other commitments. Turkey largely supported the Allies, but Germany sought to undermine this relationship by undertaking to construct the Reichbahn 2-10-0s quickly, which brought an immediate British response to fulfil the Turkish order. Although smaller than the German design, the 2-8-0s were welcomed by the Turks, who called them 'Churchills', and they remained in service for decades after the war. Some have been repatriated, for conservation. Other locomotives went to Persia (Iran), where British and American (later all-American) staffs ran the Trans-Persia Railway, helping the Allied war-effort by hauling further supplies through to the USSR.

This large commitment meant widening the 2-8-0-construction from the four LMS shops to those of the other three railways: to Darlington and Doncaster (LNER), to Swindon (GWR) and even to Brighton (SR), which had built no new engines for many years. Furthermore, the planned second-front in 1944 would require more locomotives than even these works could produce, therefore commercial builders would have to participate. The wartime Railway Executive began construction of fresh orders in 1940 with 50 engines by the North British Locomotive Company, Glasgow, 8176-8225, while Crewe built three batches up to 8175 from 1941 to 1943. Numbers 8226-8325 were officially War Department stock lent to the LMS and the GWR in 1940-41. Continuing from 8301, Crewe built 8301-8330 in 1943-44, while Horwich's share was considerably more, 8331-8399 and 8490-95. The author recalls several of the 83xx series heading coal-trains through the Calder Valley, Halifax, clearly brand-new and smart in their glossy-black with the company-insignia in gilt counter-shaded red. They were no doubt running in after emerging from erecting-shops at Horwich. Also clearly, they were in line to replace the 'Austin Sevens', which had not fulfilled expectations to replace the LNW Super Ds, an issue discussed elsewhere. The 84xx-series, apart from the six mentioned above, was constructed by the GWR at Swindon to Railway Executive order, but ten, 8480-89, were cancelled. The series was lent to the GWR for 1946-47. The LNER built 8500-59 at its Doncaster and Darlington works and officially borrowed them for 1946-47. After this gap, we come to more straightforward lots, 8600-8704, which came out of the Southern Railway's workshops at Eastleigh, Ashford and Brighton during 1943-44. Complications reappear with sixty-eight further engines being authorized in 1945-46 to LNER order at Doncaster and Darlington, but the first twenty-five had come from Brighton works in

1944. These later received LMS numbers 8705-8772. Finally, the last three were released from the Ministry as late as 1957, and allocated the numbers 48773/4/5; the first is preserved. Over the years, a few of the overseas locomotives have been repatriated. *The Railway Magazine* of March 2011 pictures two of these 'Churchills' arriving back in Britain from Turkey, 45166 and 45170, the latter standing in the Locomotion Museum of the NRM at Shildon, Co Durham awaiting restoration. The Stanier 2-8-0 holds the record for the largest number of a design constructed in Britain, 852, though not all returned to the country after the war. The complex story of the Stanier 2-8-0 as researched by Rowledge is detailed in the chapter containing 'the largest classes of the LMS'.

But even all this was not enough, particularly to fulfil post-war needs on the Continent. In order to achieve maximum output, Riddles, who had been seconded at the outset of the war to the government as Deputy Director-General, Royal Engineer Equipment, examined every feature of the 2-8-0 for ease and economy in its manufacture, in consultation with private contractors. A round-topped, parallel boiler was substituted for the taper Belpaire, and many other simplifications were made. They resulted in the WD 'Austerity', bringing a saving of 20% in production man-hours. It looked similar to the USA 2-8-0s, mentioned shortly, the design of which possibly influenced Riddles. The Stanier design however was built unaltered by the various railway-works. In 1944, Riddles designed a larger version of his Austerity-engine, a 2-10-0, to haul, as one activity, the Toton-Cricklewood coal-trains, a reflection of efforts—including the Beyer-Garratts of 1927—made over many years to eliminate the double-heading required on this heavy traffic. Immediately after the war, a coal-shortage caused Government to press the railways to convert locomotives for oil-burning. However, before the scheme could become fully operational, the crisis passed and the railways reverted to coal.

In October 1943, Symes retired, and to replace him as Chief Stores Superintendent—a vital post especially in wartime—the LMS secured the release of Riddles from his post of Deputy Director-General of Royal Engineer Equipment, for which he had been awarded the CBE in January. Railway-enthusiasts knew of him for his 'Austerity'

2-8-0 and 2-10-0 locomotives. With R.C. Bond appointed as Works Superintendent at Crewe in 1941 as well, the Stanier team was now further strengthened.

Mr Fairburn had been 'head-hunted' from the English Electric Company by Sir Harold Hartley in 1934, an explanation of this unusual entrant into railway-engineering from private industry. It recalls Hartley's head-hunting of Stanier in 1932. Actually, Hartley himself had entered the LMS from outside the railway-industry, brought over from academia by President Stamp—who himself had been brought in similarly, by Granet. This recruitment-policy says something about the ethos of the LMS management: logical organization to achieve the best possible result. With Stanier seconded to war-work in 1942, Fairburn acceded to CME, a career curtailed by his premature death in 1945. His EE diesel experience had enabled him to assist Hartley and Stanier in their pioneering promotion of the diesel-electric shunter during the 1930s, which led to their construction in hundreds by BR. His work as Electrical Engineer on the LMS provided the groundwork for H.G. Ivatt's main-line diesel-electric locomotive of 1947, both described under this heading. Fairburn had encouraged Coleman to modify the Stanier 2-6-4 tank-engine design to save weight and material, as remarked when examining this type, and hundreds of these locomotives too were built into the BR-era. Fairburn died suddenly in October 1945 aged only 58. Uncertainty over a successor caused a delay in the appointment. Finally, Hartley was outvoted by the rest of the Executive and resigned as Vice-President to join the board of British Overseas Airways Corporation (BOAC). His place as Vice-President was filled by R.A. Riddles, in April 1946, leaving the other candidate, H.G. Ivatt, to be appointed CME, in January 1946, and R.C. Bond was promoted to Mechanical Engineer, Locomotive Works.

The Americans had pioneered new devices to facilitate the servicing of steam-locomotives, and their Transportation Corps S.160 2-8-0 freight-locomotives, fitted with them and working in Britain ready for shipment to France after D-day in June 1944, gave the LMS practical experience. Major Marsh became well-known for his S.160 locomotive. Stanier may have observed these devices while in the USA leading the visit of *The Royal Scot* in 1933, and his good memory would have enabled him to recall this information years later for their introduction by Ivatt; Riddles would certainly have noted them while taking *Coronation Scot* to America in 1939. They comprised the self-cleaning smokebox, rocking-grate and self-emptying hopper-ashpan. These features had been routinely fitted to locomotives operating on American and Colonial railways. During the war, experiments were made to see how these features could be applied to LMS locomotives. After successful trials on 4-6-0s and 2-8-0s, the LMS introduced these improvements on all locomotives built from 1945, denoted by 'SC', stencilled on the smokebox-door below the shed-plate, later replaced with an oval plate. These devices fitted by Ivatt saved maintenance man-hours, an important consideration with many staff away in the services, as well as saving expense and rendering steam-operations quicker and cleaner. The disposal of locomotives after their duties was hard work, raking the grate to remove clinker and dropping the ash, as well as shovelling out the char from the smokebox, so Ivatt's innovations were popular with the loco-crews. The accepted thinking that the smokebox-diaphragm would cause a reduction in the blast and difficulties in cleaning the boiler-tubes was proved unfounded; the device allowed engines so fitted to run from one boiler-washout to the next without once opening the smokebox-door. These improvements followed Stanier's side-window cab and an improved cab-layout fitted by him to the last batch of the Derby 2-6-4 tank-locomotives (2395-2424), built at the beginning of his appointment as CME. Such advances assumed a greater importance after the end of the war in 1945, a time of full employment, when recruitment became harder to jobs which had become relatively less appealing. Earlier members of standard-classes were fitted with the SC-devices during routine maintenance.

In 1943, Stanier, along with Riddles, was knighted, and he retired in the following year. At this time, post-war plans were being formulated and, since mixed-traffic construction was permitted, the Executive decided to continue building the Class Five 4-6-0, detailed earlier. The various developments incorporated are described in the chapter covering the Stanier standard-classes. After many schemes—including diesel-trains—to replace engines for secondary services, Ivatt decided on a 2-6-0 along with its counterpart, a 2-6-2 tank, a straightforward design incorporating the latest thinking. These Class 2s represented the only modern small engines built by any railway in Britain.

The Rugby Locomotive Testing Station

This facility was started in 1938, but the war, beginning only a year later, put it on hold, preventing its completion before nationalization. It was opened by the Minister of Transport on 19 October 1948, the first year of the British Railways regime. The French and German railways had modern locomotive testing-stations, while Britain's sole example remained the GWR-plant at Swindon of 1905-vintage. So, eventually, Britain embarked on this significant project to update locomotive-testing from the traditional trial-and-error method. It was begun jointly by the LMS and LNER, following a long campaign from 1931 for scientific locomotive-testing by H.N. (later Sir Nigel) Gresley, CME of the LNER. His company lacked the necessary funding, owing to its heavy dependence on the coal-and-steel districts of the North East, hit particularly hard by the Great Depression, and so he had turned to the LMS and gained its co-operation. Significantly it was erected at Rugby on LMS territory, another demonstration of the company's determination to pursue efficiency—and of its much larger resources. The testing-facility was designed to calculate the maximum steaming-capacity of boilers, optimum designs of steam-circuits and valve-events, among other areas, by running the locomotives on rollers, where coal— and water-consumption for example could be closely monitored under controlled conditions. Henceforth, the dynamometer-cars were used for confirmatory tests of locomotives already paced on the rollers, especially on the Skipton-Carlisle line, which remained a favourite testing-ground. The Rugby tests demonstrated a further potential of some engines, for example the Horwich 2-6-0. However, it was the test of a Duchess that proved the most remarkable. The engine was pushed to a sustained steaming-rate of 41,500 lb/hr, the highest output ever recorded in Britain, but this did not reach the boiler-limit, even with two firemen. The testing recalls the myriad modifications made to many types of locomotive once built, because designs had always had to be drawn empirically. The testing arrived almost too late, after more than a century of steam-locomotive construction, but it did provide useful data for the BR standard-locomotives of the era that was dawning.

Preservation

The LMS is well represented by preserved locomotives and trains, including two of Stanier's Princesses, three Princess Coronations (Duchesses), two converted Royal Scots, four Jubilees (including one undergoing restoration), eighteen Black Fives, the pioneer 3-cyl 2-6-4 tank 2500, two Fairburn 2-6-4 tanks, and eleven 8F 2-8-0s. Ivatt locomotives comprise four 2MT 2-6-0s, four 2MT 2-6-2 tanks, one 4MT 2-6-0. Older engines include: MR 2-4-0 158A, 4-2-2 'Spinner', 4-4-0 compound 1000, FR 0-4-0 20 and *Coppernob*, three 4F 0-6-0s, ten 3F 0-6-0 tanks, three Horwich moguls (one unrestored), and two ex-S&DJR 2-8-0s. The L&Y is also well represented, with two 'Pug' 0-4-0s, 11218 & 11243, its first L&Y radial 2-4-2 tank 1008 (LMS 10621), 'Ironclad' 0-6-0 957 (LMS 12044), 0-6-0 Cl.27 12322, 0-6-0ST Cl.23 11456, *Wren* 18in gauge Horwich Works shunter, and 1, Motor-rail petrol-mechanical shunter. Some royal carriages are also held by the NRM.

Although the constituent-companies had set aside a number of locomotives for preservation, the official LMS attitude was ambivalent. It had no definite policy to preserve anything; in fact a practice had grown up to scrap the last locomotive of a class, once withdrawn from service. The few historic relics set aside for preservation were stored in the various paint-shops. When Stanier—appointed in 1932 with a remit to 'get things done'—discovered them occupying premium space at Derby, he had them scrapped. The 1948 nationalized British Railways too had little interest in the past. You may have seen the classic photograph of the last three ex-LNW express-engines, specially posed for the camera at Crewe on 20 June 1949 before scrapping: superheated-Precursor 4-4-0 25297 *Sirocco*, rebuilt 4-6-0 Claughton 6004 and 4-6-0 Prince of Wales 25752, all retaining their LMS livery. Luckily the author saw the last two, in service. Therefore *Hardwicke* remains the sole representative of an LNW express-locomotive in preservation, at the NRM. It is only through good fortune that we can still see these engines. Enthusiasts were responsible for purchasing numerous withdrawn engines, notably

Mr Billy Butlin, who exhibited three LMS Pacifics at his holiday-camps during the 1960s. These are now cared for elsewhere, in particular 6229 *Duchess of Hamilton*, which masqueraded as 6220 *Coronation* on the 1939 North American tour of *Coronation Scot*. However, of the hundreds of steam-locomotives preserved in Britain, the majority were rescued from Woodham's scrapyard at Barry, South Wales, described later, but due to circumstances, they largely represent BR standard-classes. The carers of ex-LMS engines include the National Railway Museum, the Midland Railway Trust, the Churnet Valley Railway, the Severn Valley Railway and the Keighley & Worth Valley Railway. Details are available in specialist books.

Standardization on the LMS

Owing to constituent-company rivalry during its first decade, the LMS mostly built obsolescent designs of locomotive, although their very quantities gave a degree of standardization, at least a commonality of many parts between different classes, such as boilers and cylinders, apart from the multidude of dials, levers and other fittings. Standardization—programmed by Stamp before Stanier's arrival—also simplified workshop-practice, enabling quicker servicing, so that fewer locomotives were needed altogether. The workshop-reorganizations of Ivatt and Riddles at Derby, and of Beames at Crewe, have been described. Great Western locomotives illustrate standardization: they bear a family-likeness, with their taper-boilers, brass safety-valves and so on. It explains why Stamp went to the Great Western to procure William Stanier for the CME he needed. Whereas the degree of standardization the LMS had achieved in the 1920s was based on obsolescent designs, from 1932 Stanier produced the required range of standard locomotives of up-to-date design—good-lookers too, with a more-refined appearance than those of the GWR, Stanier's training-ground.

With this, Stanier contributed hugely, not only lifting the LMS out of the doldrums, but making it the leader of Britain's railways, while demonstrating his management-qualities in the design-team he assembled. Older, non-standard, locomotives could now be withdrawn. This 'build-and-scrap' policy was aimed at achieving Stamp's long-term economies. For example, the high capital-cost of constructing a taper-boiler paid a dividend in its longevity, often lasting the life of the engine, greatly reducing maintenance. However, the threat of war in the later-1930s caused many older locomotives to be retained in stock for emergency, some positively ancient—but very interesting for fans. Stanier was active in other fields too, notably for his standard carriages with comfortable seating researched by the company's technical department. Also at Derby, the LMS School of Transport was opened on 22 July 1938, essentially a college to train the company's personnel. Now, we look at LMS progress across the board.

Ex-MR 0-4-4 tank-engine 1366 prepares to depart Earby for Barnoldswick, piloted by ex-MR 3295. A pilot is unnecessary on three carriages, but the 0-6-0 has to be taken up the branch to shunt the coal-sidings at Barnoldswick on the basis of 'one-engine-in-steam', to return later with empty wagons (author).

A restored LMS sleeping-car (author).

Chapter 5

LMS ACHIEVEMENTS: ORGANIZATION, STEAM AND DIESEL TRACTION

Organization

Chapter 2 has described the early difficulties of the LMS. The competing loyalties of constituent-company staff, in particular the rivalry between those of the the former LNWR and the MR, ran counter to the development of a corporate sentiment from management downwards. The problem was compounded by the criteria for appointments, in particular that of the CME, essentially seniority. What the company sorely needed was a long, settled period with a *company* locomotive-policy. Instead, the LMS continued with a nineteenth-century tradition of loyalty to individual engineers who pursued their own ideas. In 1926, the directors introduced new blood to reorganise the company on modern lines.

By appointing Sir Josiah Stamp as chairman, Sir Guy Granet paved the way for the new regime the company needed. Stamp introduced systematic costing, eliminated inefficient processes, plant and equipment and then, as President of the LMS, created an American-style executive of vice-presidents, each responsible for a specific activity. He had seen straightaway that his large unwieldy railway urgently needed a locomotive-policy that would produce a stud of standard, modern and powerful locomotives, initially for express passenger trains. Instead, all the company had received were obsolescent designs. In this way, the first seven years had passed uncertainly. But a measure of rationalization had been introduced, marking the first stage of Stamp's policy of build-and-scrap, beginning to make the LMS competitive.

Steam Achievements

Chapter 3 has described how in 1926, senior staff privately arranged for a GWR 'Castle' 4-6-0 to be lent to the LMS, resulting in the construction of the Royal Scot 4-6-0s to haul the heavy west-coast expresses—'The Pride of the LMS.' From 1932 onwards, Stanier created the required stud of modern, standard classes of locomotives, with long-life taper-boilers, the 5P5F 4-6-0s, 8F 2-8-0s and 5X 4-6-0s, the two classes of pacific, and the improved 2-6-4 tank-engines, all achieved within a few years, making the LMS a serious player. The conversion of the Royal Scots to taper-boiler came later. Post-war, the company planned to operate its traffic, apart from light branch-line and shunting, with five classes only. A lasting achievement was the team of able assistants Stanier assembled around him, committed men who would continue his policy. This they did, through the final years of the LMS, and well into the BR-regime from 1948.

Diesel and Electric Traction

The LMS made a significant advance from steam-trains stemming from the birth of railways, through diesel-mechanical, diesel-hydraulic and diesel-electric to pure-electric drive, along with the parallel progression from the paradigm 'locomotive-plus-carriage' leading to the multiple-unit trains of today, *EuroStar, Le Shuttle, Virgin Pendolino* and *Javelin*. Of this quantum-leap, the LMS can fully claim its fair-share, and more in the field of diesel traction.

LMS, the Pioneer: Diesel Experiments

In the early 1930s, Stamp had formed a study-group to reduce shunting-costs. He had learned that, remarkably, 50% of a freight-engine's time was spent in shunting—quite apart from the hundreds of engines dedicated to this activity. Reference was made earlier to two further study-groups initiated by Stamp: an analysis of maintenance-costs, and of shed-routine. They recommended examinations of locomotives at mileage-intervals, on the lines of motor-vehicle maintenance. Stamp was embarked on a crusade to achieve greater efficiency and to drag the company into the twentieth century. His shunting study-group led to experiments with several models of diesel-mechanical and diesel-electric shunters and to comparisons of them with steam-shunting. The success of the diesels encouraged the LMS to expand diesel-electric traction into main-line service, which in turn was to pave the way for the elimination of steam-locomotives twenty years later.

After the peace in 1945, the media called for an end to steam-trains, seen to be outmoded when compared with North America. Over there, across the Atlantic Ocean, the railways were replacing steam with diesel and electric locomotives, and it was felt Britain should follow suit. But North America had oil, while Britain still had a coal-based economy. Furthermore, Britain was still struggling to recover from the ravages of war and its severe financial constraints. However, the LMS Executive had realized in the 1930s that the steam-locomotive was incapable of much further development, since its size—the boiler—had reached the limit of the British loading-gauge. Therefore, with the aim of having the knowhow ready for the appropriate time, the LMS Executive decided to include in their busy 1947 construction-programme four special locomotives: two further Duchesses incorporating the latest refinements and, for comparison on the road, Britain's first two main-line diesel-electric locomotives. These last two Duchesses were 6256 and 6257; the diesels were 10000/1 (the first having its stainless steel insignia and number riveted to the panels, as more permanent than mere paint or transfer). Rated at 1,600 hp, the machines were built at Derby in collaboration with the English-Electric Company. Coupled together, their power represented an advance on a Duchess pacific, while one unit was roughly equivalent to a Class Five 4-6-0. The CME of the LMS, C.E. Fairburn, head-hunted from English Electric (EE) by Hartley, had laid the foundations through his discussions with British-Thomson-Houston (BTH) for a 1,500hp locomotive with a Paxman engine, capable of work equal to that of the powerful 2-6-4 tank-engine. After Fairburn's untimely death in 1945, Ivatt took over, and was officially appointed CME on 1 January 1946. In order to advance the diesel project, he immediately contacted three firms, BTH, Crompton-Parkinson, and EE, all exporters of diesel-electric locomotives. By May,

Ivatt realized that, to build a machine quickly, the only way was a joint-project with a single firm. EE, Fairburn's old company, was chosen, and great harmony was achieved from the first meeting of the LMS with EE's chairman, Sir George Nelson. Tom Coleman's staff at Derby made a fine job of designing the mechanical parts, which performed well from the outset. I considered the engine handsome and well-proportioned. Ivatt himself drove LMS 10000 out of the Derby paint-shop on 8 December 1947. With this thrilling short ride, he made history. After tests, the locomotive ran up to London St Pancras on 16 December for its public presentation, to the chagrin of the other three railways. The news of its construction had leaked out at an Institute meeting earlier that year, causing a considerable flurry among the other three railways, which were considering similar machines. Indeed, the Southern Railway had begun to construct two 1-Co-Co-1 diesel-electrics, which entered service only after nationalization, but 10000 demonstrated the LMS was still ahead, the pioneer and leader. When the twin 10001 was finished in 1948, the pair made their proving-runs on the St Pancras-Manchester expresses, before their introduction to the West Coast route.

Teething-troubles seem to have been few, remarkable on such a ground-breaking design. The pioneer 10000 kept its LMS livery up to 1951 when, on a maintenance-visit to Derby, the machine was repainted in BR 'engine-green' with the first-lion emblem. The other project, Fairburn's 800hp diesel-electric for secondary services, 10800, with a Paxman engine and BTH electrical-equipment, had been handed to the North British Locomotive Company at an introductory meeting in 1946. However, time ran out for the LMS, and it was put into service by BR after nationalization. Thus culminated two decades of LMS experimentation with diesel-traction: it produced the first and only diesel-electric express-locomotive in Britain to carry the insignia of a private company.

Diesel Shunters

The first diesel-locomotive on the LMS was the diminutive 18" gauge 5519, a diesel-mechanical 0-4-0 used for shunting at Crewe works. As an expermental locomotive, it blazed the trail for further research into diesel-shunting. Other diesel-mechanical shunters were used by the

Civil Engineer's department. It was Sir Harold Hartley, Vice-President in charge of research, who recognized the potential of the diesel-machine as a shunter, and he proposed most strongly to the LMS Executive that steam-shunters be replaced with diesels. The conversion immediately began of ex-MR 0-6-0 shunter 1831 to diesel-hydraulic drive. Next, trials were made with diesel-mechanical shunters, supervised by Thomas Hornbuckle. Two Hunslet machines, 7050/1, were successful, and three more units followed. A further eight from other manufacturers were in the 150-200 hp-range. For comparison, a Sentinel-Doble oil-fired compound steam-shunter was purchased, 7192, the last steam-shunter built for the company. In July 1934, Charles E. Fairburn was brought from the English Electric Company into the LMS by Sir Harold Hartley and appointed Electrical Engineer: through Fairburn, Hartley wanted to tap EE's diesel knowhow. First, Fairburn trialled an English-Electric diesel-electric 300 hp prototype. The favourable outcome encouraged him to order twenty production-units, upgraded to 350 hp, a power he considered necessary for shunting intensively-worked yards. On the demise of the Beardmore company in 1931, some of its diesel-team had come across to EE's Diesel Division, which produced the Model K engine, a six-cylinder design. Under the nomenclature 6KT, it later powered the BR 08 and 09 standard shunters. Trials with these twenty machines proved the diesel-locomotive definitively, certainly for shunting, so the Executive standardized on the 350hp design. The operating-departments and their staffs were delighted with the new shunters, especially with the warm, comfortable cabs and regular shifts. Forty units were ordered in 1939, of the 0-6-0 wheel-arrangement driven by a single engine with jackshaft-drive, running-numbers 7080-7119. It was some of these that the author observed at Carlisle from 1941, 7112/3/4, along with 7089 seen later at Willesden Junction. The early prototypes, the 7050-series diesel-mechanicals, were then withdrawn. In 1936, following the experimental work by the LMS, the GWR had purchased a diesel-electric machine built by Hawthorn Leslie/EE, numbered 2 by Swindon. The final LMS design, numbered 7120 onwards, was even better than its 7080-type: a double-framed, twin-engined 0-6-0 with nose-hung motors, giving significant savings on running-costs. The LMS recognized this as the shunter of the future and planned a further hundred. They managed to put a few into service during 1947, and BR continued their construction in quantity, but renumbered in the 12000 series, later reclassifying them 08 and 09. In 1942, the LNER had followed the lead of the LMS by producing three similar machines at Doncaster in collaboration with EE, numbered 8000/1/2. However, because in 1946 the diesel-locomotive was unproven except as a shunter, Ivatt had introduced his Class 2MT 2-6-0 and the tank-version, the 2-6-2, for secondary-duties, already described.

Combined Locomotive-and-Carriage: Steam Railcars

It had been before the war beginning in 1914 that the first breath of competition from the road began to be felt by the railway, which up to then had enjoyed a monopoly of traffic. The fresh competition for passengers was arising in particular from the tramways operated by many municipalities from the 1890s. The many changes after the war included the spread of road-transport, and these services expanded steadily into the surrounding townships and new suburbs. The author's home-area provides a good example. Halifax Corporation Tramways was a medium-sized operation with a fleet eventually totalling 110 cars. After 1900, the Corporation gradually extended its routes south-westwards towards Ripponden (for Rishworth), and south-eastwards into Stainland, taking the passenger-trade from these two valley branch-lines. In an attempt to counteract this kind of competition, in 1906 the Lancashire and Yorkshire Railway had introduced a 'rail-motor', commonly called a 'motor-train', using two Kerr-Stuart engines, numbered 1 and 2. When these were found to be under-powered, Hughes, the L&Y's CME, designed his own, also numbered 1 and 2, for these services The engine's front-end rather resembled the same designer's improvement of the 'radial' tank-engine. The train comprised a small 0-4-0 steam-engine and carriage combined, the locomotive-wheels acting as one bogie of the carriage. The tail-compartment of the carriage was fitted with basic controls and large end-windows for driving in reverse (propelling), while the fireman remained on the footplate. A frequent shuttle-service could thereby be operated, obviating running-round at a terminus. The Halifax time-tables show a continuous service from 7am to 11pm. The L&Y had eighteen of these units (LMS 10600-17), which all ran in Lancashire apart from these two in the Halifax district. The *Halifax Guardian* of 23 February 1907 jubilantly announced 'the forthcoming opening of motor-train services on the [two branches] on 1 March'. Since the Halifax trams penetrated only as far as Triangle village, part-way along the five-mile branch to Rishworth, it suffered less from competition than Stainland, which had a parallel tram-service all the way into central Halifax. On other Yorkshire branches, the traffic was too heavy for these small trains: they needed several carriages. In fact, a major disadvantage of the single car was its lack of flexibility. At busy times, the capacity was often insufficient, even when an extra carriage was added, taxing the locomotive-power. The trains failed to stem the loss of the railway's passengers, whose numbers continued to fall—and withered away when the Corporation replaced its trams with motor-buses. The new owners, the LMS, ended passenger-services in 1929, on 6 July on the Ripponden branch, and 23 September to Stainland, though goods-traffic continued until 31 August 1958. The LMS, in common with the other three railways, took shares in bus-companies, following the empowering Acts of 1929/30, allowing them to recoup some of their losses.

The other three railways attempted to stem the growing competition as well. The LSWR built one unit, but it was the Great Western that blazed the trail, with 99 cars in service by 1908. Acknowledgements are due to R.M. Tuffnell *The British Railcar: AEC to HST* (see bibliography) for some of this information. The LNWR also built a number of contemporary steam railcars, introduced by Whale in 1905. On Beattock shed in 1947, beside the former CR line to Glasgow and the Moffat branch, the author saw its train, the sole LNW unit remaining in LMS stock, 29988, which survived to be scrapped by BR in 1948 from that depot. In contrast with the L&Y motor-trains, the LNWR unit had a 'carriage-outline': the steam-engine was enclosed by the carriage bodywork with the chimney projecting from the roof, giving an attractive appearance. Similar in design were some Sentinel 6-cylinder steam-railcars with geared-drive. They were operated by the LNE/LMS jointly, including the lines of the M & GN in East Anglia and the Isle of Axholme. This was an inheritance of an LYR/GNR joint-arrangement. Axholme is a sparsely-populated fenland east of Doncaster, over which these cars ran from Goole (West Riding of Yorkshire) to Haxey (County of Lindsey, Lincolnshire). The important step forward made by these railcar-designs was the development of the unit-concept: it enabled a two-way operation or shuttle, obviating locomotive-shunting at each terminus, the turning of engines, and light-engine and empty-stock movements, thereby effecting operating and time economies. Different forms of petrol-electric cars were tried before and after the Great War, cued by road-vehicles, but one more idea was floated.

Although some of the branch-lines served by these machines closed owing to road-competition, the idea of the self-propelled train lived on, and some of the remaining branches were served by their successors, the pull-push train. This was a small tank-engine coupled to one or more carriages where again the tail-end was a compartment equipped for driving in reverse. While living at Earby in the mid-1960s, the author witnessed a late example of this. An Ivatt 2-6-2 tank-locomotive coupled to no less than three carriages ran from Skipton through Earby to Barnoldswick, for the selfsame reason of competing with the car and the bus. Actually, the engine often ran round its train at the Barnoldswick terminus before returning to Skipton, since the men preferred the engine at the front, particularly as the train comprised three carriages. It was certainly a rapid shuttle-service but it failed to attract passengers, was soon withdrawn and the line was closed shortly afterwards. Another chapter describes it along with an account of a footplate-trip. But in the 1930s, management and designers, still searching for increased efficiency and lower operating-costs, turned back to the petrol-electric data. The high-speed diesel-engine was well-proven, therefore the diesel railcar was the logical outcome.

Diesel Railcars

Some early contraptions had been tried, but in the 1930s, the LMS bought a diesel-car produced by Hardy Motors Ltd., a subsidiary of the Associated Equipment Co. (AEC, London Transport's bus-manufacturing arm, mentioned in the Introduction), who converted an AEC *Regal* motor-coach to run on rails in 1933. AEC was a subsidiary-company of the former London General Omnibus Company, a constituent of the LPTB, formed in 1933 by the amalgamation of the various passenger-transport companies in the London-area. AEC gained world-wide renown for its design of the excellent London Transport buses, and for their reliability in service. From 1931, Halifax Corporation had a splendid fleet of these excellent vehicles, their fluid-drive pre-selector gearboxes ideal for the hilly terrain, a move followed by Bradford, Leeds and Huddersfield. AEC manufactured at Walthamstow, London E.17, before opening its new factory at Southall, Middlesex, in the 1930s. In the late-1950s, it was merged with the Leyland group and eventually closed down. Thus began the long association of AEC with railcars. The streamlined railcars built by AEC for the GWR from 1933 are the best known and were the most numerous. Utilized at first for parcels-traffic from London-Oxford, they gave speedy passenger-services on feeder-lines of the Great Western, some operating express-services. BR operated them until 1962.

An isolated example by the LMS for a similar purpose was the rail-bus operated briefly to serve their railway hotel at Stratford-on-Avon, the Welcombe Hotel. The 'Ro-Railer', however, developed the concept differently, in that the carriage was designed to run on road as well as rail. In fact, it was a bus on rails, a Karrier single-decker mounted on a specially-designed chassis with two sets of wheels, road and rail, which swivelled to change the mode. Its road number-plate UR 7924 (Hertfordshire CC) reveals it was built in 1930-1. It thus pre-dated the AEC experimental car alluded to above. The Ro-Railer connected with the west-coast mainline at Blisworth, Northamptonshire, to transport its first-class passengers along a section of the former Stratford-on-Avon & Midland Junction Railway to Stratford-on-Avon, finishing its journey with a short run along the road to the door of the Welcombe Hotel. The hotel was well-known to LMS passengers, if only vicariously, from its sepia photographs which graced many carriage compartments.

Experimental Rail-buses

Railcars, or 'rail-buses' with petrol-engines had been tried before, by the North Eastern Railway in 1903, by the Great Western and by American railways in the following year. The first essay in diesel-power in the British Isles in regular service was made by the County Donegal Railways, a 3ft-gauge line run jointly by the NCC, an LMS subsidiary, using a converted bus, in September 1928, followed by an LNER experiment in 1931. Other Irish lines also used converted buses. A pneumatic-tyred car was tried out by the LMS and the SR in 1932, and the following year, the LMS tested the 'Coventry Pneumatic Railcar,' a 16-wheeled vehicle built by Armstrong Siddeley in Coventry. Fitted with Michelin tyres, it was a publicity-machine for the manufacturer at Stoke-on-Trent, a subsidiary of the French tyre-company, but no orders resulted. Unsurprisingly, the photographs show this one to have a rather French appearance. Two units ran in service around Coventry and Rugby for about a year, but the high rolling-resistance made the cars expensive to run.[1] However, similar cars have been widely used in France and may have spawned the idea of the rubber-tyred cars introduced on the Paris *Metro* around 1960.

Shortly before Beardmore's closure in 1931, EE fitted a Beardmore 6HT engine to their diesel railcar *Bluebird*. Their intention was to use this vehicle for trials and proving-experience as a way of entering the railcar-market. Since the car had been constructed at Rugby, the tests were carried out on the branch to Market Harborough, but later trials took place between Bletchley and Bedford, a favourite proving-ground. Nothing further seems to have been heard of this machine. Post-WW2, a few single-car railbuses were introduced from 1958 onwards by various vehicle—and engine-manufacturers: BUT/AEC; Waggon & Maschinenbau of Donauwörth, West Germany; Park Royal Vehicles; Bristol/Eastern Coachworks/Gardner; and D.Wickham/Meadows. The latter's 1958 four-wheeled models ran in Hertfordshire and in Scotland, but produced a rough ride, apparently a poor service and so were withdrawn after about a decade. The author is not alone in failing to understand why it was so difficult for BR and the manufacturers to put a bus on rails, since it seems to involve only straightforward technology. He believes a role still exists for such vehicles. Enlarged versions were exported by Wickham to the Boston and Maine RR in the USA. Railbus-operations in Britain ceased entirely on 27 Jan 1968, allowing the last wisp of steam to outlive them by six months or so. However, some cars are preserved. A final essay was made in 1974 into the single-car concept: the experimental R.3 built by British Rail Engineering Ltd. (BREL) at Derby and the joint-venture LEV 'levitation' transit system. The LEV vehicles were tested on a specially-built elevated track, later dismantled, along a section of the abandoned St Ives branch near Earith, Cambridgeshire. A version was introduced later in Birmingham to connect with the city's airport.

Diesel and Other Multiple-Unit Trains

In 1928, the LMS, through the advocacy of Alan Chorlton of Beardmore, produced a 500hp diesel-electric four-car train-set using a Beardmore engine similar to that designed for the airship R.101, with electrics by Dick, Kerr & Co., Preston, a constituent of EE, built into one of the power-cars from the LYR experimental 3,500v-electric line from Bury to Holcombe Brook in Lancashire. This was the first DEMU in Europe, possibly anywhere. Although neither a technical nor an operational success, it did encourage the EE's interest in diesel-electric traction and in the development of its own diesel-engines for rail-traction. Perhaps slightly ahead of the GWR-railcar, the LMS introduced their Leyland Diesel railcar in 1933, a similar machine mounted on four wheels of 3ft diameter and driven by a 95 hp-engine, a powerful unit for that era. Three were built, numbered 29950/1/2, entering service in 1934, and they remained in LMS stock to be taken over by BR in 1948. They survived until 1951. So far, all the railcars, superseding the earlier steam-cars, were powered by a diesel-engine with a direct-geared drive. The next step by the LMS, taken in 1938, and described below, was to upgrade the single-car into a 'set', that is, to couple three carriages together, like its Euston-Watford Oerlikon/Siemens electric trains and the electric sets of the Southern Railway, the successors to those introduced by the LB&SC on its South London Line in 1909.

Reference has been made to the L&Y as a pioneer, whose CME Aspinall firmly believed in the future of electric traction. He had therefore equipped the Manchester-Bury line with dc-electric multiple-units. This line has been rebuilt as a route of the Greater Manchester Metro-tram network. The North Eastern Railway too was an early electric-train operator, opening its North Tyneside suburban-system in 1904, and many similar schemes were being developed at this time, notably the London Underground trains, demonstrating that the principle of the multiple-unit self-propelled train, at least electrically-driven, was well established by the 1920s.

The last essay in LMS diesel-development was its experimental articulated three-car set of 1938. According to accounts, it was a handsome train finished in red and polished aluminium, numbered in the carriage-series 80000/1/2, and driven by under-floor diesel engines. This was a novel traction-layout, for it was to be well over a decade before buses appeared with this configuration. The Sentinel single-deck bus of 1950, operated by Ribble Motor Services in Carlisle, was the first noted by the author, registered CRN—, and shortly afterwards the same operator put into service a similarly-configured fleet of Leyland *Royal Tiger* coaches, registered DRN—and ECK-, marks issued by the Preston CBC, where Ribble was headquartered. Concerning the articulated train, a further novelty was that, despite unfavourable experience with hydraulic-drive in their very first essay into diesels, the converted shunter 1831 described earlier, the three-car train again had diesel-hydraulic drive, but now to an improved design. Twin Leyland-125hp engines under each car drove all axles except those at the outer-ends through Leyland Lysholm-Smith torque-converters and cardan-shafts. The streamlined-nose shape had a French appearance when viewed from the front, its design perhaps influenced by the earlier Michelin experimental train. The hydraulic train spent most of its time on the cross-country line from Oxford to Cambridge via Bedford, a favourite testing-ground, though absent from the time-tables. However, having failed to increase revenue, it was transferred to the St Pancras-Bedford run, occasionally extended to Nottingham. Its lack of buffet-facilities however rendered it unsuitable for main-line duties, and it was retired in 1940 for want of a role, later converted into an electrification maintenance-unit for the Manchester & Altrincham line, and disappeared from the LMS stock-list in 1945-6. As a passenger-carrier, then, it did not survive the war, but it pointed the way to the future. But for the outbreak of WW2, further developments may have taken place, with more sets being built.

The diesel-hydraulic 80000 paved the way for the diesel multiple-units (DMUs), introduced by BR from 1954 onwards for use on branch—and cross-country services, the first stage in the phasing-out of steam-trains. The twin-car configuration allowed trains theoretically of any length (in even numbers of carriages) to be coupled up, therefore giving economic and operating flexibility. Usually they ran as twin-car units or in fours. This move was another card played by the railway to combat increased road-competition, which, by the mid-fifties, was becoming very severe in country-areas, owing to the ending of petrol-rationing and an affluent population rapidly becoming car-owners. The former LMS/LNER joint inter-urban line from Leeds to Bradford via Stanningley (renamed New

Pudsey) was considered suitable for a trial. This former L&Y/GN joint-route was the first to receive a dmu, on 14 June 1954, which initially effected a large increase in passengers. The branch from Carlisle to Silloth in West Cumbria received its units on 29 November, extending the viability of trains on this sparsely-inhabited line for about a decade. In September 1956, the London Midland Region of British Railways rebuilt two cars of the 1926 LMS Euston-Watford electric stock with Paxman flat-six-cylinder engines as prototypes for the planned Liverpool-Leeds-Newcastle express service. However, a Swindon-built design with an Albion engine was eventually adopted for the 'Class 124 Trans-Pennine' trains, which appeared in 1960.

Electric trains

The LMS constituents had contributed several suburban-electric systems. The former LNWR Euston-Broad Street-Watford electric-trains have been mentioned. Constructed by Oerlikon in Switzerland, they entered service in 1920, having been delayed by WW1. The multiple-unit concept was by now well established, at least for local services. Following the Weir Committee's report in 1929 in favour of electrification, the LMS and LNE converted their joint Manchester suburban line from Oxford Road and London Road (now Piccadilly) to Altrincham to 1500V dc with overhead-line, opening in 1935 with LMS-designed stock. The LMS then began to electrify its network on the Wirral peninsula from Birkenhead Park, an end-on junction with the Mersey Railway, using third-rail pick-up with track-return, running to West Kirby and New Brighton. It just scraped in ahead of war-requirements, opening in 1940. Since the adjoining Mersey Railway had the third-and-fourth-rail system on 650V dc (similar to the London Underground), a dual-voltage was necessary on both trains, since, for traffic-reasons, they crossed into each other's territory. Now commuters could travel through from the Wirral coast into the heart of Liverpool, arriving at the Central Station (low level).

Also within the same area, the LMS renewed the electric-stock on its Liverpool-Southport-Crossens line, another busy commuter-route. This was another pioneering project instituted by the former L&Y railway. The new lightweight stock was of neat design internally and externally, each carriage equipped with two sets of pneumatically-operated sliding-doors on each side to allow rapid loading and unloading. Also finished in 1939-40, it was a technical leap forward and the precursor of trains to be built in the post-war era.

Mainline Multiple-Unit Trains

The APT (Advanced Passenger Train), the tilting-train, was on the drawing-board in the mid-1960s, a concept developed in the new BR Research Laboratories opened at Derby in May 1964. The laboratories themselves may be traced back to the embryo research-department begun by the LMS in 1933, initiated strictly as a service to the major operating—and engineering-departments. From that small beginning, it grew to dominate the Derby scene. This shows another area where the LMS company demonstrated its forward-thinking and the initiative to push out the frontiers of modern, economic, train-operation. The experimental tilting-train was beset with many technical difficulties, typical of most pioneering ventures, in its case ascribed to a super-abundance of new concepts included in a single project. A dispute over manning arose too with the drivers' union ASLEF. Tuffnell and Marshall give full technical details. The Italian railways however continued the British research, succeeding with a tilting-train, the *Pendolino*, and exported it to Britain. It is operated on the West Coast Main Line by Virgin Trains. In economic terms therefore, Britain now has to import the result of its initial research—a story unfortunately too often repeated.

From its humble beginnings on branch-lines, the concept of the diesel multiple-unit spread to the crack main-line services too, beginning with the Metro-Cammell 'Blue Pullman' trains of 1961, providing a luxury journey from St Pancras to Manchester, designed to woo the business-traveller back from the car to the train during the disruption caused by the West Coast electrification in the 1960s. A decade later, BR adopted overseas ideas to combat competition from the airlines, in particular borrowing from the TEE-network on the Continent. On 5 May 1975, the Western Region's InterCity 125 (IC-125) was introduced to run from Paddington to Bristol and Weston-super-Mare, and throughout the Western Region from 1977. Of all BR modernization-projects, this design has proved to be the most successful, financially as well as technically, its success underlined by the exporting of InterCity trains to Australia. This achievement is reflected in the adoption of the name by the German state railways (DB) for its new high-speed trains, though the dominance of English as the world-language was no doubt also a factor. On the East Coast main-line, the Class 55 *Deltic* diesel-electric locomotives needed replacing after giving twenty-two years of sterling service, and so here too the IC-125 diesel-electrics were introduced. Later, they appeared on the Midland line out of St Pancras, displaced from the East Coast when similarly-configured trains, but with electric-drive, were introduced in 1991. The train-sets of 2 + 8 carriages comprise a power-car at the front and a 'driving-van trailer', or DVT, which controls the train when travelling in the reverse, or propelled, direction. All these multiple-unit trains, that is, without a separate locomotive, demonstrate the evolution from the traditional steam-train to steam-railcar and rail-motor, followed by the substitution for traditional steam of diesel-traction, diesel-hydraulic, then diesel-electric, and finally electric-drive via a 25KVa catenary. A significant share of the development can be claimed by the LMS Railway, particularly in the field of diesel—and diesel-electric traction. It demonstrates that the Executive was determined to press on with pioneering-projects to stay ahead technically, pushed by its president and chairman, Lord Stamp. This active and radical-thinking leader of the LMS was killed, along with his wife and eldest son, in an air-raid during WW2, when his home in Kent suffered a direct-hit by a German bomb on 16 April 1941. Fortunately his ideas had taken root and were ably continued by his dynamic lieutenants, including the CMEs Stanier and Ivatt, and electrical-engineer Fairburn, along with their dedicated staffs.

LATER INNOVATIONS BY THE LMS

The Permanent Way

Now, it is no use designing fast and powerful locomotives to haul heavy trains if they do not have a decent track to run on. The former LNWR had standardized its rails at sixty feet and claimed to be The Premier Line, and its track was certainly among the finest in Britain. The LMS sought to extend this standard to all its main-lines. Soon after his arrival on the LMS as CME in 1932, Stanier, suspecting rail-replacement costs were too high, set up a permanent way study-group. It soon discovered that the company was losing money by rolling its own rails: big steel-producers like Firth-Brown in Sheffield were willing to supply them more cheaply through mass-production, thus retaining jobs during the Great Depression. Stamp, concerned to improve efficiency, recognized this as the way forward, so Stanier closed the Crewe rolling-mill and placed contracts for rails with outside manufacturers. The space at Crewe was needed anyway to expand other departments, in particular the specialized boiler-shop mentioned earlier, and the craftsmen were redeployed.

For generations, almost from the birth of the modern railway around 1830, 'bullhead' rail, named after its profile, had been employed, because its shape gave it stiffness. The concept was that, when the top became worn and due for replacement, the rail could be turned over, so enabling the unused edge of the rail to be put into service. This operation used to be straightforward with only short lengths of rail to be handled. However, later practice proved the theory flawed: the lower edge of the rail was not in pristine condition, but indented through pressure on the chairs and therefore useless as a running-rail, at least for a main line.

Railway-staffs were in contact with their overseas neighbours through professional organizations, whose conferences exchanged ideas and threw up new methods. Stanier's study-group focused upon one aspect in particular, the shape of the rail. All overseas railways used the flat-bottomed rail, and the obvious question to ask was, surely Britain was not right and everyone else in the world wrong? Prototype-tests of heavy flat-bottomed track were carried out successfully, followed by a main-line trial in 1936 over a length of the new rail laid at Cricklewood. Its success made it the LMS policy. The Executive decided on 113lb/yd, considering the heavier weight than the 96lb bullhead-rail that it replaced necessary to support the increasing weight of trains. The exercise overturned a tradition of a century and demonstrated the LMS was forward-looking and receptive to current thinking. The other three group-railways were watching the LMS closely, and after its success with the new flat-bottomed rail, the LNER followed suit immediately, so here we have another example of the LMS as a pioneer. Limited use had been made of flat-bottomed rail on minor lines, such as the Metropolitan Railway's branch from Aylesbury to Brill. However, preparations for the impending war halted development and widespread introduction of the flat-bottomed rail until well after the peace in 1945, but the delay allowed further research, gaining a better result than was hitherto possible, for example the great strides made during the war with electric-welding techniques. The GWR had experimented with steel sleepers, but had retained the bullhead rail.

Long lengths of welded track could now be safely laid, with expansion provided for by pre-stressing the rail during laying, and by using an obtuse-angled joint, rather like the mitre of a picture-frame, but with a shallower angle. These methods allowed rails in lengths of up to a mile, delivered on engineers' trains of flat-wagons. Earlier, the LMS had pioneered track-relaying by using rail-mounted cranes, which placed complete 60ft-lengths ahead of the crane; these could now be welded together. Several advantages accrued: the fewer rail-joints reduced wear and tear, not only on the track itself, but on the rolling-stock running over it; furthermore, the fewer rail-joints and the heavier profile reduced the incidence of broken rails. Two-bolt fishplates had been tried in order to bring the end-sleepers closer together, but this method failed through inability to pack ballast firmly enough under the end-sleepers; lengths of welded-rails solved this difficulty. It thereby enhanced safety, and reduced permanent-way maintenance at a time when wage-costs were rising, since fewer inspections became necessary.

Simultaneously, services were being accelerated, but their introduction was hampered by traditional flat junctions with their consequent speed-limits. One of these was on the West-Coast line at Stafford, where the former London & Birmingham Railway's route joined the 'new line' through the Trent Valley, the Queensville curve. To allow a high-speed transition to be made to the Trent Valley line, the LMS pioneered a new junction-design. For the diverging-road a series of two-level chairs was laid, tapering in depth, in this way introducing cant to the curve, enabling a higher-speed transition to be made. The crossing-timbers too were canted in the ballast. A further development was to use switch-diamonds, which closed the 'frogs' to support the wheel throughout pointwork.

In 1929, an improvement had been made to end congestion at a serious bottleneck north of Birmingham on the busy line to Barnt Green. Cofton Tunnel was demolished to allow the line to be quadrupled, an example of the constant upgrading by the LMS of the lines it had inherited. Some of them had weak bridges, restricting haulage to 4-4-0 locomotives. Upgrading enabled the new Stanier 4-6-0s to be employed, for example, on the Derby-Manchester line, on the Bath branch and on its continuation, the joint S&DJR to Bournemouth.

Water-Troughs

These troughs laid between the running-rails enabled locomotives to replenish their tanks. A steam engine could use 2,000 gallons in seventy miles, and the LMS had several places where this was useful. A large lineside tank fed the troughs—often set upon a building, a 'tank-house', as at Garsdale on the Settle-Carlisle line (since demolished). However, considerable spillage was found to occur through the locomotive's scoop sending water over the sides of the troughs, so a device was designed to avoid this wastage. It comprised a vane mounted ahead of the scoop, which pushed water inwards from the sides of the trough, piling it up in the centre. The scoop could now collect more water and also avoid much of the spillage over the sides—another LMS initiative.

The Travelling Post Office

The LMS carried mail for the General Post Office (GPO), since called 'Royal Mail', now 'Post Office', along its trunk-routes, inheriting a system pioneered by the LNWR during the 1850s. GPO vans unloaded their mail into a specialized train at Euston. Its carriages were painted in 'post-office red', bore the royal cipher, and were fitted with pigeon-holes for sorting letters, which could also be posted into a carriage before departure (plus a supplementary stamp) and sorted with the bulk mail en route. More was picked up with nets swung out, which collected mail-bags hung on lineside posts. In order to deliver mail as well, the reverse procedure was adopted: arms were swung out to drop bags, collected in lineside nets alongside the delivery-posts. This procedure was used at several places along the important west coast line to serve principal towns on or accessible from the line. The mail collected from the lineside was sorted immediately, so as to be ready for delivery, some perhaps destined for the next dropping-point. GPO mail-vans despatched and collected the mail at the lineside. At regional centres such as Crewe, the train stopped to unload quantities of mail to be sent forward along connecting-lines to serve more-distant places. In 1936, the Crown Film Unit recorded this procedure, beginning on Euston station, showing the last mail-bags being loaded from the red vans into the red carriages before departure. It remains as probably the best archival film of the LMS coming to its peak during the exciting Stanier years. It complements the nostalgic, contemporary cinema-film *Brief Encounter*, made later on the same west coast route.

Signalling

The 'lineside furniture' on the LMS, including signals, was no more up-to-date than on the other three railways of the Big Four. In fact, much 1923 pre-grouping equipment was handed on to BR in 1948. In the chapter on the author's observations at school in the 1940s, the author described how none of the thirty-odd signal-arms in sight had been modernized; all were still of the Midland lower-quadrant type, those with the large white spectacles. Luckily, some preserved railways have examples of them, notably Butterley and Quainton. The reason for their relative obsolescence was that the majority of the available funding had gone into updating the prestigious expresses, partly to compete with the LNER for Scottish traffic. Once again, pioneering-work had been done by the L&Y, with electro-pneumatic signals and points at Bolton in 1910, superseding the clumsy point-rodding and signal-wires of the Victorian era.

However, some updating on the LMS had taken place. After a few early colour-light signals had been erected, a quantum-leap was achieved by the 'speed-signalling' installed at Mirfield, West Yorkshire. The LMS Chief Signals Engineer, A.F. Bounds, had been so impressed by this form of colour-light signalling during a visit to the USA that he persuaded the Executive to try this experiment. The US-designed speed-signalling system was put in from Heaton Lodge Junction to Thornhill LNW Junction (near Dewsbury), replacing a forest of ex-LYR signals on this busy four-track stretch. At Heaton Lodge, two routes converged, leading from Manchester and Preston towards Leeds. Through Diggle came expresses and freight from Manchester, while the Calder Valley line was host to a succession of coal-trains from the collieries in south Yorkshire to Lancashire—plus their empties—and expresses from Lancashire to York and Scarborough.

Speed-signalling needs some explanation. It gives instructions to drive at a certain speed using a combination of coloured-lights, the top light applying to the principal high-speed route, the second light to the medium-speed route and so on. The idea was unpopular with drivers, who felt confused with several lights mounted on the same post, especially reds and greens together. Mentally, the author agreed with them, on watching the endless succession of trains passing; surely a red definitely meant 'stop'? The system was not replicated elsewhere, but, simplified versions were installed on the Euston-Watford line and the London Transport's District Line between Bow and Upminster, then owned by the LMS as part of its London, Tilbury and Southend network.

Instead, LMS replaced semaphore distant-signals with two—or three-aspect coloured lights. These could give an indication of a single yellow, a double-yellow (very useful for keeping trains moving, especially express-freights), or a green. The single-yellow means 'prepare to stop at the next signal, which may be red', the double-yellow indicates 'pass the next signal at reduced speed,' while of course a green indicates the road is clear for the maximum speed permitted on that stretch of the line. This policy of replacing semaphore-distants with colour-light signals was extremely useful during foggy conditions, when, as on the ATC-equipped GWR, fogmen could be dispensed with. The double-yellow, however, could be misleading, and caused accidents where drivers had not reduced speed sufficiently through not realizing that a double-yellow sometimes indicated a junction ahead set to cross them over slowly to another line. An example of this was the disaster on Sunday, 30 September 1945 at Bourne End, north of Berkhamsted on the West Coast route, when the up Perth sleeper derailed while being crossed from the fast-line to the slow on account of engineering-work ahead. The colour-light distant signal was showing a double-yellow and the diverging home-signal had been lowered, the splitting-home bracket before the junction-points. The train derailed at 50mph on the 20mph-crossover, killing 43 passengers and the engine-crew. The author remembers the accident, when he and his friends, schoolboys, as yet knowing nothing of the technicalities, wondered how such an accident was possible. The locomotive was Royal Scot 6157 *The Royal Artilleryman*. The LMS stopped using a double-yellow in semaphore territory, but, if the company had extended track-circuiting and put in place something similar to the GWR's ATC, this accident—and those at Charfield in 1928 and at Ashchurch in 1929—would probably have been averted, not to mention the huge disaster at Harrow-Wealdstone in October 1952, involving three trains, 112 deaths and tremendous destruction of stock. This accident did spur the railway, by then under the control of BR, to accelerate its research towards installing something like Hudd, described below. By coincidence, on that very day in 1952, BR was testing its new Automatic Warning System (AWS) on the East Coast main line, but its development, acceptance and installation took so long that another serious collision took place, at Lewisham St John's on the Southern Region in December 1956. The savings from these accidents would have gone far to financing an earlier introduction of automatic train-control. As well as replacing distant-signals with colour-lights, the LMS gradually installed new upper-quadrant semaphore-signals to replace the lower-quadrants, considering them safer in view of their inherent 'fail-safe' design. The author doubts the wisdom of this, as he knows of no accident attributed to a false clear given by a lower-quadrant semaphore; these signal-arms were counterbalanced, thereby nullifying the perceived advantage of the upper-quadrant. However, perhaps some old mechanisms were time-expired—and the company thus 'made a statement' that it was updating. The Southern Railway was also replacing its lower-quadrant signals with upper-quadrants. After some experimentation with three-position upper-quadrant arms, the GWR continued successfully with their standard lower-quadrants, except for colour-lights at a few large stations. In 1939, the LNER had made some progress: installing four-aspect colour-light signalling on its East Coast route between Thirsk and Northallerton in Yorkshire, but again the group of lights on one post was found to be confusing, almost causing a collison in at least one case. It also introduced thumb-switch interlocking panels at Leeds

(City). Elsewhere it retained large numbers of ex-GNR somersault-signals. Now let us look at automatic train-control.

ATC and the Strowger-Hudd System

As far back as the years leading up to the Great War in 1914, the Great Western Railway had introduced its pioneering Automatic Train Control, ATC. Its concept was to give the driver indications of the lineside signals in foggy conditions, while leaving the controls of the train in his hands. The system was based on the indications shown by the distant-signal, the first one encountered in each block-section where, in the middle of the track about 440 yards ahead of the signal, a ramp was installed, which made contact with a shoe mounted underneath the locomotive.

As the locomotive passed over, the ramp imparted an upward movement to the shoe underneath. This had two effects: if the if the distant was showing caution, it opened the ATC brake-valve and sounded a vacuum-operated siren in the cab. But a distant-signal at clear applied current to the ramp, which was picked up by the locomotive. This forestalled the opening of the brake-valve and the siren, ringing an all-clear bell instead. The important feature was the 'fail-safe' nature of the system; there was no possibility of receiving a false clear. Now it is necessary to explain the acknowledging-lever on the ATC apparatus. Since it was considered impractical to have a purely-automatic train-stop device as on the London Underground railways, the principle was retained that a driver keep control of his train, therefore the acknowledging-lever was introduced. When the siren begins to sound at an adverse distant-signal, the driver can silence it and forestall the automatic application of the brakes by operating the acknowledging-lever. Having been alerted and duly acknowledged it, it is then his responsibility to act upon the signal indication he has received. Only if he fails to acknowledge is the control taken out of his hands and the brakes applied. Where a warning instead of all-clear is picked up in the cab at a distant-signal showing clear—because for some reason current is not picked up by the collector-shoe—the driver operates the acknowledging-lever to silence the siren and forestall the brake-application. This happened often and was perfectly in order. At the enquiry after each collision on the other three railways, the Inspecting Officer invariably recommended the adoption of the Great Western ATC-system, but parochialism prevailed in those days, and nothing was done in this respect. Apart from face-saving, the Great War of 1914-18 halted progress. A reason for inaction by the rest of the Big Four companies later was the lack of funds at a time of financial stringency during the 1920s and the Great Depression of the 1930s. Later, the Strowger-Hudd System was taken up by the LMS to develop ATC, further refined by adding a visual-indicator in the cab of the locomotive. After successful trials on the London (Fenchurch Street) to Southend-on-Sea commuter-line, the LMS in its later days installed a modified Hudd-system throughout the London-Tilbury-Southend network. The nationalized BR developed Strowger-Hudd to produce its AWS warning-system, later enhancing it to ATP.

Steel fireboxes & other innovations

It was a later CME, Mr H. G. Ivatt, who introduced several developments, at first on 'Black Fives'. The steel firebox had been pioneered by Hughes on the LYR around 1910, and developed by Bulleid on the SR in 1941-2 on his 'air-smoothed' locomotives, the Merchant Navy and West Country/Battle of Britain pacifics. His developments followed those in America, which had brought electric-welding to a high state of perfection. Their rapidly-built welded ships of WW2 are a prime example. Ivatt also fitted Timken roller-bearings to many late Class Fives, as a further improvement to their bearings. It will be recalled that Stanier had brought the Great Western's horn-block axle-boxes from Swindon, a great advance on the Derby design, so Ivatt's essays represented further technical advances. His trials of the Caprotti valve-gear on the Black Five have been detailed in Chapter 3, but it is worth noting here that his efforts made the LMS the pioneers in Britain.

The Ivatt Class 2 locomotives

These comprised a 2F 2-6-0 and the tank-version, a 2P 2-6-2, for branch-line service. The first 2-6-0 the author set eyes on, 6401, looked a tiny machine, and was apparently struggling even to bring the pick-up goods into Apperley Bridge; did he need running in? The antique Midland 2F 0-6-0s dating from 1868 used to handle this—and much longer trains—quite readily. These observations were confirmed in the BR era by North Eastern Region experience over the steeply-graded Stainmore Summit, the former North Eastern Railway across the Pennine Hills from Barnard Castle in County Durham to Kirkby Stephen in Cumbria. Here, an ex-NER P1 class 0-6-0 of 1898 (LNER J25) regularly hauled eighteen loaded wagons, like the older NER 'C' 0-6-0s (1886-95, LNER J21), but two Ivatts together could pull only fourteen. However, the Ivatts were officially only 2F, whereas the NER 0-6-0s equated to an LMS 4F, so this comparison was unfair. The fault lay with BR management for allocating these little engines to the Stainmore line. Its enginemen nicknamed the Ivatts 'Mickey Mouse' engines. Further unfavourable comments have been made—so much for progress. Since the diesel-locomotive was as yet unproven save as a shunter, Ivatt had introduced this Class 2F 2-6-0 and the 2P 2-6-2 tank-version for secondary duties and, since no high-speed running was envisaged, roller-bearings were not fitted. The error of such forecasts was proved by the Carlisle men's nickname 'Penrith Lizzies' due to their turn of speed. Their reference was to the Princess Royal pacifics, in particular the second of the class, *Princess Elizabeth*, which had run the high-speed Glasgow-Euston test in 1936 past this spot. The Ivatts have been called 'snappy little engines.' Their performance, once allocated to Penrith during 1950 to replace the ageing 2F Cauliflowers, both classes mentioned in descriptions of the author's time in Carlisle in 1950-1, was equated in speed with the pacifics. Considering the longevity of the sixty-year-old Cauliflowers—and other 0-6-0s—the Ivatts did not represent the quantum leap in all respects that observers expected. Later, 6405 too brought the daily pick-up goods, also apparently struggling, while in Leeds, 6406 was observed as carriage-pilot at City station, and 6407 on empty stock at nearby Copley Hill sidings, duties to which they seemed more suited. Soon after nationalization, some of these engines were drafted into South Wales for branch-line duties, but ex-LMS staff were stunned to find their new 2-6-0s quite unequal to the lusty ex-GWR 'Dean goods' performing there with ease. One of the 2-6-0s was sent for analysis on the Swindon testing-plant resulting in a marked improvement in steaming. However, the Dean Goods too equated more closely in power to an LMS 4F, so here again, the management made a mistake in their allocation of the little 2F 2-6-0s. The preserved Ivatts acquit themselves well though on the preserved lines for which their axle-weight of only about eleven tons is ideal. Twenty-five were produced by the LMS, and the BR regime from 1 January 1948 continued construction until the class totalled 128. The Riddles version followed, detailed under 'Nationalization'.

That several Ivatt Class 2s are preserved is simply because they still existed, rows of them available in Woodham Bros' scrapyard at Barry, described later. From the 1950s, they became redundant following the mass-closure of the branch—and cross-country lines for which they were built—before as well as after Lord Beeching's enquiry. It is simply unfortunate that the last survivors of much older designs had only recently been scrapped before preservation had properly got under way. However, these Class 2s represent the only new small engines built by any of the big four railways to haul secondary-traffic. The other companies invariably used superannuated goods-engines or pilots, so this essay represented another pioneering achievement by the LMS.

The third Ivatt newcomer arrived a year after the Class 2 mogul, another 2-6-0, this one classed 4F, an ugly-looking customer with a double-chimney. The new class, numbered from 3000, was intended to replace the 4F and older 0-6-0 designs—many coincidentally also in the same numerical series. Some staff nicknamed these locomotives 'Doodlebugs', a reference to the stubby, German pilotless planes, the 'flying-bombs' of the second war, over only recently in 1945. Others called them 'flying pigs.' With construction of several classes of locomotive proceeding simultaneously at the different works, the LMS managed to put only three of the 3000-class 2-6-0s into traffic before nationalization; 'the author saw several of the later examples during his last two years at the school. Its outstanding feature, the high running-plate, gave improved access for maintenance and foreshadowed the standard BR-classes. A flexibility built into their frames achieved another aim, to work sharply-curved sidings. The steaming of these 2-6-0s was indifferent at first, but was improved—like their appearance—by converting them to single-chimneys. The improvement to the draughting recalls the initial difficulties with the Jubilees back in 1934, when double-blastpipes were also tried. Railway historiography contains many examples of new designs that were not exactly right at first, for example Gresley's A1 pacifics in 1922. Without the benefit of the facilities offered later by the

Rugby testing-station, designs were based on past experience. I felt, as a layman, that these 2-6-0 machines too were inadequate replacements for older and well-tried designs. General opinion seems to be that the Ivatt-designs were not a great success initially.

Ironically, it would be early in the BR-era when scientific investigations could at last replace information arrived at experimentally—in particular on locomotive front-end design and steam-circuits: the testing-station, having been delayed by the 1939-war, was completed by BR in 1948. The details are in Chapter 3.

Devices Introduced by the LMS

The Ivatt engines did, however, incorporate labour-saving devices, in particular the self-cleaning smokebox, rocking-grate and self-emptying hopper-ashpan, all denoted by the plate 'SC' below the shed-plate on the smokebox door. Stanier may have noticed these devices during his promotion of *The Royal Scot* tour of America in 1933, but Riddles certainly would have, on following him with the *Coronation Scot* streamlined train in 1939, so this information was on file, ready for incorporation into the standard types. The LMS was continually seeking ways to reduce the labour-costs of maintenance, as well as to make the steam-locomotive a more attractive job for the men. An example of the latter is the side-window cab provided by Stanier on the last batch of the Derby 2-6-4 tank-locomotives (2395-2424) in his early days as CME. The SC apparatus was introduced by his successor, Fairburn, and appeared on engines built from 1945. This was one of several areas of design where the LMS was a pioneer, a subject explored in depth under 'Steam and Diesel Developments of the LMS.'

Certain other aspects of these new designs seemed retrogressive, rather than progressive. I, along with contemporary observers, expected a definite advance on all fronts. After all, fourteen years had elapsed since Stanier had begun to introduce his new designs, launching the LMS into the forefront of steam technology—and with aesthetically-pleasing machines too. By contrast, the three Ivatt designs, with their boxy transatlantic look, were utilitarian in design to enable easier maintenance, but it is a pity that this detracted from their appearance.

On this count too they seemed to represent an ending unworthy of the LMS Railway. Probably they were utilitarian in looks simply because they were conceived in a 'utility' era, those difficult years immediately after the second war. Indeed, during that conflict, the Riddles 2-8-0 and 2-10-0 designs were officially called 'Austerity' locomotives; they too showed transatlantic tendencies, such as their two-box tenders, maybe setting a new trend. The Southern Railway's Q.1 0-6-0s built during that war are another example. But a photograph of an LMS Beyer-Garratt 2-6-6-2 makes one think again: because of the necessity to work this engine both ways, 'tender-first', if you like, a view from the footplate was provided over the large coal-bunker—which was cut away into a box-shape, and that was back in 1927. Again, the bunkers of the Stanier 2-6-4 tank engines were cut away to allow a clear rear view when travelling bunker-first, but these seem to be generally accepted as aesthetically pleasing.

By contrast, one has only to glance at Stanier's effect on the Company compared with the infighting of its early years, when it largely multiplied obsolescent designs. His locomotives, with their efficiency stemming from the proven boiler-technology and steam-circuit layouts absorbed during his GWR career, revolutionized LMS motive-power at a critical time—and his engines *looked* right too, with their shapely, well-proportioned lines. An experienced engineer recognises that a machine which 'looks right' invariably 'performs right' as well.

4-6-0 6399 *Fury* represents LMS 'lighter' 4-6-0 developments (H.C. Casserley collection).

L M S LOCOMOTIVES 1923 to 1951

The table lists chronologically locomotives built during this period.

Wheel Arrangement	Non-std pre-group built by LMS	LMS standard-designs	LMS designs by or for BR	TOTALS
0-4-0T:	11	5		16
0-4-4T (CR):	10	20		30
4-4-2T (LTS):	35			35
0-6-0T:	432	432		432
0-6-2T (NSR):	4 ‡			4
2-6-2T		208		208
2-6-4T	—	502	143	645
4-6-4T (LYR):	10	-	-	10
0-8-4T (LNW):	30			30
2-6-6-2T:		33		33
4-4-0:		333		333

0-6-0:		575	575
2-6-0:		285	162	447
4-6-0‡‡	62†	1056	100	1218
4-6-2:		51		51
0-8-0:		175		175
2-8-0:		852*		852
TOTALS	162	4527	409*	5094

* Includes 133 built during WW2 which never ran with LMS numbers.

† One 'Prince of Wales', experimental with Walschaerts-gear (a 'Tishy'), 5845 (25845 after 1934); CR '60' class 14630-54 and further LYR 'Dreadnoughts'.

‡‡ Leftovers from constituent-companies, but excluding Dreadnoughts, which were continued as standards by Hughes as the first CME of the LMS.

— 128 —

This list of locomotives constructed by the LMS makes fascinating reading, but ignores the vast army of 10,300 machines in almost 400 classes taken over from its constituent-companies at the grouping of 1923. The 5,000 new locomotives replaced 7,000 of these, which shows some advance in maintenance and availability. The table now leads on naturally to a consideration of those locomotives which became dominant-stock because of their efficiency, availability and utility.

The Largest Classes of the LMS

In this review, my intention is to present the facts so as to set these large classes of locomotives within the company's total stock picture. Immediately before nationalisation vesting-day on 1 January 1948, the total stock of LMS locomotives still stood at well over seven thousand. This position appertained despite the management policy of replacing old designs with more efficient machines, which in turn worked longer running-diagrams, therefore requiring fewer engines in total. On the other hand, apart from a few minor closures, the huge network remained intact, requiring a large fleet of engines to haul the cross-country and branch-trains, the whole served by a dense network of depots, over 170 in total. Furthermore, the threat of war in the late 1930s had caused the retention in reserve and reinstatement to stock of locomotives scheduled for the breakers in 1939-40. These constraints militated against much shrinkage of the total stock during the 1940s. Nevertheless, the heat of the day was borne by the construction of the 1920s and the new stud of Stanier-standards, leaving the older, non-standard engines in a supporting-role.

Isolated Older Designs Remain in Stock

Looking back five years from the eve of nationalisation, I was agreeably surprised to note in my *ABC of LMS Locomotives* (Ian Allan, 1943) that, despite this standardization of motive-power, a considerable number of classes of engine were listed where only a handful of examples remained, often of previously numerous classes. The Johnson 2-4-0s from the former Midland Railway, already alluded to, are typical: only three remained and were probably little used; certainly, 20155 was stored at Nottingham and 20216 at Kettering. The same is largely true of many other classes where only a few engines remained, such as the nine double-framed Kirtley 0-6-0s of 1868, the rump of a class originally totalling hundreds. Was the management trying to 'postpone the evil day' of scrapping the very last example of a design?

The result was that the LMS stock-list was virtually a living museum—if only the author had known where to find that elusive survivor; usually the author did not, or were unable to travel to see it. At the take-over by BR on 1 January 1948, the LMS stock therefore comprised as many as 144 classes. However, the author's business-experience leads him to conclude that the company had not gone soft in the boardroom but was simply obeying the *diktat* of the accountants by retaining some old motive-power as a reserve for unknown problems—much less romantic, but realistic. Finally on this point, this situation casts a sidelight on a facet of the British character: the underlying urge to 'make do', to prolong the life of every artefact to the ultimate—even at the cost of efficiency—and to buy nothing new, except when compelled to. The design of the Claughton, the Hughes 2-6-0 of 1926 and a glance at former traditional British industries underline the point.

The Standard 4F: the Final Development of the Ubiquitous 0-6-0 Goods Engine

For more than a century—since the first, *Atlas,* by Robert Stephenson for the Liverpool & Manchester Railway in 1834—the basic British maid-of-all-work had been the inside-cylinder 0-6-0 locomotive. The emergence of 4606 onto LMS metals in 1941 (a wartime-contract for forty-five simple, proven, goods-engines) represented the final construction of more than 2,000 machines of this wheel-arrangement by every constituent-company of the LMS. The 4F derivatives formed easily the largest class on the LMS with no less than 772 examples, i.e. *ten per cent of the entire fleet.* The 4Fs comprised the Midland class of 1911 numbered 3835-4026, built in batches up to 1922, and the LMS-built engines 4027-4606. After 530 engines had been put into traffic (up to 4556), the five from the Somerset & Dorset Joint Railway were added to stock and given the numbers 4557-4561 on the absorption of that railway's motive-power into the LMS during 1930. Following them, the war-time batch of forty-five was built as late as 1941, and thus these engines were new during the author's observations. The class was chosen on account of its being the most-numerous 0-6-0 and reasonably straightforward to maintain, despite rather unsatisfactory axle-boxes. Its boiler was that of the 2P 4-4-0.

It is fascinating to reflect that this class represented the ultimate development of the 0-6-0 goods engine on the LMS and its constituents, from the earliest examples. The power of the 0-6-0 had been developed steadily from 1F through 2F and 3F to 4F. The running-numbers of the MR/LMS locomotives even followed this order, from around 1600 to 4606. But of course all the railway companies of Britain had participated in the development of the 0-6-0, as well as Continental railways. The Great Western even brought out a new design as late as 1930, the lightweight '2251' class—of course with a taper-boiler.

Old predecessors of the 4F still at work during the 1940s, the Kirtley double-framers of 1866, originally totalled hundreds too, worn out on those heavy coal trains from Toton to Brent: the 2Fs and 3Fs succeeded them. This is not to ignore the LNW 'Coal Engines', 'Cauliflowers' and many other much-loved engines of other companies. Crews reported that the 4F's boiler needed careful firing in order to steam freely and that they preferred the earlier 3F 0-6-0s—nick-named 'Bulldogs' on the SDJR. However, at this time, the men still had over three hundred 3Fs to drive, some recently upgraded from 2F. Conflicting reports have circulated concerning the maintenance costs of the 4Fs—but certainly their axle-boxes were unsatisfactory.

Analagous cases have arisen earlier, where an outstandingly-successful class is succeeded by an 'improved' design, bigger and more powerful. This happened on the GWR, where the outstanding Castle locomotive was a development of an earlier 4-6-0, the 'Saint' of 1903, but the final development, the King, theoretically a superior machine, was proportionately less successful. Compared with the numerous Castles and Halls, only 30 Kings were built, but this was partly because of restricted route-availability owing to their heavier axle-loadings. The Castle however, a design of 1923, was still being built up to 1950 under the BR regime. The preserved 7029 *Clun Castle* is one of them. A sidelight on this is a remark that amused me by a Yorkshire friend of the author, Arthur Kinder of Honley, who was born in 1911 and died in 1996. You have read his anecdotes earlier. The greatest fan of the LMS the author ever knew, one day, referring to the Castles, he announced in his forthright Yorkshire way that, "The GWR produced nothing new after 1923!" This is true, particularly when one considers Gresley, Bulleid and Stanier, among other pioneers. Yet the GWR had—and still has—an army of devoted fans, probably due to its sailing unruffled through the Grouping of 1923. Three 4Fs are preserved, a Midland-built example, 3924, running on the Worth Valley Railway, 4422 from the Somerset & Dorset lines, at Cheddleton, and 4027, the first LMS-built example, preserved at the NRM.

The Fowler 3F shunting-tanks (total 422)

The next-numerous class, also an 0-6-0, the shunting tank locomotive, was a design continued by the LMS, following the sixty Fowler examples introduced on the MR in 1899, 7200-59, an advance on the 1Fs of the same wheel-arrangement designed twenty years earlier. During the regime of Fowler as CME of the LMS from 1925, these sixty tanks, like other Midland designs, were multiplied considerably, starting with 7260, the series ending eventually at 7681. the author saw few of them, even in his later travels; quite naturally, their shunting-role scattered them in penny-numbers across the system. However, large depots such as Edge Hill, Liverpool, had considerable allocations. Few worked in the West Riding of Yorkshire, but one, 7562, was allocated to Skipton (20F) late in the LMS regime. Photographs resulted, and later his colleague 47427 (BR number) many hours of recordings while shunting the down exchange sidings. This is another example of an obsolescent design multiplied as a standard-class. Incidentally, the author never heard them called 'Jinties' during his observations; this was confirmed in a letter to The Midland Railway Trust's magazine *The Wyvern* (Summer 1991) from a retired engine-driver pointing out that the staff never used this name either. The same applies to the so-called 'Crabs', called 'Horwich moguls' in this book. Such nicknames are copied by successive authors, thereby gaining credibility.

The 'Fowler' 2-6-4 tank, derived from the Horwich mogul

The origin of the Horwich mogul mixed-traffic locomotive has been described in Chapter 2. Painted red as a passenger-engine, it was so successful—and popular with the enginemen—that a tank-engine version was built, the 2-6-4. Retaining the Midland boiler, it was also outstanding, its speed and acceleration due to the long lap-and-lead arrangement of the Walschaerts gear—a last-minute suggestion by H.G. Ivatt. It was developed into the equally-successful Stanier/Fairburn 2-6-4 that appealed to the author so much.

It is important to underline here a point made earlier: the majority of contemporary locomotives had *inside* cylinders, making the Horwich mogul with outside cylinders and Walschaerts valve-gear a new departure on the LMS, and one that paved the way for *all* its other standard-classes—and those built by BR. Like the moguls, some Derby 2-6-4s remained in service almost to the end of steam.

Stanier's Achievements on the LMS

In the few short years from 1932 to 1937, William Stanier had made his indelible mark on this railway, the largest of the big four, bringing technology from the GWR, including their ideas imported from overseas, modified and updated with his own persuasions. He quickly saw that it was not a matter of adopting GW practices lock, stock and barrel, but rather of adaptinng them to LMS requirements. Examples are his abandonment of the jumper blastpipe on his 5X 4-6-0s and his increase of superheat on all designs. In the design of his first pacific, too, the Princess Royal, rather than adopt the GW conjugated valve-gear, Stanier went for four separate sets of gear—but then, with the benefit of this experience, he reverted to the GW-principle on his masterpiece, the Princess Coronation 4-6-2 (Duchess), fitting conjugated valve-gear to operate the inside-cylinders with rocking-arms from the outside Walschaerts gear. But at the heart of his achievements lay his 4-6-0/2-8-0 designs, though also notable is his excellent 2-6-4 tank-engine—the third-largest class on the LMS. To all his designs, he brought the Swindon taper-boiler and improved axleboxes, while Horwich contributed its heating-surface proportions. Stanier's talented chief draughtsman Coleman, trained on the NSR at Stoke-on-Trent and on the L&Y at Horwich, was a vital aid in his designs and his efforts to improve performance and appearance. The rough-riding and heavy maintenance were solved by the substitution of the horn-block axle-box of the GW for the existing Midland type. These actions demonstrate that Stanier utilized the best from the GW where appropriate, otherwise he used his own experience, allied to test-results and calculations, in order to achieve the desired end: 'adopt and adapt.' Before listing the largest classes of the LMS, a note is necessary on some remarkable heavy-freight engines inherited by the new company at the 1923 grouping.

The LNWR 'Super-D' 0-8-0 coal-engines

As mentioned earlier, the freight-operations of the LMS—like those of the other three railways—continued largely unchanged following the grouping, since the majority of the available capital was directed towards the prestigious express passenger-trains in the name of competition. The existing freight-locomotives were quite competent to continue their tasks. The sole new heavy-freight engine contructed, the 7F 0-8-0 'Austin Seven' of 1929 had failed to live up to expectations, partly on account of its poor Midland-type axle-boxes, which increased maintenance-costs. These locomotives had been designed to replace the LNW Super-Ds; to modernize these was now the better option, one adopted by the LMS Executive.

The Super-Ds comprised three classes, G.1, G.2a and G.2. The oldest G.1s, with saturated 160lb boilers, derived from 3-cylinder Webb compounds dating from 1892, rebuilt as G.1s in 1908 by Whale. He added similar new engines, and the class was superheated by Bowen-Cooke from 1912. His G.2 of 1921 was an upgrade with a superheated 175lb boiler, most receiving Belpaire fireboxes later. This is where the LMS enters the picture. After scrapping pre-1894 G.1s, the new owners gradually rebuilt many of the remainder with the G.2 boiler and Belpaire firebox, reclassifying them G.2a, since they now conformed closely with the G.2. The successive rebuilding concentrated the several types into two power-categories according to boilers, 6F and 7F. In the 1943 stock-list, their numbers 8892-9454 reveal over 500 fine heavy-freight engines which, although non-standard, fulfilled a vital role in freight-haulage, many of them relatively-new rebuilds. As late as 1961, only six years before the end of steam haulage, ninety-two G.2a rebuilds and forty-one G.2s remained in stock.

THE LARGEST STANDARD CLASSES OF THE LMS

Class	Number built	Stanier standards[#]
4-6-0 Class 5P5F/5 mixed traffic	872	872¶
2-8-0 Class 8F heavy freight	c.852	666*
# 2-6-4T Class 4P heavy suburban-passenger	645	645
† 0-6-0 Class 4F freight (MR- & LMS-built: Fowler)	772	
† 0-6-0 Class 3F shunter (" ")	422	
	3,563	2,183

¶ About 100 built by BR. † Fowler designs. ‡ The initial 125 by Fowler.
* Figures given by Rowledge. # Including the Fairburn-type.

Although less numerous, important Stanier standard-classes should be included:

4-6-2 Princess & Duchess pacifics	58
4-6-0 Class 6P 'Royal Scot' class (not all converted yet)	71
4-6-0 Class 5XP 'Jubilee' (including two converted)	191
4-6-0 Class 5XP 'Patriot' programmed for conversion	18
	338

Therefore, 2,183 + 338 = 2,521 comprised Stanier standards, plus the 3,563 good older workhorses.

Rationalization and Standardization of the locomotive stock

In 1923, the LMS had inherited 10,300 locomotives, many of them standards of large constituent-companies. Construction of these continued, mostly left-over lots, but Stamp's subsequent policy of 'build-and-scrap' in order to rationalize the stock for greater efficiency and therefore reduce running—and maintenance-costs saw an additional 5,000 machines constructed, the majority to LMS standards. Because of increased availability for work, the new engines would operate up to eighteen hours a day, thereby reducing the total number required. The ex-LNWR Super-D class added another 500. By the early-1940s, the LMS had reduced the total stock to something over 7,500, reflecting two eras of build-and-scrap, the Fowlers in the 1920s and the splendid 'high-tech' stud by Stanier from 1933. The above table shows that, out of a total stock of over 7,000 locomotives in 1951, about a third (almost 2,500) were Stanier standards—the majority still relatively new. This was surely an outstanding achievement by the LMS, particularly when one considers the slack trade of the 1920s, the Great Depression of the 1930s, the years of interruption caused by the Second World War and the continuing severe shortages afterwards.

Therefore at nationalization, the LMS possessed a fleet of locomotives largely of modern design, many of which were capable of hauling every type of train from express-passenger to loose-coupled mineral with equal competence. They were light on maintenance and could achieve high mileages between repairs. Many of the latest features had also been incorporated on the residual pre-grouping locomotives (including rebuilding), for which Coleman also deserves great credit. Sir William A. Stanier's genial personality had harmonized his staff, dissipating their animosities and encouraging them to develop their talents. In this way, he built up a new loyalty to the company and a formidable team, preparing the LMS to adapt readily to the changing circumstances ahead, fitting it far better than the other three railways to lead British locomotive-development into the new, uncertain, era. This is evidenced by the appointment of many of Stanier's lieutenants to high rank in the nationalised British Railways. Riddles, Coleman and Bond in turn became CMEs of the whole of BR, while Stuart Cox worked for all of them.

The main object of this chapter has been to chart the advance, much of it made by the LMS, of new *types* of train, from the early steam railcars as a cheap substitute for steam-trains on secondary-lines to their successors the dmus. Acknowledgements are made to Tuffnell, p.49, and John Marshall *The Guinness Railway Book,* p.142 (see bibliography), who give fuller details of diesel railcars and multiple-unit trains. The parallel development of the diesel-shunter led to the ground-breaking LMS/EE 1,600hp diesel-electric mainline locomotive 10000, put on track by the LMS in 1947 on the eve of losing its identity in the nationalized

BR. This achievement was the culmination of almost two decades of experimentation with diesel-traction.

Summary of LMS Achievements

On the locomotive side, Stanier's standard-classes, with the SC apparatus and other improvements added later, represented the latest practices and technology of the steam-locomotive, a great leap forward in the modernization of the LMS fleet and in these respects ahead of those of the other group-companies. The pioneering 'Turbomotive' too must not be forgotten; it represented the sole example of a turbine-driven locomotive on the railways of Britain. In the field of diesels, the LMS 10000/1 paved the way for the introduction, almost a decade later, of powerful diesel-electric locomotives across British Railways, such as the Type 4 'Peaks', 37s, 40s, 45s, 46s and 47s constructed by BR, Vulcan Foundry and Brush/Sulzer, plus the Deltics built by English-Electric/Napier. These, the most-powerful single-units in the world at 3,300 hp, would for two decades haul the express-passenger trains on the East Coast main-line. From its early days of experimentation with diesel-shunters by the diesel-development arm, this was the ultimate achievement of the LMS. The company's 1938 multiple-unit train blazed another trail, this time for the diesel InterCity-125 trains from Paddington to the West in 1975, followed by its diesel-electric locomotives and the later multiple-units with diesel-electric, and later electric, drive, on both West and East Coasts from London to the North. The LMS can therefore claim to be the leader in British traction-matters for much of its twenty-five-year existence. Its pioneering-work, unique among the Big Four railway companies, laid the foundations for BR motive-power, first the steam standard-classes by ex-LMS locomotive-engineer Riddles, followed by the dmus, then by the diesel-electric mainline locomotives and the diesel and electric multiple-units of the 1990s and the new millennium. Furthermore, the LMS was unique among the Big Four in sending a locomotive and train to the USA on two occasions. It was also unique in approaching the impending nationalization positively, a significant factor in its influence within the new management.

We have traced the progress of the LMS from 1923 when the large locomotive was just appearing, through the lack of definite purpose caused by internal rivalry in the 1920s, to the production of its first large locomotive, the *Royal Scot*, and then, initiated by Stamp's Executive, the final breakaway from old traditions and personal loyalties into the Stanier-regime, which produced the standard locomotives the company urgently needed. We have seen the art of steam-locomotive design progressing to efficient boilers giving reliable steam-production, and to higher standards of servicing and maintenance. The boiler no longer controlled the repair-schedule of an engine, while hot-boxes, fractured tyres, constricted steam-passages and internal leaks had been consigned to history. Further work was indicated on laminated springs and frame-fracture, to be carried out in the new LMS/LNE joint Locomotive Testing Station, which BR would complete and open in 1948.

The other aspects of the company must also be brought into focus. An industrial empire, it controlled harbours and ships, hotels and refreshment-facilities—including many restaurant—and sleeping-cars—as well as properties. It rationalized these in the 1920s, eventually renewing two-thirds of its fleet of freight-wagons and passenger-carriages; the latter were the most comfortable to be found anywhere. The LMS freight-wagon control was a pioneer too, one of many of its practices adopted by BR from 1948. Its track was as good as any, and it pioneered the mainline flat-bottomed rail in Britain in 1936. Its re-designed water-scoop reduced wastage when picking up from water-troughs, and the new coal—and ash-handling plants at depots—plus the drop-grates and rocking-ashpans (borrowed from America) fitted to the Duchesses, leading to the improved SC-devices on the other standard locomotives—made the job of servicing easier and cleaner. Signalling was improving, with many colour-light distant-signals replacing semaphores, and the modified Hudd-system of the LMS advanced the GWR's ATC-system, paving the way for BR's AWS-control. The LMS publicity-department did notable work: its posters now conserved in museums testify to an equality with the other railways in publicizing its work and what it had to offer, including excursions to holiday-resorts, often using joint publicity with those towns.

Stanier's genial disposition had rapidly dissipated the rivalry lingering among the employees of the LMS constituents, bringing out the best in them. In this way, he raised their morale and encouraged a corporate company image. His lieutenants possessed the potential he had identified to carry out his programme: his creation of a positive, forward-looking team of engineers, men who would continue the modernization-programme after his retirement. This they did amply in the last years of the LMS, updating his designs with new devices appropriate to the time, and actually outliving the company to become the heart of the new BR management from 1948 onwards. In December 1947, Stanier's highly-motivated school of engineers—unlike those of the other three railways—stood ready for the challenges of the new BR nationalized regime in the New Year, epitomizing a company that was positive, and a leader technically.

Consider all the constraints the company suffered: the internal rivalries and the sluggish economy of the 1920s, followed by the Great Depression of the 1930s and the second world war from 1939 to 1945, finally by restrictions and shortages. Hampered by all these, it seems the company made considerable progress in its short existence—a mere twenty-five years. Wartime difficulties merely slowed it; in the peace after 1945, austerity ruled, but the company's considerable resources enabled it to continue to inaugurate new projects. It pressed on relentlessly with its modernizations even before the war ended, in the following years running out its life on a steep upward trajectory, looking positively to the future. Like its 6220 *Coronation Scot* in 1937, the LMS Railway at the very end of its existence was still accelerating.

Stanier 3-cyl 2-6-4 tank-engine 2532, of the 37 designed especially for the London-Southend commuter-line in 1934, departs Plaistow for Shoeburyness (H.C. Casserley collection).

Ex-MR 2P 4-4-0 509 piloting a Horwich mogul on *The Pines Express* through Radstock, Somerset, S&DJR (R.K. Blencowe). Several of these 4-4-0s ran on this line.

Ex-HR *Loch Tummel* 14389 & 4-6-0 14681 *Skibo Castle* at Wick, North of Scotland (H.C. Casserley collection).

Claughton 6004 heads north on a Manchester express near Rugby.

PART II

A SELECTION OF LMS OPERATIONS (1)

No. 19
LMS
ONE SEAT RESERVED
in
3rd Class Restaurant Car

Passengers when proceeding to the Restaurant Car are requested to take their Railway Tickets with them.

Passengers are also desired to leave the Car as soon as the meal is finished, in order that the Attendants may serve another meal.

FIRST SITTING

ERO 89109/3
511

LMS reservation-ticket for the buffet-car to take afternoon tea (author).

Ex-MR 2-4-0 express locomotive 158A restored at Butterley, Derbyshire in 1993 (author).

Derby-designed 2-6-4 tank-engine 2390 at Swansea (H.C. Casserley collection).

Chapter 6

THE LEEDS TO SKIPTON LINE AT APPERLEY BRIDGE

My years here at Woodhouse Grove School completed my introduction to the LMS. If I had been living in Manchester or Sheffield during 1942, I would have spent a considerable amount of my time crouching under my school-desk as the German bombs rained down. As it was, I was further north, at school beyond Leeds, beside the southern end of the Leeds-Carlisle line, later well-known nationally because of the struggle to save the splendid mountain section north of Settle, in particular the Ribblehead Viaduct. I immediately became fascinated with the railway.

Four tracks leading from Leeds to Shipley. There, the left pair continued to the Bradford terminus at Forster Square; the sharp right-hand curve led through Bingley and Keighley and on to Skipton, then Settle, the junction for Morecambe and Carlisle. In addition to the four-tracked main line at Apperley Bridge, the branch line to Ilkley, climbing as it left the Aire Valley, curved away at the back of the goods yard, fitted neatly into the triangle of land. This was my view over the low, dry-stone wall of our Top Field, and several of us spent innumerable happy hours there.

Soon after arriving in the school, a Prefect in my house, Vinter, Neville Kirkman, introduced me to the trains and taught me a lot about LMS operations. But then he had the luck to live at Berkhamsted, on the crack West Coast Route, whereas my home was on the cross-country lines of Halifax during the holidays, described later. Kirkman wrote out lists of LMS named engines for me, before I could get my hands on—and afford the 2s.6d (12½p)—for that vital Ian Allan pocket-book,

The ABC of LMS Locomotives, 1943. In that period during the middle of the war, the line was immensely busy with trains carrying the munitions of war. Troop trains mingled with them, both slotted somehow into the ordinary time-table. On dark evenings, we identified engines by torchlight when the trains were checked at our signals.

The heavy wartime-traffic certainly gave a wide variety at Apperley Bridge. Trains of well-wagons carried tanks from the Royal Ordnance Factory at Barnbow, Leeds; flat-wagons carried guns, and mysterious van-trains all sorts of stores and munitions of war. Engines were often commandeered for these tasks, or had to work through to distant destinations without the normal change of locomotive. This provided an immense range of motive-power for us to see, with engines appearing from all parts of the extensive LMS system, indicated by their shed-plates. Examples are 5504 *Royal Signals* from Crewe South, Jubilee 5576 *Bombay* from Polmadie one Sunday morning, while colleague 5670, the picturesquely-named *Howard of Effingham* from Patricroft, was identified by torchlight one winter's evening after a signal-check on the near-line.

Regular Passenger Trains

These comprised the Morecambe residential-trains and the Glasgow/Edinburgh expresses bringing Jubilees, and later, Royal Scots, and the Bristol or Paignton through-trains. A 'Belpaire' 4-4-0 used to haul the Paignton-Bradford on its last leg from Leeds, worked as a stopping-train after reversal had trapped its train-engine in Leeds (City) station, usually a Jubilee of Bristol Barrow Road (22A), sometimes 5690 *Leander* or 5699 *Galatea*, after its seven-hour journey. It was the same routine on the last leg of the London (St Pancras)—Bradford, which arrived soon afterwards. Leeds Holbeck was home to Belpaires 720/9/36/48/58/9, but I saw almost all the remaining members of the class pass the school at one time or another. The sole example that I saw near my home in Halifax, 711, on the former Lancashire & Yorkshire Railway, underlines the fact that locomotives from the LMS constituents largely remained in their own area. This method of operation was even more marked on the freight side. Bradford-Leeds non-stop passenger trains were in the hands of ex-MR 4-4-0s while the locals were hauled, exceptionally, by ex-L&Y 'radial' 2-4-2 tanks, plus a few Stanier 2-6-2 tanks.

Regular Freight Trains

One was the Saltley Goods, down in the late evening and returning up to Birmingham at breakfast-time, often providing us with some interest. One morning, this was ex-MR 383, a saturated (non-superheated) 2P 4-4-0 from Sheffield (19A), piloting the new Stanier Black Five. To see a fresh engine from this small class of Johnson/Fowler rebuilds was a rare treat. I describe the 2P 4-4-0s later. Every day, 1.30pm saw the mineral-empties from Barrow-in-Furness pass by, the unique 'coke-racks,' painted yellow, with 'Barrow' in black. They evoke memories of the great fleets of privately-owned wagons, many by collieries, that ran on the railways before nationalization. Names like *Firbeck, Denaby, Coote & Warren, Bickershaw, Llay Main* and *AAC* come to mind. The slatted-sides of the coke-racks sloped straight out from the solebars, giving an unusual appearance. This train occasionally produced a treasured stranger, such as an ex-LNW 'Cauliflower' from the Barrow district. In 1944, 28603 came along, and in the following year, 28505. I was exceptionally thrilled in December 1945 when ex-LNW 'coal-engine' 28104 headed the coke-wagons. I only ever saw six of the fifty-seven remaining of this class built in 1873, as they lived on the Western Division 'A', like the Cauliflowers. Boys could not travel around the country then to spot engines. Apart from the radial-tanks, an ex-LYR engine too was rare at Apperley Bridge. Mundanely, an MR/LMS 4F 0-6-0 was usually turned out for the coke-racks, say 3893 or 4197 of Skipton (20F). Indeed, it was one of these ubiquitous locomotives that headed this train one day with eighty-eight wagons behind the tender. Near my home, along the Calder Valley, Halifax, I was used to seeing the down mineral-empties routinely comprising seventy-five wagons plus brake-van—but headed by an 0-8-0, rather than an 0-6-0, so this Barrow train created a record for me in two respects. It was the longest train I had ever seen; when the brake-van was passing our field, the engine had shrunk to a speck in the distance. But this record was broken in the Midlands when a 4F deputized for a failed Beyer-Garratt on ninety mineral-empties, as noted by a correspondent of *The Wyvern,* the magazine of the Midland Railway Trust. I have discussed the 4Fs earlier, in the context of the largest classes on the LMS. The coke-racks were often delayed by an Ilkley-branch local, also bound for Leeds. The coke-racks would crawl past the school, hoping the advance-starting signal would come off to avoid stopping, while on his left, the little branch-train spun merrily down the incline to the junction. Then the coke-racks were signalled off and steadily accelerated away.

Signals

All the signals were of the Midland Railway design, those with the large white spectacles and ribbed steel arms; even a few arms of the earlier wooden variety remained. There were no upper-quadrant signals in view at all; two home-and-distant pairs were down the line behind the station at Apperley Viaduct, which I describe below. The ground-signals for crossovers were of the early-LMS swivel-design. Only three signal installations in the two sections of Apperley Bridge/Junction were replaced up to 1948, six arms out of twenty-six. While out for a Sunday-afternoon walk along the towpath of the adjoining Leeds and Liverpool Canal, we witnessed one of the replacements being connected up, the 'splitting' two-arm bracket for the crossover at the junction. The tubular steel post and bracket had been erected in front of the old structure and, once connected up, sadly the old Midland arms and mechanism were dismantled and the teak post sawn down. But you can still see splendid examples of Midland signals rescued for posterity, re-erected by preserved railways such as the Midland Railway Trust, Butterley, near Ripley, Derbyshire. The ex-MR lines were routinely characterized by approach-controls, that is 'splitting-distant' signals warning of a junction or a crossover ahead. Other railways had similar arrangements.

At Apperley Bridge, the far-line up starting—and advance-starting signals had these splitting-distants, and we were always interested to watch a train switched from the the far to near line in the distance at Apperley Junction, and then whether the Junction 'bobby' would have time to pull off his inner distant to show the crossing-movement. It happened occasionally—and even more rarely to pull off his *outer* split-distant, bracketed on the station starting signals behind us. One afternoon though, the Scotsman was switched, evidently because of a freight ahead on the far line. He braked hard in the station, where the distants were 'on', but the junction's inner split-distant came off, allowing him to coast down to cross over without stopping. On another occasion, this express again met the station starting-signals at half-peg. The Jubilee slammed everything on so hard, causing sparks to fly from the wheels, that he could almost have stopped at the advance-starter— that is, in just a few hundred yards. This time though, the freight ahead had crossed over, and the Scotsman was signalled straight ahead at the junction as usual. The two pairs of metals were not utilized specifically for fast and slow trains as on the West Coast Route, and on the LNER and the GWR too, therefore we naturally referred to them as the 'near' and 'far' lines. But, generally, the expresses ran on the far lines; the exception was the morning Leeds-Glasgow, which always came past on the near line, probably for operating reasons. Similarly, the pick-up goods had to arrive on the far line in order to reverse direct into the yard. You can see how the network of tracks made a theatre for our observations.

The Branch to Guiseley and Ilkley

I alluded to this branch-line earlier to show how it affected the main-line operations. The passenger rolling-stock was ex-MR or early-LMS panelled non-corridor carriages, hauled by 0-4-4T locomotives. This was the traditional MR type for local passenger services, a practice that continued well into the BR-era. Indeed, most companies had used a similar type, but more on this in a moment. Five 0-4-4 tank engines, 6400-4, of a Derby 1932-design, replacing similar old Midland locomotives, headed these Ilkley trains, the same group week in, week out, boring for us, waiting to cop fresh numbers. Their Derby outline certainly betrayed their drawing-office origin. The ten-engine class was however credited to Mr Stamer, since he had been appointed CME to the LMS in that year. Over the years a couple more did come along, 6405/6, no doubt drafted in temporarily while regulars were undergoing repairs. A protracted correspondence on the class took place in *The Railway Magazine* during 1994, noting that some ran in the Nottingham area, and picturing some members of the class withdrawn and in store at Barrow. The diameter of their driving-wheels followed that of their MR predecessors but they had a longer piston-stroke and a considerably-higher tractive-effort at 17,099 lbs. They were of a neat appearance and seemed free-running. In 1946, the class was renumbered 1900-9 in order to free the 6400-series for the new Ivatt 2-6-0s. Later that year, an interesting interlude occurred: the 1900-class 0-4-4 tanks disappeared, to be replaced by five strangers, ex-Caledonian McIntosh 0-4-4Ts no less. This was startling, and made us sit up and take notice again, after watching the same motive-power on the branch literally for years. I noted 15130, 15192 and 15195 passing the school in December 1946 bearing 20E shed-plates (neighbouring Manningham). However, a later outing with my parents to Morecambe explained what had occurred. We called at the Promenade Station, the seaside terminus built by the Midland Railway to compete with neighbour LNWR at Euston Road. The white art-deco Midland Hotel nearby was built by the LMS in 1933 to replace the Midland Railway structure. The electric-stock of the Morecambe-Heysham-Lancaster triangle was stored in the carriage-sidings. The Jubilee *Newfoundland* also posed for my camera as he waited for his special return-working. This locomotive was shedded at Leeds for many years, working to Carlisle as well as Morecambe and Lancaster (Green Ayre). I have an anecdote on him much later on. Then I spotted 'our' 0-4-4Ts working the trains on the Lancaster-Morecambe-Heysham triangle. A 1990s-redevelopment of the Morecambe sea-front moved the Promenade terminus back with the inevitable reduction of tracks.

What had evidently happened to our tanks was that 1900-4 had been borrowed to replace the electrics during refurbishment, though at least one lingered at Skipton for a while. Their places at Manningham were filled by drafting in the Caleys from Scotland, though they did not reign long; I guess the men disliked them. This was a common occurrence when locomotives were transferred from a 'foreign' area, like the transfer of ex-London Tilbury & Southend 4-4-2 tanks in 1947 to Dundee. The men up there heartily disliked them and Dundee quickly rid itself of these interlopers. The McIntosh 0-4-4Ts were pretty with the flared chimney but the fitting of a stovepipe-chimney to one engine greatly detracted from its appearance. On contemporary visits to Scotland, I noticed many ex-CR engines altered like this, probably in the quest for fuel economy during that difficult time of coal shortages. Goods-traffic on the Ilkley-line was minimal, to say the least. The 2F and 3F 0-6-0s hauled mainly coal for the mills in the townships such as Yeadon along the line, reached by a short single-track branch, extended during WW2 to serve the aircraft-works of Messrs A.V. Roe Ltd. (Avro). The modern upper-quadrant signals along the branch betrayed its construction, confirmed by Ordnance Survey maps. Here, Avro made wings for their Lancaster bombers in 'underground' machine-shops—actually factories landscaped and camouflaged to avoid detection by German reconnaissance-aircraft. RAF articulated lorries—60ft long, huge for that era—used to pass the school each carrying one wing cradled upright, destined for the assembly-line at Woodford, Cheshire, or the nearby Ringway airfield, Manchester, now its international airport. Post-war, Yeadon too became an airport, serving Leeds and Bradford.

Stopping Trains & 4-4-0s

The Midland 4-4-0s hauled many local-trains and were in fact used as maids-of-all-work; we called them 'simples' to distinguish them from the compounds. The origins of the varied 2P 4-4-0s need explanation. By 1882, the 1860s Kirtley and Johnson 2-4-0s had evolved into 7ft 4-4-0s, both of class 1, but even these soon became inadequate to haul the increasingly-heavy trains, including Pullman-cars. As a remedy, in 1890 Deeley, the Midland CME, began a comprehensive rebuilding-programme, resulting in a mixed bag. Four of the eighteen locomotives received 6ft 6in driving-wheels, replacing their 7-footers, and straight footplating (the '332' class), such as 391, based at Manningham. The rest became the '483' class, so-called after the first rebuild in 1912, all vastly changed from the originals of 1882. Fowler continued the 2P rebuilding and added superheaters, the '483s' forming the basis for the LMS 2P 4-4-0s, the '563' class, with running-numbers 563 to 700, the last three for the S&DJR. In 1905, Deeley had introduced his three-cylinder 'compound' 7ft 4-4-0 (superheated by Fowler up to 1927), based on the 1901 Smith/Johnson patent and superficially similar to the 2P 4-4-0s but, at 4P, much more powerful and a good performer. The Midland Railway constructed forty-five, 1000-44, superheated under Fowler from 1913-28. During the Midland-dominated years of 1925-32, the LMS classed them as 'standards' and built many more, now with 6ft 9in driving-wheels and left-hand drive, giving an eventual total of 240.

The 2P 4-4-0s passed constantly, 351/3/9 (332-class) and 323/6, originally S&DJR (322-6), all based at Skipton (20F). From the 483-class came 401/6/9/14/45/6/52/53 also of 20F, and 434/6/7/46/55/519/62 of Holbeck (20A). Fewer of the 563-class, built by the LMS from 1928-32 with 6ft 9in driving-wheels and left-hand drive but otherwise little changed, appeared past the school. Many ran on the old G&SW line, but a long resident of 20A was 633, one of the three (633-5) taken over with the S&DJR locomotive-stock in 1928-30. We could always recognize 633 approaching by its Dabeg feed-water heater mounted on the offside of the smokebox. Members of this class were much more numerous in Scotland where their introduction from 1928, along with new Compounds, had allowed the rapid scrapping of the non-standard—especially saturated—engines of this wheel-arrangement, particularly those from the G&SW Railway, as a start on rationalizmg the multiplicity of designs.

The mystery of why these weak engines were constructed—particularly with such large driving-wheels—is explained by the strong Midland influence in the LMS during the 1920s. David Jenkinson, in his *Rails in the Fells*, calls them 'unoutstanding and rather feeble', an opinion shared by others. Some believe that the Johnson Belpaire, described below, or '990', 4-4-0s would have been a better LMS standard, but they were fewer than the 2Ps. I cannot see the logic of this numeric argument; a similar situation arose decades later, when the 'Western' diesel-hydraulics were scrapped in favour of the much heavier diesel-electrics, because these were more numerous. This topic is expanded later. However, the 2Ps performed tolerably well, the crews liked them and firemen have told me they were easy on the shovel. The other 4-4-0s, the 3P Belpaires, were a Johnson 6ft 9" design of 1901 comprising eighty engines. Some were superheated under Fowler, but by 1928 the LMS had scrapped the others, along with the majority of the saturated, unrebuilt, 2Ps (428/9/31/5/40-2/5/9/51/7/60/7/9/73-6/81, plus 465 scrapped in 1931, along with the 990s. Leeds Holbeck (20A) had Belpaires 720/9/36/48/58/9, but I saw almost all the remainder. In 1943, the Belpaires were listed as 707-775, but the class totalled only 35; in mid-1946 there were 32, and further withdrawals meant that by 1947 I had seen more than the 22 remaining to be taken over by BR. The last went for scrap in 1953. I describe elsewhere the use of the

Belpaires' boiler on the Hughes 2-6-0 of 1926, and on its derivative, the equally-successful 2-6-4 tank-engine introduced in the following year.

Accidents and Diverions

The Ilkley branch was useful to the operating department as a diversionary-route whenever the main line was blocked between Apperley Jct and Skipton. Just such a need arose in Spring 1943 when a night Scots express was wrecked north of Keighley. I was still in my first year at The Grove when we were all awakened at dawn one morning by the sound of a locomotive slipping violently as it struggled to 'find ts feet'. Kirkman was our sub-prefect—the railway fan who had taken me under his wing earlier—and so he allowed a few of us to join him at the window to see what was making the racket. It was a Horwich 2-6-0 stalled on the Ilkley branch with a long goods train. But why was he going up there? Later that morning, we learned the details of an accident, which had blocked the line at Steeton & Silsden, the first station north of Keighley.

The overnight Glasgow-St Pancras express had collided with a local goods which was shunting, wrecking the express. The tracks were torn up and both lines blocked by spread-eagled carriages while the engine, one of our Jubilees, 5581 *Bihar and Orissa*, lay overturned on the level-crossing at Steeton & Silsden. Immediately all traffic had been hurriedly diverted, leaving the unfortunate footplate-men to try to struggle up the bank without assistance—at first. Both lines were blocked at Steeton for a few days, necessitating the diversion of all traffic up to Ilkley, then through Bolton Abbey over another watershed to return down to the main line at Skipton. But Leeds Control soon got organised with banking-engines on goods trains and pilots on the expresses, Compounds, and of course 2P 4-4-0s. The goods-bankers were the usual 2F, 3F and 4F 0-6-0s. What pictures we would have had if only films had been obtainable! It made a fascinating interlude for us—but much more for those living along the branch who had probably never seen so much traffic passing. On the way home months later, I saw 5581 at Shipley, repaired and finished in wartime black, evidently running-in on a Bradford-Skipton local-train. Later, this locomotive worked from Farnley Junction, Leeds (25G) on the LNW 'new' line to Manchester, and was still performing strongly near the end of the steam era—possibly because of his renewal. Unfortunately, this good candidate for preservation went to the scrapyard.

During my seven years as a lineside observer, these diversions of traffic occurred a number of times, usually of short duration through a minor incident such as a derailment of wagons down the line. However, in November 1947 an incident potentially much more serious occurred when the bridge over the Eastburn Beck suddenly collapsed as a train was passing over it. Coincidentally, this culvert lies only a mile or so north of Steeton, the scene of the 1943 disaster. An unusually-wet spell of weather had built up the placid streams into raging torrents, and the Eastburn Beck, a small tributary of the River Aire, had scoured out its banks, the pressure of the floodwater undermining the bridge abutments. When Compound 1004 ran on to the bridge at about 2.30am with the Bradford-Skipton connection for the following night-express, the second abutment gave way. Although the engine managed to cross, the tender did not, breaking away and slipping back into the stream, fortunately leaving the carriages on the far side, as the press duly reported in pictures (the *Craven Herald & Pioneer*, Skipton, and the *Yorkshire Post*, Leeds). Luckily, the few passengers were merely subjected to a shaking; the train stayed upright, its moderate speed obviating any telescoping, but the line was blocked for days until a temporary structure could be thrown across the stream. This produced another bout of hectic activity on the Ilkley branch. But suppose the bridge had held under that train, giving way only when the following Scots express had run onto it? This must be counted as a hair's-breadth escape: a relatively minor accident had prevented another which could well have been infinitely more serious.

Incidents

The only incident that I actually witnessed was a goods van with one pair of wheels derailed in the neck of the goods yard opposite the school. The sweating goods-staff managed to re-rail it with old sleepers, jacks and levers (brain)—plus human-power (brawn).

The Daily Pick-up Goods

At about 1.45pm, the daily pick-up goods used to arrive, usually hauled by an ex-MR 3F 0-6-0, very often 3351. "Ooh, it stinks!" we cried, wanting to cop a different engine. These 3Fs were in four different classes, and we saw many over the years, notably 3456, 3579 and 3705. Fowler 4Fs appeared too, such as 4041 or 4245. Near the end of the LMS era, an occasional 8F 2-8-0 did this duty, the newish 8547 being one. It was a sign of the times: the 2F and 3F 0-6-0s were being steadily superseded and withdrawn.

The little train started in Leeds and worked its way steadily up the Aire Valley, shunting the wayside yards at Armley (of jail fame), Kirkstall (see its Cistercian Abbey from the train or the main Leeds-Ilkley road), Newlay & Horsforth (1930s Leeds ring-road) and finally Calverley & Rodley (Smith's Cranes of Rodley) before arriving with us at Apperley Bridge. Clearly, the gentle routine had hardly changed for generations—probably not since the construction of the line a century before. Stopping in the station, the short train, often consisting of only three or four wagons and brake-van, would set back into the neck of the small yard directly opposite my dormitory and the brake-van was unhooked to roll down into the outer siding. The gradient-post indicated 1:225. The handful of wagons would then be allowed to run down, occasionally inside the goods depot, more usually into the rear siding for unloading with the large hand-crane, a standard Midland feature. You may remember them: a cast-iron jib and frame holding a large block of stone as a counterweight. My grandstand-position in the second-floor dorm was great for photographs, the engines stationary and in full sun—both factors important for my 1930 Brownie 2A box-camera with a limited range of exposures and a slow or grainy film. New cameras were of course unobtainable, and films too were scarce until well after after WW2.

It takes only seconds to describe these operations, but the crew of three took well over an hour for the job, usually not starting straightaway—well, there was little to do. The engine would stand there simmering, the crew with their feet up drinking tea. Then suddenly he would burst into life with a bout of frenzied shunting, couple up, puff quickly through the station and up the line at some speed. They had evidently honed their timing almost to split-seconds—but of course, they had to fit into a narrow path between trains—including time for the reversal at Apperley Viaduct for shunting there. I read decades later in *The Wyvern* that these handy little engines were preferred by the train-crews to the heavier Class 4F, which the LMS went on to multiply in very large numbers, described elsewhere. However, in the 1940s, the men still had over three hundred of the smaller 3Fs to drive. Those running on the S&DJR were called 'bulldogs' by the men. The little train's destination, Apperley Viaduct, short of Thackley Tunnel, half-a-mile up the line, was where the Esholt Sewage Works wagons were collected from the sidings. A short inclined branch ran down into the sewage-works, and here a word on the works is of interest.

The plant was of a new design when opened in 1932 by Bradford Corporation. The effluent pumped from the city was particularly greasy, the outflow from the wool-scouring and dyeing processes of which Bradford had become the centre in the previous century. The school's Science Society took us on a visit, which showed us every stage, from the raw, noxious, input, to the final settling-lagoons, from which the clear water ran into the River Aire. However, we declined their offer to drink a glass of it! By-products were produced, gaining revenue for the corporation in order to offset their operating-costs. These were pared still further by employing water-turbines, one for each set of coke screening-beds. Here, the filtered effluent drove the spraying-trolleys over the beds before the same fluid passed through the spray-nozzles. This ingenious mechanism cost almost nothing to run, and was one of the pioneer-aspects of the works shown off to foreign dignitaries with a view to stimulating Britain's exports.

The principal by-product was fertilizer produced in bulk, a khaki powder which was loaded by hopper into the usual 10-ton four-wheeled wagons. These were then hauled up the branch by one of the corporation's two tank-locomotives through a five-barred gate on to the main-line exchange-sidings at Apperley Viaduct. A rake of these would arrive daily. The corporation locomotive would then withdraw down the branch and the gate was locked till the following day. The rake of up to twenty wagons was picked up daily by our pick-up goods, who often had little else on, and the engine would steam quickly through Apperley

Bridge station tender-first to Leeds non-stop, so ending another day's shunting-routine. The opening of the works in 1932 had necessitated the sidings and a controlling signalbox—interestingly, a traditional Midland timber structure—which explains the two pairs of upper-quadrant signals on the up-line. The warning distant stood at the far end of Thackley tunnel.

End of Term Luggage

In that wartime-era, I must remind you, practically all traffic went by train; motor-cars were few, and little petrol was available anyway. On the day before the end of term, we all received our train-tickets and packed our trunks, labelled 'unaccompanied luggage'. The prelude was, on the previous day, the pick-up goods-train had brought an extra vehicle, a bogey passenger parcel-van. This was shunted inside the goods depot, ready to receive our trunks, transported by the local carrier's horse-and-cart. With its high load firmly roped on, they would walk up our back-drive to the main Harrogate road, cross the railway and down Back Lane into the goods depot opposite the school, a U-shaped trip. The depot was little-used on account of its small catchment-area, despite its important-sounding name 'Apperley Bridge and Rawdon.' The former comprised a few houses near the school, and the village of Little London up the hill towards Rawdon, since the 'bridge' in the valley was served by the blue buses of Bradford Corporation, goods being transferred to and from Shipley or Bradford by motor-lorry. Once loaded, the parcel-van would be taken on the pick-up goods to Leeds, which despatched our trunks to their destinations all over the country. I soaked off some friends' labels for my archive. Our local goods depot delivery-lorry, an Albion of 1936 vintage, is pictured parked in its usual spot just inside the entrance to the yard, its starting-handle hanging below the large radiator.

Only occasionally there did I witness a wayside feature that was soon to disappear: horse-shunting. It occurred when the staff needed to unload a wagon inside the depot, but the wagon had run through to the middle of the yard, and the pick-up goods had gone for the day, leaving it stranded. Then the faithful dobbin would be roped to the buffers of the wagon, which he slowly pulled to the required spot, helped by the sweating goods-staff. I assume that the LMS hired the horse from a local farmer—perhaps from the carrier who took our luggage, since local goods deliveries were made by the Albion lorry. The once-numerous Scammell 'mechanical-horses' were also used in some places to pull wagons in this manner. I have more to say about them later, when I describe large goods-depots using them as adjuncts to the horses-and-carts, some kept on and others reinstated because of the fuel shortages caused by the war, and kept on for some years afterwards.

Unusual Trains

We had a novelty one day, when a long ballast-train was shunted down the front siding. Its brake-van was the first plough-van we had seen, and so was worth a photograph along with the side-tipping wagons. Then, one afternoon, another ballast-train suddenly appeared. To us, it indicated that track-maintenance work was about to start nearby. It was the usual miscellany of ballast-wagons, some hoppers, a few old 10-ton coal-wagons and the brakevan, in charge of one of the simple 2P 4-4-0s, 446. These were 'pensioned-off' on all sorts of jobs as you see. But what intrigued us was that the train arrived on the near-line, and proceeded to reverse over the crossover in front of us. To our knowledge, no train had crossed there for years, and we were relieved that the points—and the swivel ground-signal—worked perfectly. No doubt a signalman had secretly tried them out one quiet night. The train then ran forwards over the middle crossover to the down far-line, reversed again onto the up far-line and finally ran over a little-used crossover into the yard. You can imagine that this performance took some time, particularly as through-traffic was allowed to pass between manoeuvres. It was quite a relief to us when he cleared the main-line. Even now, in these well-equipped days of AWS/ATP, I become nervous when my train is held standing on the main line for more than a minute or so.

The Inspection Saloon

This short train occasionally appeared in the afternoon, comprising one carriage only, a rather grand affair with two large windows at each end. These special windows gave the carriage an unusual appearance, especially on first sight, because the engine was propelling it. You may have seen one, with a personage like the District Engineer, inside with assistants, examining the line expertly through the big windows. For this reason, it passed fairly slowly. I assume it was equipped with mechanical track-testing sensors, recording faults on a paper-roll in the saloon, and making white splashes on the track to indicate any deviations from the straight and level. The ganger or lengthman and his team would then be called on to rectify these faults and reinstate a good 'top.' Newer, electronic measuring has consigned him to history. The LMS used to award prizes for the best-kept lengths in each Area. The motive-power was again one of the ex-MR 4-4-0s, such as 362 or 489.

The Weed-Killing Train

This came along once a year, in the spring, with the inevitable 3F or 4F 0-6.0 hauling the short miscellany of vehicles including a couple of ancient ex-MR clerestory-carriages marked 'ED', and the key tank-wagons of chemicals, one vehicle carrying the sprayer underneath, the obligatory brake-van bringing up the rear. You younger readers will see a goods-train with one nowadays only on preserved lines, but all goods-trains had a brake-van at that time. Foreign goods-trains, seen on the silver screen, looked weird ending in 'nothing', a flat truck or an open wagon, looking really incomplete. On the subject of these interesting vans, a great variety passed the school during the war. Whereas the government's Railway Executive policy left the Big Four companies to run their own networks with their own locomotives, this did not apply to brake-vans apparently. We saw the 'island' type marked NE, even similar models from the distant SR, but those that I recall most vividly were the large GW vans with a wide rear-opening. They bore the names of their depots, such as Treherbert or Aberdare.

E.C.S.

During this middle period of the war, empty-carriage trains frequently made an appearance. The normal maximum length was twenty carriages, but once we did see twenty-one; several of us counted them to make sure. No doubt, the mass of troop-movements at that time would leave the stock 'in the wrong place', the phrase used now after some hitch in services, hence the movement to 'the right place.' In the

North of England, we had large contingents of troops for years, starting immediately after Dunkirk, when the men had been bundled into their trains at Dover or Ramsgate and sent off to apparently any destination away from potential air-attack; in Halifax, we received the entire Corps of Royal Engineers, who made the town their headquarters. Later, in 1944, when the troops were being trained and assembled ready for D-Day, more troop-trains were employed, the best way of moving masses of people. Almost always, the motive-power on the ecs was a Horwich mogul, very often 2762 or 2850, since only a few of these excellent machines ran locally—and hardly any of the Stanier type, which lived in Lancashire and the Midlands. Thanks are due to the retired driver who, in *The Wyvern*, (Summer 1996, p.8), declared that the staff never used the terms 'Crab', nor 'Jinty' for shunting-tanks. We never heard these either, so this confirmation was welcome. Such nicknames are copied by successive writers and so gain credibility.

The Red Cross

Speaking to you about the troop-trains reminds me of the Ambulance-trains which passed now and again. Painted olive-green, the carriages had been suitably converted into mobile sick-bays; nowadays, they would be 'intensive-care units'. Perhaps they had an operating theatre as well. Each vehicle bore a large red cross on a circular white ground on its side, and also on the roof, warning off any enemy pilot. But, for once, the 2P 4-4-0s were not officiating; these trains were too heavy of course, and were accorded some importance by receiving a 4-6-0, either a Jubilee or a Mixed-traffic as their motive-power.

The Circus

On a lighter note, it was after the war was over that I happened to spot, one Sunday morning, a special coming down the line from Apperley Jct. Class Five 4792 was brand-new and its destination probably Bradford. The wagons were specialized vehicles, with cages and boxes dedicated to particular animals and of course to the Big Top equipment, the whole train vacuum-braked with two passenger/luggage brakes at the rear. That was the only time I saw the circus on the railway, and it took me by surprise with no camera at the ready; Sunday morning was not for train-watching, but for chapel and I should have been getting ready. In contrast, the other travelling-attraction, the showman's fair, went by road.

'Dead' Engines

It is a pity we use this term for a locomotive out of steam; he is only sleeping! The only occasion when I saw a locomotive being towed like this was about 1945. To cap it all, it was 1177 of the Southern Railway, a small tank-engine going up towards Leeds, and naturally marshalled next to the train-engine. It was an 'H' class 0-4-4, and I discovered later that this little engine had been doing duty as station-pilot at Ayr in Scotland.

Locomotive parts

To end this section, an interesting consignment on a down-goods during 1945 was not a special-train or engine, but the collection of parts for one, a 2-6-4 tank locomotive of the Stanier/Fairburn type. The ready-painted parts told us clearly what it was and where it was bound: 'N.C.C. 3', read the lettering of the tank-side panels on a maroon ground; the frames and other parts were laid out along several flat— and tube-wagons. Evidently, it was a 'ckd' locomotive and heading for the docks at Heysham on a regular goods-train to that port, ready for assembly at the Belfast locomotive-works of the Northern Counties Committee, an LMS subsidiary.

The LMS Renumbering Scheme of 1933-4

Early in the Stanier-era, in order to prepare for the new standard-types of locomotive now planned, the Executive had decided that all machines deemed to be standard were to carry numbers below 10,000, that is, the simpler four figures. The two classes of 2-6-2 tank were renumbered from 15501-15709 to 1-209, Horwich moguls from 13000-13244 to 2700-2944, the Stanier version from 13245-84 to 2945-84 and the standard 3F shunting-tanks from 16343-16754 to 7260-7681. The Horwich moguls had been numbered from 13000 as some were built at Horwich, numerically following the L&Y 0-8-0 coal-engines. The first new standard Stanier Mixed-traffic 5P5F was numbered 5000 with the following five hundred numbers reserved. The Patriots followed from 5500-51 and the Jubilees continued from 5552. Earlier you have read my analysis of Stanier's development of the 4-6-0 express-locomotive to replace the Claughtons and others, leading to his rebuilding of the Royal Scots. In order to make space for the standard classes, some older, non-standard engines, such as the 2F 0-6-0 goods mentioned above, were placed on the reserve-list by moving them from the 0-9999 series by adding 20,000 to their numbers, effectively a prefix 2, so that 3018 became 23018 and the Kirtley 2-4-0s 2 and 12 became 20002 and 20012. But renumbering was not a new idea, for it had been necessary at the Grouping in 1923, when all LMS engines other than ex-Midland were renumbered to avoid duplication. On the LNER, GNR engines received the prefix 3 to their number, allowing NER engines to retain theirs. The Southern Railway added the prefix E to South Eastern & Chatham locomotives and B to the Brighton ones. The renumbering of the other LMS constituents has been explained.

Spotting Trains Brings Punishment

Now, here is a little anecdote. In 1944-45, our first-floor form-room faced the railway with a clear view of passing trains, causing our studies to suffer somewhat . . . We would 'get it in the neck' if our master spotted us turning to took out of those convenient Vinter building windows while he was endeavouring to teach us, especially at the prize morning Leeds-Glasgow express. It needed only one boy to note the engine-number; for the rest of us, placed further from a window, it sufficed to have a mere glimpse of the top of the boiler. Now, our Latin master was a gentleman by the name of Mr A.E. Reed, nick-named 'The Hun' because of the straight-backed, Teutonic, shape of his cranium. Well, if there was one thing that The Hun detested above anything else, it was the sight of little boys turning their heads to look out of the window at the *bon moment*. He gave us lines to write as a punishment. We might be noting Latin verb-conjugations from his blackboard, when he would turn and catch us looking out. Then he would call in his peculiar, high-pitched voice: "Boy, pay attention! Verbs, not trains! Twenty puff-puffs" This is what we had to write out as a reminder of the importance of Latin. It is poignant how, decades later, his very phrase is part of history. He had a car that looked as ancient as he did, though built only about ten years earlier, before they had evolved into rounded, pressed-out bodies. It was an 'Austin Six' with wire wheels and registered WX 8763 (West Riding CC).

Jubilee 5XP 4-6-0s on expresses

However, the afternoon trains we could see legitimately after the end of classes at 3pm. Some were the province of the much-loved Jubilees introduced by Stanier in 1934, a class which totalled 191 locomotives. Nicely-styled and well-proportioned, the first eighty-seven bore names of the Dominions and their Provinces, followed by the Colonies and Other Territories, in this way helping our geography and history considerably. The next forty-eight bore the names of famous admirals of the fleet and naval battles, a further fifty-two carried heroic names from mythology and the last four the Irish provinces—further educational value. We soon saw a good number of them, but some remained obstinately domiciled elsewhere, inaccessible to boys who could not yet travel around the country. However, wartime specials bringing visitors from those depots, along with family-visits to Scotland, Preston and Nuneaton, enabled me eventually to see every one; 5663 *Jervis* was the last I ticked off.

Claughtons and Patriots

The unrebuilt Claughtons had been withdrawn following the introduction of the Jubilees in 1934. Even the large-boilered rebuilds had gone by 1942 (6017 *Breadalbane* was the last), save 6004, which was retained for years. Formerly *Princess Louise*, its name was taken in 1935 for the new 'Princess' pacific 6204. The large-boiler Claughton formed the basis for the Patriot. Chapter 4 has described its development through 5X Patriot 4-6-0 to the Jubilee/Royal Scot conversions. The Patriots appeared frequently, but here tended to be employed more on parcels and fitted-goods workings. However, the Patriots still reigned on West Coast expresses. Passing the school we saw 5510, 5529 and 5545 (all unnamed), 5530 *Sir Frank Ree*, 5536 *Private W Wood, VC*, 5537 *Private E. Sykes, VC* and 5539 *E.C. Trench*. Holbeck was home to 5526 *Morecambe and Heysham*, 5534 *E. Tootal Broadhurst* and 5538 *Giggleswick* which therefore gained the reputation of 'stinkers.'

Unnamed 5542 sported a Patricroft shed-plate (10C) when passing with a troop-train in 1944, and 5520 *Llandudno* came past from 8A, Edge Hill.

Against Convention

Some Leeds and Bradford stopping-trains boasted unusual motive power, namely a group of ex-LYR 2-4.2 radial tanks, unusual because, as remarked, the Midland lines remained largely worked by engines emanating from this constituent company, as indeed the LYR lines were with theirs. The long-bunkered example 10885 appeared, and the more-powerful superheated versions, classed 3P, 10910 and 10911. The variants of the radial-tanks are detailed in the chapter on Halifax. All of them were hearty performers, accelerating a train of six carriages very smartly from a stop. At the end of term, it was usually one of them that took me to Bradford (Forster Square) and another from the Exchange-station on to Halifax. Their alternate turn was the Bradford-Keighley-Skipton locals, described in my chapter on Skipton.

This is the outline of our daily railway-experience, though as constant watchers, we did see occasional novelties. In March 1945, the Compound off the Edinburgh-St Pancras afternoon express provided one. This locomotive returned from Leeds on a Bradford local in the evening, its fill-in turn, and on this occasion it was 901, its tiny cab-numbers matching the Polmadie (27A) shed-plate on the front, quite exciting. Many of the 900-939 Compounds, along with the LMS-built '563' 2P 4-4-0s, displaced GSW 4-4-0s in Scotland, and family visits up there did enable me to see a number of both types, some lettered in this St Rollox style. As we had only 910/27/8/31/2 locally, a freshman of the forty was always welcome. Conversely, a decade later in the 1950s, the St Rollox works was noted for turning out its locomotives with *large* cabside numbers. Crewe used to paint its numbers rather smaller and higher on the cab-side, the tenders with closely-spaced initials. About 1945, one works, I believe Horwich, was painting its digits high on the cab, level with the tender-insignia, 'high-numbers' we called them, aesthetically a much more attractive style and one that became standard from 1946—more Horwich influence. 'Crewe-numbers' and 'the Derby-style' were terms we used to describe different styles of lettering. All this is evidence of a lack of standard company-policy throughout the railway: the constituents continued to go their own way. Also, a few engines retained their insignia and numbers in the short-lived 1936 *sans-serif* style.

Unusual Visitors

Class 2F 0-6-0s

The first of these was more out-of-the-ordinary than an actual rarity: it appeared on the daily pick-up goods. I stared in delight at an ex-MR 2F 0-6-0—and with Salter valves too. Most had been rebuilt with regular domes, or even into the numerically-overlapping 3F goods class and were quite numerous, but 3173 was well worth seeing. This engine was shedded at Hellifield from 1942-47. The earlier part of this class had been renumbered in the 1934 scheme, gaining the prefix 2 to make way for the Stanier 2-6-0s, numbered 2945-2984. One was 22977, shedded at Stourton (20B), and was also one of several rebuilt with a Belpaire firebox and a large cab in 1917 to replace the spartan affair of 1875. Others of the class appearing were 22901/65/74/5,23002/14/6 and 23018. Three more came my way en route to visit a school-friend in Leicester in 1947, 22950/69 near Sheffield and 23009 at Leamington Spa.

1F 0-6-0s

This one really was a rarity, also arriving with the pick-up goods. I could scarcely believe my eyes when I saw 22822, a Midland IF 0-6-0 dating from 1868, a Kirtley class with double-frames (only fifteen LMS locomotives had these) and only nine of these 1Fs remained from over three hundred originals, the rest worn out hauling those heavy coal-trains from Toton to London. They are worth a look now, so long afterwards: 22567, *22630, *22818, 22822, *22834, 22846, 22849, 22853 and 22863 (* round-top boiler; the rest, Belpaire). We spotters were tremendously excited. It was 9 January 1945. During 1945, 22567, 22818, 22834 and 22849 were withdrawn, and in 1946, 22822 as well. Four of the class survived to be taken into BR stock in 1948, 22630, 22846, 22853 and 22863, with numbers 58110-3 allocated, but only 22630 was re-numbered 58110, the sole Kirtley engine to be so treated. This rarity was crowned soon afterwards by the appearance on the same train of 22630. This one was even rarer, as noted retaining a round-topped boiler with Salter safety-valves on the dome; it was the 'icing on the cake.' And they all still sported a tender with springs above the footplating. I used to wonder whether Control sent these visitors from the south along to us for a treat? However, a more likely and practical reason is that they were running in after repairs at Leeds.

Even Rarer

These really rare episodes stand out particularly vividly in my memory. One day we were routinely watching a typical 'Midland front' approaching, a light-engine coming down the near line one summer afternoon in 1943, apparently a 3F 0-6-0 goods engine. Imagine our amazement when a MR 2-4-0 sped past, 20185. It was one of only five ex-MR 2-4-0s left in service, only three in its class. Where it was bound for we had no idea and we did not see it return, but I know we were tremendously excited. Years later, I discovered that Barrow was noted as a home for old engines, so perhaps he was going there. This class dating from 1876 comprised 20155 and 20185 of Nottingham 16A, with 20216 at Kettering 15B[1]. In 1947, I saw 20155 on his home shed. All three survived to be taken over by BR in 1948. 20216 was the last to be withdrawn by BR, still in LMS livery, in 1951. The other two 2-4-0s still in stock in 1943 were even rarer and I never saw them, the older double-framed Kirtley examples dating from 1866, 20002 and 200012, by then the oldest unrebuilt engines on the LMS (if we exclude 27217, the ex-North London Railway crane-engine of 1858, since this locomotive had been extensively rebuilt). Although intended for preservation (as No. 156A), 20012 was broken up in 1944 by Stanier, and so the last example remaining in service, 20002 (MR/LMS 2 until 1934), took its place, preserved as 158A in MR crimson lake livery, pictured elsewhere in this book. I saw it for the first time in 1993 in the Midland Railway Centre's splendid new museum at Butterley.

---

[1] Thanks to a Wyvern correspondent in 1990 for this information in a super article on Kettering shed in the 1930s.

The Milk train

This interesting working ran through up to Leeds around 9.30 in the evening, and so we were restricted to the lighter evenings if we wanted to see any detail. You will now see why I always ensured that my bed was on the railway-side of the dorm. The train comprised six-wheeled Express Dairy 3,000-gallon glass-lined/stainless-steel milk-tankers and a six-wheeled passenger-brake, operated as an express-parcels. The milk-train varied a good deal in length from two or three to twenty vehicles, which affected its make-up. A short train would have the passenger-brake marshalled next to the engine, but in a longer formation it brought up the rear. The milk tankers were tripped from a wide area of Galloway and south-west Scotland, from Carlisle, with a final rake picked up from the Appleby Dairy sidings, for their run up the Midland line to Cricklewood depot for trip-workings to their destinations around London. On a dark night, we could always identify this train through the distinctive sound made by the six-wheeled tankers over the rail-joints—only sixty-foot lengths then. Even the sound of the rail is different now. A variety of motive-power was utilised on this train, from Compounds to the more usual Stanier 5P5Fs or Jubilees. But one summer night in 1945, I received a lovely surprise, when an ex-Highland Railway 'River' class headed the train. Whether a shortage of engines at Carlisle had caused this, or the authorities wanted to give us (and the crew) a treat remains a mystery—probably the former. Only three remained of these handsome 4-6-0s, and it was a double stroke of luck to see 14760, stationed at Ayr and possibly named *River Tummel* earlier, because he was withdrawn shortly afterwards, his colleague 14758 soon following to the scrapheap.

Foreign Locomotives

No, not French engines, but S.160 American 2-8-0s arriving in the middle of the war, seeing service before shipment to the Continent after D-Day on 6 June 1944. Officially the property of the United States Army Transportation Corps, they were numbered 23xx—24xx; most had the WD emblem on their tenders, though a few carried 'USA'. They disappeared once the 'Second Front' was launched in Normandy, France, needed for motive-power over there after the war-devastation wrought on the SNCF. Their appearance suggests that they influenced Riddles' Austerity designs of the 2-8-0 and 2-10-0, a subject explored elsewhere.

Locomotives seen at Apperley Bridge after nationalization

Horwich 2-6-0 LMS 2779, Ivatt 2-6-0 43030, Derby 2-6-2T 40075, 2-8-0s LMS 8743, 48748, 0-6-0s 43933, 44595, Black Fives LMS 4790, 44721/3/7, 45179, 45365, Stanier 2-6-2T 40203 and Austeritiy 2-8-0s 77027/70.

Beyer-Garratt-built 2-6-6-2 locomotive 4997 hauling coal from Nottingham to London (A. Coulls)

Ex-LNW steam railcar 29988 taking water at Moffat, Dumfries-shire, the terminus of the branch to this little Scottish hydro (spa) from Beattock, wcml (H.C. Casserley collection).

Ex-LNW 0-6-0 'Cauliflower' 28417 – a much-liked class of engine - is relegated to be the steam- raiser to power the gas-lighting at Upperby, Carlisle (author).

Chapter 7

LEEDS—SKIPTON (2): SKIPTON IN THE 1940s

From Apperley Bridge to Skipton is a short step of less than twenty miles along the Midland main line towards Settle and Carlisle. It was also during the 1939-war when my associations with the Skipton area began when father used to take me, from the age of 11, on lengthy cycle-rides from our home in Halifax. These sixty-mile trips mostly passed through Skipton, there branching off, usually through Gargrave to different village—or farm-destinations. We had overnight-stops and short holidays up there too, since, during the war, many seaside hotels had been requisitioned for military use, and some coastlines became restricted as well. 'Holidays at Home' was the government slogan. We were able to venture further up the Settle-Carlisle line after father was directed by the Ministry of Labour late in 1944 to work at the Rolls-Royce jet-engine research-factory at Barnoldswick, south-west of Skipton. I therefore had plenty of opportunity to watch trains along the whole stretch from Leeds to Ribblehead at one time or another. It was a lucky that father was a railway-enthusiast too! Cycling from Keighley to Skipton, I used to stare across the valley at the railway to pinpoint the location of the signals.

Opposite Skipton South Junction, we used to lean over the drystone wall at the roadside to look at a 3F or 4F 0-6-0 on the goods-loop, the engine often taking water before continuing on the goods-lines behind the station to rejoin the main-line at Skipton Station North Junction box, or turning on to the main line straightaway, according to the traffic. Occasionally it would be a Class 5P5F 4-6-0 (Black Five), less numerous then. The loop was operated as a permissive-block, so we would often wait to look as the second train drew up. Therefore, when the family removed to Earby, also south-west of Skipton, to be nearer father's work, I was already well acquainted with the routine and continued spotting trains to fill the gaps in my Ian Allan *ABC of LMS Locomotives*, spending hours at both the sheds and the station.

Skipton, the centre of 'the Craven country', lies in the Aire Gap, the great limestone fault running from north Lancashire to the outskirts of Leeds. Skipton's title 'The Gateway to the Yorkshire Dales' implies it is also a route-centre for rail and road. The rails ran in four directions, with further branches forking further out, Earby to Barnoldswick, Embsay to Grassington, and Settle Junction to Morecambe, with a further junction at Clapham for Low Gill, giving access to several stations on this alternative route to Carlisle, and a final fork further on at Wennington for Lancaster/Morecambe and Carnforth. They all fed in traffic to the Skipton hub. While the exchange sidings to the north of the station were extensive, the station was a modest affair of three through platforms, with a bay for local-trains to Keighley and Bradford. The down through goods-lines passed behind platform 4 but up goods-trains ran through the station. It was a tight squeeze for the signalmen fitting in the traffic, particularly with the summer-extras, and as an observer I could sense the tension and excitement in the air, which I describe below. Behind the goods lines, the platforms serving the Ilkley/Grassington-lines lay at a slightly higher level, the tracks beginning their climb to the overbridge half-a-mile further on, to turn sharply north over the main line towards Bolton Abbey. This is the diversionary-line described in the previous chapter. The branch turned off southwards at the grandly-named Skipton Station North Junction signalbox. It was used as a through-route for North Eastern trains from York and the North-East to Blackpool, and on week-end summer-evenings I would see an LNER engine, a B.16 4-6-0 or a humble J.39 0-6-0, on Skipton shed awaiting the return-working.

Near Skipton South Junction box, where we leaned over the wall, was the small goods-yard for local merchandise and coal, but the more interesting section lay to the north of the station. This half-mile of line funnelled all traffic from the south and east to the north and west via Engine Shed

Junction, re-named after 1948 by BR, 'Skipton North Junction'. To all this through-activity were added the movements through both the up and down exchange-sidings and on the depot itself, situated on the down-side. Engine Shed Lane was an ideal vantage-point for all this; we railfans are often lucky in this respect, for I found a similar situation obtained at other sheds. The LMS Sports Club, then on the other side of the lane, was later relocated at the station, but retains its old name.

Like other junctions, Skipton was a busy place until mass-motoring took off in the late 1950s, and I have happy memories of the station on many a summer Saturday. Crowds of people, luggage and parcels had to be moved, as well as lots of those noisy but jolly milk-churns. Stamped on them were the names of their owners, West Marton Dairy, Leeds Dairy or CWS. The churns were brought in by the local trains from the north and west, and by lorry locally, which collected the churns from platforms at the farm-gates. The milk was destined for the populous markets further south, so that the Skipton platforms acted as exchange-points. Fascinated, I would watch the porters wheeling them along the platforms by holding the pivoting-knob on the top, an effective idea. However, the milk-churns have long gone, the milk now transported from the farms direct to Leeds by road-tanker. The local dairies have been absorbed into large groups, and bear another name, for the familiar Milk Marketing Board was replaced by 'Milk Marque', the spelling betraying its Brussels origin. 'Cravendale' milk (Arla Foods plc, Leeds) is sold nationwide in supermarkets. The station was also a changing-point for passengers to and from Bradford, as well as from the branches. Later in this chapter, I describe my first journey along one of them, from Clapham (Yorkshire) to Low Gill, the scenic line through Lonsdale, and then the last train before its closure in January 1953, plus a look at the history of the line. The link to Earby, (with the branch to Barnoldswick), Colne and Burnley, is described later in this chapter.

From the track-diagram, you can calculate the many route-possibilities, available then through a network of railways. It must have been quite a problem for the signalmen coping with all the movements, trains, empty-stock and light-engines to and from the shed; the staff contributed with plenty of smart platform-work. Much later, in the BR-era of 1952, I recall the first electric luggage-trolley, replacing a hand-barrow. The porters had to lower the handle to release the brake, then squeeze the pistol-grip. It must have been over-sensitive, for they had quite a performance at first, the barrow nearly overtaking them down the ramp into the subway with the risk of luggage falling off as they tried to turn the corner at the bottom. Fortunately, they went *under* the line rather than across it . . . Here is typical summer Saturday operation.

Early in the afternoon, Compound 1020 arrives in the back platform, 4, with the Bradford-Morecambe portion of four carriages. Some passengers alight, either to catch the following down Thames-Clyde Express or a train to Lancashire or the branches. The engine uncouples and runs ahead to the shed for turning and servicing; later, he will work back on a Bradford local from the bay platform. A few minutes on and the Leeds-Morecambe express arrives, headed by another Compound, perhaps 1005 (the original Deeley compound, renumbered from 1000). He runs into the main down-platform, 3. The passengers alighting are again for Lancashire or perhaps one of the wayside-stations on the Settle-Carlisle line or along a branch. They would have to wait for the Bradford-Carlisle stopping-train. Now the platform is crowded with people, including relatives and friends seeing their folks off; the crowd surges round the trolleys of luggage, parcels and milk-churns. Behind this *melée*, 1005 has quietly drawn the Leeds-portion forward, reversed into platform 4 and coupled up to the carriages from Bradford. People and luggage are sorted out, the doors slam, the whistle peeps and the Compound, echoing its deep Midland exhaust, hauls out the combined express for Morecambe.

Returning in the up direction, the train would be split on platform 2, the Bradford engine waiting in the bay or behind the goods-lines in the engine-yard opposite Skipton Station South Junction signal-box, where a turntable was available. However, the up portions were often run as separate trains. These residential-expresses ('the resi') formed a feature of life then in those parts, enabling the Leeds and Bradford businessmen to live in Morecambe, rather like their southern counterparts commuting daily from places like Brighton, Herne Bay or Littlehampton. A parallel to these expresses over in Lancashire were the Club Trains from Blackpool, Southport, and also Llandudno, North Wales, which were run for many years by the L&Y, the LNW, and later, the LMS.

Bradford was also served by the 'Carlisle stopper' departing from 'woolopolis' at 4.25 pm, balanced by a departure from Carlisle at 4.35 pm. While doing my National Service at Carlisle later, I often travelled from Carlisle on this train which, over the years, produced a wide range of motive-power, from the MR/LMS 2P 4-4-0s, through Compounds, Black Fives and, to end the steam-era, Jubilees. Typical engines on these trains were 4-4-0s 422, 446, 603 and 683; Class 5s 4853, 4855 and 5080, and in BR-days, Jubilee 45742 *Connaught*, the last of the class.

The line is so well-documented that I confine my remarks to personal observations. The up evening run in summer along the backbone of the Pennines was scenic beyond description. The stopping-train gave the traveller the time to pick out well-known mountains and rivers, as its locomotive steamed peacefully over the viaducts and through the tunnels. It thrills me now to write about it. I recall such a journey in the summer of 1950 so clearly, when I was travelling home from my army camp at Durranhill, Carlisle. Atop the Pennines, Garsdale station, the tank-house and signal-box were aglow in the level rays of the setting-sun as we stopped to set down passengers for the NE branch to Hawes and Wensleydale. The train was waiiting in the bay-platform, headed by one of the old faithful ex-NER G5 0-4-4 tanks, possibly 67345, which saw out the passenger service in 1954. A later run in the same year was especially poignant: in the autumn twilight this time, I watched the guard blowing out the platform-lamps at Crosby Garrett; the station closed shortly afterwards. Where are those lamps now, I wonder?

However, the freight-traffic through Skipton were just as interesting, and there was so much of it, as the account of Hellifield rel;ates. As elsewhere, very little had changed from pre-grouping days. There were still the fitted-freights from Leeds and points south destined for Carlisle, Glasgow and beyond, the Durranhill (Carlisle)—Stourton (Leeds) for example, the Heysham petrol-tanker trains, the Barrow coke-racks, local goods for the Morecambe and Lune Valley lines, and loco-coal for the Skipton and Hellifield depots. And of course there was the endless shunting. While convalescing in the former Whinfield Hospital opposite Skipton South Junction, my mother used to complain of the clanging and banging that went on all night. Similar activities occurred in the extensive exchange-sidings north of the station, with short trip-workings between the up and the down sides, and also through the station to the local yard beside the Keighley Road. This has long been redeveloped into a Tesco store.

These workings were in the hands of ancient 0-6-0s, 2F 3477 (fitted with Belpaire firebox but retaining the spartan cab) and the 1F tank engine 1855, both of 1878 vintage. Others of this type appearing over the years were 1734, 1767, 1802 and 1859. A standard 3F shunter, 7562, came on the scene late in LMS days to work the down exchange-sidings, which provided photographs; later, colleague 47427 gave me recordings of apparently endless shunting. Oddly, these two were the only ones of the class to be seen for miles, yet they belonged to the standard LMS shunter-class, which totalled no fewer than 422—plus 60 of MR origin. Clearly, as in MR days, engines worked at the same place for years. The shunter or pilot from the sub-shed at Keighley, nine miles up the line, another 1F 0-6-0 tank, 1820, occasionally put in an appearance, like his mate, the 0-4-4 tank detailed to work the Worth Valley branch, for light repairs or adjustments and servicing, since Keighley was merely a signing-on point. At different times, 1275, 1361, 1413 and 1430 all turned up. Also of this class, we saw daily 1358 and 1366, one to work the Garsdale stopper, the other the Earby-Barnoldswick branch, some six miles down the Colne line, an interesting little corner of the LMS described later in this chapter.

Ivatt 2-6-2Ts replaced the MR tanks in early-BR days, belatedly consigning the old stagers to the scrapyard. The Ivatts 41241, 41251, 41326 and 41327 appeared at different times, as well as the Riddles standard-version 84013/28. Both types served all over BR, including running on the Oxted-Cranleigh-branch in Surrey, a non-electrified enclave of the former Southern Railway. You may have seen 41241, now in the maroon livery of the Keighley & Worth Valley Railway and running on that line. This preserved railway has acquired many items from the Skipton-area, such as the turntable from Skipton Station South engine-yard, the swivel-bar signal at Barnoldswick, the stockaded turntable at Garsdale and the small signalbox plus gates from Earby Crossing close to my former home, described later.

The marshalling in the local goods-yard mentioned earlier was shared among the MR shunters, but in 1947, incomer 11484 came on the scene, an ex-LYR 0-6-0 saddle-tank. The only other representatives of the LYR were the radial-tanks, based at Manningham (20E), working Bradford-Skipton local-trains, as related in the previous chapter chapter. Earlier, ex-LYR 0-8-0s used to work up from Burnley through Colne on the daily mineral-empties arriving in Skipton at about 2.30 pm. These 'Class 31s' were numbered 12841-12981, every one of which I saw on the Calder Valley line, Halifax, hauling coal from South Yorkshire collieries to Lancashire, also described in another chapter. In the BR era however, I did see their successors on the Skipton-Lancashire line, the 'Austin Seven' 0-8-0s, particularly when heading the balancing-working at about 8.30 pm from Skipton-Colne and East Lancashire. I noted 49508, 49673 and 49674, which also provided attractive recordings passing our house in Skipton Road, Earby.

The LMS code for the Skipton shed was 20F, but the BR-regime changed it to 24G on the division of the Leeds Area (20A) between the Midland and North Eastern Regions. The dividing-line was between Skipton and Shipley. Leeds Holbeck became 55A, while the northern depots of Skipton, Hellifield and Lancaster (Green Ayre) were placed under Accrington (24A), hence the strange 24G shed-plates appearing in the vicinity. With such minor changes, BR retained the LMS scheme of shed-codes, even adopting it for the whole system; for example Nine Elms became 70A and Banbury 84C. These sounded strange to us, accustomed to sheds numbered only up to 32. It represents one of several examples of Midland Railway practice perpetuated by BR, described in the chapter on nationalization.

Goods-trains were arriving and departing from the exchange-sidings constantly, in charge of 4F 0-6-0s, Horwich moguls, 5P5Fs and 2-8-0s, later headed by Jubilees and later still even by Clans and Britannias. Fitted-freights passed through from the south for points north and west, the Barrow coke-racks and the petroleum block-trains from Heysham, not forgetting coal for the depots of Skipton and Hellifield, the wagons marked LOCO COAL, some in *bas-relief* lettering. Many 4Fs were stationed at Skipton, like the old faifhfuls 3893, 3960, 4041 and 4197, all fitted with weatherboard-cabs against that harsh northern climate.

They hauled the heavy stone-trains from Swinden Quarry near Cracoe on the Grassington branch and even continued to work some main-line freights almost to the end of steam. Of course, long before that, this 1911-design was outshone by newer and more powerful locomotives such as Stanier 2-8-0s, Britannias, Clans and 9F 2-10-0s. The 4Fs were used as maids-of-all-work, and so were seen on all kinds of trains: trip-workings, branch-lines and even excursions to Morecambe and Blackpool during the Wakes holidays of the manufacturing towns. The class totalled 772, and so was the most numerous on the LMS, actually ten per cent of the entire locomotive-fleet. I have already discussed large classes and old survivors. The local population was swelled when the Hellifield contingent arrived on the closure of that depot in 1963. On the main-line, few tank-engines were to be seen, not even the ubiquitous 2-6-4s: the radial 2-4-2s were soldiering on, such as 10671 and 10795. Even rarer were ex-LNWR engines: no Super-Ds, but the afternoon up Barrow coke-racks would occasionally produce a 'Cauliflower' or more rarely, a 'Coal Engine.'

Under the BR regime, Ivatt light 2-6-0s soon replaced the old 1F and 2F 0-6-0s which were withdrawn for scrapping; after all, they had served for some seventy years. More 2-8-0s, of both the LMS and Austerity varieties, came in too, as well as Horwich moguls until they too were withdrawn in the sixties. The once-ubiquitous 4Fs followed them to the scrap-heap; their replacements turned out to be the last stud of engines at Skipton, the Riddles Standard Class 4 light 4-6-0s, including 75019, 75039 and 75048. But the 'spider's-web' was shrinking: the Barnoldswick branch closed in October 1965, the Skipton exchange sidings and the sheds in 1967, the line to Colne in 1970, described later. Even the expresses to Carlisle and Glasgow/Edinburgh vanished in favour of an occasional dmu to serve the surviving and now-unstaffed wayside-halts such as Gargrave and Kirkby Stephen. But the Grassington branch remains open, to serve the now-enormous limestone quarry at Swinden, near Cracoe, a mile short of the original terminus of the line at Threshfield/Grassington. The Tilcon company removed almost an entire hill, opening up vistas of Wharfedale towards Kettlewell from the Skipton road near Cracoe. Standard 4 light 4-6-0s took over the stone-trains, giving way in turn to class 31 diesels, two working in tandem. The former Skipton engine-shed yard and exchange-sidings site on the south-west side of the main-line is fenced off, a factory-estate, the fate of many a former railway-site. The line has been slimmed to a mere double-track with loops, complete with 25 KVa catenary from Leeds, which ends here. Marshalling was concentrated in the big yard at Healey Mills, at Horbury near Wakefield, but even this became redundant on the ending of single-wagon loads; freight runs in block trains now.

Hellifield in the 1940s

The origin and significance of this junction arising apparently in the middle of nowhere through an accident of geography will become clear as you read on. A number of similar isolated junctions exist both in Britain and abroad. After brief glimpses of the junction and engine-shed on family trips to Scotland during the second war, father and I often visited the station later while in the Dales, cycling up past the modern council-houses lining the long station-approach and walking through the echoing, tiled, subway under goods-lines to reach the single island-platform. Now a listed-building, its ornate Victorian cast-ironwork awning-supports have become familiar to railfans through the initials MR cast into the scrollwork, all now restored. It is sad to see it now, deserted, with the engine-sheds gone and many tracks ripped up.

Hellifield was a super place to watch trains. Now let us roll back time to those glorious days of the '40s, despite—or rather because of— the 1939 war. 'For the duration', Hellifield was a tremendously busy place, with troop-trains and overcrowded expresses on both the Carlisle and Morecambe/ Carnforth routes. Then there were the munitions-trains that ran day and night—and all the time the hard-pressed crews had to make do with locomotives often in need of maintenance. The island-platform would be crowded with both service-people and 'civvies', arrived from or destined for the Manchester area along the ex-L&Y branch through Blackburn. Knots of enginemen and guards congregated here too, coming off duty or waiting to sign on. Well into the post-war period, a bookstall operated here, as well as a busy refreshment-room, to cater for the travellers changing trains. Hellifield's *raison d'être* was created by the junction of the Midland Railway with the L&Y branch up the Ribble valley from Blackburn. The MR had encouraged Manchester and Lancashire traffic generally at Carlisle in order to compete with the West Coast line of the LNWR. After both the Midland and the West Coast routes were brought into the LMS Group, the new company, to rationalize operations, closed the L&Y shed, in the vee of the junction, in 1927, concentrating the motive-power at the former MR shed. This explained the frequent appearance of an ex-L&Y engine there, a radial-tank such as 10675 and sometimes an Ironclad/Jumbo 0-6-0. I noted 12131, 12260 and 12615 but by the later 1940s their work was often carried out by ex-MR 0-6-0s, 2Fs, 3Fs and 4Fs. Ex-L&Y or LMS 0-8-0s too appeared on goods-traffic from the Blackburn line.

At the south end of the station, we would see a stopping-train for the branch in the bay-platform, headed usually—and appropriately—by a Horwich mogul: 2845 was one example, but often a Derby 2-6-2 tank would fulfil this duty, such as 21, pictured. The tank engines worked only to Blackburn, the moguls through to Manchester. In 1946, one of the new Ivatt class 2MTs of the same wheel-arrangement, 1205 pictured, was allocated to replace a Derby 2-6-2. The big Hellifield South signal-box controlled the junction, the goods-loops and sidings with brackets of signals, many fitted with upper-quadrant arms by then, and we would look up the two lines for trains approaching. However, the main line curved sharply up to the left towards Otterburn and Bell Busk, cutting off our line of sight. Set into the hill facing the platform was the coaler, an antiquated affair. It comprised simply a loop-line where the engines received their coal from wagons set as usual on a higher level behind, and inside a long shed. Far from the ease and efficiency of those coaling-towers erected by the LMS in the 1930s, the coal was shovelled out of the wagons into tubs, which were pushed along narrow-gauge tracks out to two coaling-points to tip their contents into the tenders and bunkers. That was a heavy, dusty job, the demise of which no one will regret.

'The Hoodoo Engine'

This was the name given by the *Halifax Courier & Guardian* newspaper to the unfortunate 2-6-2 tank-engine, 183, that you have read about earlier. He had been transferred from Sowerby Bridge to Hellifield, but the poor engine kept on derailing, and so evidently he had not 'learned to do better.' Here he is, standing on his new engine-shed opposite the station platform. I do not know the further career of this unfortunate engine.

Hellifield Shed

The north end of the platform afforded a grandstand-view of the depot where a few engines could usually be seen on shed, 4F 0-6-0s, an ex-MR 3F 0-6-0, perhaps a Horwich mogul or a Derby 2-6-2 tank, while on the siding alongside the shed, a 3F 0-6-0 would be standing next to the large snowplough, which bore the title LMS writ large. Examples I saw standing ready for this task were 3332, 3381/7, 3665 and 3774. The 2F 0-6-0s were rarer by this time, but, up to about 1946, we saw one now and again, for example, 3038, 3144 and 3173, the latter shedded there for years. A Black Five, perhaps 5049, 5054 or 5184, would be preparing for a departure to Carnforth, or to pilot a Royal Scot to Ais Gill en route for Carlisle, and once a 20A Jubilee, unaccountably taken off one of these down expresses—*before* The Long Drag. Perhaps he was failing, or was commandeered to run to Morecambe or Blackburn. The Scots expresses, the morning down from Leeds and the afternoon St Pancras in both directions were highlights of interest with their Royal Scot or Jubilee officiating. The up afternoon trains were usually marshalled separately, the Edinburgh portion normally hauled by a Compound from Carlisle to Leeds. Hellifield was home to 927/8, 931/2, 1004/5/6 and 1014, while visitors included: 910/1/3, 1002, 1020/22/40/3-5/62/79/92/7, 1119/21/36/45/92/6; with so many around, it was a good thing we liked Compounds. The Morecambe business-express, 'the resi', arriving at around 6pm, often too late for us to see, was the province of another Compound, a task later taken over by a Holbeck Black Five as the compounds were gradually withdrawn. The first to go for scrap, in 1946, were 1002 and 1029, of the original Midland class.

I well recall an exciting glimpse of a Royal Scot back in 1945. I had been staying overnight with my father at his Rolls-Royce hostel in Barnoldswick during my Easter holidays. This gave us a flying-start to Dales-cycling, avoiding the five-mile climb out of Halifax, and the thirty-mile ride altogether. We did not call in at Hellifield on that day, bypassing it on the A.682 road Gisburn to Long Preston, the first wayside-station to the north of the junction. Its name derives from the mile-long village straggling along the A.65 trunk-road. We sat there on the platform-seat, since the down Scots express was due, and we expected to see it working hard to get up speed after its stop at Hellifield. Not a bit of it—the Royal Scot 4-6-0 came flying through—only a mile or so from its standing-start; it was only afterwards that we noticed the gradient-post indicating a gentle descent from Hellifield to the valley-floor of the Ribble and along to Skir Beck and Settle Junction.

Taper-boiler Scot 6132 *The King's Regiment (Liverpool)* was doing 60mph we estimated, and the crew certainly looked all set to make a valiant ascent of The Long Drag to Blea Moor, the engine newly converted and the fireman having carefully built up the fire, the steam-pressure and filled the boiler. I remember the scene as if it were yesterday, and my father really enjoyed those few seconds too. It is worth mentioning that the overbridge before Long Preston (over which we had cycled from Barnoldswick) is used nowadays to park a road-tanker in order to refill the thirsty water-tanks of the enthusiasts' specials, such as *The Cumbrian Mountain Express*. After the rebuilding of 6103 *Royal Engineer* in 1943 with a Stanier 2A taper-boiler described earlier, more locomotives had received the treatment, as steel became available after the war. At this time fifteen had been 'converted', to use the official term, but none of the last twenty, newer, members of the class; 6146 *The Rifle Brigade* was the highest-numbered engine converted at that time.

The Midland 4F 0-6-0s, numerous at both Skipton and Hellifield, were mostly fitted with weatherboard tender-cabs against inclement weather. I noted 3893, 3960, 3989, 4008, 4009 and LMS-built 4042 appearing among many others. They hauled the loco-coal trains to supply the depot, through-goods to Carlisle and Morecambe/Lancaster/Carnforth, as well as servicing several wayside yards down the branch, such as Gisburn, Clitheroe and the cement-works at Chatburn. In addition to these, to the north was a further branch to be serviced, the Lune Valley running from Clapham through Ingleton to Low Gill on the West Coast route. Ingleton, Kirkby Lonsdale, Barbon and Sedbergh needed house-coal like everywhere else, a steady traffic on most lines at that time. The ubiquitous 3Fs and 4Fs were in charge of these pick-up trains too, the passenger-services being hauled by Derby 2-6-2 or 2-6-4 tanks. I cover the history of this line in detail further on, a branch that is central to the saga of the Settle-Carlisle route. The wayside-stations on the S & C main line, all open then except Scotby and Cotehill, had also to be served with pick-up goods-trains, conveying coal, general merchandise, plus farm-implements and feedstuffs for the isolated hill-farms of the central Pennines.

Five miles down the Blackburn branch lay Gisburn, its station a hive of activity during World War 2, used as a depot to receive bombs and shells for storage. Frequent trains brought these munitions, which were transhipped into lorries for the last stage of their journey to storage-points along quiet wooded byways nearby. The Nissen huts have gone, but their concrete bases remain among the trees. One of these byways, Carter Lane, was closed to the public completely 'for the duration'. The special trains must have made big demands on the local motive-power: from our vantage-point on the road-bridge, father and I often saw three engines in the spacious goods-yard, usually two 3Fs and a 4F. Locomotives from further afield would appear up the branch too, such as Jubilee 5678 *De Robeck*, which trundled into Hellifield one day in 1945 with a long mixed-goods off the Blackburn branch. To this schoolboy, the consecutive number was interesting. The engine may have been shedded at Upperby (12B) at the time, working a triangular diagram to return home.

The Hellifield main line was constantly busy with through-freight, both general merchandise and fully-fitted van-trains, often diverted into a loop to leave the platforms clear for the Scottish or Morecambe expresses. The goods, such as the Durranhill-Stourton, were hauled by 4Fs, Horwich moguls or Stanier 8F 2-8-0s. Most of them carried a small snow-plough fitted below the buffer-beam, against the expectation of some snow on the line during several months of the year on the 1,200ft plateau from Ribblehead through Garsdale to Ais Gill. Some Class Fives were similarly fitted. Regulars were the Heysham tanker-train, headed by a 4F, and from the same direction would come the Barrow coke-trains, already described. Stanier 8F 2-8-0s would roll through bound for the West Midlands (then called 'The Black Country') with heavy trains of steel-products from the Lanarkshire industrial area between Motherwell and Glasgow.

The Ingleton Branch Line (The Lune Valley Railway)

I was missing Carlisle and my friends there and so visited army-pal Smudger as soon as I could after his demob in January 1952 and the worst of the winter-weather. A sunny Friday evening in April saw my departure. As no through-train ran on the Settle-Carlisle line in the evening, a cross-country journey provided the answer: Skipton to Clapham (Yorkshire), change there for Low Gill on the West Coast main line, and finally, a local-train over Shap to Carlisle. This is what could be achieved when there was a rail-network.

The first train, departing at 5.39 pm from Skipton, was a Bradford/Leeds to Morecambe 'resi' express, the business train I had often seen passing my school further down the line. Compound 41005 took me past Settle Junction to the tiny junction of Clapham, where the author crossed, alone, to the back platform to await the branch train up the Lune Valley to Low Gill. It was nice to see its motive-power was a Derby 2-6-4 tank-engine. He ran round the two carriages smartly, coupled up, and set off promptly at 6.36 pm. He sped along the branch, calling at its wayside stations, Ingleton, Kirkby Lonsdale, Barbon and Sedbergh, all picturesque, traditional, stone-built stations. Almost an hour later, we curved to the right over the long red-sandstone viaduct approaching the junction with the West Coast route at Low Gill. The little train terminated in the back-platform to leave the main-line clear, but the trains continuing through to Tebay ran straight into the down main platform. The connection, in charge of a Black Five, was again an all-stations affair, stopping at Tebay, Shap, Clifton & Lowther, Penrith, Calthwaite and Southwaite. It arrived on time, and, sure enough, friend Smudger was waiting on the Citadel station. Local trains no longer run on the wcml, after the closure of the country stations in the '50s and '60s and the electrification afterwards. Here is a brief history of the branch line and its relationship with the neighbouring Settle-Carlisle line, starting with the trip the author and his father made one cold January night. The poster on the station at Ingleton read:

Closure of THE INGLETON BRANCH LINE
(The Lune Valley Railway)
on 30 January 1954

This time, it was not the closure of a branch-line, but of a complete through-route. In the Skipton paper, the *Craven Herald & Pioneer*, we had read these details, and this is why my father and I found ourselves in the station yard at Ingleton on that cold January evening for the last train to Low Gill and back. There were not the crowds that turned out for the numerous railway closures a decade later, when there often had to be several 'last trains' on the particular line, with the local notabilities riding on the very last one. In 1954, most people did not have cars and therefore could not participate, so in this sense, the author was lucky to be at that isolated spot that night. All the same, a surprising number did turn up, considering the venue and the season.

Of the 150 who booked at Ingleton that night, not all actually travelled, but merely kept their tickets as souvenirs. Instead of the usual two non-corridor carriages, BR had sportingly turned out for the 6.52 pm train five corridor compartment-coaches, but it was still a squash sitting crushed together, four-a-side. Very probably more passengers were on board that night than on any train since the opening day of the line. Many boarded in Victorian costume and some of the ladies even wore mourning veils. Although we were unaware of it at the time, Lord and Lady Shuttleworth and Mr and Mrs Roger Fulford had invited a number of people to join their private party on board the train. More were squeezed on at the intermediate stations, but nothing was visible in the darkness along the Lune Valley. How different from that lovely Spring evening trip only last year!

Many passengers stepped out on to the draughty branch platform at Low Gill to watch the big tank engine run round the train for the last journey. It was one of the usual Derby 2-6-4T locomotives based at Tebay (11D) serving this branch; they also acted as bankers on the Shap incline. Twenty years earlier, the surviving ex-LNW 4-6-2 'Prince of Wales tanks' had been pensioned off here. Other habitués of the line were the smaller Derby 2-6-2Ts, 64, 67, 41, 21 and even 1. The LMS 2313 *The Prince* had been another regular 2-6-4, but tonight it was (BR) 42396. Interestingly, the newspaper photograph showed the engine-headlamp still bearing its LMS number 2396.

A wreath was presented by Mrs Fulford to Mr Jack Bird of Ingleton, who placed it on the front of the engine while a piper led the Kirkby

Lonsdale Brass Band playing *Will Ye No' Come Back Again*? Some spectators were in tears. Refreshments were served to the private party, while, sadly, we boarded on the very last regular passenger train on the Lune Valley line. No one said much, each occupied with his or her own thoughts. Once back at Ingleton, the 2-6-4 tank was put into the engine-shed for the last time, while the crowd gave a cheer and sang *Auld Lang Syne*. They melted away to their cars and the station became deserted—permanently. The only exceptions were the termly special trains, run for the benefit of the boarding—and county-schools along the line, but even these were eventually withdrawn, as the children were increasingly transported by car. The goods traffic continued for over a decade, when the line was maintained in first-rate order as a relief route. This proved invaluable in the severe winter of 1962-63, when the Settle-Carlisle route became blocked by snow at the usual spot, between Dent station and Garsdale. In 1965, the Clapham-Ingleton goods service was withdrawn and the track lifted two years later.

During the 1950s, BR had examined the north-west railway network, in particular seeking the most satisfactory route from Leeds to Carlisle. At first, it seemed the Lune Valley railway would be chosen, rather than the longer Settle-Carlisle; this could then be shut, with a saving in maintenance-costs. A plan was drawn up for a Freightliner-route and to equip the Lune Valley with colour-light signals. However, the view prevailed that a closure of the S&C would cause a greater hardship to its many rural communities than to close the Lune Valley, and so this line received the axe. With hindsight this decision is hard to understand now: the further increase in motor-traffic now transports both the S&C inhabitants and their goods, at greater convenience and more cheaply; several stations were in any case distant from the communities they purported to serve; and the preponderance of goods-traffic then was coal, no longer an issue. So, from the economic viewpoint, the higher maintenance-costs of the S&C have to be met.

A further plan, to electrify the East Coast Main Line, with the fastest journey-time to Scotland, would downgrade the West Coast route. This would now focus on London-Manchester/Liverpool, nullifying any advantage in retaining the Ingleton link as a relief line; furthermore, the planned closure of the Settle-Carlisle route north of Skipton, along with the Lune Valley would allow the whole of the Midland north of Leeds to be downgraded—and closed north of Skipton, particularly after the lifting of the Earby/Barnoldswick/Colne branches. The preservationists of the Ribblehead viaduct however gained the support of Mrs Thatcher's government—especially with transport-minister Michael Portillo in favour; the great viaduct was upgraded to a standard higher than when it was new, and so the Settle-Carlisle and Settle-Carnforth routes remain open. Furthermore, in September 1995 a new electric service began on the Leeds-Bradford-Skipton/Ilkley lines.

On a visit to the Lune Valley line during the 1970s, the author noted even the trackbed had gone in places, taken for road-widening, as is so often the case. The narrow railway-arch north-west of Ingleton had gone, carrying the line over the A.65 Keighley-Kendal turnpike road at Thornton-in-Lonsdale, enabling the narrow kink in the road to be straightened. The S-bend bridge over the railway south of Kirkby Lonsdale had been swept away also for a new road alignment, straight and level, partly over the old trackbed. This may well have been the original line of the road before the railway came. And so the wheel turns full circle, one might say.

However, the line had had its swansong, for its last few years saw traffic passing along it of a density previously undreamt of. In the 1960s, British Rail's London Midland Region was busy electrifying the West Coast Route from Weaver Junction (north of Crewe) to Carlisle, necessitating closure of this artery every Sunday for months. The result was the diversion of all traffic on Sundays through Blackburn to Hellifield (another cross-country line threatened with closure, but surviving as a single-track), to bear left at Settle Junction to Clapham, right there for Ingleton to regain the wcml at Low Gill. Because all the trains were by then diesel-hauled, especially after the end of most of BR steam in August 1967, the author paid little attention to it, apart from one photograph of a 'Peak' at Newsholme, approaching Hellifield. But in an earlier era, the family had been lucky once, on returning from an outing to The Lakes. On driving home from Windermere, they had the extreme good fortune to meet a West Coast Route express headed by a Princess Royal Pacific. It ran right alongside—an ideal spot for train-watching—a million-to-one chance to see it there. Such power had never been seen even on the Settle-Carlisle line, owing to weight restrictions, let alone on a cross-country link such as the Lune Valley. One must assume that the train had been diverted via Hellifield and Ingleton because of a mishap on the West Coast main line and that the local bridges had been strengthened.

The Lune Valley Line: A Historical Perspective

Here is an outline of the origins of this railway and its relationship with its famous neighbour, the Settle-Carlisle line, on which detailed reading is available. The diverted expresses recall the situation immediately before the building of the Settle to Carlisle line through the Pennine Hills a century earlier, a time when the Midland Railway Company, expanding rapidly in all directions, urgently wanted their own route to Carlisle and Scotland. Elsewhere, the MR's relentless expansion is described. The 'Little North Western' had intended to continue its line to join the LNWR at Low Gill but, following the end of the Railway Mania in a financial crisis, it pulled in its horns to terminate its single-line branch from Clapham at the village of Ingleton. The MR take-over of the Little North Western in 1852 clearly highlights the fact that, if only its further section had been there, the MR would have gained their through route to Scotland at a stroke. For years, the LNWR had denied the MR even a through-carriage beyond Tebay. It was alarmed at the Midland's unending expansion, exemplified by syphoning-off its traffic further south—and at the manoeuvrings by other companies, for example the GNR and NER, to build the missing link to gain a foothold in the region. It therefore took the initiative and pre-empted the matter by bridging the gap—with a double-track line too—from Low Gill to Thornton-in-Lonsdale. Opening in 1861, it scowled across the viaduct at Ingleton and the MR, firmly blocking its progress to Carlisle and Scotland.

In 1868, the Midland again proposed to the LNWR that the its traffic pass along from its terminus at Ingleton via the LNWR to Low Gill and on to Carlisle. Its proposition was rejected, so the MR put its Settle & Carlisle bill to Parliament. No sooner was this passed than the LNWR had second thoughts, accepting the MR proposition. But the Midland's Act for the Settle-Carlisle line was now on the statute book and, unfortunately for them, Parliament would not allow a Withdrawing Act. The S & C was seen as an obligation which, if not carried out, would undermine confidence in railway development. This decision is hard to understand now, since by 1869 all the main routes had been built, but it has to be seen from the perspective of the Victorians. They loved their railways, which after all were the latest means of serving their expanding industry, as well as carrying passengers quickly and cheaply. With the wisdom of hindsight, it is all too easy to make a judgement. First, one must reflect that the internal combustion engine was not yet invented, would not come on to the scene for another two decades, and not appear commercially on the roads for more than three. So the railway remained the unchallenged mode of transport. The inference was that considerable potential still remained for railway-building to fill the gaps in the network, hence the House's attitude.

But two more points deserve attention. First, that the large majority of lines built since 1860, rural links, did not have the necessary traffic potential, particularly freight, to break even financially or make small profits, but were seen by managers as important feeders to the trunk routes. The branches' lack of traffic potential was a major factor in their early succumbing to road competition, while the original trunk lines of the 1830s remain open and increasingly busy, and have therefore been upgraded. Second, both the LNWR and the MR were put into the LMS group in 1923, *de facto* demoting the MR's Settle-Carlisle line to a second-rate status, in effect questioning the soundness of the rationale for its construction in the first place. The Great Central Railway through the East Midlands to London (Marylebone), opened in 1899, represented a further example of wasteful duplication in the name of competition, proved by its failure to attract the traffic envisaged when planned.

Both projects demonstrate the arguments concerning Private Sector versus Government railway development. With the latter in charge, competing and therefore loss-making lines would not have been built, thereby saving a great deal of private capital, which could have been more effectively utilized elsewhere in the economy. This situation largely pertained abroad, where a desirable network-plan was drawn up at the outset. They, however, had the advantage of building later, having other countries' mistakes—notably Britain's—from which to learn. But if the S & C had not been constructed through Ribblehead and over Ais Gill summit, what a loss it would have been aesthetically, quite apart from its tremendous strategic value in two world wars.

Developments on the S & C line

Following accidents in the early days of railways caused by facing-points, the Midland had developed such an aversion to them that not one was laid along the whole seventy miles of its new railway between Settle and Carlisle in the 1870s. The lack of these points, which would have allowed a switch straight into through-loops, was a disadvantage when a goods-train needed to be side-tracked because of a following express. The only way was to put it into a siding by careful and slow setting-back to clear the main line. We saw a good example of this one morning at Horton-in-Ribblesdale, the station before Ribblehead going north. Father and I had taken a rest from cycling the hilly road to watch trains for a while—particularly as the morning Thames-Clyde Express was almost due. As we arrived, a long goods-train came up the incline and stopped opposite the signal-box. The bobby told him to 'go in', that is, back the long train into a siding. Horton had two sets of sidings, a group for the limestone quarry on the down-side, and a refuge on the up-side. The Black Five first had to draw forward to clear the points and then reverse his train carefully across both main-lines into the up-siding. The train was too long to be accommodated as the siding was already partially occupied, so the guard had to uncouple the front section, which the engine hauled back to the down-line and then set back into the quarry-sidings. As you can imagine, all this took some time, but there was a sufficient margin before the Glasgow express. All the same, we felt nervous, but the bobby had no doubt ascertained from control the expected time of the express and calculated he had the time to complete the manoeuvre. I guess the loop ahead, at Blea Moor, was already occupied, leaving Horton as the only option.

The same laborious procedure had been necessary at the Long Meg anhydrite-quarry sidings near Lazonby, in the Eden valley on the way down to Carlisle, but here the operations had been streamlined by laying facing-points with loops for arriving and departing trains, since this was such a busy spot, often having more than one train at a time. The 1955 flat-roofed brick signal-box (now closed) is reminiscent of the war-time air-raid shelters, contrasting with the timber Midland signal-cabins along the line.

Accidents had happened in the past when a goods-train, slowly reversing into a refuge-siding, had not cleared in time. Examples are the well-known disaster in a snowstorm in 1876 on the GNR at Abbots Ripton, East Coast main line, and on the LMS at Charfield, Glos., one night in 1928. In both cases, a following express had run through the warning signals. These accidents may well have been averted if the goods had been able to run straight into a loop over facing-points, leaving a margin of time.

The quarries at Horton and Long Meg recall several other limestone developments along the line. The quarry at Stainforth, north of Settle, became the first S & C freight-customer in 1873 even before the completion of the line, allowing the MR to begin recouping some of its vast construction-costs. It was controlled by the Stainforth Sidings signal-box but, when the quarry was closed, the sidings and box were removed. Between Stainforth and Horton is another quarry with sidings, at Helwith Bridge, also without a station, lying on a short stretch of level track (a former glacial lake of the last ice-age), a brief respite for hard-working locomotives and their crews pounding up 'The Long Drag'.

Looplines put in north of Skipton formed another wartime development on the S & C. While cycling the five miles from Skipton to Gargrave with father on the way to a welcome lunch of boiled eggs at Mrs Bell's farm, Otterburn, Bell Busk—a delicacy during the food-rationing—the author was continuing to glance at the railway across the valley and spotted an unusual brick-arched structure. It was supporting a water-tank. A Mr Delaney had opened a limestone-quarry beside the line and later he developed another, further back on Copy Hill. From here a tramway carried the stone down to the main line, where the Delaney's Sidings signal-box controlled the points and signals. Here, up and down loops were put in during WW2 as accommodation for goods-trains to hold them clear of the Skipton yards, now extra-busy with munitions-trains. However, following the post-war decline of traffic, BR issued a notice on 4 May 1970 proposing to close many stations on the S & C. It is thought that the loops, sidings and signal-box were removed around this time. The electric pump to lift water from the river Aire, along with its generator and the lineside tank were also dismantled. Following the closure of the Lune Valley line, already described, BR's agenda was to close the railway completely north of Skipton, to avoid the costly maintenance of the S & C mountain-section, or even north of Leeds, to concentrate Scottish traffic on the east-coast main-line. However, the Friends of the Settle-Carlisle Line who had the Ribblehead viaduct refurbished put paid to these plans, and later the Leeds-Bradford-Ilkley triangle and the Shipley-Skipton line were electrified for commuters. The author is indebted to Mr Jeremy Taylor, who volunteered some of this information on 7 September 2012, and whose family has owned the Small House Farm at Copy Hill for over two hundred years. Grateful thanks are due to the author's old friend John Wolfenden of Linton-in-Craven for his research by perusing old maps and investigating the site amongst the undergrowth and mud.

Finally on S & C developments, another development for the second war, a munitions-factory, was constructed beside the down-line about four miles west of Keighley, on the stretch where the railway runs approximately westwards. Sidings were laid with a ground-frame, 'Steeton North', controlled by the Steeton & Silsden Station box. The Airedale General Hospital now occupies the site. On the subject of these ground-frames—put in to control sidings in occasional use—the S & C had several. The Milk Depot south of Appleby station has been mentioned, and another was the Strong Close Siding up the line from Keighley station, serving the eponymous foundry of the CWS (Co-operative).

Skipton-Earby-Colne & the Earby-Barnoldswick branch

Leaving Skipton, the Carlisle line, the 'Little North Western', runs west for half a mile, then swings to the right in a quarter-circle at North Junction (formerly Engine Shed Junction), before diving under the Niffany Bridge carrying the road to Colne, Preston and Blackpool, while the branch from Skipton to Colne continued straight on from the North Junction. Built before the Little NW to Settle and Lancaster, the line to Colne formed the north-western tip of the Leeds & Bradford Railway, opened in 1848. This double-track line represented a convenient trans-Pennine link between East Lancashire and Leeds, as well as forming part of a useful route across the Pennine Hills through Skipton to Bolton Abbey and then York for destinations such as Darlington and Scarborough. The Colne East signalbox was the last of the Midland timber structures, for here the MR branch made an end-on junction with the East Lancashire Railway, later the LYR, afterwards the LMS. It was in this yard where, in the early days of the railway, an engine exploded. The increasing steam-pressures of locomotive-boilers, compared with the older stationary-engines, had overtaken metallurgical technology. Furthermore, safety-valves were unreliable and capable of abuse, rendering boiler-explosions fairly common. Soon after the official opening on 1 February 1849, a viaduct was built across the North Valley in Colne to enable through-running from Skipton to Burnley, Manchester, Liverpool and Preston. Some trains ran through this way from Leeds/Bradford, in an attempt by the Midland to compete with the direct L&Y trans-Pennine route to Lancashire further south.

Between Skipton and Colne, the line ran through a sparsely-populated dairy-farming district, with stations serving the villages of Elslack, Thornton-in-Craven, with a short branch serving Spencer's limestone quarry, closed before my observations, Earby and Foulridge (pronounced 'Foal-'), all provided with sidings. Elslack and Earby had a goods-depot as well, but Elslack and Thornton did little business during the 1940s-50s. Thornton's siding/cattle dock was removed around the end of the LMS-era, allowing signalling to be reduced to a ground-frame on the up platform, but the ex-MR signals remained operational into the 1950s. A mile or so south-west of Thornton, the line crossed the A.56 Skipton-Colne road at Earby Crossing, not a block-post however, but provided simply to control the crossing. It forms an anecdote later. Half-a-mile further lay the largest intermediate station, at Earby (pop c.5,500 in.1949), a township where cotton-mills had been erected in the 1840s. Additional importance had accrued in 1871 when it became the junction for the short branch to Barnoldswick (pop 10,000 in 1949). Facing the sidings at Earby, the back-platform (the track leading to the goods depot) was the usual base for the branch-train, but for flexibility the up-platform was signalled for down departures as well. This was useful to handle the Wakes Weeks (annual holidays) specials to west-coast resorts. During the week preceding the holidays, the stock for the specials was stabled in the three coal-sidings. The signals were almost all of MR design, the tall bracket for the down-line departure/siding from the up platform especially outstanding with wooden arms. The large signalbox stood beyond the level-crossing over the minor road to Salterforth, nicknamed 'Klondyke' after a nineteenth-century cotton boom—and the 1940s pre-fabricated houses—with the only upper-quadrant signals in the vicinity, a standard LMS home-and-distant on steel tubular post, the up home-signal at Earby.

Passing Barnoldswick Junction box, the line continued on a gentle rise following the trickle of the Earby Beck through pastoral country, crossing County Brook into Lancashire, before reaching the wayside station of Foulridge. At this point, the Leeds & Liverpool Canal converges as the valley narrows to the low watershed, crossing with a short tunnel near the two reservoirs—Lake Burwain is one—which feed water into the summit pool of the canal here. The railway however needed only a cutting, before curving left to descend into Colne and the beginning of the industrial belt that ribbons sporadically along the small Pendle Water/Lancashire Calder to Nelson and Burnley. Despite the through-station at Colne, the LMS frustrated through-passengers by continuing the LYR practice of terminating most trains from Manchester/Accrington/Preston here, including the through-carriages from London (Euston). Returning to Earby from visits to relatives in Preston and having already changed at Accrington's triangular station, the author's family had to change again at Colne for a local to Skipton, some of which were extended to run all-stations to Bradford. The large goods-warehouse at Colne had the usual large notice painted under the eaves:

LONDON MIDLAND & SCOTTISH RAILWAY COMPANY
GOODS & GRAIN WAREHOUSE

After my father was 'directed' to Rolls-Royce to work on jet-engine development during the 1939-war, we travelled from Halifax to Barnoldswick several times, a journey involving four trains: the ex-LNER (GNR) branch to Keighley, described in my chapter on Halifax, a local to Skipton, then another for Colne, which we left at Earby for the final stage, the branch-train to Barnoldswick. It was quite feasible providing we had good connections, and the parallel journey today by bus would be little quicker. The antique roads of the West Riding ensure that the thirty miles still take an hour by car; no wonder lorries are called 'waggons' in the vernacular. This train-journey again highlights the possibilities of travel when the country had a proper rail-network. The traffic is outlined on both lines together, but first, a word on the geography of the branch.

The Barnoldswick Branch

Since 'Barnoldswick' is such a mouthful, it had become abbreviated to 'Barlick.' in the usual English way. However, the full name is used here. The branch turned to the right off the main-line to Colne at Barnoldswick Junction, where the fireman would lean out to the left to take the ringless single-line staff from the signalman standing at the lineside. Becoming single-track immediately, the line curved sharply to the north-west, climbing through a shallow cutting to the village of Salterforth with its cotton-mill, but no station. The gradient increased over the Leeds & Liverpool Canal to the watershed, the iron bridge being the principal structure. A short descent through a cutting and under two roads including Rainhall Road, took the tracks into the single-platform terminus.

The signal controlling movements over the level-crossing immediately beyond the platform, was an ancient rotary board-and-disc. Such rarities derived from the early days of railways in the 1840s; the author did see one other, in Manningham goods-yard, outside Bradford. During his observations, the signal at Barnoldswick was not used. The road-traffic was light over the Station Road-Wellhouse Road crossing, and the footplatemen could see when it was safe to open the two long gates. The 0-4-4 tank would then draw forward into the coal-yard, where the fireman altered the points for the engine to run round its short train into Rainhall cutting. A ground-frame here controlled the run-round loop-points, from where the engine drifted back onto its train for the return-journey, all-stations to Skipton. The branch-engines were ex-MR 0-4-4 tanks, either 1358 or 1366, the first rather faded, but the latter smart in gilt counter-shaded-red lettering. The author's 1947 photograph shows this engine preparing to leave with the mid-morning train from the branch-platform at Earby, piloted by 3295, a 3F 0-6-0, also a long-server at Skipton. The trains did not run on an interval-basis but gave an occasional service in the morning and in the afternoon. Between the passenger-services, an ex-MR 3F 0-6-0 (earlier, a 2F 0-6-0), such as 3295, would run through from Skipton with the goods for Barnoldswick, the train consisting mainly of engine-coal for the mills and house-coal. Sometimes, however, the mid-morning departure from Earby took the 3F as a pilot engine, as shown in my photograph. Its purpose was not to assist the 0-4-4 tank with its three carriages, but to enable it to run up the line in order to shunt the coal-yard, since the branch was operated with a single-line staff on the basis of 'one-engine-in-steam'. The staff would be handed to the pilot on its outward-run at Barnoldswick Junction to enable it to return legitimately down the branch with empty wagons after the passenger-train had departed. This routine occurred when the stock of coal in the yard sufficed for immediate needs, as in this summer picture. After the returning passenger-train had cleared Earby, the 3F would bring his rake of empty wagons down the line and run through Earby to Skipton, where he deposited them in the up Broughton Road exchange sidings.

Main-Line Trains: passenger

The Skipton-Colne trains were composed of a mixture of ex-MR and early-LMS stock, non-corridor as befitted a stopping-train, but on an early journey, in 1945, we travelled in a 'family-compartment.' The seats were the normal five-a-side bench-type, except that one corner was occupied, unusually, with a small WC. They had been designed to take a family, including servants, on holiday. The carriage was ex-MR 17328. These three-coach trains were usually hauled by one of Skipton's 2P 4-4-0s, maybe 406, 414 or 519, the numbers writ large in gold/gilt-counter-shaded red, easy for identification at a distance. The line was also served with semi-fast trains, also hauled by the 4-4-0s, succeeding ex-LYR radial 2-4-2 tanks. However late in 1946, one of the 1932 0-4-4 tanks from the Leeds-Ilkley branch, 1904, was in evidence for a period, before being moved to Lancaster to haul trains on the

Morecambe-Heysham—Lancaster triangle, as observed by M.N. Clay and pictured by D. Binns (see bibliography). In my account of Apperley Bridge, I mentioned the posting away of the 0-4-4Ts to Lancaster to replace the ex-MR electric-trains. Gradually a few Derby and Stanier 2-6-4 tanks came along, in particular on the 3.50pm Skipton-Blackpool. Two Stanier regulars were 2475 and 2483. It was well into the BR-era when the 4-4-0s were scrapped, to be replaced by the odd Compound; I saw 41063 and strangely enough, 41163. Occasionally, a Horwich mogul would appear, possibly due to a shortage of the usual motive-power. A regular task for the 4-4-0s was the early-morning train from Skipton to Manchester, departing from Earby at 7am, which I took frequently in the 1950s. It is hard to understand now how these engines with 7ft driving-wheels hauled seven-coach trains, but they would have had rear assistance up the Baxenden Bank from Accrington over into Rossendale. At Bury, a crowd would be waiting on the platform, business-people, who were all delivered to 'Cottonopolis' for 9am. Well into the BR-era, in 1955, I saw the first diesel-train passing through Earby. A Craven four-car set, it was one of the first put into service in 1954, though here they appeared only as specials.

Goods Trains

The mixed-traffic Horwich moguls also put in their usual sterling work on through-goods workings; I noted 2762 and 2875. I used to watch out for the long afternoon mineral-empties, passing Earby at about 2.30, headed by an 0-8-0 coal-engine, either a Derby 9500-class ('Austin Sevens') or an ex-LYR, the powerful 'Class 31' 7Fs, referred to above. These were numbered 12841-12981, by then reduced through scrapping to twenty-three locomotives only. Numbers 12873 and 12916 we noted on these trains in 1946. After being turned and serviced at Skipton, this engine would work back to Rose Grove (24B) at around 8.30 pm hauling mainly coal, but with some mixed merchandise. The remaining LYR 0-8-0s were soon scrapped by BR, which replaced them for a while with the LMS Austin Sevens. I noted 49508, 49673 and 49674 on these workings shortly before they too were scrapped, around 1962. However, a 4F could manage over the easily-graded line, and this task became a regular one for them until their withdrawal too, years later in the 1960s. A down mineral ran also in the mornings, which accounts for the 50-wagon empties arriving in Skipton on the afternoon balancing-working. This train too would be headed by one of Skipton's 4F 0-6-0s, such as 3893, 3999, 3960, 4007, 4422 or 4197. It reveals the quantities of coal burnt by the cotton-mills and domestic grates at that time. The local, or pick-up, goods was in charge of one of the habitués of Skipton, an ex-MR 2F 0-6-0, such as 3018, or 3554. The range of numbers reveals the original size of the class. They served the branch too, but they were gradually replaced with the larger 3Fs, popular with the crews, including 3295 mentioned above, and 3408, both based at Skipton for years.

Business, never brisk at the small stations on the route, Elslack, Thornton-in-Craven, and Foulridge in Lancashire, was tiny by the mid-1950s, though Earby continued to produce a steady demand, mainly for coal. A considerable parcels-traffic too was generated here by the plastic-sheeting firm Armoride Ltd. in Shuttleworth Street, which usually went out on the Blackpool express around 4pm—and Colne East yard would continue to take a significant tonnage of coal for many years yet.

Special Trains

The annual holidays, the two 'Wakes Weeks', traditionally from the first week-end of July, shut the mills and other industries of the local area and East Lancashire: whole towns became deserted on the migration of their populations to the seaside. The excitement started to build when, a few days before the holidays, three ten-coach trains were stabled in the Earby coal-sidings. These were specifically for the local people, and connecting-trains ran down the branch to bring the passengers from Barnoldswick. From about eight o'clock on the Saturday morning, it might be 5 July, the three trains were drawn out and propelled successively into the platform for departures to Blackpool, Morecambe, Southport and the North Wales resorts of Prestatyn, Rhyl, Colwyn Bay or Llandudno—even to Pwllheli, where Billy Butlin had a holiday-camp. From the author's home in Skipton Road, the manoeuvres could be heard clearly. The motive-power would be a Horwich mogul or a Black Five.

From home though, the departures could be seen for the Yorkshire Coast, to Bridlington and Scarborough, with similar locomotives. As time went on, bigger and more glamorous power appeared in the shape of Jubilees, an occasional Royal Scot or unrebuilt Patriot, these locomotives having lost out to the Type 4 Peak diesels on the West Coast Route. These were almost the sole occasions when named engines came through Earby. A couple of westbound expresses would run through too, probably coming from their stabling-point and destined to haul the crowds from Colne and other East Lancashire towns to the coast.

This account of the holiday-specials recalls a mishap that happened to one of them. It was late in the steam-era, and the author was at the station on the Saturday morning watching the departure of a Southport special, but clearly something was wrong with the engine, judging from the fuss and the expressions on the crews' faces. Suddenly, there was a warning shout from the footplate, and the fireman started throwing out shovels of blazing embers onto the track: he was dropping the fire, not good for the timber sleepers . . . The injectors had evidently failed on Black Five 45205. Urgent telephoning summoned a replacement engine—and they were quick about it too. In less than an hour, a much newer Class Five arrived hotfoot from Skipton, 44667, one of the later batches built in 1949, though he would have been cautioned by the signalman, since he made 'two trains in one section', a cause of accidents in the past. Once arrived in Earby, he had to manoeuvre carefully around the stranded train over the two crossovers. 'Carefully' because a derailment now would have been the last straw. Then he shunted his failed colleague into the rear coal-siding and took the excursionists off on their trip. The disabled engine was towed away to Skipton a few days later.

Other specials are recalled with pleasure. In 1953 and again in 1955, the staff and friends of the Rolls-Royce jet-engine factory (Bankfield Shed) ran a special from Barnoldswick direct to Farnborough in Hampshire for the SBAC Air Show. The ten-coach train—yes, in Barnoldswick, and corridor coaches too!—was eased gently down the branch to Earby by a 4F goods-engine, where the author's party boarded and the train-engine came on, a Horwich 2-6-0, for the first leg to Leeds. The route overnight was down the Midland line towards St Pancras and presumably along the link past Olympia to reach the Sou' West Waterloo-Farnborough, where a fleet of buses ferried the thousands into the showground. There were static displays alongside the airfield and exciting flights of the latest jet-fighters from the many manufacturers. The huge Blackburn *Beverley* freighter was marvellous, capacious enough to carry lorries. Most dramatic though was the flight of the Avro 707 Vulcan V-bomber, plus smaller sisters, the 707a, b and c. The air-shows make a story in themselves, already told by air-buffs. It was all splendid, with lots of pictures, followed by an evening seeing the lights and action 'up west', before another overnight journey brought the party back to Earby station. On stepping off at Earby on that quiet Sunday morning, it was almost inconceivable that yesterday this same carriage was standing in Farnborough, Hampshire, and now it is here! Perhaps some of you feel this way about your cars, but one still feels that life was—and remains—more exciting when travelling by train rather than by car: one meets people—and it is safer.

Another eight years were to pass before Barnoldswick was to see another ten-coach train in its tiny terminus. That was on 4 May 1963 when Lord Garnock, a director of Crossley's Carpets in Halifax, sent his LNER-type mogul *The Great Marquess* on a RCTS railtour of West Yorkshire and East Lancashire. The packed train came along from Skipton to Earby and up the branch to Barnoldswick. It was quite an afternoon, with photographers everywhere to record this milestone near the end of the steam era. The author was not aware that it was also the twilight of both the branch and the whole line from Skipton to Colne. Old pal John, also from Halifax, had come over for the week-end, and so it was a matter of cameras and spare films, monochrome then, before the colour-film was an everyday commodity.

John and the author went to Barnoldswick and saw the train arrive, and luckily only a few had the same idea, leaving the tracks free for viewpoints of the engine running forward over the crossing into the coal-yard, now much quieter than earlier. Someone even operated the swivel crossbar-signal mentioned earlier, just as a gesture, before the mogul reversed and ran round the long train. Before he left, the author's party drove fast to Salterforth for a shot of the engine, now tender-first, coasting back down to the junction. Then they drove quickly the mile over Klondyke to park near the crossing at Earby Station, and watched the train arrive. The 2-6-0 then manoeuvred over the two crossovers as he ran round the train again, while the crowds milled around. Using the occasional routing of the branch-train, the special finally departed 'wrong line', being immediately crossed over, before accelerating for Blackburn and Great Harwood in Lancashire. It had been another fascinating experience providing several good photographs. At least, the weather had been fine. There was more activity around the line that day than any day since its opening. Platform gossip later said that the mogul was in fact over the weight-limit for the branch. The governing-factor would be the iron bridge over the canal.

As remarked, many ex-MR signals remained well into the BR-era, those distinctive arms with their white spectacles, such as those at Thornton-in-Craven and at Foulridge—including even some of the older wooden variety. Thornton's two home and two distant signals and the points were controlled from a ground-frame on the up-platform adjacent to the tiny level-crossing. But, after the removal of the goods facilities, the passenger-traffic too was miniscule, resulting in the closure of the halt in 1953. After all, it was not much of a service to offer potential passengers: a walk from the station past the cricket-field, then up the hill, possibly on a wet and windy night, to the village at the top; here, the Ribble 281/X.43 routes and Laycock's Barnoldswick buses brought the folks almost to their doors.

Unusual Trains

On Sunday afternoon, 21 January 1963, winter came suddenly: the snow drifted heavily in a few hours, closing both the road—at Wysick—and the railway, in the Thornton cutting. Snowploughs were sent out, one pictured the plough pausing near Earby Crossing for cleaning and adjustment, the plough of course attached to one of the Skipton 4Fs, a fresh one today, 44603. Snow blockage did not happen every year by any means, probably because of the mild, damp air that blew over the watershed from Lancashire, a reason for the location of the cotton-industry over there and in Earby and Barnoldswick. One summer Sunday in that same year at about eight in the evening, the author was preparing to return to his digs for work on the Monday but was on the lookout for an engineers' train spotted the previous week. Fortunately it came along, a train of rails for relaying track somewhere in Lancashire. But what a train! *Two 2-10-0s* doubleheaded, a tremendous concentration of power, but necessary to haul eighteen bogie-wagons loaded with rails, possibly approaching two thousand tons. These Austerity engines were a common sight all over the West Riding and Lancashire for many years.

And now a little cautionary tale on Earby Crossing. Some of the signals had been modernized by fitting upper-quadrant arms to the old teak posts, which signalmen have told me were virtually indestructible. This happened to the two home-signals at Earby Crossing, where the A.56 road crossed the line half-a-mile north of the station. The distant on approaching from Skipton was quite visible from the crossing, only a quarter-mile away, because it shared its post with Thornton's distant. When Thornton closed in 1953, the opportunity was taken to set a new distant for Earby Crossing further out, past the bend beyond the Punch Bowl Inn, and electrically operated. Enginemen had long complained about the over-short warning given for the crossing, where the closing of the gates could be delayed by road-traffic, increasing fast as the austerity of the nineteen-forties gave way to the affluence of the fifties and sixties.

The crossing-gates were not operated with the familiar large handwheel, but manually. The double-tongued bolts had to be shot fully into their sockets and turned down a half-turn before the locking-lever and signals could be operated. Decades ago, the A.56 road was quiet, only a subsidiary main road, therefore hand-operation was quite feasible. But in the 1960s, the traffic was rapidly increasing, car-drivers often a nuisance by persisting in driving over the crossing when the signalman was trying to shut his gates. Even odder was the fact that all three signalmen were disabled, two of them with artificial legs! Godfrey and especially 'Owd Bob' Richardson had many a tale to tell me, as I spent a happy hour or two with them on a Saturday evening. It was not simply a matter of keeping them company; they were glad of my help with the gates. Between trains, Owd Bob would tell me of events in the Great War, when he received his injury at Arras in 1917. Mind you, like many old soldiers, he talked little of the great battles and the slaughter, but more about his mates, where they came from, what they talked about, and their hopes and fears.

At this period in 1963-64, we had two or three trains an hour, plus the Barnoldswick branch-traffic. The through stopping-trains from Manchester were now hauled by Ivatt Class 2 moguls of the 6400-series; I noted 46403/27/40/2. The last evening-train was one of these, passing at about 10.15 pm. After it had gone, the signalman would lock the cabin and go home, as the line was closed at night by this time. You will remember how these trains had for years been pulled by the Johnson 2P 4-4-0s. The same designer's 0-4-4 tanks on the branch-line trains, described earlier, went for scrap early in the BR-era, replaced by Ivatt's 2-6-2T-version of his 1946 moguls. Several of them appeared over the years, 41241, 41251, 41326 and 41327, later two of the Riddles BR-Standard version, 84015 and 84028. Three 2-6-2Ts were allocated to Skipton, one for the Barnoldswick branch, the second for the Skipton-Garsdale-Hawes service, while the third was out-stationed to work the Worth Valley branch from the Keighley sub-shed. It is fascinating to reflect that 41241 has been rescued and so has the branch-line where he still works, residing at Haworth in the red livery of the KWVR.

In the early-1960s, a demand had been voiced for a decent passenger-service to Barnoldswick, especially useful for mothers with prams, for invalids and the disabled, so the plea went, as boarding a bus was awkward. BR obliged with a shuttle-service, comprising a three-coach set fitted for pull-and-push working and one of the Riddles 2-6-2Ts. It ran constantly to and fro between Skipton and Barnoldswick and was dubbed locally 'The Barlick Spud'; whenever we looked out of our windows in Skipton Road, this train seemed to be passing. Mother called it 'the fussy little train' as it puffed swiftly past the house. This made life at the crossing quite arduous for Owd Bob and Godfrey, who were glad of a hand occasionally from locals like me, on a Saturday evening at home for the week-end.

Over-confidence

I quickly became used to the routine of obeying the bell, warning us of a train coming from Skipton, and jumping down the steps to close the gates and pull off the signals; this routine went on whenever I was home. However, then came my *bon moment*: 'pride comes before a fall.' For a Skipton-bound train, the routine was easy: hear the warning-bell from the Earby Station box, watch for his signals coming off and the train arriving in the station, then open our gates to the railway and pull off the home and its distant. However, the trains coming from Skipton on a non-stop run of six miles were a different matter. They rang our bell through a track-circuit at the site of Elslack station, about three miles away, giving us enough time to 'set the road'—providing the road-traffic was not heavy; however, we had to be smart about it, for the little train would cover that distance quickly. Well, on this particular evening, the bell rang as usual, I leapt down the five wooden steps and ran over to the far gate. I let a couple of cars straggle through, closed and bolted the gate, then the nearer one and ran up the steps into the little cabin to set the signals. However, I found that I could not return the locking-lever and consequently was unable to pull off the home-signal. I dashed out to the gates again to check the bolts. I had just rectified the faulty one, which I had not fully shot—it had to be the *far* one—when the engine whistled at our distant-signal, which of course was on. I managed to pull off the home just in time to avoid bringing the train to a dead stand. He puffed past, the crew staring down at us, no doubt wondering what we had been playing at. I hoped they were blaming some selfish or tardy motorist. But they had plenty of time at the Barnoldswick terminus to absorb short delays. Not long afterwards, the Spud was withdrawn following lack of support, and the line became very quiet; it closed in October 1965. We often experience a similar situation now: an outcry for or against something, then it turns out to have been only by a vociferous minority, when the majority is quite satisfied with the *status quo*, and the whole exercise was a waste of time and money. But, in all fairness to the travelling-public, the station in Skipton is quite a step from the High Street, no joke in wind and rain—and perhaps pushing a pram. Again, by that date Mr Everyman had got his hands on the car, so that the buses too were beginning to feel the pinch. However, the motto when using equipment is: 'Don't become complacent; every occasion can be different and often is.' My last anecdote on this line, recounted in Chapter 12, describes an event a year or so later, when I was lucky enough to have a footplate-trip up the branch,.

To conclude the story of the railway south-west of Skipton, even the main-line to Colne was closed about four years later, officially after the last passenger-train on Sunday 1 February 1970. Since there *was* no

Sunday-service, effectively it closed on the previous evening, the usual way these closures are done. The track was lifted in December of that year. At Earby too, the station site has been redeveloped, under a government Job-Creation Scheme by demolishing the station and replacing it with grass and paving, bordered with conifers and flowering shrubs on the north, or country, side. Preston's Transport leased the goods-yard area including the commodious stone-built depot, underlining the defeat of rail by road, as at many other locations. The main A.56 Skipton Road, now much busier with roadstone lorries from the Swinden Quarry near Cracoe among other traffic, has been straightened at the double-bend over the former Earby Crossing, leaving this corner looking very different— and bare. In 2003, the steep, twisting Wysick Hill was improved for the ever-increasing traffic. Some items from the railway survive however. The small six-lever Earby Crossing cabin with its gates, scene of my little contretemps that night—and of many pleasant chats with the old MR/LMS retainers—plus the antique rotary disc-and-board signal from Barnoldswick and items from Skipton—are now in the care of the Keighley & Worth Valley Railway. Acknowledgements for some details are due to D. Binns *The Skipton-Colne Railway, the Barnoldswick Branch.*

Sir Harold Hartley, Executive Director from 1930 (National Rail Museum).

Chapter 8

THE LMS IN HALIFAX

My appetite for watching trains around Halifax was whetted in 1940, when my school-friend David Robinson, a year my senior, showed me the main Halifax goods yard down at Shaw Syke. 'Down' is appropriate, because the railway lies in the valley below The Shay, the Halifax Town football stadium. Holdsworth Bridge, a little further west, takes Simmonds Lane across the tracks approaching from the west and south, but the best viewing-spot was the long metal footbridge leading from Lilly Lane over the goods-yard. At the far end, a steep flight of stone steps dives under the railway, the path for workers at the mills and factories along the River Hebble, especially the thousands clogging down to Mackintosh's Toffee Works, now owned by Nestlé. If the wind was from the east, we spotters gained an added advantage, the sweet smell of toffee being made. The top step gave us a grandstand view of the western ends of the platforms, while the middle of the bridge spanned the series of goods lines fanning out beside the Halifax West signal cabin. Apart from a newish gantry of ten upper-quadrant arms controlling the junctions when arriving from the west, every signal was of Lancashire and Yorkshire design. The westbound starter of platforms 1 and 2 was a bracket of the type 'left-up-right-down', the latter placed low for sighting below the platform two awning

The trains comprised express—and local-passenger, through—and pick-up goods, as well as the local shunting. The expresses ran from Leeds and Bradford to Manchester or Preston, the routes diverging in the Calder Valley at Stansfield Hall junction, Todmorden: straight on for Rochdale and Manchester, right, over the top past Copy Pit for Burnley and Preston. Westbound, the two portions from Leeds and Bradford combined at Low Moor, on the Calder slopes above Brighouse. Low Moor was an exceedingly busy place, with a double-track branching down the Spen Valley with exchange-sidings alongside, and its engine-shed, the LMS 25F. These fast trains were infrequent, one being the quoted business train originating in Manchester and departing from Halifax at 8.22am, timed to bring passengers into Leeds or Bradford comfortably in time for business. In the 1940s, while the local express motive-power would be a Class Five, the 8.22 usually had a Jubilee, such as 5642 *Boscawen* of Newton Heath (26A) or 5697 *Achilles* of Blackpool (24E). However, occasionally we got a bonus when a 'Dreadnought' 4-6-0, also from Blackpool or Preston, was turned out as in earlier days. Now it was usually when the rostered engine had failed, an occasional occurrence caused by poor maintenance, understandably below par in wartime. The Dreadnoughts were by then relegated to stopping-trains, but more on them later.

We therefore saw few 'namers'; their homes were the crack North-South routes, traditionally more prestigious. Very few locomotives of the former Midland Railway put in an appearance either, an occasional standard 4F 0-6-0 or 2P 4-4-0, with a Compound now and again on a Manchester-Leeds express. One I noted was 937. As for ex-LNWR engines, I never saw one in Halifax, and only an occasional one on the Calder valley trunk-route, described shortly.

The Local Passenger-Trains
On these ex-L & Y lines, the stopping-trains were in the charge of the redoubtable and long-lived radial tanks, the 2-4-2s designed by John Aspinall in 1889, pictured earlier. In 1943, the 2P class was listed with running-numbers 10621 to 10899 but totalled only 156, evidence of considerable scrapping, but it was still a substantial class for those days. The first of the class, 10621—the first engine to come out of the new Horwich works in 1889—is preserved at the NRM. The exigencies of World War 2 undoubtedly prolonged their lives and it was only after the war that considerable inroads began to be made into the class by the many new standard 2-6-4 tanks.

In addition to the Class 20 radials, twenty-nine further engines with larger cylinders and Belpaire fireboxes had been built in 1898, following the success of the original class nine years before. They had 20½" x 26" instead of the original 18" x 26"; 10903/23/5/38/43//5/52 however had cylinders of 19½" x 26". These superheated 3Ps, numbered from 10835 to 10953, totalled twenty-nine in 1943. To explain overlap of the numbers, the first few were rebuilds by Hughes of class 2P engines, evidently to prove the design, before more were added as a new class. One of these, 10882, was a regular at Halifax. Some 3Ps I noted were 10901/3/9/21/34/42/3/4/51/2/3, including a few at other locations, so that eventually, like the 2Ps, I had seen almost every one. Some of the latter had smaller-bore cylinders, 17½ in x 26 in of which we saw 10634 and 10804 (25B) in Halifax, while others had been fitted with the longer bunkers, so that they resembled the 3P class, for example, 10842/52/55. There were thus several variants of the radial tanks, locally shedded at Low Moor.

The stopping-trains ran from Todmorden or Hebden Bridge to Leeds/Bradford. A few started from Sowerby Bridge, giving intermediate connections for passengers on Manchester/Southport-York/ Scarborough expresses who were travelling to Halifax or Leeds/Bradford, and the return workings. They all ensured a busy time in Halifax's three main platforms. We also had the link from Huddersfield and Sheffield which ran through to Bradford/Leeds, often headed by 10873 of 25B.

Goods Traffic

Through-goods were hauled by Horwich moguls or Class Five 4-6-0s. These would be 'double-pegged' on the upper-quadrant gantry to run Leeds-bound through the station, while the pick-up goods would turn off before the West cabin and terminate on one of the loops directly under Lilly Lane bridge, when the engine would begin its shunting operations. My pictures show 0-6-0 Jumbo 12099 beside the West cabin. Saddle-tank 11503 had arrived on the inner goods-loop opposite, standing with its rake to be sorted and shunted into the large covered goods-depot. Another 0-6-0ST-visitor was 11429, while near the end of the LMS era, 11381 was drafted in. 'Visitor' is appropriate, since these engines were based at nearby Sowerby Bridge (25E) in the Calder Valley. They would return there once operations were finished at teatime, or sometimes earlier, when they could be spotted trundling along to Dryclough Junction, through Bankhouse Tunnel and Copley, to drift down past the rhubarb-fields and over the long viaduct to Milner Royd Junction on their approach to Sowerby Bridge. These engines were termed by my father 'the errand lad.' It is amazing that the same Jumbo 0-6-0s and 0-6-0 saddle-tanks that he used to see as a boy were still employed on the same job, demonstrating that life had changed little on the cross-country lines or on the goods-traffic of the LMS since the 1914 war. And father was forty years older than me.

The Shaw Syke covered goods depot in Halifax had several roads and was equipped with an overhead travelling-crane. Here, complete wagon-loads and loose merchandise were trans-shipped or delivered with horses-and-carts, some of which had been hurriedly retrieved from retirement with the fuel-shortage on the outbreak of war in 1939. The depot did have, though, some of the useful 'mechanical horses' with flat—or van-trailers of the two-wheeled variety. These had been introduced in 1933 by Scammell of Watford to supersede the horse-and-cart, and consequently had a similar, small-radius, turning-circle, for constricted locations such as goods-depots and factory-yards. After the end of the war in 1945, an upgraded model of this tractor was brought out, and the horses-and-carts were finally consigned to history. Like the majority of LMS vehicles, our mechanical-horses were registered in Hertfordshire, many bearing the registration-mark ANK, issued from June 1934.

The 'LNER side' of Halifax Old Station

This was the beginning of the LNER branches to Bradford and Keighley. Whitaker and Cryer's *The Queensbury Lines* (see bibliography) describes the network in detail. The Halifax Chamber of Commerce pushed strongly for the construction of this branch, made feasible on the completion of the new North Bridge in 1871, built eleven feet higher than the previous structure of 1770. The line was opened as far as Ovenden on 17 August 1874. North Bridge Station was opened in 1880 and closed in May 1955. The section to Bradford was constructed later, jointly by the Great Northern and Lancashire & Yorkshire Railways, the former anxious to gain a share of the business in the important, expanding industrial-areas of Halifax and Bradford. The equally-difficult extension to Keighley followed, converting the wayside station of Queensbury in the Halifax outskirts into a triangular junction, with a platform on each curve. That timber-built junction, at almost a thousand feet above sea-level, was one of the most miserable places at which to wait anywhere. The station before Queensbury, Holmfield, became the junction for the Halifax High Level Railway (HHLR), which terminated at St Paul's, Queen's Road, close to King Cross, 3½ miles away—and 300 feet higher—with an intermediate station at Pellon. It was opened on 4 September 1890 by Alderman Charles Booth. The HHLR was closed to passengers in December 1916, owing to competition from the Halifax Corporation tramcars following their opening in 1898. At only a mile or so from the town centre, it was clearly nonsense to travel five miles in a semi-circle on two trains to reach Pellon. Apart from The HHLR, another limb was added for goods, the mile-long Brick Lane Branch down into Bradford (Hammerton Street).

The HHLR was built between 1888 and 1890. A large workforce made rapid progress through difficult terrain, with a tunnel, then a viaduct over the Hebble valley. It was planned to serve the thriving and expanding industrial district west of the centre of Halifax (locally termed 'the top end of the town'). The opening of the High-Level in 1890 was unfortunately too late for a long and useful life. It was needed two or three decades earlier, like the whole route to Keighley, and several schemes had been mooted. The plans fell through, because of capital construction-costs facing the LYR/GNR, or financial crises, such as that of 1866. The coming of the Halifax Corporation tramways a few years after its opening curtailed its usefulness for passengers, but it continued for goods until 1960, carrying mostly engine-coal for the mills. On 12 August 1947, I saw 8469, a Swindon-built Stanier 2-8-0 shunting at Pellon, an unusual visitor, since the motive-power was normally a Riddles Austerity 2-8-0. Before closure, a few specials had run to the St Paul's terminus and along the main line, dubbed 'The Switchback' or 'The Alps' on account of its gradients of 1:50 or steeper.

The dusty ex-GN four-carriage trains used to arrive in Halifax from Bradford or Keighley in platform 4, then the engine would uncouple and draw ahead to clear the points beyond the West cabin in order to run round his train ready for the return journey. Regular performers were

9443 and 9478 (1946 numbers). This N.1 class of 0-6-2 tank-engines, built by the GNR and renumbered by the LNER 9430-9485, had lost only a handful of engines to the scrapman by this date, demonstrating that LNER operations too, outside the prestigious expresses, were continuing pre-grouping practices. This was confirmed by my visits to different places. The line was called locally 'the GN branch.'

But the LNER had an express-service from Halifax too, through-carriages to King's Cross from as early as 1882. I often saw two Gresley East Coast teak-bodied carriages standing on the spur between platforms 3 and 4, awaiting the daily through-service to London demanded by local businessmen, timed to allow a day in the capital with a return in the evening. They were worked to Low Moor and down the Spen Valley line to Dewsbury and Wakefield. I understand that later the two carriages were coupled to an ordinary train for the short journey to Huddersfield to serve that town too, then worked to Wakefield Kirkgate and up the spur from the ex-L&Y lines to the LNER at Westgate, where they were attached to a King's Cross express. During the 1950s however, a through-train to London, later named *The South Yorkshireman,* ran from Bradford (Exchange) via Halifax, Huddersfield, Penistone and Sheffield, before continuing to London on the old Great Central line to Marylebone. While working for the David Brown Companies at Huddersfield in the 1950s, I often handed the guard a parcel of documents, which was collected by our company secretary at Marylebone a few hours later, a real express service. This train ceased to run soon after 1960 on the diversions of services away from the GC, as a prelude to its complete closure in 1966.

For the goods service on the GN branch, an ex-GNR J50 0-6-0 'Ardsley tank' engine (also called a 'Tango' tank), 8947, was rostered and, like his N1 stablemate, stayed overnight in the small former ex-GNR shed to the north of Halifax Old Station. Both the shed and the station are now listed buildings. We would look across from Lilly Lane bridge to watch the J50 shunting in the middle of the spread of sidings between the station and Church Street. This has been landscaped to form the approach to *Eureka! The Children's Adventure Centre,* with patrons Prince Charles and Princess Diana. With shunting completed, the tank would couple up and puff out over the viaduct towards North

Bridge, the small station half-a-mile up the valley. For this reason, the main station was renamed Halifax Old Station, since it was the original. Beyond North Bridge station a private siding branched off into the vast complex of Dean Clough mills, then the home of Crossley's Carpets. From North Bridge, the severe climb began to Ovenden and Holmfield. Latterly, the goods on the branch was mostly coal, for both domestic-grates and engine-coal for the local mills and for those at Queensbury, Thornton and Bradford, as well as those at Denholme, Cullingworth and Keighley on the extension-line. Denholme had a substantial coal-yard serving the large mills of Foster's nearby; their relatives' mill, the former Black Dyke Mills at Queensbury, is well-known on account of their famous brass band, if for no other reason.

The third station out of central Halifax, Holmfield, but well within the borough, was the junction of the High Level Railway, described above. The mills at the top end of the town had sprung up from the 1840s, standing on the different roads which had led the development of the town up from the Hebble valley, radiating out like the ribs of a fan from the shopping-centre above the ancient Minster, the medieval market and Woolshops, the former home of wool-merchants. King Cross Lane, Hopwood Lane, Hanson Lane, Gibbet Street, Pellon Lane, and the long Queen's Road connecting them were peppered with mills. The HHLR, coming off its long viaduct over the valley of the river Hebble, ran into Pellon station to terminate half-a-mile further on at St Paul's, King Cross. Each station had several sidings, mainly for coal, including private coal-drops for some mills, though merchandise was also handled until the motor-lorry captured this trade from the 1920s. It was too easy for the lorry really, only a mile or so from the town-centre, rather than hauling the goods around a semi-circle of five miles via Holmfield by train. The station-sites have gone the way of many: Pellon has a timber-yard, other industrial units and car-parks, but an approach-road bears the name 'High Level Way' a historical reminder of the line.

The Calder Valley Line at Norland

I had been spotting trains outside Halifax Old Station for a couple of years or so when David left school to train in the textile mills of Marriott & Muff Ltd., Horley Green, Halifax, where his father was a manager, and we drifted apart. Then, quite by chance I met John Wolfenden, who lived nearby in Heath Avenue. We knew the Wolfendens distantly through seeing John and previously Frank, his elder brother, walking down Manor Heath Road on their way to the 'Brown School', so-called after its school-uniform. John and I met one day during the holidays while I was playing about on my bike and we started talking about trains, so he suggested we walk over to the Calder Valley line and that was it. We crossed Skircoat Moor (Savile Park), passed John Henry's corner into Birdcage Lane and then Woodhouse Lane, the cobbled road down the steep escarpment, to emerge onto Wakefield Road at the bottom. From here, a few minutes took us through Sterne Mills, a right-of-way lane through the works, where we watched wire-drawing. Once through the mills, a concrete bridge crossed the River Calder, then the lane, by now reduced to a mere cinder-track, passed under the four-track railway through a gloomy tunnel. At the other side we found a cosy little corner where a stony farm-track turned up the hillside to Norland Moor. This was the origin of our name 'Norland.'

We had a grandstand-view of the main line and of the Halifax line, the two tracks at the far side that had just branched off at Milner Royd Junction, just out of sight to our left, explaining the tunnel we had just walked through. The Halifax tracks led over a twenty-three-arch viaduct, passing above Copley village while rising up the escarpment and curving left from the Calder Valley to gain that of the its tributary the Hebble. After Cow Lane, the line passed through the short Bankhouse Tunnel cut through a spur of rock, to emerge short of Dryclough Junction, the meeting-point with the steeply-graded link from Greetland Station, a mile or so east of Norland on the main line. This completed the triangle, running straight down the Calder Valley past the complex of engineers' sidings at Greetland No.1 and half-a-mile further to Greetland Station, the junction at the foot of the steep link, the other corner of the triangle, described shortly.

Goods Traffic

During the school holidays, we spent hours at Norland watching the endless procession of coal-trains plodding up the valley, balanced by the corresponding mineral-empties eastbound. The westbound trains comprised sixty wagons of coal hauled from the collieries in South Yorkshire to the power stations and mills in Lancashire. The mineral-empties comprised seventy-five wagons; their length was such that, as the brake van was passing us, the engine had shrunk to a speck in the distance. The previous owners, the L&Y, had developed 0-8-0 'coal-engines' especially for this traffic, powerful locomotives with small wheels and large boilers. Indeed, we could hardly fail to notice the stages of development in the three classes: the boilers had become fatter and fatter and the chimneys shorter and shorter; the same could be said of express engines of the period but on these old L&Y goods-engines, this feature was more apparent because of the contrast between their small wheels and their huge, fat boilers. Their appearance caused them to be dubbed 'teddybears' by the staff. The original design, the 6F Class 28 of 1900, by the 1940s comprised only a handful of engines, of which we saw 12723, 12727 (which reached BR stock in 1948) and 12729; the Class 29s had similar dimensions save for the larger boiler, with running-numbers 12771 to 12839, and most of these fifteen ran through the Calder valley. The wide span of numbering reveals that the majority had been scrapped. The last development, by Hughes in 1912, the L&Y Class 30, was the superheated version with the fattest boiler of all, 12841 to 12981, but this class too had been drastically reduced through withdrawals. For example, the last two in the class were 12971 and 12981. Like many others, these 0-8-0 coal-engines were saved by the war, and we saw every one of the twenty-seven engines. In fact, several already withdrawn were brought back into stock to cope with the increased war traffic expected. These 0-8-0s were shedded in Lancashire, at such depots as Springs Branch (10A), Bank Hall (23A) or Newton Heath (26A). It was a bonus to see one before they were gradually withdrawn from service.

Superseding them was the other class of 0-8-0 locomotives, the LMS 7Fs of 1929, numbered 9500-9674, having slightly smaller cylinders but larger wheels. Dubbed by the staff 'Austin Sevens,' the large boiler showing a gap below gave them a superficial resemblance to the L&Y engines. These 0-8-0s were essentially an enlargement of Derby's ubiquitous 4F 0-6-0s. Intended as replacements for the LNW 'Super D' 0-8-0s, described elsewhere, and the L&Y 0-8-0s, they headed the majority of the mineral traffic on the line at this time. Although I saw a few elsewhere, by far the majority appeared on these coal trains up and down the Calder valley, and eventually I had seen every one of the 175 in the class; 9611 was the last to be underlined in my Ian Allan *ABC*. I gathered they were not particularly popular with their crews, nor did they live up to expectations—especially because of their undersized axleboxes. The LNW Super Ds long outlived them.

An occasional local goods train passed us at Norland, mostly loco-coal, also from pits around Wakefield or Castleford, bound for the engine-sheds at Sowerby Bridge (25E) or Rose Grove (24B, near Burnley), headed by one of the still-common Jumbo 0-6-0s. These too comprised three classes, listed here with principal details and running-numbers:

2F Barton Wright, 1887, cyls 17½ in x 26 in (Ironclads), 12016-12064, total 29
3F (L&Y Cl 19) Aspinall 1889, cyls 18 in x 26 in, 12086-12529, total 291
3F (L&Y Cl 22) Hughes 1909, cyls 20½ in x 26 in, superheated, Belpaire boilers, 12528*-12619,
   total 45. * This engine rebuilt from Aspinall 3F class.

The L&Y class 25, 26 and 27 were hearty little engines and certainly the Belpaire version could almost hold its own with the L&Y 6F 0-8-0. Its nominal tractive-effort of 27,405 lb was more than the Mixed-traffic 4-6-0! However, here very clearly the comparison ends. They have however been recorded hauling 750 tons, evidence of the efficacy of a strong, simple design. As on other railways running similar machines, the Jumbos were used on a variety of duties from pick-up goods and shunting to empty carriage-stock—even being pressed into use to haul excursion expresses to Blackpool. Apparently, they were considered 'good enough' for that task, like the carriages they hauled, non-corridor low-roofed stock—without lavatories. Their cabs have been described as Spartan; my view of 12258 on up loco-coal passing Norland in a blizzard says everything about crew-comfort. But these simple engines did their work well and without fuss for over sixty years. Others of the ninety per cent of the total that I saw were Sowerby Bridge's 12108, 12229, 12355, 12375, 12400, 12411, 12515 and 12376, this last being a 'stinker' as it remained at 25E for years. Mirfield (25D) possessed 12408 among others, and Lees (26F) had 12454, which we saw in the Horwich works scrapyard later. The earlier Class 25s (Ironclads) were less common along the valley, but years later, in the 1960s, we went to

Wakefield shed (25A) especially to see 12044 (renumbered by BR to 52044), the last Ironclad remaining, as he had been put aside for private preservation. He can be seen running on the Worth Valley Railway, Keighley, close to his native area, as L&Y 954 and in that company's livery, in lined-out black—smarter than ever he was in service. By the way, I did see the consecutively-numbered 12345. Two of the Class 26s I saw most unusually passing my school on the Leeds-Carlisle line were 12244 and 12252, and two more in ex-Midland territory in 1947 on a trip to a school-friend in Leicester were the palindromic 12121 at Nottingham and 12135 at Loughborough, some of the few shedded outside their native area. When the LMS had sent some of them out beyond their former homes, it was reported that their simplicity and dependability made them popular with the staff.

The Class 27s, the Belpaire version, were very common, and again we saw nearly every one. Shed 25E was home to 12574, 12590 and 12616; the latter will figure later in a little anecdote at Greetland Station. His neighbour 12615 was allocated to 24C Lostock Hall late in 1947, 12441 to 24D Lower Darwen, while Newton Heath, Manchester (26A), was home to 12541 and others; indeed, the majority of these handy engines, of all three classes, were based in the more-numerous Lancashire sheds, but each Yorkshire depot of the former L&Y had some. A engine of this class could easily be recognised approaching by its cab-glasses: they were not round spectacles like the earlier versions, but arrow-shaped to fit around the Belpaire firebox. Although the 2Fs soon went to the scrapyard under the BR regime from 1948, strangely soon followed by the Belpaire 3Fs, thirty of the Class 26 3Fs remained in stock as late as 1961, though I suspect that by then they were mainly in store. However, this means they had served for more than seventy years, a remarkable life-span.

The 0-6-0 Saddle-Tanks

The same remarks apply to the 0-6-0 saddle-tank locomotives, and here I must not forget the errand lad! It would be late afternoon when we spotted the 0-6-0ST rolling towards the old L&Y signal, Milner Royd's outer-home. He had finished his day's work in the Halifax Shaw Syke yard and was returning home to 25E. We have noted 11503 on this task under the Lilly Lane bridge; 11482, 11500, 11381 and others performed there at one time or another. The nickname was given to this engine, returning light from duty, by my father—or maybe by *his* father. Copley station closed in the 1920s, its passengers taken by the Halifax Corporation tramcars from Skircoat Green at the top of the hill, and later by its buses from Copley village in the valley.

Passenger Services

The freight side has taken so long to describe because it dominated the line. As for the passenger traffic, a couple of expresses ran daily from Manchester/Southport to York/Scarborough, according to the season, hauled by Class 5P5Fs, and these locomotives also headed the Manchester-Halifax-Leeds/Bradford expresses; 5207, 5225/6 and 5210 of Low Moor (25F) appeared regularly on these trains, and 4964, 5153, 5161, 5325 and 5436 represent others seen. A very occasional Jubilee appeared for us in the Calder valley, mentioned shortly under Greetland, but with over five hundred Class 5s in service by 1945, they were beginning to dominate and reduce the variety of classes appearing. The local passenger trains ran from Todmorden/Sowerby Bridge to Normanton, the junction beyond Wakefield on the former Midland main line from Leeds to London (St Pancras), and were mostly worked by the still-ubiquitous radial 2-4-2 tank locomotives, including 10695, though the occasional 2-6-2 tank appeared, such as 183, shedded at 25E for a while, but was quietly despatched—to Hellifield. That section contains an anecdote about this 'hoodoo' engine, so-called because of his propensity to derail.

Some Rarities Along The Calder Valley

I have mentioned the rare appearances of LNW engines at Halifax—in fact I never saw one there—but occasionally a Super-D, prolific in Lancashire and the Midlands, would put in an appearance along the Calder valley, making a change from the 'Austin Sevens'. One was 9394, the last of the G2a class, creeping up to the Milner Royd outer-home signal, hauling not coal however, but empty-stock, probably a return working to his home shed in Lancashire. But, one day, John and I had a great cop. We had to catch the 5pm bus at Copley so as to arrive home for tea. Discipline in our families was strict in those days. We had walked along the cinder-track, crossed Norland Stream and were climbing the path towards the woods above Copley with a broad vista of the Calder Valley. It was a lovely sunny afternoon and, hearing a train coming, we looked back. We could not believe our eyes, for it was *the Claughton*, heading down mineral-empties. By this, I mean that it was the sole remaining locomotive of the formerly-numerous class, 6004, its pre-war paintwork showing dull red. The development of the Claughton, eventually into the converted Scot, was detailed earlier. Even without reading its number, writ large anyway on the cabside-sandbox in the older style, we would have recognised this engine, even at this distance. It made our day—and we had seen a complete class at a glance. While waiting at Copley for the Halifax Corporation single-decker 27 routed to Warley, we would continue to watch the eight-coupled engines rumbling over the arch on the mineral-trains.

GREETLAND STATION

This is the other corner of the triangle, around two miles further down the Calder valley from Norland/Milner Royd. The village lay another half-a-mile further along Ha'penny Bar (since renamed 'Stainland Road') The railway, having passed Greetland No.1 with its fan of engineers' sidings, shaves under the hillside south of the river Calder, passing through the junction and the station, then out onto an embankment. It crosses Ha'penny Bar, then the river, before diving under the A.629 and into Elland Tunnel, penetrating a spur of sandstone blocking the line's direct path down the valley to Elland and Brighouse.

The broad yorkstone platforms made a modest but comfortable station at Greetland, with its stone-built waiting rooms on both sides, the nearside (the down-line) up the cobbled approach accommodating the stationmaster's office, porters' room, parcels-office and lamp-room. At the top of the approach, the timber brown-and-cream booking office faced the traveller, who often was also greeted by pigeons cooing softly in their stack of baskets. Pigeon-fancying was a local hobby. The birds were waiting to be transported to some distant destination, in a guard's van or by 'pigeon-special', to be released at their destination by railway-staff to fly back to their home lofts. Passengers walked across the siding and up the platform-ramp—or crossed the bridge to the up-side. Officially, the metal footbridge was intended for the use of all passengers, but no down passenger used it, because normally the siding was clear and they simply walked over it and up the platform-ramp. Shunting took place here in the mornings, and this was the location where I experienced my first-ever footplate-ride. I was standing beside the booking-office watching a Class 26 Jumbo 3F shunting, 12616, when the driver leaned over and called me up. I was only about eleven and must have looked wistful, so he took pity on me. On his "Coom oop lad!" I needed no second bidding: I was up and on that footplate in a flash. I was thrilled, even to run up and down a few times.

The up-sidings lay under the hill behind the station-building with access onto the main line westwards, one of them also continuing in a long headshunt away into the distance opposite the engineers' sidings. Twin L&Y shunting-signals controlled these movements, the top one usually pulled off for the shunting-spur, allowing long rakes of wagons to be hauled up to clear the points at the neck. The tail-end of these sidings curved around following the hill, and the coal-chutes (spelt *shoots* in the local dialect, which also calls them 'coal-drops') were built over a yard set into the embankment alongside the main road. Their site remains visible. The double-track branch continued beyond the coal-chutes to the intermediate station of West Vale, and over a lengthy viaduct to terminate at Stainland & Holywell Green, opened in 1875 to serve John Sykes' large Brookroyd Mills at the head of the valley. Earlier, the branch had been a haunt of one of the L&Y motor-trains, introduced before the Great War to compete with the Halifax Corporation tramcars, but they failed to stop the haemorrhage of passengers. Passenger-traffic ended on 23 September 1929. These small trains were used mostly in Lancashire; the only other such service on the Yorkshire-side of the L&Y was on the Rishworth branch. Of the original eighteen, the last, 10617 survived on the Blackrod-Horwich branch in Lancashire, to come briefly into BR ownership. I described earlier the evolution of these trains into the present multiple-units. Durng the 1940s, a daily train of coal ran for the mills and houses in the two villages of Stainland and Holywell Green. The sidings were dismantled early in the BR regime and the long viaduct spanning the valley was demolished, its site typically covered with industrial buildings. Back along the main line, a long refuge-siding lay approaching the station in the up direction, coming from Elland.

Highlights of the Day at Greetland

Again, it was my friend David Robinson who introduced me to train-spotting at Greetland—just as he had in central Halifax. We would take one of the 51/51a/b/c buses, which transported us down to the station, a ten-minute ride. He had noted some likely times for copping a worthwhile engine, including the rare 'namers' on two down stopping trains, the 10.15am and 6.12pm. The first time we went together, the morning down stopper produced a Hughes Dreadnought. I explain our glee by reminding you that only ten remained of these 4-6-0s of the L&Y/LMS; they had not solved the motive-power demands in the 1920s, and so many had a short life. O.S. Nock *The Railway Enthusiast's Encyclopedia* (Arrow Books Ltd., 2nd impr 1971/Hutchinson, 1968) describes them as 'one of the most complete failures of all time: heavy on coal, mechanically unreliable and sluggish. However, a rebuild in 1920 with superheaters and Walschaerts valve-gear improved them enormously into fast, reliable engines, though still heavy on coal'. Some railwaymen called them 'Lanky Claughtons'. The last one, 10474, was displayed by the LMS as their newest express-engine at the British Empire Exhibition from 1924 at the new Wembley Exhibition Centre. These engines figured in LMS publicity during the mid-1920s.

That morning, it was 10437. I can see it now, bright and clean, with the large gold/gilt figures counter-shaded red on the sandbox ahead of the cab in pre-war LMS maroon as he stopped beside us. We also saw 10412, this one in black, no doubt after being shopped during the war. On another occasion, it was 10460, the highest-numbered locomotive remaining. The ten remaining engines were shedded at Blackpool (24E), so the semi-fast train had originated either there, or at Preston using the Dreadnought to deputize for a failure, or a fill-in turn to Normanton and back. His return-working up the Calder Valley to Lancashire would be that evening.

Following the successful rebuilding of the Claughtons and the mass-production of Jubilee 5XP and Class Five 4-6-0s, the writing was on the wall for these coal-eating 4-6-0s, and all were scrapped from 1933-7 save eleven, which were, remarkably, given a new lease of life in 1937 with copper fireboxes and the latest type of lubricators to replace their Wakefield mechanical ones—and painted in LMS maroon. Our 10437 was one of these. They shared top-link jobs with Jubilees and Black Fives, such as the 'club trains' and the Manchester-Leeds business-service departing at 8.22am from Halifax. After the war, Blackpool refurbished the stud for a few more years' use. Six of the class remained at the BR takeover, but only one, 10455, survived to be renumbered 50455 and painted black in 1949.

The 6.12pm was just as interesting, for it invariably produced a namer, a Jubilee, also bound for Normanton. It was well worth going down to see this train for, shortly afterwards, another Jubilee would drift quietly down the Halifax incline tender-first, to reverse in the station, cross over and steam away to Sowerby Bridge. In this way, the triangle was utilized to turn the engine for its return westbound on a parcels from Sowerby Bridge to Manchester. The Jubilees came from Longsight (9A) or Newton Heath (26A). Those appearing at different times were 5702 *Colossus*, 5710 *Irresistible*, 5711 *Courageous* and 5726 *Vindictive*. However, only the long summer evenings allowed us to be out so late.

My enforced absence from school for seven weeks in 1944 with a fractured shin-bone gave me plenty of time for train-spotting. I had only a lower-leg plaster-cast, which soon became quite comfortable for walking. This meant that I was a constant visitor at Greetland station. As it was March, the weather was still cold, so I would be invited into the porters' room to sit in front of the roaring fire with a mug of their strong tea. Actually, owing to the war, only one porter was on duty. After enjoying a good warm-up at the fire, we would emerge to have a look when a train was coming. If it was a down local, the fireman of the radial-tank would throw off a cob, which landed with a crash on the 'flags' of the platform, fuel for the porter's fire. This was no doubt one aspect of railway-operations which escaped the attention of the accountants. The routine time-table was similar to that described at our Norland spot just up the line, mineral-trains and local passengers, but with the addition of the trains up Greetland Bank serving central Halifax and Bradford/Leeds. The radial-tanks hauled ex-L&Y 'three-sets', three low-roofed carriages closely screwed-up. On the services up the unusually-steep bank, inclined at 1:48, it probably taxed the power of a radial to drag its train over the summit at Dryclough Junction. Years later, towards the end of steam, long after the radials had been replaced by Mr Fairburn's version of the splendid Stanier 2-6-4 tank locomotives, these too found the tremendous incline severe collar-work. Later, I relate a ride up this incline behind one of them.

The branch advance-starter was standard LMS on steel post, and the station signals were also upper-quadrant, but fitted to the original timber bracket (down starter) and gantry (up starters for main/Halifax junction). The down advance-starter, of L&Y-design with shadow-boards behind its two lower-quadrant arms, stood in front of the A.629 road-bridge and tunnel. The signalman often used to leave the home off after a train, reversing it only when called by the 'attention' bell, after which he would often pull it off again in setting the down-road. We were often invited into the box, as the men got to know us through our long sojourns on the station. The box was a new structure, built in the wartime brick-and concrete design around 1941, like the air-raid shelters of that time. Father had a picture of the tall, old cabin, standing high to look over the station roof up the line towards Norland.

The afternoon-shunting of coal-wagons, brought up from South Yorkshire collieries, went on in the sidings opposite, under the hill. I have a poor photograph, a time exposure with the Brownie placed on the platform, showing another Cl.27, 12587, pausing between movements for my benefit. Those enginemen were really decent types. With the train marshalled, the Jumbo would haul the train, complete with brakevan in those days, out on to the main line. In the meantime, a similar engine had appeared from Sowerby Bridge shed or from the engineers' sidings, 12159, 12203, or very often 12375. He coupled to the rear of the train to draw it back with its train-engine, and together they set back slowly through the station into the long refuge-siding where the buffer-stops overhung the River Calder. The task of 12375 was to bank the long train up to Dryclough Junction, and it was quite a performance.

The train, fired up to maximum steam-pressure, would wait in the siding for a path between main-line traffic. Then the L&Y shunting-signal would be pulled off, the road set for Halifax, and we were treated to the crowing for a banker, *Cock-a-doodle-do!* three times by the train-engine, with the banking-engine answering. They would advance out of the siding, accelerating hard through the station, leaving the whole place smothered in a fog of black smoke. Charging the bank, they roared over the bridges spanning the river, the Calder & Hebble Navigation and Wakefield Road, their speed falling off as the gradient steepened below Bankhouse Tunnel on the upper, Manchester, line. Their syncopated exhausts gradually faded up Salterhebble as they muscled over the summit at Dryclough Junction. By then, it was our tea-time, so reluctantly we turned and walked down the Yorkshire-sett road for the 51 bus home. But I had seen plenty; quite often, an unusual visitor would turn up, like Stanier 2-6-2 tank 171 running light up the valley one day, shed unknown. It was not one of the four with larger boilers (148/63/9/203), but welcome all the same; we rarely copped members of this class, since they naturally remained in their local area. They are described under the Stanier standards.

Reminiscing about the coal-trains reminds me of an anecdote told by a friend of mine, Charles Hibberd, a retired Chartered Engineer in the coal industry. It illustrates that workers are always on the lookout for 'something for nothing', or 'freebies' in today's vernacular.

'The colliery's own locomotive would pull the loaded train slowly over the weighbridge to register the weight of each wagon. The clerk had only to deduct the tare-weight of each wagon, around seven tons, to record the amount of coal taken out. However, the colliery-crew, working as a team with the railway staff, had discovered how to 'make a bit on the side.' Before the train drew forward to be weighed, the guard in the van at the rear screwed down his brake hard. The resulting tension in the couplings had the effect of raising the wagons very slightly so that the weighbridge recorded about five hundredweight less than their actual weight of each wagon. This allowed the 'surplus' coal to be removed later. Beyond the colliery, men in overalls with faces blackened to resemble pit-workers, were waiting beside the line with lorries and sacks, into which they quickly shovelled the five hundredweight of coal from each wagon. This they disposed of, either into their own coal-cellars or by selling it, thus making a bonus for themselves.' Pilfering is rife across industry, and this trick was only one of many used to obtain coal without paying for it—a valuable commodity in the days when homes were warmed with open fires and people received low wages or were unemployed.

At Greetland, the approach of the afternoon down York/Scarborough express was exciting to watch, the engine and tender oscillating over the trailing-points of the down loop, then over the double-junction crossover at the station. It would be a Mixed-traffic; 4941, 4967, 5012, 5262 or 5351 were some I noted. Unexpectedly one summer evening in 1945, I saw a modern smokebox approaching on a down mineral-empties. The Stanier 8F was clearly brand-new, both in its appearance and in its absence from my Ian Allan ABC, which deliciously announced that the class was 'still being delivered.' It was one of several batches of the Stanier 2-8-0s built at Horwich in 1945, giving us a change of power from the usual Austin Sevens. Its glossy-black paint and the number 8394 in gilt, countershaded red, impressed me. It demonstrated the change that was coming: the gradual withdrawal, not only of the earlier L&Y 0-8-0s, but soon of the Austin Sevens too.

David used to continue watching the trains when I was away at school, and I felt envious when he told me he had seen a '19-inch goods' on an up mineral. Now, only six of this LNWR-class remained out of the hundred and seventy built from 1906-9 (8786, 8801, 8815, 8824, 8834, 8858) and he had seen 8834. But luckily, I did see 8824 later, and so felt relieved. This was also working up to Lancashire, and I was pleased to be able to cop a fresh class without going to look for it. Age and lack of cash prevented us from travelling far anyway. Years later, I did see 8834 on his home shed, Springs Branch (10A) just before withdrawal in 1950. The other two taken into BR stock were 8801 and 8824. One of these represented the last ex-LNW 4-6-0 in service. I understand they were domiciled there or at 10C Patricroft.

Another rarity that pleased me greatly was the appearance on an up mixed-goods train of a 'Cauliflower'. I only ever saw a handful of the hundred remaining of these 'crested express-goods' engines, as they worked mainly in the Western Division 'A' (West Coast route and the Midlands), out of my reach at that time. It was 28598, and in 1944 a probable shortage of motive power had brought him over to Yorkshire, and luckily I saw the return-working. I liked the look of these dear old engines, an opinion shared by others. In the following year, 28603 made another bonus.

Summary and Reflections of the Halifax area

Saddle-tanks, Jumbos, 0-8-0s, radial-tanks, Horwich moguls and Black Fives were my world in the mid-1940s around Halifax. I witnessed practices and routines hardly changed since before the First World War—partly because of that huge expenditure on armaments—goods deliveries to the local stations and to the big depot at Shaw Syke, with shunting by two railway-companies on the extensive sidings below Church Street; the horses-and-carts—and the Scammell mechanical-horses that had been gradually replacing them in the inter-war years; but the 1936 Morris Commercial parcel-vans parked at the Old Station were clearer signs of change.

The rolling-stock too, was slowly being replaced on the expresses to Manchester, Leeds and York, but the local carriages, mostly of the low-roofed type, still bore the lettering LYR cast on the axle-boxes of their distinctive bogies. I remember the clean, spacious booking-hall at Halifax Old Station and the timber steps leading down to the six platforms, with the wartime-notices warning us that *Careless Talk Costs Lives* and asking, *Is Your Journey Really Necessary?*; the big bookstall on platform 3 and the smell of Mackintosh's toffee, as I waited for my train to Bradford on returning to school, watching the old signals swing down, then up again to danger; the homely voice calling out, "Halifax, 'alifax", that distinctive squeal of brakes as the train jerked to a stop. Then the doors would slam and we felt the lusty pull-pull of the radial-tank as he puffed out strongly past Patons & Baldwins woollen-mills and into Beacon Hill Tunnel, out into the daylight again with the view of Shibden Park, and of Hipperholme with its neat goods yard and the private-sidings with yellow shunting-signal—the upper-quadrant type evidencing the wartime-branch to the former Brooke's Chemical Works on the other side; Lightcliffe, another clean, well-used little station; Wyke was similar, but with tracks branching down to Clifton. Then we were in Low Moor's busy platforms, where the train was divided, the front portion leaving for Leeds while my rear portion was taken on to Bradford by another radial-tank from the shed (25F) through the smoky Bowling Tunnel, past St Dunstan's and down into the gloomy Exchange Station.

Coming home, I felt that eager anticipation of the holidays as the train ran into Beacon Hill Tunnel, hearing the clang of its warning-gong as the train slowed, before we emerged into the Hebble valley and nearly home, with the centuries-old Parish Church (elevated to a Minster in 2009), Patons & Baldwins mills on the right and Mackintosh's toffee-works below on the left. Then it was up the steps with my suitcase, through the clean, echoing booking-hall, over the station-bridge with its parcel-vans and up Horton Street for the comfortable AEC corporation-bus home.

EXCURSIONS FROM HALIFAX TO PRESTON, LANCASHIRE

Before and during the Second World War, we made family visits to my mother's brother Uncle Morland and his wife Auntie Nan, and cousins Norman and Margaret. Our family visit was often simply mother and I, as father had been 'directed' by the Labour Exchange on to munitions. The train from Halifax was Black Five-hauled and classed as semi-fast, as it stopped at Sowerby Bridge, Hebden Bridge, Burnley, Accrington and Blackburn. Therefore we passed the sheds at Rose Grove (24B) and Accrington (24A), so plenty of fresh engine-numbers on the way, the same classes I was used to on the Calder Valley lines, with odd engines shunting in wayside yards too; Burnley produced shunters 3F 7575 and 0-6-0ST 11497. But often we went via Bolton and Chorley. On a visit in 1938, we came this way, and, as we approached Farington Junction to join the West Coast route, we noticed several large, new, brick factories, with blank walls. To me, they looked strange, but father, who was accompanying us that day, announced that they were 'shadow factories'. They formed part of the official preparations, mainly for the motor—and aircraft-industries, against the war that the authorities had reluctantly admitted was inevitable. Father was interested since, as a machine-tool engineer, he visualised the engineering-shops to be set up inside them.

We were welcomed with tea and cakes at Hollywood Avenue, Cop Lane, Penwortham, but, after a decent interval, I was allowed to be anti-social and leave the house for a while. This was because I wanted to walk around the corner to the little station at Cop Lane. It was the first stop out of Preston on the West Lancashire line to Southport, and sometimes I saw a fresh radial tank there, for example 10728 and, the numerically-similar 10872, both of 10B Preston. From 1941 onwards, I was old enough to be allowed to go spotting in Preston itself—an entirely different matter, translating me at a stroke from a quiet country line to the crack West Coast route. The *Ribble* bus dropped me in Fishergate at the station, I bought a platform-ticket for a penny (1d = about 2.5p) from the slot-machine and walked down the ramp onto the wide island-platform 5/6, to the far end. This gave a panorama of the all the movements at the south end of Preston station: expresses, stopping-trains, through goods and behind them the shunting, including the branch emerging up its ramp from Preston Docks. Behind me were the platforms serving the Blackpool and East Lancashire lines.

Express Trains

On my first visit, the up 'Perth' express yielded 6204 *Princess Louise*, and sister locomotive 6207 *Princess Arthur of Connaught* hauled the down 'Royal Scot' train. I was so excited because I had never seen a 'Princess' before. The Leeds-Carlisle line, my usual hunting-ground, could not support the axle-weight of pacifics at that time, leaving the converted Scots as the most powerful locomotives we saw there. On my next visit, 6212 *Duchess of Kent* appeared on the up 'Perth' express. Then there were the 'Duchesses' (officially *Princess Coronations)*—we called them 'Streamliners,' the class running from 6220 *Coronation* to 6245 *City of London*, again delightfully listed by Ian Allan as, 'still being delivered.' These further pacifics represented a tempting goal. We read in *Meccano Magazine* about the construction of the next three, *City of Manchester/ Liverpool/ Leeds*. The original *City of Leeds, 6244,* had had to relinquish his name in order to be re-named *King George VI*; the new 6248 *City of Leeds* was the replacement, and the last streamlined locomotive built by the LMS, in red with gold stripes. The non-streamlined style re-adopted from 6249 onwards was similar to 6230-4 back in 1938, though each batch showed detail differences up to the final engine. The self-cleaning smokeboxes and rocking-grates exemplified these, with the 'SC' plate on the smokebox below the shedplate, 6249 being the first of a batch of four. From 1946 onwards, the streamlined casing was progressively removed from all the members of the class, leaving *City of Lancaster* the last to be 'defrocked' in 1949. The de-streamlined engines could be instantly recognized on approach by the chamfered top to their smokebox, which I thought attractive, until routine maintenance replaced them with standard circular smokeboxes, which gave a heavier look. I saw 6251 *City of Nottingham*, one of the non-streamlined batch, when new in 1944 and finished in wartime black, heading a Birmingham-Glasgow express and eventually I had ticked off most of the class. These pacifics headed the crack Birmingham/Manchester-Glasgow, Liverpool-Glasgow and the direct Euston-Glasgow trains. Among these West Coast expresses, it is odd that I saw no more Princesses, but some obstinately remained on the Euston-Manchester/Liverpool trains, giving my school-friends living at places like Berkhamsted, Hemel Hempstead and Northwich advantages over me. One that favoured them was turbine-pacific 6202, unnamed but dubbed *Turbomotive*. This Princess was rostered regularly on *The Merseyside Express* and so I never saw it. At Preston, I was constrained by time as well as by space, with only an hour or so at the station, in order to be back at Penwortham in decent time for tea, so that we could leave afterwards for the train home. On a visit years later in the BR-era, I noted 46206 *Princess Marie Louise* and the last two LMS pacifics built, 46256 *Sir William A. Stanier, FRS* and 46257 *City of Salford*. This very last one was finished by BR in May 1948, both constructed to Mr Ivatt's amended specification. It was fitting that Sir William, as he had then become, was honoured by the LMS in its last year; the ceremony is detailed elsewhere.

The much-loved Jubilees appeared on the lighter expresses, such as the Euston-Windermere/ Barrow/Morecambe/Blackpool, including holiday extras to these resorts, as well as piloting Royal Scots on exceptionally heavy trains. They were often seen heading parcels and fitted-freights too, such as banana-vans from Avonmouth Docks to Glasgow. Among others already seen elsewhere, 5628 *Somaliland*, 5629 *Straits Settlements*, 5637 *Windward Islands*, 5687 *Neptune*, 5692 *Cyclops*, 5720 *Indomitable*, 5733 *Novelty* and 5737 *Atlas*, appeared at different times. Patriots too headed these trains, many demoted from their express-duties owing to wartime conditions. Patriots were common: 5502 *Royal Naval Division*, based at Preston, was restarting a through goods southbound, while 5515 *Caernarvon* stood in the bay with a Manchester local and the unnamed 5550 passed through on freight. The Patriots were not rebuilt at this time—in fact, only a few Scots had been so treated by 1944-45. In 1947, I saw *Royal Scot* itself, 6100, still unrebuilt, heading an up Euston express. Other Scots I noted were 6123 *Royal Irish Fusilier*, 6133 *The Green Howards* (which later appeared for us at school as one of the first rebuilds sent to Holbeck, Leeds, 20A), 6136 *The Border Regiment*, 6139 *The Welsh Regiment* and, as a bonus, the unique 6170 *British Legion*. The very names are consigned to history now: the regiments they represented have disappeared after repeated reorganisations of the army. Even the famous *Black Watch* regiment is phased out, after returning from heroic service in the second Iraq war—and every year seems to bring further cuts.

In between spotting the passenger trains, I was watching the goods traffic passing on the through-roads behind the station and the dock-branch movements beyond. Super D 9141 was emerging from the docks up the steep incline, which had a service of about twelve trains per day, keeping several of these capable 0-8-0s in employment. Class 5P5F 4936 was accelerating an up through-goods as he met 4F 4399 on a similar operation. Shunting-tanks were numerous too, some on trip-workings to Burscough Junction, Greenbank Yard or light-engine to Lostock Hall shed (24C) up the line; 7291, 7383, 7386 and 7357 I noted. The latter has survived to become one of a pair of these 3F 0-6-0Ts preserved by the Midland Railway Trust, at Butterley, Derbyshire. While I was thus engrossed, behind me 2P 4-4-0 631 (23E Lostock Hall) was preparing to depart on a Manchester local, and as soon as he had cleared, Black Five 5142 clanked through the adjoining platform 6 on up mineral-empties This class was already a significant presence by 1944, with more than five hundred locomotives in traffic, 5000-5499, plus some of the 4800-series.

Further over my shoulder at the Blackpool/East Lancashire (ex-L&Y) platforms, Stanier 2-6-2 tank 191 was busy marshalling carriages. On the way to Manchester, I saw Fowler 63, and more Staniers, 182, 186, 192 and 198. Fresh ones were always welcome, since these small tank-engines usually worked near their home so travel was necessary to see them. There were the Blackpool arrivals and departures to keep an eye on, usually led by a Black Five such as 5147 or 5448, this one still new. Occasionally I received a treat, when a Hughes 4-6-0 'Dreadnought' was turned out, recalling earlier days. The motive-power of the East Lancashire trains gave a variety: a radial-tank, perhaps 10692, a 2-6-4 tank such as 2643, 2661, or, very occasionally, a 2P 4-4-0, like 584. These LMS-built engines had probably replaced the former L&Y 'High-Flyers,' scrapped in the rationalization following the Grouping of 1923.

But all the time, main-line carriage-marshalling was being handled by two carriage-pilots in the centre-roads under the overall roof, and had time to pose for my camera. They were radial-tanks—not boring however because of their ubiquity—but a scoop: 10676 was admittedly a very ordinary 2P-machine, the basic design without even a Belpaire boiler or extended bunker, but the other engine was unique: 6762 was listed as Wirral Railway, the sole member of its class. Preston (10B) was its home and workplace, so it was unlikely to be seen elsewhere; even its birthplace, Horwich works, was quite near, so only a short trip was required for heavy repairs. Built by Aspinall in 1890 for the L&Y as a normal radial-tank, it was sold to the Wirral Rly later. It made an extra interest, in rarity-value almost paralleling 2290 'Big Bertha,' the distant Lickey banker. Another little item that came my way in 1946, though not a rarity this time, was an inspection-car, but hauled by one of the new Ivatt 2F 2-6-0s, 6409. The occasional inspection-car I saw passing the school was usually hauled by an ex-MR 2P '483' 4-4-0.

Our usual train home left from the East Lancashire platforms, but quite often we would take a local to Manchester, so as to take a train from there direct to Halifax, and so avoid awkward changes to cross East Lancashire. The engine could be a 2P 4-4-0, such as 631 seen earlier; others encountered were 640, 677 and 691; they would be based at Lostock Hall or at Preston itself. In contrast with these LMS-built examples, once we had 483, the original rebuild of ex-MR 4-4-0s, giving his name to the whole class, more likely to be met with around Leeds; perhaps he was working back there after a special duty. Twice we had a Compound, 1157 and 1192; they were fairly common on the West Coast line and in the Manchester area, usually later members of the class like these; many of the 900-series stayed in Scotland, but I did note 900 and 925 at Preston. These could have been pilots off overweight expresses from Carlisle, and shedded there (12A Kingmoor) or even at Polmadie (27A), Preston being a convenient point to detach them to work back later as useful pilots over the Grayrigg and Shap banks. I have mentioned several of the series closer to home at Skipton and Hellifield. But, as I have pointed out earlier, the wartime period did produce some very unlikely comers—good cops for us lineside-observers.

Often in the darkness, these return-journeys produced little in the way of locomotives to note, perhaps an occasional engine in Manchester or one standing in a yard if the lighting was bright enough. Summer return-journeys did however produce a few: 0-6-0ST 11519 at Bolton East, Ironclad 12016 and 2-6-4 tank 2455 in Manchester, and another saddle-tank, 11516 at Accrington are some examples. 'If only . . .' is the saddest phrase in the world! I should have gone down to the docks or round to the engine-sheds for more; I did not know that the unique 7862 and 7865, ideal for dock-shunting, were based there, but information was sparse in those days, travel was awkward—and I was short of time.

Here are the locomotives noted around Preston-Manchester other than those mentioned:

2-6-4Ts: Fairburn-type, 2209, 2210, 2216, 2225, 2229, 2230, 2259, 2265, 2279, 2284, 2286, 2288, 2292, 2293; (after 1945-6, these new 2-6-4s were clearly displacing the long-lived radial-tanks); Stanier-type: 2475, 2476, 2492, 2528, 2537, 2550, 2557, 2559, 2564, 2565, 2614, 2622.
Stanier moguls: 2952, 2955, 2979.
Ex-MR & LMS 4F 0-6-0s: 3912, 4105, 4393.
Ivatt 2F moguls: 6403, 6417.
Ex-LNW Super Ds: 9102, 9115, 9119, 9150, 9198, 9252, 9299.
Ex-L&Y 0-6-0STs: 11318, 11323, 11327, 11336, 11345, 11436, 11481, 11514, 11519.
Ex-L&Y 'Ironclad' 0-6-0s: 12034, 12051, 12064, 12118, 12123, 12164, 12189, 12279, 12412.
Ex-L&Y 'Cl.28' 0-8-0: 12828.

When considering this list, it is fascinating to reflect on the relatively-large number of constituent-company engines that were still running, on mainline duties too; subtract the Fairburn 2-6-4Ts which appeared only in my later years at Preston—when the Black Fives became more dominant too—and you are left with crowds of LNW Super-Ds, L&Y

radial tanks, Ironclads/Jumbos, saddle-tanks, and standard 4F 0-6-0s. The new locomotives had been built mainly for the prestigious express-duties, and so the goods-trains continued much as before, as remarked on my Scottish adventures. The lineside furniture too dated largely from pre-grouping days.

Gordon Biddle's slim volume *The Railways Around Preston. An Historical Review* (Foxline Publishing, Romiley, Stockport, 1989), a softback of monochrome photographs, shows the development of the town through its canals and docks, its early railways and branch-lines, while for those interested in industrial history, Mr Biddle has included a brief industrial history of Preston, illustrating how it grew into a large cotton-manufacturing town.

TO SCOTLAND ON THE L.M.S. 1945 & 1947

For conciseness, I have noted my experiences of 1945 and 1947 together, since I saw largely the same classes of engine on both trips and at the same locations. As my mother was Scottish, we went quite frequently to visit her mother, 'nana', and her two sisters, travelling from our home in Halifax to Leeds for the morning Leeds-Glasgow express. For many years, this train departed from Platform 6 at around 10.25am. This station is now devoted to parcels-traffic, after the 1960s amalgamation of the Central and City traffic at Leeds City, renamed simply 'Leeds.' As father was on munitions, mother and I travelled together. I know we both felt it exciting to find a comfortable seat at a table beside one of those large windows. Then I would dash up to the front to look at the engine, but I had to be quick, or mother would become anxious. Often it would be a powerful *Royal Scot*, preparing a good fire for its slog up to Blea Moor, one of the four newly converted with taper boilers and allocated to Holbeck for the purpose, 6103 *Royal Scots Fusilier* (the first to be converted) 6108 *Seaforth Highlander*, 6109 *Royal Engineer* or 6117 *Welsh Guardsman*. Of course, Leeds (City) had several other locomotives on show for me, Compound 1043 and 2-6-2T 195, and 'Belpaire' 4-4-0 720; on the LNER-side, G5 0-4-4T 7240 was shunting Gresley teak-bodied stock bound for York.

Ten minutes or so after leaving the City Station, we would flash past my school where I had so often watched this very train, reaching Skipton in half-an-hour. Here several engines were to be noted, 4Fs including 3893, 3999 and 4007 (all with tender-cabs), 2P 4-4-0 519, 1F 0-6-0T 1855 shunting the up exchange-sidings, Horwich Mogul 2851 and 1P 0-4-4T 1358. The latter, I discovered later, was allocated to serve the Earby-Barnoldswick branch, already described. I had seen the Keighley pilot, another 1F 0-6-0T, 1820 outside that station, and in the bay-platform there, waiting for departure to Oxenhope, Worth Valley, was another 0-4-4T, 1430, the last member of the class.

Ten miles further and we were curving down into Hellifield, a busy junction, also described earlier, with more locomotives on the shed to the right as we departed. They included more 4Fs, 3902, 3939 and 4108, another Horwich mogul 2869, probably preparing to haul a branch-train to Blackburn or Manchester, Compound 1045, Mixed-traffics 4828 and 4829 (the latter converted to oil-burning) and, luckily, a Derby 2-6-2T, 41. This would be the Carnforth-based locomotive preparing for his return-working along the Clapham-Lowgill branch, a lovely line again already portrayed in detail. The topography of the Settle-Carlisle line has been so extensively documented that I will concentrate instead on what I saw and where. Our next stop, Appleby, was brief, with nothing to see. We had run past too close to the engine shunting in the down sidings to see it distinctly, but it would often be a 4F 0-6-0 to be 'copped' on our return-journey.

Another half-an-hour saw us rolling into Carlisle Citadel Station, that mecca for enthusiasts, with routes converging from seven directions. In fact, Citadel was worked as a separate entity, shared by the seven companies up to the grouping of 1923, each with its own yard and engine-shed, not all visible from the Leeds express. Durranhill was the first, the closed Midland depot, with diesel-electric shunter 7114 at work in the South Sidings, then the North Eastern at Petteril Bridge, before I was trying to look both ways at once as we ran past the big Carlisle No.4 box into the station. Here is a selection of what I saw: 4Fs 4184, 4251 and 4346; 2-6-4Ts 2570, 2581, 2630; Compounds 904, 1149; ex-MR 2P 483-class 4-4-0s: 448, 492, 513, LMS-type 596, 642, 656; Black Fives: 5167, 5350, 5368, 5409; 8Fs: 8150 and 8151. Patriots were represented by 5518 *Bradshaw*; Jubilees by 5653 *Barham* and Royal Scots by 6131 *The Royal Warwickshire Regiment*. In Carlisle, I even saw a a Black Five shunting. It was in the Viaduct Yard and it certainly proved they were 'maids of all work' as the magazines put it. This sight became commoner towards the end of the steam era, more than two decades later.

Twice, including the 1945 trip, we had taken the stopping-train departing from the Number 3 Bay, in order to arrive direct at Wishaw Central, only a short bus-ride from the aunties' home. This three-coach train would usually be hauled by one of the many LMS-built 2P 4-4-0s stationed in the south-west of Scotland, or with luck, an ex-Caledonian Railway Dunalastair 4-4-0, a 'Caley bogey' to the men, each giving way to a Black Five as time went on. Caley 4-6-2 tanks had headed this service earlier, their coal-bunkers being replenished at Beattock for the remainder of the hundred-mile trip. The slower journey gave an opportunity to identify the wayside stations, which often boasted a Caley 'Jumbo' 0-6-0 shunting his pick-up goods. Approaching Beattock, I was on the lookout for a banking-engine on the shed or the spur, where a 4-6-2 tank was often waiting. Later some McIntosh 0-4-4 tanks took over this task. The last four of the second, and largest, class, 15237-40, built in 1900, were listed as 'fitted with cast-iron front buffer-beams for banking-purposes' which accounts for my spotting them there. One or two of the ten more-powerful successors built by the LMS in 1925 came on duty here later, of which I saw 15262 and 15269. The Fairburn version of the Stanier 2-6-4 tanks replaced them along with, near the end of steam, some standard 2-6-4 tanks.

In 1947, we stayed on platform 6 in Carlisle, for a speedier journey on a west-coast express to Motherwell, though it was a longer bus-ride from there to Cambusnethan, the village beyond Wishaw which was the aunties' home. Departing from Carlisle behind 6231 *Duchess of Atholl* for Glasgow, I rejoiced in the power of the big locomotive as we accelerated over the junctions. Soon, on our right, we were passing the huge Kingmoor sheds (12A), simply a forest of chimneys and domes; even the front row contained too many engines to note. Ex-CR Jumbos, 0-4-4Ts and a 4-6-2T stood there; Duchesses 6221 *Queen Elizabeth* and 6244 *King George VI*—most appropriately standing together. Significantly, on the 1947 trip, the two ex-GSWR 0-6-2Ts were in the front row. In 1945, seven had been listed, but now only two remained,

16905 and 16920. They actually survived to be taken into BR stock in 1948, the only ex-GSWR locomotives to do so. Its last two 2-6-0s, 17821/9, had been scrapped only a few months earlier. So at a glance I saw not only a whole class, but the rump of a complete LMS constituent-railway of a generation before.

Symington was a traditional stop for some West Coast expresses, to allow passengers to take the link to Edinburgh. This train could be seen standing in the branch-platform on the right; on my 1947-trip, it was one of the 'Improved Dunalastairs' designed in 1916 by Pickersgill, 14471. This time-consuming-stop was phased out later in favour of a connection at Carstairs, not far ahead. But Symington had demonstrated its own need for a special service, the *Tinto Express* of the old Caledonian Railway, put on for the benefit of those who wished (and could afford) to spend a holiday in the invigorating air around the eponymous mountain. Lamington, Elvanfoot, and particularly Crawford drew people on this bent, the latter village becoming a thriving little spa (a 'hydro' in Scotland) for Glasgow folk at the turn of the century.

But the outstanding moment of both journeys was the sight of the engine-sheds at Carstairs. It was almost incredible. From our standing train, the depot on the Edinburgh curve to the right was laid out as if for viewing by enthusiasts, particularly on my 1945 trip in brilliant afternoon sunshine. A long row of engines that I could not believe: two complete classes of 4-4-0 at a glance, 14434, the sole remaining Dunalastair III (rebuilt in 1916) and 14438/9, the two Dunalastair IVs of 1907, rebuilt with superheater in 1917/15 respectively; and then Jumbo 0-6-0 goods engines, McIntosh 0-4-4Ts, and Dunalastair IVs 14461, 14464, 14505; I had only just time to note them all down before we pulled out for Motherwell past McIntosh 0-4-4 tank 15261 marshalling carriages.

From our aunts' house at Wishaw, the 'small end' of the Large Burgh of Motherwell & Wishaw, I went for a look-see at Wishaw South, the little-used station on the West Coast route. To me, it was like nectar to a bee. The lighter expresses were in charge of a Jubilee, a Patriot, or a Royal Scot, the last two still with their parallel boilers, often piloted by a Compound or LMS-built 2P 4-4-0. The Patriots and Jubilees also did duty on parcels and ecs workings. But it was the pacifics I wanted to see. Around 10am, I would see The Royal Scot, headed by a Princess Royal, and other expresses brought out the Duchesses; the only pacifics I had seen previously were those on our visits to Preston. But, I soon discovered that if I went out before ten o'clock, and to the nearer Wishaw Central on the Motherwell avoiding-line via Coatbridge, I would gain a bonus with a Princess hauling the up Perth express, the other crack train of the morning. I can see it now, that first time, 6203 *Princess Margaret Rose*, piloted by Compound 903, both in LMS red, splendid. Then it was back on the bike for the short hop to Wishaw South. The few trains that stopped at this station were hauled by the improved Dunalastair IVs, the superheated McIntosh design of 1910 (14440-60), the similar Pickersgills of 1916 (14461-14508) or his rather poor 4-6-0 of 1916, the class expanded by the LMS in 1925, the '60 class' (14630-54). I noted nearly all the latter at either Wishaw Central or South; 14649 was on Carstairs shed in August 1947—probably on the same service—and 14630 at Beattock. He may have hauled a stopping-train from Carlisle, as I saw him later on Kingmoor shed, or possibly was pressed into use as a banking-engine. It is remarkable that, barring 14633/55, only recently scrapped, every one of these ninety-four locomotives remained in service. But the appearance of an occasional 2-6-4 tank on local—and branch-line services was evidence that the writing was on the wall for these old CR engines, now that the exigencies of war had passed.

On the 1945-holiday, we went on the bus to Lanark to see a friend of Auntie Eleanor's. Passing the terminus-station, and with permission to take a quick peek, I sprinted up the wooden steps to the one-platform terminus; the branch-train was in, the engine looming over me. It was one of the 1916-Pickersgill 4-4-0s, 14504—splendid, as so far I had seen only 14484 out of those forty-eight engines. I was highly delighted and it stuck in my memory. Later, I did see a few more of these handsome 4-4-0s, including 14508 heading Dumfries goods up to Carlisle one afternoon.

The signals at Wishaw South, mostly ex-CR, with a few upper-quadrant arms on those same distinctive lattice-posts, were usually pulled off, as very little shunting took place in the few sidings, allowing the box to be switched out. The situation was similar a mile up the line at Pather (pronounced with a long *a*, like 'may'), where sidings served a small ironworks. Suddenly its distant, mounted 'double-peg' on our starter, would swing up to caution, followed by his home signal snapping up to danger. This told me that the signalman had arrived, and that I could expect a pick-up goods, bringing coal or steel-scrap to the works. This small factory near Newmains closed down later, too small to survive as competition hotted up in the cold post-war climate. The train, like the other local goods traffic, was headed by one of the sturdy ex-CR Jumbo 0-6-0s, which comprised three different classes:

> Drummond 1883 2F Nos. 17230-17473, total 244
> McIntosh 1899 3F Nos. 17550-17645, total 96
> Pickersgill 1918 3F Nos 17650-17691, total 24 (superheated)

The dimensions were similar, save that the 3Fs had larger-bore cylinders and consequently were more powerful.

It can be readily seen that the Caledonian lines, when compared with the LNW, MR and L&Y systems, had changed even less under LMS ownership in terms of freight-haulage, reflecting the individualistic Scottish management of the LMS. It was the passenger-department where change had come about, where the emphasis had been on upgrading the expresses and their motive-power, mainly to compete with the LNER's East Coast route, a policy driven by prestige. The result was that, up to my visits in the mid-40s, very little change had occurred to the Scottish freight motive-power over the twenty years of the LMS; indeed, the two largest classes of Jumbo 0-6-0s, over three hundred locomotives, were intact, *and remained so well into BR days.* Even the 96 Pickersgill 3Fs had suffered few inroads, with only eleven scrapped during the last two years of the LMS, but now, with the war well over, replacements were becoming available. The express—and through-goods were hauled by standard locomotives, Jubilees, Patriots, Black Fives and Horwich moguls. Compound and 2P 4-4-0s often piloted Jubilees; 5584 *North West Frontier* was one I noted at Wishaw South, distinctive in the 'St Rollox' style of small lettering. Particularly after 1945, the Black Fives were everywhere, helping the 2-6-4Ts to displace various classes of Caleys, 4-4-0s, 4-6-0s and the 0-4-4 tank-engines, as the new 4-6-0s were pressed into service for almost everything.

Before our 1947-holiday ended, I was allowed to go to Motherwell on the SMT bus to watch the trains for the morning. Passing the station, I noticed the cut-out sign on the roof, a steel fretwork: LONDON MIDLAND & SCOTTISH RY Had it replaced a similar-style sign, spelling 'Caledonian Railway.'? Beyond the station, ex-CR 3F 0-6-0 tank 16285 was shunting the sidings of Bridge Engineering Ltd. and Hurst, Nelson & Co. Ltd., another big engineering-works and a manufacturer of railway-wagons. You may remember those standard 16-ton four-wheeled steel coal wagons that replaced the plank-built models. Many were made here, and a few are preserved. I saw whole trains of them being hauled out brand-new in works-grey being despatched to the south.

Then I headed for the sheds, close by on the Coatbridge/Airdrie turnout and what a sight it was. Rows and rows of old Caleys: Jumbos, Caley bogies, 0-4-4 and 0-6-0 tanks and even a CR 'pug' 0-4-0, 16032, my first view of this class of fifteen. However, some had gone to the scrapyard—but they did date from 1885 . . . The stock-list shows the 0-4-4Ts, numbering 124 engines in three different classes and, remarkably, *not one of them had been withdrawn* by that date—and only a few went just before the BR take-over in 1948. But *all* the 147 0-6-0Ts (16230-16376) remained intact well into BR days. Looking back now, it is remarkable that the Scottish operations of the LMS remained so stable for so long—partly because industry remained stable too (and old-fashioned), but partly because the LMS Executive allowed its Scottish directors considerable latitude to conduct their affairs north of the border. One detail of working they retained was the Caledonian route-indicator, two white pivoting-arms mounted on the top lamp-bracket of the locomotive. They appear in photographs, often on Princess pacifics, set horizontally, indicating the West Coast main line.

I recall our journey home in September 1945 very clearly. We went to Motherwell to catch a West Coast express to Carlisle, where we would change for Leeds. The up platform was crowded as the train swept in majestically, headed by pacific 6211 *Queen Maud*. A Princess—what a thrill—my first close-up view and haul by one of these lovely pacifics. Only the stop at Carstairs for Edinburgh passengers—with many more engines to note—interrupted our speeding progress and, after a swift climb from the River Clyde bridge near Lamington and up through Elvanfoot to Beattock Summit, we swooped down off the hills, probably at 90mph plus, through Wamphray and Dinwoodie, continuing fast to Lockerbie. But running into the Borders, I felt the train slowing and went to the end-window to look out. We were rolling towards Ecclefechan's tall outer-home signal, which was 'on'. The driver was staring down the track too, and we saw in the distance an engine backing slowly into the sidings; clearly the pick-up goods was late in finishing his shunting, and had overlapped our path in the time-table. The signal swung up just before we came to a stand, then the exhaust of the four-cylinder pacific attested the power as she pulled away strongly.

"Well" you ask, so you suffered a routine signal-check?" No! It was significant there and then because earlier that year, 1945, at that very spot, precisely the same situation had arisen, but on a wet morning *Duchess of Atholl* had run through the Ecclefechan signals and caused a tremendous collision. Beyond the sidings, we saw the rebuilt brick retaining-wall of the A.74 trunk-road skew-overbridge which had been damaged in that accident. A former Inspecting Officer of Railways, Captain Tyler, while investigating a similar accident on the GNR in 1876, the well-known disaster at Abbots Ripton north of Huntingdon, referred to two accidents on the Midland Railway—in particular, Arlesey Siding—where a train had been accepted up to the home signal while shunting was taking taking place in the station, the normal rule at the time. In his words, "The margin of safety had been reduced to the thickness of a signal-post." In our case, it was *two* signal-posts. This is food for thought: even with the provision since then on all main-lines of AWS followed by ATP, accidents still occur. The accident was attributed to smoke obscuring the driver's view, always worse in wet weather when steam tended to condense along the top of the boiler; deflector-shields (smoke deflectors) were fitted to the Duchesses to lift the exhaust from the top of the boiler, just as they had been on the Royal Scots. We ran smoothly down to Carlisle, where I walked up to inspect the engine, before she hooted and left on her way to Birmingham.

I had had plenty of time to do this, because this platform, 5, would shortly be hosting our train which would take us over Ais Gill Summit to

Leeds. I thus had the opportunity of observing the other engines in the vicinity: an LNER C15 4-4-2 tank-engine stood in the adjoining bay-platform ready for Newcastle; on the adjoining centre-road, our Royal Scot, 6117 *Welsh Guardsman* and Compound 1022 were standing, the compound awaiting the Edinburgh express arriving over the old North British line through St Boswells, Galashiels and Hawick, the 'Waverley Route', now closed. It duly arrived behind the gleaming A3 LNER 2568 *Sceptre*, a habitué of Carlisle. I watched the uncoupling after which the pacific went off to his shed at Carlisle Canal, the former NBR depot. In 1947, the Pacific was 91 *Captain Cuttle* (renumbered from 2745 in the LNER 1946-scheme, and used by BR in 1948 to display an experimental livery). Director D.11 4-4-0 *Luckie Mucklebackit*, evidently an earlier arrival from the North British line, had just gone off to Canal shed too. He was probably shedded here, as we often saw this engine in Carlisle.

When our train arrived—over the old G&SW route through Kilmarnock and Dumfries—we did not board straightaway, for the LMS had adopted the practice of adding two extra carriages to the front of this train. The *cognoscenti* would await this manoeuvre, to be sure of gaining a seat in the empty stock. Mother and I did this and boarded what even then looked a very old-fashioned carriage. Once seated comfortably, we looked round the compartment and noticed the mirrors bore the insignia G&SWR. The sepia photographs typically showed scenes from south-west Scotland, the countryside of Galloway and the Kirkcudbrightshire coast. That was a bonus to add to a super trip, where I had seen so much. Over the Settle-Carlisle line we arrived back in Leeds (City) and walked down Wellington Street with our suitcases to the Central Station for our humble stopping-train behind a radial tank to Halifax and home. This inconvenience has since been removed with the closure of Central in 1967 and the diversion of all trains into City, renamed simply 'Leeds.' I had seen hundreds of fresh engines to add to my collection, and so the journey became a milestone in my experience. The 1947 visit was similar, but more Class Fives were in evidence.

These are the locomotives I saw on the two trips, apart from those noted in the account:

McIntosh 0-4-4Ts: 1895:	15118/23/34/8/45
" " 1900:	15164/7/79/83/8/204/7/11/20/1/7
" "	1925: 15261/2
Pickersgill 4-6-2Ts: 1917:	15352/5
Drummond 0-4-0 'Pug' 1885:	16032
McIntosh 0-6-0 Dock Tank 1912:	16169
" 0-6-0T 1896:	16241/5/68/76/327/32/4/5/58.
Drummond 1883 0-6-0 'Jumbo':	17267/72/91/332/40/63/93/429/32/5
McIntosh 3F 0-6-0 1899:	17588/95/600/3/6/8/13/45
Pickersgill 3F 0-6-0 1918:	17653/4/68/70/81 (24 remained of the 74)
" 3F 0-6-0 1919 superheat:	17688 (one scrapped of the original seven).

To Leicester & Nuneaton, December 1947

This was my last chance to watch the LMS in action before it was nationalized. I had invited a school-friend, John Lines, home to Halifax for a few days before Christmas. Among other activities, I took him to my train-watching haunts, then we went off on the exchange-visit to his home in Leicester. I confine my remarks here to our train-spotting on that trip, John noting ex-L&Y types at Low Moor (25F) and Leeds Central. This trickle became a spate as we continued from Leeds (City); I mention the engines seen on the way in numerical order at principal places, which, however, do not include those I had already seen. Leaving Leeds, 3F 0-6-0T 7538 was standing in Stourton yard, then approaching Normanton came a scoop, rare 'freshers', ex-MR 4-4-0 397 and 1F 0-6-0Ts 1793, 1794, 1842 and 1855 and the brand-new Fairburn 2-6-4T 2187, 3F 0-6-0 3497, 3F 0-6-0Ts 7334, 7421 and 7443, followed wonderfully, by my first Beyer-Garratt, 7993. The list continues with 2-8-0s 8443, 8450, 8532, 8544 and 8547, ex-L&Y 0-6-0s 12088 and 12108, ex-MR 2F 0-6-0 22969; in the Sheffield area, Stanier 2-6-2 tanks 82, 139 and one of the four fitted with a larger boiler, 169; 3F 0-6-0Ts 7423 and 7634, and another Garratt 7982. More 3F shunters 7276, 7277 and 7545 graced Millhouses shed (19B) along with two more comparative rarities, 4-4-0 Belpaire 728 and especially 0F 0-4-0T 1531, probably in from the Staveley Works (Barrow Hill, 18D) for running repairs. Also on shed were 1P 0-4-4T 1344, 2F 0-6-0s

3058, 3140 and 3156; 3Fs 3191, 3661; 4F 4101; 2F 0-6-0 22940 and 22950. This was a very good haul, but better was still to come.

Trent Junction with its array of Midland signals produced further ex-MR engines, 2P 4-4-0 548, 1P 0-4-4T 1324 and 0-6-0T 1682. More 3F tanks were shunting here, 7274, 7422, 7442, 7534, 7539 and 7582. At Nottingham appeared 3Fs 3235, 3242, 3441, 3529, 3538; 2F 0-6-0s 3511, 3648 and 3687; 4Fs 3958 and 4433; more shunters 7552, 7629, 7637; yet another Garratt, 7977, and the palindromic ex-L&Y 0-6-0 12121 some way out of his area. Two 2-8-0s, 8390 and 8434, were heading coal trains. The Trent-Nottingham stretch started me on another new class, the ex-LT&S 4-4-2 tanks. The first, 2093, was at Trent, and two more stood at Nottingham, 2096 and 2103. As if this were not enough, one of the second class of 4-4-2Ts, 2120, built by the LMS in 1923, was standing outside Leicester as we ran in. I was thrilled to see these strangers. They had been transferred from the Tilbury lines on the arrival of the replacement Stanier 3-cylinder 2-6-4 tanks. The rarest cop of all though, was one of the last four ex-MR 2-4-0s, 20155, which we knew to be shedded at Nottingham. Fortunately, he was standing in full view alongside the shed, at a guess mostly held in reserve for occasional outings, rather than placed there especially for the benefit of passing spotters! At Loughborough, another exiled ex-L&Y 0-6-0 came our way, 12135, a further 3F shunter 7534 and 2-8-0s 8402 and 8549. Leicester produced several 2-6-4Ts, Fairburn 2228, Fowlers 2320, 2330 and 2373 and Stanier, 2660, 4Fs 3956, 3965 and 4419. New Class Five 4997 was about to depart with a Leeds semi-fast.

Although John was a confirmed Great Western supporter, he looked after me, once ensconced in his comfortable home, by taking me by bus to see LMS trains, as well as to the GWR at Leamington Spa. Here, the local engines were naturally fresh to me: Derby 2-6-2 tanks 3 and 9, and Staniers 135 and 144. Ex-MR 0-6-0 2F 23009 was shunting, while Super-Ds 9319, 9409, 9410, 9412 were hauling coal. His kindest gesture though, was to take us on another bus to Nuneaton, that butt of the stand-up comic—but nothing comic for us, just the bliss of the West Coast route. The town stood in a mining-area, and consequently at the head of several mineral branches. One always has regrets, though— mine simply the continuing scarcity of films for the box-camera preventing me from taking any pictures. I retain instead the images of that day printed indelibly on my memory, seen from our vantage point beside the Leamington branch south of the station, with views of the spread of tracks under the huge ex-LNW signal-gantries. The crack expresses always take pride of place, and we saw a similar selection of motive-power to that I had spotted at Preston, the trains augmented at Nuneaton by the Euston-Manchester/Liverpool trains. Duchess 6239 *City of Chester* on a Glasgow express and 6247 *City of Liverpool* most appropriately hauling one to that city, almost completed the class for me. However, we could not stay to see The Merseyside Express and so missed seeing *Turbomotive*. We had strict instructions to be back in Leicester in time for tea; John's father was a Methodist minister and he ran his home to a time-table, so discipline was the watchword.

Other expresses were headed by Royal Scots, 6115 *Scots Guardsman*, 6130 *The West Yorkshire Regiment*, 6148 *The Manchester Regiment*, 6159 *The Royal Air Force*, 6164 *The Artists' Rifleman* and 6165 *The Ranger (12th London Regiment)*, a splendid haul, leaving very few still to underline in my ABC. As I had seen all the Jubilees by this date, I did not note those we saw, but I did see three fresh Patriots, the unnamed 5509, 5521 *Rhyl* and 5533 *Lord Rathmore*. They were by then employed more on semi-fast expresses and parcels-trains. Again, after years of daily observations, they left few that I had not seen. Class Five 4909 sped through on an up fully-fitted van-train, possibly banana-empties, and colleague 5431 trundled through on down ecs. Intensive local services were running, both on the main line and on the branch to Leamington Spa diverging beside us. This enabled John to see at least a few Prairie tanks and one of the GWR diesel-railcars built by AEC. LMS 2-6-2Ts were in evidence too, Derby 18, Staniers 109, 145, 190, 202 and 205, all from shed 2D (Nuneaton), ex-MR 4-4-0s, 322, a rebuild of an 1882 original for the S&DJR and so quite a cop, 447 and 508 of the '483'-class. Several 2-6-4 tanks were also in evidence, a Fairburn, 2262, still new, and Stanier 2606. But the cream on the cake was the appearance of the sole member of the 'Prince of Wales' class remaining in stock, 25752, typically on a branch-train. It was one of only a handful of ex-LNWR express-locomotives to be taken into BR stock only a week later. Fans of the LNW/LMS may recall the photograph in the railway press in the spring of 1949 of three locomotives standing together at Crewe, condemned, and posed for the camera on the rear siding: 'Prince of Wales' 25752, 4-4-0 'Precursor' 25297 *Sirocco* and 4-4-0 'George the Fifth' 25376 *Snipe*, each the sole survivor of its class, the three representing the last LNWR express-passenger engines remaining. They still carried their LMS numbers and insignia. This list of locos for branch—and cross-country traffic seems numerous now, but at that time, Nuneaton, like other junctions on the West Coast route, was the hub of several routes, apart from the colliery branches, necessitating many duties with a wide range of motive-power. It was the role of the local shed, 2D, to provide these.

The colliery-lines needed the ubiquitous 0-6-0 goods engines, including ex-MR 2F 3161, and ex-LNW 'Cauliflower' 28487, another treat. The consequent marshalling required 3F shunters, 7286, 7594, and the trains were hauled out by Super-D 0-8-0s 8896, 8940, 9068, 9080, 9190, 9239, 9242, 9272, 9318, 9351, 9368, 9415, 9435, 9436. Stanier 2-8-0s 8438, 8465, 8550, 8660 also appeared on mineral-traffic, clearly still very much in the minority against the LNW engines. Three Stanier moguls, rarely seen on the Midland Division, but here on home territory, passed on express goods-trains, 2950, 2974 and 2978. The rarities speak for themselves; both in this respect and generally, I had a super haul in just a few days. Of the impressive list, many aspects are striking when surveying the locomotives and the classes they represent: so many Super-Ds still evident, and not idling on secondary duties either, but typically working hard on main-line mineral-trains, a feature of the Midlands; the large number of constituent-locomotives still in service generally, Midland 2Fs and 3Fs still numbering many hundreds, an army of 3F shunters and other tank-engines. The paucity of Black Fives, by then numbering over seven hundred, seems remarkable, but I had seen a good number of them previously and therefore do not include them here.

This was my last big outing to watch trains before the LMS was swallowed up by BR only days ahead on 1 January 1948. Back at home in Halifax, 31 December 1947 was tinged with sadness. I obtained permission from my parents to cycle down to my old haunt Lilly Lane Bridge, a mile from home. My friend John came with me. Close to midnight, we watched a Manchester-Leeds express run in, the engine's number, 4807, just discernible in the yard-lighting around Halifax West Box. It had to be a Black Five—but the company had produced over 700, so it was only to be expected. Melancholy at the end of the LMS, we cycled home up the hill.

In 1928, ex-LYR railmotor 10614 has arrived at the Stainland terminus, Halifax. (National Rail Museum/SSPL).

An LMS 4-6-0 in America. #6100 *Royal Scot* pauses during the 11,000-mile tour of the USA in 1933 (H.C. Casserley collection).

Ex-LNW 0-6-0 coal-tank 7822 awaits duty on Edge Hill MPD, Liverpool (author).

Horwich mogul 42835 on through-freight coasts through Gargrave heading a Carlisle-Leeds freight on a sunny July afternoon in 1959 (author).

A brand-new example of the BR Standard '5', 73010, stands on Leeds Holbeck MPD in July 1951 (author).

PART III

NATIONALIZATION 1948

At Grayrigg, Cumbria, wcml, in 1960, Stanier 2-6-4 tank-engine 42449 drops back from the freight he was banking up the gradient from Oxenholme. Several of these splendid 2-6-4s were employed as bankers, both here and on the Shap gradient, a little further north. This engine was still here five years later (author).

The first Royal Scot 4-6-0 to be 'converted': *Royal Scots Fusilier* about to leave Leeds Holbeck MPD to haul the afternoon express to Glasgow (St. Enoch) in 1947 (author).

Stanier 2-6-0 2966 passing Berkhamsted on up freight, wcml (H.C. Casserley collection).

Chapter 9

THE LMS AND BR. PERSONALITIES AND INFLUENCES

The Lancashire & Yorkshire Railway

Let us look now at the men leading the London Midland & Scottish Railway from from its birth in 1923 and its successor British Railways, from 1948. A year before the grouping of 1923, on 1 January 1922, the London & North Western Railway had amalgamated with its smaller neighbour the Lancashire & Yorkshire Railway. Paradoxically, several of the smaller partner's senior staff continued in their positions after the amalgamation, largely through seniority. The L&Y general manager, secretary and its CME, George Hughes, received the same appointments on the enlarged system. Furthermore, at the Grouping occurring just a year later, a similar situation occurred: Hughes became CME of the entire LMS, making Horwich its centre of design, and other other L&Y men gained leading-positions. On the further reorganisation occurring a generation after the grouping, the nationalization of all the railways, several LMS men were appointed to leading-positions on BR. Some, including Riddles, its CME, had received training on the L&Y at Horwich, thus some of its traditions and practices lived on. Hughes, in his papers read to the Institution of Mechanical Engineers in 1909 and 1910, had demonstrated that he was a profound thinker, receptive to modern ideas, well aware of railway developments evolving around him, and always prepared to innovate to keep the 'Lanky' ahead technically. It was a pioneer in several fields. First, its locomotive-works had not grown *ad hoc* like most of its contemporaries, but had been planned as a modern engineering—and erecting-shop when constructed on a greenfield-site in the 1880s. Second, in 1906, it built the first British locomotive fitted with the high-degree Schmidt superheater, which was proving itself on overseas railways; third, it introduced steel fireboxes in 1902, fourth, its electric shunter of 1906, fifth, further electrification projects: Liverpool-Southport in 1904 and the Manchester-Bury-Holcombe Brook suburban-lines; sixth, in 1903, electro-pneumatic points and signals at Bolton West; seventh, the only dynamometer-car with integrator to come into LMS stock—and the best car, therefore worth updating in 1929; and eighth but not least, its Staff College, moved to Derby later, in 1938. There are other examples. Aspinall, Hughes' predecessor on the L&Y, remained highly respected in engineering-circles, in fact a railway 'guru' who was frequently consulted in his old age, for example during the enquiry on the Southern Railway derailment in 1927 near Sevenoaks in Kent.

Midland Railway influences on the LMS

The traditions and expansionism of another leading constituent of the LMS, the Midland Railway, were also significant. These words are merely a reminder of the relentless and determined spread of the MR throughout its eighty-year life. The drive of the directors is evidenced in a constant expansion in all directions from the Leicester & Swannington, a local mineral-line; its amalgamation in 1844 with two other companies created the Midland Railway. It gained importance through its stretch of the first London to York main line, before the GNR opened its own direct route in 1850. At the southern end of its system, the MR instituted the first through route to London, from Rugby through an agreement with the LNWR. Midland freight-traffic was growing rapidly and in 1853 the company submitted a Bill to Parliament proposing amalgamation with the LNWR. The Bill failed through government's worries over monopolies, a concern that pervaded the nineteenth century.

An earlier scheme to connect Leicester with the GNR at Hitchin was immediately revived. The line opened in 1857. However, similar difficulties arose, namely a lack of priority and congestion. The MR needed its own line to London. This, their first big expansion, terminated in the splendid Victorian-Gothic St Pancras Station opening in 1868, overshadowing the insignificant GNR train-sheds next door at King's Cross. Great Eastern trains from Cambridge and SECR services from Kent came into St Pancras as well. The GE agreement also gave the Midland access to London docks via Stratford, which it also also reached along the Widened Lines of the Metropolitan Railway; MR coal was now unloaded at points such as Walworth Road and West India Dock, Poplar.

Through the GE agreements, the Midland ran through to Tottenham and Forest Gate, and a further extension linked with the LT&SR. From 1899, this allowed MR trains to reach Tilbury to serve the Orient Line's ships sailing to Australia. The next step was to take over the entire LT&SR network. It took place in 1912—under the noses of the GE, so red trains now ran to Southend-on-Sea as well. This was the Midland's last big expansion. Tilbury also enabled steamer-services to places such as Gravesend, Herne Bay, Margate and Ramsgate, competing with other boats. Later, one route even crossed the English Channel to Dunkirk by means of an agreement by its new owners, the LMS, with the French line Angleterre-Lorraine-Alsace (ALA) in 1929, in an attempt to compete with the Dover and Folkestone ferries. This initiative however, proved unremunerative and was abandoned after a short period.

The MR operations over the S&DJR line have been described. To summarize, the MR outmanoeuvred the GWR to absorb the Birmingham & Gloucester Railway, then extended their operations to Bristol to gain access to the south-west. The MR branch onward to Bath encouraged the S&DJR to extend northwards to link up there, so allowing MR trains to run through from Birmingham to Bournemouth, a flourishing and fashionable watering-place. The LMS moved its Birmingham departure-point back to Manchester in 1926 and later named this through-train *The Pines Express*. Other northern towns had through-trains or carriages. After BR diverted traffic away from the S&DJR and closed it in 1966, the track was lifted, but some traces are visible, including preserved sections at Midford and Shillingstone. North of this village, the Sturminster Newton station-cutting has been filled in to create a park. Its gates bear the legend in white scrolled-iron

'The Somerset & Dorset Joint Railway.' A nearby pillar carries sculpted scenes, including a MR 4-4-0. Further south, the museum at Blandford Forum has memorabilia of the S&DJR and a model layout of the line in that locality with working LMS trains.

Immediately following the St Pancras opening, the Midland began to complete the difficult route through the High Peak from Rowsley in Derbyshire to Manchester, where its new terminus, Manchester Central, gave it access to Southport, Liverpool and the Wirral peninsula through the Cheshire Lines Committee, on which it partnered the GNR and the GCR. Not content with the London-Manchester line, the company now wanted its own route to Scotland. As detailed in chapter 6, it had found an agreement impossible with the LNWR, its end-on neighbour at the Lune Valley terminus at Ingleton, as the way forward to Carlisle.

Consequently, in 1869, the company embarked on its Settle-Carlisle line. The project became an expensive struggle to overcome the difficulties of driving an express-line over a summit of almost 1,200ft through the Pennine Hills. After its opening to passengers in 1876, the MR, now a substantial network, digested the huge construction-costs with the aid of its big coal-haulage revenues, and continued its expansion at a slower pace. An agreement with the GSWR at Carlisle enabled through-services to Glasgow over that company's line via Dumfries and Kilmarnock. At Dumfries, the MR gained a through-route to the port of Stranraer in order to secure some of the Northern Irish traffic to Larne. This was achieved by yet further agreements, including one with the Portpatrick & Wigtownshire Railway, to run through-carriages over that company's single-track from Dumfries south-westward across Galloway to the junction with the GSWR line from Glasgow near Stranraer. The short crossing of the North Channel to Larne made it popular with travellers who disliked sea-voyages.

If Midland policy meant anything, it was, 'one thing leads to another', one of life's true sayings. The Stranraer agreements enabled a further step in 1903: a leap across the narrow strait to take over the Belfast & Northern Counties Railway, which it reorganized as the Northern Counties Committee. It was of course equipped with Derby products. Another project which needed a considerable capital outlay was the development of another packet-port, to use the contemporary term, at Heysham in Lancashire (pronounced like 'key'). By absorbing a small local company, the MR began to construct a deep-water terminal on this muddy inlet south of the seaside-resort of Morecambe. They rebuilt the lines to form a triangle, Heysham-Morecambe-Lancaster—and equipped it with DC 1500v overhead-line electric multiple-unit trains. A power-station at Heysham fed the system, which opened in 1907. It lay at the cutting-edge of technology. The MR was now able to run steamers (ferries in today's language) which began to ply to the Isle of Man and Ireland. The shipping-company that inherited the former route, 'The Isle of Man Steam Packet Co. Ltd'., retains the name, though its ships are now mostly powered by the ubiquitous diesel-engine. The one exception is a preserved steamship, which still operates. 'Packet' indicated that the boats carried the mails. The IOM Steam Packet Co is the oldest ferry-company in the world. The Midland became able to compete with the LNWR further in the holiday-trade with its bright and airy Morecambe Promenade station. From Lancaster Green Ayre station, an MR line served Leeds, merging at Settle Junction with the Settle & Carlisle line. From the intervening Wennington Junction, it ran westwards jointly with the Furness Railway to Carnforth, also on the West Coast route, north of Lancaster. This allowed MR trains from the south to serve destinations in Cumbria via the FR main-line: Barrow-in-Furness, a booming shipbuilding-town, and Millom with its haematite mines and ironworks. Further along the coast it reached another coal-and-steel district, Whitehaven, Workington and Maryport. Here, the MR made an end-on connection with the Maryport & Carlisle Railway, providing another access to Carlisle.

The Midland made numerous further agreements to gain running-powers over neighbouring-companies' lines in order to reach out to further markets. A big development of this concept was the joint venture with the Great Northern Railway to tap the wide acres of East Anglia. The Midland & Great Northern Joint Railway of 1893, an amalgamation of several local companies, enabled the two railways to run through-trains from Manchester and the East Midlands via Peterborough to Norfolk, including Norwich and seaside-resorts such as Cromer and Great Yarmouth, as well as Norfolk Broads holiday-spots. A smaller project was the MR extension from Normanton, south of

Leeds, to Dewsbury, in order to tap this expanding textile-area, with a branch to Huddersfield, which, however, was opened for goods only. The Dewsbury line was also the stump of an unfulfilled project for a new north-south line to place Bradford on a through-route. Another line in which the Midland was interested was the Midland & South Western Junction Railway, running from Andoversford Junction near Cheltenham on the Midland route from Birmingham, across country, coincidentally to Andover on the London & South Western Railway. The M&SWJR thus connected the two systems. Although its rolling-stock was painted in 'Midland Red' and it received MR loans and through-traffic, the MR interest never approached ownership. Eventually, Midland tentacles spread from Shoeburyness to Swansea and from Great Yarmouth to Stranraer.

The London & North Western Railway

The progress of this company, incorporated in 1846, the other major constituent of the LMS, is less dramatic, since it was formed early in the railway age with an amalgamation of the London & Birmingham Railway and the Grand Junction Railway to Warrington (already amalgamated with the Liverpool & Manchester), making it a considerable network. Its progress continued with absorptions and extensions. One was the leasing of the seventy-mile Lancaster & Carlisle in 1849. With extensions and agreements, the LNWR threw out branches from its spine from Euston, for example, through the east Midlands to Peterborough, west to the Cambrian coast and from Crewe to Chester, Shrewsbury, and then through central Wales to Swansea. Finally in 1921, the year of the Act grouping the railways, it developed its association with its smaller neighbour, the Lancashire & Yorkshire Railway, into a full amalgamation.

The Great War, beginning in 1914, put paid to major expansions, and time would soon show that the Edwardian era was the pinnacle of the railways' importance as prime-movers of people and goods, and that the rail would be unable to expand much further. It would rather have to struggle to retain its existing traffic against road-competition, as explained in Chapter 2. The culmination, after another war, ending in 1945, was the wide ownership of private-cars and the door-to-door convenience of moving goods by lorry with which the railways could not compete—even with containers—either logistically or financially. The Clean Air Act of 1957 brought about the decline of coal-burning in factories and houses, with the consequent loss of this lucrative business to the railway: coal-carrying represented over fifty percent of receipts. These factors contributed to the closure of many branch—and cross-country-lines from that time, explained elsewhere.

This summary indicates the constant quest of the Midland Railway to extend itself in a competitive market. Its continual expansions and agreements had taken it to practically all corners of England, and into Wales, Scotland and Northern Ireland. In this way, the company had achieved equality with the LNWR, 'the Premier Line', at the Grouping of 1923. Furthermore, after only two years, its CME, Henry Fowler, was appointed CME of the whole LMS Group. Thus its influence strongly swayed the policies of the new company, visible to the public in its 'Midland-red' carriages and passenger-locomotives.

The very name of the new Group fully reflected MR influence: 'London' (from the LNWR), 'Midland' (MR), while 'Scottish' acknowledged the companies north of the border. The LMS continued other Midland practices. The cast-iron number-plates on the smokebox-doors were considered useful and adopted, but disliked by the staff at Crewe, who refused to fit them to many ex-LNWR engines. Also bolted on the smokebox-doors were MR-type shed-plates, at first a simple number; for example 7 denoted Rugby as the locomotive's home-shed (changed later to 2A). The suffixes were introduced in the 1930s, so that 'A' denoted the principal shed of a group having heavy-repair facilities, the subsidiaries, or 'garage' depots, indicated with 'B', 'C' and so on. For example, 20A denoted Leeds (Holbeck), 20B Stourton, the suffixes continuing to 20H for Lancaster (Green Ayre). Both smokebox-plates were two of several MR traditions continued by BR from 1948. To avoid duplication after 1923, most locomotives had to be renumbered. Midland locomotives were numbered in blocks of numbers allocated to each class, and the strong Midland influence caused the LMS to follow this practice, allowing Midland engines to retain their numbers. For example, Kirtley double-framed 2-4-0s began at 1 and the 4-4-0 compounds ran from 1000 to 1045. The other details of LMS renumbering have been described.

Influence of the LYR and MR on BR

A generation later, on the nationalized British Railways, it was fortunate for LMS fans that R.A. Riddles became its CME. This engineer, trained at Horwich (LYR), Derby (MR) and Crewe (LNWR), produced a stud of standard locomotives based on the best of his mentor, Sir William A. Stanier, but including Fairburn's improved ash-disposal devices, the rocking-grates, self-emptying ashpans and self-cleaning smokeboxes, denoted by a further plate on the smokebox-door, 'SC', fixed below the shed-plate. The LMS shed-numbering system, explained as originating on the Midland Railway and extended by the LMS, was also adopted by BR, suitably expanded so as to include all the depots of the former LNER, GWR and SR, resulting in the appearance of numbers such as 73A (Stewarts Lane), south-east London, and 83D (Laira, Plymouth), startling at first to LMS followers, used to shed-numbers only up to 32. The other smokebox-plate, the number, was also continued by BR, but was unpopular at Swindon, just as it had been after 1923 at Crewe—and we have seen that Swindon was reluctant to repaint its stock, resenting its loss of integrity on nationalization. As for locomotive—and carriage-liveries, BR experimented for a while with blue or green engines and the attractive carmine-and-cream, or plum-and-spilt-milk, ('blood-and-custard' in the vernacular) express-carriage livery, before standardizing on the rather smart 'BR maroon' lined out in yellow-black-yellow, almost identical to the former LMS livery. This too, it is recalled, had been inherited from the MR after 1923—and so the Midland influence lived on. It was very visible too in the name of the region. The majority of the former LMS network in England became the London Midland Region of BR, usually abbreviated in the English way to 'Midland Region', some engines for a short time bore an 'M' prefix, but the wagon—and carriage-numbers carried the prefix 'M' permanently. So the former Midland Railway was now effectively the name of almost the whole of the former LMS! In the 1990s, the various privatized train-companies naturally adopted their own liveries and logos, but a few rakes of carriages were maintained in the plum-and-spilt-milk and in 'BR red' (or 'LMS red', depending on one's sympathies) and reserved for excursions. These chartered-trains, operated by the preservation-societies, can often be seen hauled by preserved steam-locomotives. One of these excursion-trains forms the subject of a delicious anecdote.

Down in Kent in 1992, I had been attending the 'Ashford 150', a two-day celebration of a hundred and fifty years of railways in the town, when a poignant scene occurred. On the Sunday, having steamed up the branch from Hastings via Rye to Ashford in stock consisting of one of these rakes in red, behind preserved Standard 4 light 4-6-0 75027, admired the preserved West Country light-pacific 34027 *Taw Valley*, also in gleaming Brunswick-green, and toured the depot at nearby Chart Leacon, my party was sitting on a sunny platform-seat awaiting the train home to Folkestone. Opposite, the red chartered-train was being propelled into the back platform (the normal Hastings branch-platform) by 75027, at the moment when a group of railwaymen were walking up the platform towards us. One was an elderly guard, at a guess near retirement, equipped for duty with his satchel and flags. He glanced across the station at the excursion-carriages, then turned to his colleagues and muttered, "I see they've brought a Midland train, then." This, of course, was said at Ashford, a stronghold of the SR, whose carriages of course used to be green. Old traditions die hard: red carriages meant Midland—of *seventy* years before, or at least, the LMS, of fifty. Mind you, the guard probably meant (London) Midland (Region), but I smiled at him anyway, and to myself, at this significant and poignant remark. It brought a sweet feeling: the Midland Railway lives on . . .

The Railway Grouping & Nationalization Compared

Key dates
Part I gave an account of life on the LMS in the 1940s, and now younger readers can establish some benchmarks, important dates. The two principal ones are the Grouping on 1 January 1923 and the Nationalization on 1 January 1948. These reorganisations followed each World War of the twentieth century; wars were always factors to accelerate change in many aspects of life.

1923, the Grouping

The details of this milestone in the railways of Britain have been described in Chapter 2. In the LMS Group, the MR and the LNWR vied with each other from the start in attempting to dominate affairs. Exploration has been made of 'Midland' in the title 'LMS', while outlining the Midland Railway's policy of relentless expansion throughout its eighty-year history. The name geographically described the new LMS territory maybe, but it can be seen as the prize for the MR's last throws of expansion, almost up to the 1914 war, to equal the mighty LNWR.

The Big Four, like their constituent railways, were statutory companies, that is, each was set up by its own Act of Parliament and so the company name did not include 'Ltd'; the concept of limited liability was incorporated into its own statute, like a water-company, for example. The Act empowered the companies to issue their own shares, debentures and by-laws and regulations covering different aspects of operation. Excerpts from these can occasionally be found on old lineside cast-iron signs or in collections purchased from BR. The railway trade unions were disappointed at this outcome: they had been campaigning strongly for a single, unified railway system, above all one owned by the state. However, they had to wait another generation for this to come about, nationalization—a grouping the trade-unions had wanted a generation earlier, in 1923.

1948, Nationalization

During parliamentary discussions during 1946 on nationalization as a prelude to the Transport Act of the following year, the other three companies of the Big Four adopted a negative approach, resenting the coming loss of their identity and traditions. Names and status are important. But to Parliament, nationalization seemed the only way forward for an industry on its knees after six difficult years of war, when no fresh projects could be tackled and only essential maintenance was carried out. Furthermore, the bedrock of Labour policy was state-ownership of public utilities, therefore the election of a Labour Government in 1945 made railway-nationalization a certainty. The LNER in particular was in desperate financial straits and proposed to its shareholders that it cease trading, a proposal they rejected. They, along with the GWR and SR simply marked time, awaiting the financial bail-out. However, the LMS, with its greater resources—and a resolute Executive—was continuing to push its modernization-programme forward determinedly as already detailed, with the most advanced rolling-stock technically, and organized by a positive, forward-looking team, from its management to its engineers. In so doing, it confirmed itself as the leader of the Big Four, standing ready for the challenges that lay ahead. This explains the strong LMS influence in the new BR from 1948. The Transport Bill received Royal assent in August 1947, with vesting-day to be Thursday 1 January 1948.

This second reorganization merged the big four railways into one state corporation, British Railways. The umbrella-organization of the British Transport Commission had an Executive (a name borrowed from the LMS) for each activity: Railways; Railway Hotels; Docks; London Transport; and the bus interests. The Transport Act 1947 incorporated only those docks owned by the railway companies, for instance, Heysham in Lancashire, one of the MR's late developments, and Folkestone Harbour in Kent. They contrasted with the Felixstowe Docks & Railways Company, The Mersey Docks & Harbour Board, the Port of London Authority and the Dover Harbour Board, examples of several retaining their independent status as statutory companies. One consequence of 1948 was that BR found it owned two or more locomotives with the same number. A similar situation had occurred at the Grouping of 1923, where, for example, under the new LNER regime Great Northern Railway engines had 3,000 added to their numbers, allowing the North Eastern Railway locomotives to retain theirs. The LMS renumbering-scheme has been described. Evidently this had been overlooked, so again locomotives were renumbered.

The BR Renumbering Scheme of 1948

The locomotives of the GWR were not renumbered because the brass number-plates on the locomotives were more permanent than the other companies' numbers in mere paint or transfer. This meant that the locomotives of the other three companies of the Big Four had to be renumbered to avoid confusion. At first, a letter was added to engine-numbers with BRITISH RAILWAYS lettered in Gill Sans broken-white on the tenders or tanks. In 1923, the South Eastern & Chatham locomotives had been given the prefix 'E' and those of the Brighton company 'B' by the new Southern Railway group. The 1948 scheme added the regional letter 'M' (London Midland Region) to LMS engines, LNER numbers took 'E' (Eastern and North-Eastern Regions), 'S' (Southern Region) to Southern Railway locomotives and 'Sc' to those in Scotland. The letter appeared before, above or under the number on the cab, and welded to the smokebox numberplate. However, the Sc produced a conflict between former LMS and LNER engines stationed in Scotland, now merged into a single Scottish Region, a difficulty evidently unforeseen by the British Railways Board. A revised scheme avoided this by adding 40,000 to LMS numbers, e.g. 2-6-2 tank 1 became 40001 and 'Black Five' 5000 became 45000, the longer number painted in smaller, 8in, Gill Sans, broken-white figures. The regional letters were used from 2 February to 15 March 1948, superseded by a '3', '4 & 5' or '6' prefix from 16 March. Southern Railway locomotives were prefixed with '3' and LNER with a '6'. But LMS numbers above 20,000 (officially the reserve-list, old, non-standard machines), could not take the prefix '4', as this would overlap into the LNER list, so they were converted in a special series from 58000; e.g. the Lickey Banker 'Big Bertha' 22290 became 58100. But, many of these antiquities were scrapped without receiving their new numbers.

You can see that how the GWR had been favoured: no renumbering on account of those number-plates! Was some influence also brought to bear? After all, the company served prestigious parts of the country such as the Thames valley and the West Country. It had, as a company—almost as a family—continued unruffled in 1923, merely absorbing some minor railways, and so the Swindon tradition had continued unbroken and undiluted for more than a century. Now it can be seen how one thing led to another, and why, in 1948, on the nationalisation of *all* the railways, where the GWR became simply the Western Region (WR), the repainting was unpopular and for some time the men at Swindon refused to conform. For generations, they had been brought up in the unbroken tradition of the GWR—which had begun in 1838 at the dawn of railways. The company had virtually created the Borough of Swindon (incorporated in 1897), the New Town anyway, and practically ran it, with its schools, surgeries, the the Mechanics' Institute with its evening-classes, feasts and excursions for the huge crowd of families connected with the works. In fact, Swindon's reluctance to conform continued for years, refusing to repaint engines and carriages in the new colours decreed by the new management, especially since this top brass was based in a foreign land called Marylebone or Euston Road! It was reminiscent of the LNWR after 1923. As late as July 1955, *over seven years after nationalization*, as an occasional visitor to Western Region metals, I saw a 'Castle' class locomotive still in full GWR livery and hauling a train of the traditional chocolate-and-cream carriages, the *Torbay Express*. They should have been in plum-and-spilt-milk by that date and the locomotive-tender relettered.

Swindon's last throw of individualism was in its diesel-hydraulic express-locomotives. Leaving aside the unsuccessful D.600s, the 'Warships' were followed by the last class, the much-loved 'Westerns', and when they were constructed from 1961, no less than *thirteen years* into the BR-regime, the works *still* fitted the traditional Swindon cast number-plate on their cab-sides—*including more than half of the class constructed at Crewe*. The plates were in aluminium now, not brass, but this is irrelevant: it demonstrates the deeply-rooted GWR traditions. Furthermore, because of these plates, they were able to resist a further renumbering consequent upon the full computerization by BR in 1967, which required a simple nomenclature to replace the complicated 'Type 1, 2, 3 or 4' plus horse-power capacities and 'D' plus locomotive-number.

The numerical description was achieved by introducing the TOPS nomenclature, for example, the 'Class 25' and 'Class 47' designations. These were logically extended to include the engine-number that we are familiar with today, such as 47704—which had been a Continental practice for generations. Thus the 'Type 4 diesel-hydraulic Co-Co' officially became simply 'Class 52' when diesel locomotives lost their 'D' prefix in favour of the class number but, perhaps for reasons of nostalgia and certainly loyalty to tradition, the Class 52s retained their number-plates, now with the 'D' painted over. The foreword to J.A.M. Vaughan's *Western Diesels in Camera* (Ian Allan, 1977), is a fascinating introduction to a sympathetic, nostalgic illustrated book on a well-loved class of locomotive.

Awareness of these two important dates, the Grouping of 1923 and the Nationalisation of 1948, renders an account so much more interesting when it concerns, say, a class of locomotive that was being constructed in 1947 and on into the BR-era as many were, such as LMS Class Fives, LNER B1s (and all their A1 pacifics), Southern light pacifics or Great Western Castles. Looking now at the preserved.7029 *Clun Castle*, resplendent in its Brunswick green, with its 'Great Western' title on the tender, burnished brass (including of course its number-plate) and copper-capped chimney in the precise Swindon-tradition, it should be borne in mind that this locomotive was actually constructed not by the GWR but by BR, because it was built in 1950, and therefore it never ran in this livery. Several preserved LNER engines also fall into this category. Purists may argue that *Clun Castle* should at least appear with the title BRITISH RAILWAYS or the 'first lion' on the tender, possibly on the Brunswick green ground, as a 'halfway livery-change.' The argument surfaces from time to time in preservation-societies and the press concerning which livery a certain locomotive should carry, according to its date of construction or rebuilding, receiving a different chimney and so on—a debate that is virtually insoluble.

The Locomotive Exchanges of 1948-9

The official aim of this was to evaluate modern locomotives of the 'big four' railways as a basis for new standard designs, not to run a sporting contest between the various classes of engine. However, the press and especially the personalities of the crews intervened. Some were rather 'gung-ho', others lacked confidence, while a further group seemed to be 'coal-dodging.' These factors affected the Black Fives in particular. The LMS engines comprised two Duchesses, two Royal Scots, two Black Fives and a 2-8-0 freight-engine. In a mini-exchange during 1949, Stanier 2-6-4 and 2-6-2 tanks operated suburban services from Leamington Spa to Birmingham Snow Hill. All in all, the LMS designs acquitted themselves well, though the Black Fives ran below their potential best. They were 45253 and 44973, the latter on the Highland line. On the former Great Central and Midland routes, 45253 gave adequate performances, depending on its crews. But it was the Converted Royal Scots that stole the show: 46154 *The Hussar* and 46162 *Queen's Westminster Rifleman* looked wonderful to their supporters in their post-war lined-out 'straw' livery, glossy-black complete with LMS insignia. Since the SR lacked water-troughs, *The Hussar* headed the 'Atlantic Coast Express' from Waterloo with a larger-capacity tender borrowed from an ex-WD freight-engine. However, someone, very likely Cox, had had it lettered 'LMS' to show the flag as it were, a brilliant move. *Queen's Westminster Rifleman* was rostered on expresses from Paddington to Plymouth, its standard tender still bearing 'LMS'. Each locomotive was coupled to an ancient dynamometer-car, the old SR and GWR cars. They contrasted with the new LMS car, used with exchange-locomotives on their tracks, another example of the company's continuing drive towards modernization. The two ex-LMS pacifics, 46236 *City of Bradford* headed expresses from Kings Cross to Leeds and from Paddington to Birkenhead, and 46237 *City of Bristol* hauled the 'Cornish Riviera Express'. As expected, both engines acquitted themselves effortlessly, demonstrating the advantages of a wide firebox. In the summer of 1949, the two tank-engines ran their trials. The weak 2-6-2 was no match for the brisk GWR 'Prairie' tanks, normal on this route, but the 2-6-4 demonstrated its usual competence on the stop-and-start services. With the exchanges over, the ex-LMS men were justifiably proud of their engines' achievements.

In 1956, the ex-LMS pacific 46237 *City of Bristol* was lent to the Western Region and underwent a series of dynamometer-car trials. This was not a locomotive-exchange however: Western men worked the engine with their own inspectors on the footplate. Comparisons were made with recent dynamometer-car tests of 6013 *King Henry VIII*, the usual motive-power from Paddington to Plymouth. The King had been worked consistently hard throughout. It is noteworthy that this class was the progenitor of the LMS pacific. Both runs now had to reach Plymouth in exactly four hours, a much-sharper timing than in the 1948 exchanges, and each engine had the same load, 420 tons from Westbury, the beginning of the stiff uphill-work. *City of Bristol*, even with the Western crew aboard, men unfamiliar with the engine, left the King's timing behind at several stages of its run. However, since the tonnage over the Devon banks far exceeded that allowed for an engine of the 8P power-class, a pilot-engine was taken from Newton Abbot, but notwithstanding this, *City of Bristol* produced an excellent performance.

The B.R. steam era

First, I describe my railway-visits in the early-BR era, then more such outings and observations from approximately 1957 onwards, as the grip of diesels tightened on the system, squeezing steam into ever-fewer and smaller enclaves. Some of these later visits were to the Eastern, Western and Southern Regions, since the whole BR-network was involved. This leads towards the climax, a review of declining steam-haulage during its last four years or so, with a summary of the LMS diesel pioneering-work beginning three decades earlier. I call the final steam enclave *The LMS Triangle, Steam's Last Redoubt.*

My tour of national service, 1950-51

I was called up in November 1949, travelling to Oswestry (Salop) from Earby near Skipton, West Yorkshire, by seven different trains through Lancashire, Manchester, Cheshire and into Shropshire. After seven weeks' basic training at Oswestry, our squad was sent on the administration-course to Woolwich, London, in January 1950. A tiny pull-push train (the seventh of the above), hauled by an ex-GWR 14xx 0-4-2T, took us from Park Hall Halt to Gobowen. This rural junction lay on the line from Birkenhead to Paddington via Chester, Wrexham, Ruabon and Birmingham (Snow Hill).

Two months at Woolwich saw us ready to be posted to the units where we would serve the rest of our eighteen months (later extended to two years). We had ridden on the electric-trains of the North Kent line to London Bridge and Charing Cross; my opinion of the emus then was the same as it is now, living on them in Kent: 'boring, trains without engines'—and no numbers either, except very long ones on the carriages. But any photos would have been collectors' items now, 4-SUBs, 2-BILs—and the Southern Region's experimental double-deck business-trains (the word 'commuter' had not yet appeared in British English), running from the City along the North Kent line. Did Britain pioneer the type? The SNCF certainly adopted it in a big way for the Paris commuters and the DB too took up the idea in West Germany. The situation seems similar to that of the tilting-train: an idea abandoned by the British, but developed by the Italians as the

'Pendolino', operated by Virgin on the West Coast Main Line—and with trains built in Italy.

In the bidding during August 2012 to run west-coast trains, Sir Richard Branson failed to renew his franchise. He announced immediately that, following two earlier unsuccessful bids to run east-coast trains, he would stop wasting money and pull out of the railway-business altogether. Then, supported by the passenger-lobby, quite satisfied with Virgin's service, he decided to appeal against the verdict. The successful bidder, First group, declared that it had won 'fair and square'. The government has now granted Branson another two years to continue running his Virgin service in the interim to allow time for further negotiations.

After nationalization on 1 January 1948, the re-numbering and repainting of stock began almost immediately. However, you will notice that many of the locomotives observed on my journey to Carlisle and seen during my stay there still bore their LMS number, and some renumbered engines retained the LMS insignia. I remind you that BR had added 40,000 to the LMS numbers. At Euston on 24 March 1950, we started for Carlisle from an old timber-platform. I had my pencil and notepad ready for my first thrilling ride on the famous West Coast Route about which I had read so much, and I intended to make the most of it. I just had time to run up to the head of the train while my pal Brian watched my kit. The engine was 46137 *The Prince of Wales' Volunteers (South Lancashire)*, still unrebuilt and from shed 1B, Camden. This Scot became the last to be converted, in 1955. As we set off up the Camden Bank to pass his home-shed, I spotted 2-6-2 tanks, Derby 43, Staniers 40138 and 204, Black Five 5191 and Patriot 5532 *Illustrious* (1B shed-plate). As we ran past the shed, I saw only 2-6-4T 42117 and 3F 0-6-0T 7572; the choice motive-power was evidently out on duty. But Willesden Junction produced 7089, one of Stanier's pioneer diesel-electric shunters of 1939 and so quite a cop, and soon afterwards we overtook Super-D 8915 plodding along through Bushey on mineral-empties. At Hemel Hempstead, we met another of these still-numerous 0-8-0s, 9155, hauling coal up to the capital, while Ivatt 4MT 2-6-0 43021, only about two years old, was shunting his pick-up goods in the yard.

We ran into Rugby under the double-sighted signal-gantry and the great lattice-girder bridge carrying the Great Central line, which had its own station and yards on the eastern side. Rugby LMS was a busy junction, with routes radiating in seven directions, The various branch-duties were evident from the motive-power observed as we rolled in. 2P 4-4-0s 471 and 40672, 2-6-4Ts 2235 and 42304, all busy marshalling carriages or waiting for their roads. Ivatt 4F 2-6-0 43024 was shunting coal-wagons, while Super-D (G2 class) 9440 was ready to leave on coal from the exchange-sidings. The only note that I took after Rugby were 8895, a Super-D 0-8-0 hauling coal at Nantwich, and ex-LNW '19-inch goods' 8834 on Springs Branch shed, Wigan (10A), a great rarity, and soon to be scrapped. Only a handful remained of this class of a hundred and seventy. You will remember that my school-friend had seen this engine, back in 1942 at Greetland, Halifax, heading minerals up the Calder Valley bound for Lancashire. I was on the alert as we stopped at Oxenholme, the junction for the Windermere branch but, for us, the halt to take on a banking-engine. As we ran in, I observed 42314 on the bankers' spur so he probably pushed us up to Grayrigg station. These parallel-boilered 2-6-4Ts did banking-duty here for years, one of them also filling in with an afternoon run to Windermere with the four carriages detached from a London-Glasgow express. The smaller 2-6-2Ts from the same stable also worked as bankers, both being supplanted by the Stanier/Fairburn 2-6-4Ts, and finally, near the end of steam, by Ivatt 4MT 2-6-0s and standard 4MT light 4-6-0s.

The slowing for the Penrith stop was lucky, for it enabled me to note Cauliflower 28583 on the shed (12C), another great scoop, since I rarely saw one of these 'crested-goods' express-freight engines, despite the LMS still listing eighty-four in service in 1947. I fear that in the interim many had been scrapped. The engine we saw at Penrith was one of the handful retained for the stopping-trains to Carlisle and the branch-duty to Keswick and Workington, the latter soon to be superseded by Ivatt Class 2MT 2-6-0s, which I saw later. The Cauliflowers can be seen in many photographs on local and cross-country passenger-trains. Most of the class worked in the Midlands and North London, so I rarely saw one. The last three at Penrith lasted to January 1956, when their withdrawal saw the end of a well-liked and long-lived class. A smooth, fast run took us down into Carlisle and we were nearly there, at our camp, and the butterflies started fluttering. No doubt for this reason, I paid no attention to the Upperby yards, but I come to them now, since once settled in at Durranhill Camp, I had a little time at week-ends to explore Carlisle, that mecca of railways. To avoid tedium, I will report on each spot once and list what I saw there over a period of eighteen months or so.

CARLISLE

Leaving the camp on the A69 road to Newcastle-on-Tyne, I had only to walk a short distance and turn left through the housing-estate at Botcherby to the bridge over the Settle-Carlisle line beside the Durranhill yards. The former Midland shed had been closed for fourteen years, but the yard was still used for servicing engines, and for storing them. This brought me an incredible stroke of luck for, on a rusty siding behind the shed was a line of engines, not ex-Midland goods either, but four former LT&S 4-4-2 tank locomotives. Most of these 'Tilbury tanks' had been replaced on the LT&S lines of the LMS by the 3-cylinder Stanier 2-6-4 tanks in 1935 and moved to other locations. I have told you of those I saw at Nottingham and Leicester in 1947. Now comes the mystery. In December 1947, 2154/5 were sent up to Dundee West, and in January 1948 a further two, 2153 and 2156, from Shoeburyness and Plaistow respectively. They were greatly disliked by the Scottish crews who wanted rid of them, and 2153 was sent off to Stirling during the week ended 20 March. After being renumbered 1971-4 (to clear the 21xx series for new 2-6-4 tanks), they were sent south during June destined for Skipton, but ran no further than Carlisle Durran Hill shed. Here, they were shunted down this siding, 'out of sight, out of mind' but a splendid stroke of luck for the lucky spotter who happened upon them. Apparently they stayed there among the weeds for years, being sent to the scrapyard only in February 1955.

Continuing my walk, I crossed the busy A6 trunk-road and soon reached the spread of the Upperby yards on the West Coast main line. Upperby was a mecca in itself, with a wide variety of locomotive-types on the shed and shunting in the large yard. Behind the shed, another surprise greeted me: Cauliflower 28417 standing on a rusty spur, the cover of his dome removed to connect a pipe running into an adjoining building; out of service, he was the steam-raiser powering the gas-plant for the yard-lighting. There was a strange aroma near it—something like burnt-almond—that I could not properly identify and which I have never smelt since. He was withdrawn from stock and kept for this task, since he was not officially listed as one of the three final survivors. You can barely read his number on the author's picture: I should have cleaned the panel first, but railfans were not so bold in those days.

He had been, however, I *was* bold enough to creep inside the large concrete roundhouse, built by the LMS, for a little look and—this was the cream of my visit—for what did I see, but *Silver Jubilee* stored inside, and still bearing '5552 LMS' in raised chrome. I could not believe it at first, after more than two years of nationalisation, because most express-engines were renumbered during the first few months. I tried to improvise time-exposures between the concrete columns. I was too shy to ask when the locomotive would move out—as I had no permit to visit. My guess is that he was stored pending a decision on the style of livery. When the renumbering, to 45552, was eventually carried out, it was again with figures in raised chrome, but without the boiler-bands. The tender merely received the lion-and-wheel emblem.

Outside, rows of engines in store faced the main line, including two 3F 0-6-0 shunters 7391 and 7403 and 2P 4-4-0 ex-MR 403, this one possibly condemned. Further on were examples of the LMS-built '563-class', 40694 and 40699, as well as Compound 40909 and Stanier 2-6-4 tank 42429. Two Black Fives, precisely drawn-up level made another picture, the front engine the nearly-new 44685, very smart in lined-out black. Locomotives of the express-link arrived daily; Patriots 45519 *Lady Godiva*, 45525 *Colwyn Bay,* and Royal Scot 46110 *Grenadier Guardsman* made their appearance. In October 1950, I noted converted Scot 46147 *The Northamptonshire Regiment*, still without smoke-deflectors but retaining the LMS title on his tender, so probably due for a works visit.

The main line was of course busy with summer extras: unnamed Patriot 45542, also with an LMS-lettered tender, running down past Carlisle No.13 box, the first of the complex and controlling the neck of the Upperby yards and the Denton Holme goods-line avoiding the station. Scot 46101 *Royal Scots Grey* softly accelerated an up express past the same spot. I believe this engine was shedded at Carlisle, as he passed regularly, and later hauled me to Glasgow for a spell of duty up there. From another vantage-point opposite Upperby sheds, a favourite of photographers, I watched The Royal Scot train approaching from Carlisle No.4 box, 46221 *Queen Elizabeth*, in 'first-BR-lion' livery, and slowing for the crew-change. The West Coast line was of course the speeding-ground of these lovely engines: two fresh to me were 46226 *Duchess of Norfolk* and the newer 46254 *City of Stoke-on-Trent* both heading Glasgow expresses. Members of this class were shedded in Carlisle, not at Upperby but at Kingmoor, which I come to later.

Opposite Carlisle No.13 box, the yard fanned out and was inaccessible, but I did get a distant picture of another rarity, the very last ex-Furness Railway 0-6-0 'Jumbo' 12499, and Horwich-mogul 2899, both still in LMS colours and based here. The shunting, which continued night-and-day, was in the hands of diesel-shunter 7112 and a group of 3F 0-6-0s, LMS 7295, 47340, 47556 and 47666. These guys also did duty as carriage-pilots at the station. Swindon-built Stanier 8F 2-8-0 48436 ran in on a down mixed-goods, and occasionally a Super-D would appear on a trip-working—two were 49030 and 49311—but these 0-8-0s largely remained on mainline freight.

Occasional visits to the Citadel Station always produced engines fresh to my collection: one was unnamed Patriot 45506. The cente platform was the favoured spot for watching trains, with signalling for each-way working of the West Coast trains. This method of operation was forced on the authorities, as the Citadel Station handled all its passenger trains serving seven directions with only three through platforms, all signalled for bi-directional working. In order to maximise accommodation, a bracket of signals (ex-LNWR) stood halfway along each one, to permit a second train to be 'called-on' from the home signal into the platform when space was at a premium, such as at summer week-ends. Crossovers, too, were provided to let the second train 'escape'. The mid-point signals and points were controlled by a small signal-box in the stone station-building on platform 6, Carlisle No. 4A, placed aloft for a good view along the curved platforms. It is strange that so many of our principal stations are set on a curve. How many can you name?

Jubilees or Royal Scots were powering the Leeds expresses opposite, which I had seen regularly passing the school during the preceding years. On 7 August 1950, 4-6-0 Royal Scot 46117 *Welsh Guardsman*, with tender still lettered 'LMS', was easing out of the centre-roads ready to back onto the Glasgow-St Pancras express via Leeds. The following express would be from Edinburgh, hauled by a Scottish Region A.3 pacific over the North British 'Waverley Route', often *Sceptre* or *Captain Cuttle*. These engines were detached here to run light to the Canal Shed. A Compound would haul the Edinburgh express as far as Leeds. Class 2P 4-4-0s or 2-6-4 tanks heading the West Cumberland (Cumbria) trains used the M & C Bay at the south end. Nearby, Ivatt Class 4MT 2-6-0 M3007 was shunting vans one day at Carlisle No.5 box just off station-limits. On 27 October 1951, Ivatt 2MT 2-6-0 46455, very smart in 'first-lion' lined-out black livery, was working as a carriage-pilot. The two city-side up-bays, numbered 1 and 2, formed the terminus of the North Eastern Region trains to Newcastle, sharing their line with the Midland as far as Petteril Bridge Junction. A 4-4-2 C15 tank, 67481, still lettered 'LNER', was manoeuvring in front of Carlisle No.5 box. Of course, many Class 5s appeared: 44676, 44696, 44724, 44725, 45163 and 44880. You will notice that the first four of these belong to new batches built in 1948-49. This is evidence of the number and dominance of the Black 5 from that time, superseding several pre-grouping classes—and demonstrating that the rationalization planned by the LMS was continuing.

Once I had taken my bicycle to the camp I became more mobile, and rode around at week-ends when I had some time off. During long, sunny, summer evenings in 1950, I again visited Durran Hill, where I copped 48659; shunter 7114 was still at work in the sidings. Two neighbours, 7113 and 7115 were also stationed at Carlisle for many years, usually working in the Viaduct, Etterby Junction or Denton Holme yards, noted from observations made on our visits to Scotland earlier. A longer, scenic, ride took me around the northern part of the Lake District, to Bassenthwaite, Derwentwater and the town of Keswick. From here, the road undulated to Penrith, and at the village of Penruddock, I was fortunate in seeing two branch-line trains cross at the passing-place, the new Ivatt 2F moguls 46446 and 46447, allocated to Penrith (12C), replacing the Cauliflowers. But with evening drawing on I could not visit the Penrith shed, as I was due back at camp.

On another day I cycled out northwards, to Kingmoor depot (68A, the LMS 12A), some distance out of town on the A.7 road to Scotland, where a mass of motive-power stood, unimaginable now, simply a forest of chimneys and domes: Duchess pacific 46223 *Princess Alice*, two compounds, 40907, LMS 1121 (68A); two Horwich moguls, 42808, 42910; a host of Class 5s, 44669, 44718, 44720, 44762, 44931, and LMS 5029; an 8F 48464 and ex-CR 4-6-2T 55350. This engine had been withdrawn from banking-duties at Beattock, and was probably condemned. However, the ex-CR Superheated Dunalastair IV 4-4-0 54438 (a 1917 rebuild), one of a class of two, was in steam and apparently in good order. My account of Scottish trips describes my view of him at Carstairs in 1945. The Superheated Dunalastair IV 54444 of the earlier class of twenty-one smaller-cylindered locomotives built in 1910 was also in action, just finishing his servicing, ready to run down to the Citadel station or the Viaduct yard. One of the ex-CR 0-6-0 shunting-tanks, 56327, was undergoing maintenance out in the open, and the crew and fitter kindly posed on the footplate for my camera in the bright sunshine. Evidence of new routines brought by nationalisation was J.39 0-6-0 64888, its tender still lettered LNER. Unnamed Patriot 45547 slipped by on an up express-parcels and at the nearby Etterby Junction yard, Austerity 2-8-0, still carrying his WD-number 77388, was marshalling his train, as seen in my photograph. Another Austerity, a 2-10-0, was standing at the top of the yard, having finished his stint. This locomotive, 90774, was of especial interest, since he bore the name *North British*. Nowhere have I ever seen any reference to this engine, but perhaps you have.

Carlisle Canal Shed

The J.39 and 'North British' recall another visit I made, to the nearby Carlisle Canal shed. Built by the NBR to serve their Waverley Route (since closed), this shed was quiet, but did produce two notable engines, an ex-Great North of Scotland Rly 4-4-0, a D.40, quite a catch—especially in England. The other was J.36 0-6-0 goods engine named *Byng*, both probably facing withdrawal. On another occasion, I cycled further, to an overbridge north of Kingmoor, and saw one of the class of forty-eight 4-4-0s built by Pickersgill in 1916-20 to similar dimensions as the Dunalastair IVs already noted. In the evening of his life, 54507 was steaming easily through the cutting bringing in the afternoon freight from Dumfries. Amazingly, the whole class was still intact in 1950, though depredations were soon to begin. I have remarked on this concerning many ex-Caledonian classes of locomotive. Some Scottish operations too, particularly freight, had scarcely changed for decades.

Here are the other engines I noted during 1950 on Upperby shed or passing on the main-line.

Austerity 2-8-0 90229, Royal Scot 46165 *The Ranger (12th London Regiment)*, in original form, Duchesses 46247 *City of Liverpool*, 46254 *City of Stoke-on-Trent*, 3F shunters 47327/408/556/ 664/6, Black Fives 44685 & 45106, Patriot 45519 *Lady Godiva*, 2P 4-40 40652, Super-'D' 49228 and ex-CR 3F shunter 56248. In the summer, I was sent to Garelochhead to run a small camp for three weeks. My train from Citadel was hauled by converted Scot 46101 *Royal Scots Grey*, and the following paragraph lists locomotives I saw up there.

Noted around Glasgow during 1950

2-6-4Ts 42163/74, Royal Scot 46121 *Highland Light Infantry*, Duchess 46255 *City of Hereford*, Black Five 44701 and the twin diesel-electrics LMS 10000/1; at Glasgow St Enoch: larger-boilered 2-6-2T 40169, 0-4-4T LMS 15269 & 2-6-4T 2279 and ex-CR 4-4-0s 54479/508; at Ardrossan sheds: dock-shunter LMS 16169, 2P 4-4-0s LMS 607 & 40609/25/68, 4-4-0 Compound 40919, 0-6-0 shunter 56311; passing Beattock, Patriot 45527 *Southport* and 46210 *Lady Patricia;* on shed, ex-CR 4-6-2Ts LMS 15350 & M15352, bankers for the incline; 15350 I have noted as seen on Kingmoor shed later, probably withdrawn from service.

Carlisle to Skipton by Train in 1950

The WCs in the vestibule of each carriage had hinged seats, oak-varnished and lettered in gilt: 'Gentlemen Lift The Seat.' This reflected the customs of the 1930s, a gentler age, when these carriages were built by the LMS. The same applies to the afternoon tea in the restaurant-car, served to those who had ordered it. These features soon disappeared from the scene, ending practices and traditions going back decades.

The 6.50pm Express

Departing from Glasgow (St Enoch) at 4pm, this was my regular train if I had managed a 48-hour week-end leave-pass. Direct and quick for that era, with stops only at Appleby and Hellifield, it deposited me in Skipton at about 8.45 pm, where my faithful dad would meet me, having come out for a bus-ride—and to watch trains. My journey was a very good example of integrated public-transport, about which we hear so much nowadays—because towns cannot accommodate people's cars. From the camp-gate, the *United* bus took me into English Street, close to the Citadel Station, the train brought me to Skipton with the *Ribble* bus-stop outside, and the bus let me off a hundred yards from our house, one stop short of Earby bus-station—almost a door-to-door service. I could not ask more of public-transport than this.

On The Stopping-Train

During that summer of 1950, I went home several times and it seemed to be sunny all the time. With a 48-hour leave-pass, I occasionally was fortunate enough to leave the camp especially early and able to catch the earlier 4.35 pm stopping train from Carlisle to Bradford. This served me fine, for it dropped me at Skipton just the same, ready to take the *Ribble* bus home. There was not much time-advantage in taking this slow train, but the lineside interest was greater, since the slower speed with stops at the wayside stations facilitated observation of the sidings, signal-boxes and other lineside details. In this way, I gradually completed my list of all the signal-boxes from Carlisle to Leeds, including ground-frames, many of them in isolated locations and therefore identifiable only from a train. At that time, only one station had recently been closed, Cotehill, the second stop out of Carlisle, though freight was still handled. I had seen the notice of closure posted at Apperley Bridge Station outside my school around 1948. Scotby, the first station south of Carlisle, had been closed n 1942 during the second war. All the other wayside stations remained open.

One trip I remember particularly well. On a lovely summer evening, 414, an ex-MR 2P 4-4-0 based at Skipton, puffed placidly up the Eden Valley, with Dufton Pike and Cross Fell on the left dominating the Pennine hills. The sidings at several places were busy with wagons of anhydrite or gypsum, minerals that are mined all over lower Edendale, for transport in daily bulk-trains to distant destinations, for example, the anhydrite to the Imperial Chemical Industries' General Chemicals plant at Widnes. A long stop at Appleby enabled milk churns and parcels to be loaded, then it was a short hop to quiet Ormside. In Edendale, I recall seeing more than once the phenomenon of the Helm Cloud. This patch of cloud hangs over Cross Fell in the shape of a helmet, hence its name, but often spreads out into broad swathes stretching for miles. It is caused by the Helm Wind, a gale that springs up suddenly, winding into fierce gusts strong enough to rip a tarpaulin from a goods wagon and fling it down miles away—to be picked up by a grateful farmer. This wind can be felt over a wide area of the northern Pennines and has evil associations. From Ormside, the collar-work started in earnest, the slog, much at 1:100, up to the famous summit of Ais Gill. Shortly afterwards, we stood in Garsdale, the rays of the evening sun levelling in my eyes and highlighting the tank-house and signalbox. It was perfect up there on top of the Pennines at almost 1,200 feet above sea-level, the roof of Yorkshire, rare weather for those climes, I must remind you. The ex-LNER branch train for Hawes was waiting in the bay behind our up platform, headed by a veteran ex-NER G5 0-4-4 tank-engine, waiting to take passengers for that long valley of Wensleydale ending at Northallerton on the East Coast main line. On a later trip during the autumn on the slow train, I watched the guard blowing out the lamps before we pulled out of Crosby Garrett station, in the Eden Valley. I was not aware that the station was shortly to close; where are those oil-lamps now? It was almost dark as we ran along the Mallerstang Valley, its striking eastern escarpment lit by the afterglow, while the engine slogged up the last few, stiff, miles to Ais Gill box. I noted just one engine on Hellifield shed, a Stanier 2-6-2T, 40162, preparing to haul either the Clapham-Low Gill local along the Lune Valley line or a local down the ex-L&Y branch to Blackburn.

On the Night Express

After a week-end at home, I used to return to Carlisle either on the Sunday afternoon or early on Monday morning, in order to be in camp for breakfast-time, around eight in the morning. Four expresses called at Skipton daily: the 1.1am and 10.30am Leeds-Glasgow expresses, and the two London-Glasgow trains, by coincidence around 3pm and 3am. I therefore had two choices: take the afternoon train and lose half of my Sunday at home, or sit it out and go to Skipton for three in the morning, my usual choice. In order to carry out this plan, I used to cycle the seven miles from Earby to Skipton station and leave my bike in the left-luggage office. My dad would come in on the bus that evening after his work at Rolls-Royce and ride my bike back home for me. In retrospect, that was not an unreasonable request because father was only 58 and loved cycling. We carried out this exercise a number of times and I remember bowling along on those lovely nights in 1950 with the Hammerstein and Rodgers song 'June is Bustin' Out All Over' from the musical *Carousel* going round and round in my brain, like the roundabout in that show I had seen recently in London. At that hour, the roads were deserted; few people owned cars and anyway petrol was still rationed. It was really dark—no big street lights then—and the silence was so deep it could be heard. Shortly before the express was due, the connection from Bradford and Keighley would run into the back platform to disgorge its handful of passengers, after which the Compound ran forward to the shed to be turned for his return trip. For this, he would haul the carriages across the station to the bay-platform after we had departed for Carlisle.

On arriving there, the first bus was yet to appear so I used to walk to the camp, about a mile down Warwick Road, passing Brunton Park, the home of Carlisle United F.C., in the Fourth Division of the Football League at the time. It never occurred to me to take a taxi—probably because I had no spare cash and anyway I had plenty of time to walk. But people did not ride about in taxis then like nowadays: taxis were a luxury. 'The luxuries of today are the necessities of tomorrow' says the adage, and very true it is. It was very quiet at five in the morning, with practically no traffic. The morning mist was hiding the legs of the cattle in the fields near the camp, so that they appeared to float in the air—really odd.

BILL HORSFALL

Re-signalling at Carlisle

I have mentioned that the railway had largely the same appearance as thirty years earlier, at least, the trackside, because most of the limited capital available, including Government loans, had gone into new passenger locomotives and carriages, in particular on the prestigious routes to combat competition. No exception to this was Carlisle, that hub of railways, where from the south, lines converged from four directions, necessitating forests of signals controlled by several large signal-boxes.

I was unaware that some signals on the Midland line approaching the Citadel Station were to be replaced one week-end when I went home on a leave-pass, but as I was returning to the camp on the night express, it started slowing early, from Durran Hill South Sidings out on the fringe of the Citadel-complex, the spot where I had watched the shunting on first arriving in Carlisle. From Petteril Bridge Junction through London Road Junction we crawled more and more slowly, finally coming to a halt before the junction with the West Coast line, the home-signal of No.5 Box outside the Citadel station. A momentary stop was usual here for operating reasons, but, after several minutes, I became curious and looked out of the window.

At that moment, we rolled forward, and in the dim light of dawn I saw that the tall semaphore bracket-signals had gone and a flagman was controlling us. Even stranger, a platelayer was peering down intently at some points as we rolled at a snail's pace over them; he appeared to be holding them closed with a crowbar or a clip, indicating that neither signals nor points were yet connected. The time was a quarter to five on a Monday morning and I assume the week-end engineering-work would be due to finish at six ready for the day's traffic. I saw the new colour-light signal the next time I came back from Skipton, an insignificant short post showing a red or yellow light plus a small banner platform-indicator of white lights, replacing the tall structure carrying several signal arms, rather boring, for I loved those old signals. But the new lights, at driver's-eye level, were easier and safer, and represented progress towards greater safety on the railway.

Engineering Track-Work

On another occasion I returned to Carlisle from Skipton by the afternoon Scots express as I was doing nothing special at home and wanted to avoid a sleepless night through travelling back twelve hours later. If you have travelled on a Sunday, you will know that the journey is invariably interrupted by engineering work on the line somewhere, and in my case on that Sunday, it was at Dent. Nowadays a village well-known to tourists who love its conserved cobbled streets, at that time it was fairly isolated—even from its station, high on the hillside over four miles away. The station, built where the old Coal Road from Dent to Garsdale crosses the railway, lies between Ribblehead's great viaduct, and Garsdale, the level stretch atop the gradients on each side. At this wayside station, the express reversed, that is the Royal Scot locomotive propelled his ten carriages back over the Dent crossover, a ticklish business, and therefore carried out dead slow. Then, guided by a pilotman on the footplate, he steamed steadily along the wrong line for over three miles, including passing through the long Rise Hill Tunnel, to Garsdale, where we were able to run straight over another trailing crossover to regain our correct line, stop to drop off the pilotman, accelerate past Ais Gill and coast fast down to Carlisle. I have never experienced this elsewhere, neither before nor since. The sidings, crossover and signal-box at Dent have since gone and the station is now simply an unstaffed halt for an occasional dmu, the 'Dales-Rail' and summer excursions.

One of the many anecdotes about this famous railway line may amuse you. A visitor arriving from the South of England to Dentdale asked one of the locals in his 'posh' southern accent why they had built the station so far from the village it purported to serve. The local stared at the southerner for a moment and then gave a typically dour Yorkshire reply: "Appen they wanted it near t' railway lines." Under the 1974 Local Government boundary changes, Dent and nearby Sedbergh were severed from Yorkshire and added to the new county of Cumbria, itself the amalgamation of Westmorland, Cumberland and the Furness district of Lancashire.

Assisting Engines

There was often something interesting to see in the operation of the expresses from Carlisle to Skipton. Ais Gill is now famous through figuring in many train excursions, though the signal-box is closed. It was a wayside box more important than it would otherwise have been, owing to its location at the summit of the line, and was provided with a refuge siding at each side and crossovers. The sidings were used to accommodate the pilot engines which were taken off the expresses once up the incline. I saw this happen several times when travelling on the 6.50 pm express; the pilot, a simple or compound 4-4-0 would be uncoupled, run forward and reversed into the siding, leaving the express to depart towards Garsdale. Then the pilot's crew—especially the fireman—would have a relaxed, easy hour or so, once crossed over with a clear run to Carlisle as a light engine and mostly on a downgrade for almost fifty miles.

Shortly afterwards, this practice of many decades ceased as more powerful locomotives became available, and the overloaded trains of the war and its immediate aftermath became lighter. And so another little piece of railway working became history, the necessity to double-head all expresses, inherited by the LMS from the Midland. The consequence of this practice was crowds of pilot engines waiting to return down the inclines to either Hellifield or Carlisle, the ultimate cause of the terrible disaster near Ais Gill on Christmas Eve, 1910.

Annual Camp at Bude, Cornwall, Autumn 1950

Before leaving Carlisle and the Army, I must tell you of a few locomotives I saw on this long train journey. I ought to have noted more, particularly on the last fascinating stretch from Okehampton, through Halwill Junction to Bude—alas, long gone now—but I was constrained by duties. After all, I was paid (though not much) to be on National Service. The special train transported the seven hundred-odd bods of the 50th HAA (heavy anti-aircraft or 'ack-ack') Regiment RA with their small equipment; the 'heavy stuff', the 3.7" AA guns, were provided on Cleave Camp.

Travelling overnight, I awoke to see the station-sign 'Pontypool Road'; evidently we had been routed via Hereford and the Welsh Marches line, since popular with excursions. We passed through the Severn Tunnel, then Bristol, and ran down to the west to follow the twisting branches to Bude. Our private airfield provided useful photographs of light-aircraft, a De Havilland 'Gemini', and the visiting-brigadier's Avro 'Anson', but I had to await our return-trip on 14 October to see any railwayana, since I was kept well-occupied at Bude, running my Battery-office and organizing rosters of bods for various duties. From the carriage-window on the way home, I snapped the double-headed motive-power at Meldon Junction but nothing else till Exeter (St David's), where 5321, a '4300' class 2-6-0, obliged my 'Purma special' camera. Bristol (Temple Meads) produced prairie tank 5555 (now preserved), while the sheds displayed a group of 4-6-0s including a 'Castle' and some 'Halls.' My photography restarted at Whitchurch, Salop, where ex-GWR 0-4-2T 5813 was marshalling carriages, probably—and typically—for a branch-line service. Another of the same ilk was shunting in the former GWR yard on the Chester line outside Crewe, while on Crewe South shed, I saw two Class Fives, newly repainted with the red-maroon-grey lining on black. This is the sum-total of my observations, but it was a super train-ride, impossible now, with the lines in north Cornwall long closed.

A Week-end in Liverpool 1950

On Friday 24 August 1950, I got a week-end pass at Durranhill Camp, Carlisle. I even wangled an early start, catching the 1.1pm Glasgow-Leeds train, resulting in my arrival home at Earby, near Skipton, in the late afternoon. This allowed me to set off that evening, to spend all day Saturday in Liverpool with old pal John, who was travelling by express from Halifax to Manchester, where we had arranged to meet. I set off by slow train across Lancashire, starting straightaway to note 'freshers' for my collection. Again, you will notice that some of the engines seen still bore their LMS numbers. Nelson, on the former L&Y East Lancashire line, produced, unusually, 4F 44103, Accrington ex-L&Y 0-6-0ST 51376, Haslingden ex-L&Y Jumbo 52440. John met me in Manchester Victoria, where 3F shunter 47638 was standing by as carriage-pilot. We spotted more Jumbos/Ironclads, 52094, 52102 and 52136, bankers for

BILL HORSFALL

the Miles Platting incline, and shortly afterwards received a bonus in the shape of ex-L&Y 0-4-0ST LMS 11230, the first of these diminutive 'pugs' we had seen.

Having changed trains on the long Victoria/Exchange platform of the combined station, we set off across Chat Moss. Patricroft shed (10C) gave us 2-6-4T 42561, Black Five LMS 5373. 3F shunter 47657, ex-L&Y 'Ironclads' 52022 and 52024, Super-Ds 49293 and LMS 9400; nearby were 8F 2-8-0s 48441 and 48474. Earlestown No.5 box was looking after Jumbo 52366 while Earlestown Junction revealed two gems: ex-LNW 2-4-2Ts 6603 and 6727—and both still in LMS colours. The three I had seen at Nuneaton and Leamington Spa in 1947 were my firsts of this class, and here were two more. Stanier 2-6-4T 42426 and 0-6-0 saddle-tank 51491 were near St Helens Junction No.5, Super-D 49205 and 3F shunter 47444 at Lea Green; Ivatt 2-6-0 4MT 43040 was shunting at Rainhill. Now we were approaching Liverpool and around Edge Hill were crowds of engines. Stanier 2-6-2T 40080, Compound 41108, 3F shunters 47294, 47353 and LMS-liveried Super-Ds 8932 and 9192 were all we could note; while Lime Street had another 2-6-4 tank 42453 and more 3Fs, carriage-pilots 47416 and LMS 3F 7437 as well as Black Fives LMS 5028 and 45243. We resolved to return on the morrow and reap a harvest.

We settled easily into the commercial-hotel used by John's parents near the Adelphi at the foot of Brownlow Hill and slept like logs—no wonder, after all that train-smoke! A full English breakfast set us up for the day, and we walked down to Pierhead to ride on the Liverpool Overhead Railway for a look at the docks. Our vague plans allowed us enough time to go to the terminus 'Seaforth LMS', where ex-LYR saddle-tank 51462 was busy collecting wagons for a trip-working. Riding back on the Overhead, things became even better: a lucky strike at Brocklebank Dock was 47001, built in 1932 as one of five dock-shunter 0-4-0STs in Stanier's early days as CME; five more would be constructed in by BR at Horwich in 1953. Needless to say, this was another new class for us. Returning to Pierhead, we took the Mersey ferry to Birkenhead, where Cammell-Laird's giant shipyard-cranes leaned over the river. We headed for Hamilton Square station, which was disappointing. Stanier 2-6-2T LMS 132 as carriage-pilot and 2-6-4T 42568 ready to depart on a local down the Wirral peninsula were all that were offered. But a boat-trip is always refreshing, and we had enjoyed the blow on the water. We returned to Liverpool for the next stage, determined to see the Edge Hill sheds properly, that magical 8A previously seen only on smokebox-doors, the depot itself merely glimpsed from our train on the previous evening.

The local-train from Lime Street dropped us at Edge Hill station, much used by those since called commuters. As soon as our train had cleared the next section, the Edge Hill signals swung down again, including the 'branch splitting-distant' indicating that the train would be crossed over to the Euston line on the right, ready to turn off for London at Wavertree. It was an unrebuilt Royal Scot, working hard, 46156 *The South Wales Borderer* accelerating his heavy London express after the tough climb through the Olive Mount cutting. Shortly afterwards, the signalman lowered his down-line signals, allowing Patriot 45507 *Royal Tank Corps* to coast through, his trip from Euston almost over, and downhill now into Lime Street. After this auspicious beginning, we found our way to the sheds, even going inside, where we were allowed to walk around; we must have appeared responsible. Luckily, the original Princess was here, and fortunately near the doorway, thereby giving our cameras a chance. The tender of 46200 *The Princess Royal* still bore the LMS insignia, so no doubt the locomotive was going into workshops for a scheduled overhaul. Further inside a real gem was waiting, another of those ex-LNWR radial 2-4-2 tanks to add to the two seen on the way: here was LMS 6688 under repair. Another road held LMS-built 2P 4-4-0 '563' 40626 and Compound 41153, both awaiting attention.

Outside again now, we turned down the shed-yard for a look: another Compound, 41166, Derby 2-6-2T 40007, Black 5 45149, and L&Y 0-6-0 Jumbo 52330, simmering down after their work. Edge Hill was probably home to all these engines. Rounding the line of locomotives, we came upon another class new to us, a coal-tank, standing clear in the open and so ideal for the cameras. This was a lovely surprise: the dainty little LMS 7822 (8A) made a fine sight standing there in its LNW setting. Indeed, the outstanding thing that struck us about this visit was the number of ex-LNW engines still at work. The next new class for us was one of the powerful 7F 0-8-4 tanks, LMS 7939, busy on heavy shunting. The power-output of these tank-engines, expressed in foot/pounds, was marginally greater even than the Super-D rebuilds, the G2a 0-8-0s. Built to Beames' design by the LMS in 1923-24 (Lot 3), the thirty locomotives were derived from the Super-D design and worked here, on Manchester-Buxton trains and at Abergavenny. Only sixteen had remained listed in LMS stock in 1947, and my notes say several had been scrapped shortly afterwards, leaving possibly fewer than ten in service in 1950. Indeed, 7939 itself went later that year, so we were lucky to see any. We saw none of the smaller 6F 0-8-2 shunting—tanks, but at least I had seen one three years before, 7876 at Mold Junction in Flintshire, North Wales. Their big brother 0-8-0s were working around the Edge Hill yards in force as we stepped carefully over rails and points, watching the shunting while keeping clear of the movements; we did not want to be thrown out as we had been at Holbeck. Super-D LMS 9239 was the first we happened upon, an engine I had seen at Nuneaton in 1947. The group of standard 3F shunters keeping him supplied we had seen on the previous day except LMS 7597.

We had given ourselves the luxury of another night in the hotel and so it was Sunday morning when we checked out. At least we would travel in the comparative daylight of an English summer: the weather was dull; typically, when the camera comes out, the sun goes in. Lime Street Station greeted us with Black Five LMS 5095—our train-engine for the run to Manchester, and the last time I was hauled by a Class Five in LMS colours. We were all agog for a last glimpse of Edge Hill yards, that mecca for enthusiasts. We managed to note two fresh 3F shunters, 47320 and LMS 7325, and L&Y 0-6-0 Jumbo 52111, plus a further 3F shunter, 47547 in the neck of the yard. A bonus was another 0-8-4T tank, 47931, making our total two. Super-Ds, it seemed, were everywhere: LMS 8898, 9079, 9094; and 49355 and 49399 without insignia. Lastly, ex-L&Y saddle-tank 51353 was collecting wagons for a trip-working, then we were past, an unforgettable scene. We swept by so swiftly that it happened in seconds. We were accelerating into the suburbs now, and yet another Super-D, 49301, was held with his train in the loop at Broad Green for us to pass; Roby produced 8F 2-8-0 LMS 8457, one of the batch built at Swindon 1944. There was nothing fresh for us at Patricroft, then we were jolting and swinging into Manchester.

We parted company here, as John went for the Leeds express to Halifax and I walked to the slow-coach—literally—that would take me on a ramble through South and East Lancashire. Immediately on leaving Victoria station I spotted ex-L&Y Ironclads LMS 12059, and 52137 and 52266, all pilots or bankers for the Miles Platting incline. A fairly-new Black Five, 44766, was at Deal Street, then Irwell Bridge Sidings gave me the last Super-D on that trip, LMS 9426, rather unusually a G2. Bolton produced 4F 44512 and Blackburn L&Y saddle-tank 51499. Church East Siding must have been on double-time that Sunday, because another saddle-tank, 51410, was marshalling wagons there. The last engine I noted was 3F shunter LMS 7576 on Rose Grove sheds, before running into Burnley. This shed also had neighbour 7575. As it was Sunday, there was nothing to see at Nelson nor at Colne, but I arrived home on the BCN corporation-bus with a full notebook. It had been a splendid week-end, unbelievable now in hindsight for the sheer number of locomotives that I saw. It was also a novelty, as we had never travelled so far, nor stayed so long, simply to spot engines.

Looking at the list below (which significantly omits locomotives seen before), the number of pre-grouping classes still at work is notable, both LNW and L&Y. As I have mentioned in other accounts, the goods traffic of the LMS was still largely handled by these dependable workhorses; it was the prestigious passenger-traffic that had mostly received updating in the form of new designs such as the Royal Scots and the Stanier Pacifics, the Class 5s and 2-6-4 tanks. For instance, Super-Ds far outnumbered 8F 2-8-0s, and the 6F G.1s were still being rebuilt to the 7F G.2a specification, clearly considered a better option than the Fowler Austin Sevens. Even the LNW 2-4-2Ts were still common, though much reduced in numbers by the crowds of new 2-6-4Ts. They, like the coal-tanks and the 0-8-4 heavy shunting-tanks, had had their day and would soon be gone—and the age of the BR Standard Classes was soon to dawn. It was the last serious railway outing I made, and I should have continued, but that's life. Other interests were claiming my attention: the army took most of my time, and then there was the matter of young ladies . . . On arriving home to a meal with my parents, I then repacked—different gear ready to return to the army at Carlisle on the night express from Skipton. I list here all engines noted on the trip that I had not previously seen.

2-6-2T: 40007, 40080, 132;
4-4-0 2P: 40626; Compound: 41108, 41153, 41166;
2-6-4T: 42426, 42453, 42561, 42568;
Ivatt 4F 2-6-0: 43040; 0-6-0 4F: 44103, 44512;
Class 5: 5028, 45095, 45149, 45243, 5373;
Patriot: 45507 *Royal Tank Corps;*
Royal Scot: 46156 *The South Wales Borderer.*
Princess: 46200 *The Princess Royal*
LNW 2-4-2T: 6603, 6688, 6727;
0-4-0 Dock Tank: 47001.
Standard 3F shunter: 47294, 47320, 7325, 47353, 47416, 7437, 47444, 47547, 7576, 7597, 47638, 47657.
LNW Coal tank 0-6-2: 7822.
LNW 7F 0-8-4T: 47931, 7939.
8F 2-8-0: 48441, 8457, 48474.
Super-D: 8898, 48932, 9079, 9094, 49205, 9192, 49293, 49301, 49355, 49399, 9400, 9426.
L&Y 0-4-0ST: 11230. L&Y 0-6-0ST: 51353, 51376, 51410, 51462, 51491, 51499.
L&Y Ironclad/Jumbo 0-6-0: 12059, 52022/24/94/102/11/36/7/266/3 30/66/440.

Stations and Lines Closed: Thornton-in-Craven (Skipton-Colne line)

When the *Craven Herald & Pioneer* reported in December that the tiny station at Thornton-in-Craven, a mile down towards Skipton from our home in Earby, was to be closed, it stimulated us to have a final look. The Christmas weather was mild as usual, so, after helping with the dishes, father and I walked our Christmas dinner off down the valley past the small sewage-works. At Thornton, I took a couple of photographs of the platforms and signals and had a good look round. No trains were running owing to the Bank Holiday. The siding had been lifted and the passenger traffic could be described as minuscule, considering the half-mile climb past the cricket field to the village on its ridge, no joke on a wet and windy night. The village was better served by the Laycock's and Ribble buses which stopped at the tiny post office right in the centre. Another photograph, in Earby this time, of a pair of MR home-and-distant signals (pictured earlier) has proved to be a collector's picture, for they were soon replaced by upper-quadrant arms mounted on the same teak post.

Back to Yorkshire from T.A. Camp at Stiffkey, North Norfolk

I accompanied the road-convoy down to Norfolk, but returned by train. At the end of the annual fortnight, the regiment, spread over different camps, packed up and prepared to leave. I had been busy making the usual two lists of personnel in 'Q' Battery, one to travel in the road convoy and the other by train. I was a member of the latter, and, when all the equipment had been loaded, the Lieutenant-in-charge and I took our seats in the long special train in Sheringham station. It was 5 July 1953.

We took a circuitous route through north Norfolk along the M&GNR lines via South Lynn, all closed in 1959. I remember the acres of sidings full of wagons at March in Cambridgeshire—and, incredibly, the *two-hump* marshalling-complex of Whitemoor Yard—an amazing railway-centre apparently in the middle of nowhere—well, March is only a small market town. But a glance at the map shows that March is an important route-centre, having tracks in six directions at that time. It has survived the railway-closures well, with five still open. After that, our line closely followed the road through Lincolnshire, before turning west to Sheffield along the old Great Central Railway. But I was nurturing an idea, which I put to my accompanying officer, who had charge of the train. He gave me permission to go ahead, so I walked up the platform at Sheffield (Victoria) to the front of the train.

The engine had been taken off, so I watched the coupling-up procedure of the replacement, a Black Five from Low Moor MPD. Then I turned boldly to the driver and asked if I could accompany him. Now this was against regulations without a footplate pass, but he could see that I was *bona fide*, an officer too as we travelled in uniform, and learned I had permission from the officer i/c train—which was a special anyway. "OK, lad, up yer get," he responded, adding warningly, "Yer'll 'ave ter keep yer 'ead down though, as we pull out." It was certainly "Yes" to this, then we were off. I obeyed him as the engine passed signal-boxes and threaded junctions to reach the ex-GC Manchester line, which we would follow as far as Penistone.

It was a good load for a Black Five, but 45210 responded readily to the call for power as these engines do and slogged steadily up the gradient on half-regulator and 35% cut-off. It was super. On the footplate, the din was terrific, a clattering and roaring, accompanied by a tremendous shaking and oscillating. As we pulled out, I had to leave the fireman space by standing partly on the footplate between the engine and tender, holding on as best I could, as the two swayed to and fro. But up the incline to Penistone, with the fireman stoking continuously, I was able to sit on his seat at the right of the engine and look ahead through the cab-glass. He was able to maintain 215lbs/sq.in, proving how well this type of locomotive steamed. It was my first main-line footplate trip, and therefore a milestone in my railway experience. It also brought this particular journey to life for, having travelled scores of miles over the flat lands of East Anglia and Lincolnshire, we were entering the most challenging part of the long journey, two steep inclines, but the locomotive and crew were fresh and so had a good opportunity to 'make the job shine.' After passing Penistone, the hard work was over for the moment and we coasted down through Stocksmoor, Shepley and Honley, a district I was to know later through my work. 'R' Battery left us at Huddersfield to be picked up by their MT for the last leg to Mirfield, while I, feeling like royalty, descended from the footplate of the Class Five, thanked my cheery crew and rejoined my colleague in his compartment.

After passing Holliday's Sidings signal box, the train gently threaded the sharp curve to the Calder Valley line and, entering the Halifax outskirts, passed through Brighouse and Elland to Greetland, the scene of many hours' train-spotting. Up Greetland Bank, the tremendous incline of 1:48, we must have had a banking-engine, probably one of the old Jumbo goods engines. I did not notice the stop for it to buffer up to our rear, since my colleague and I were busy checking the nominal-rolls of our Headquarters staff, who were leaving at Halifax to report to the barracks there, the Duke of Wellington's HQ. On arriving, we were switched into platform 6, one of the former LNER (ex-GNR) Keighley/Bradford platforms at the back, where the Class Five, too heavy for the branch, was uncoupled to run light to his home shed, Low Moor, LMS code 25F, for servicing.

As replacements on the branch line to Keighley, we had two Ivatt 2-6-2 tank-engines, running chimney-to-chimney, brought light-engine from Keighley especially; 41241 was one. Since preserved by the KWVR, it now runs on their Worth Valley branch, also preserved, to the Brontë Country at Haworth and through to Oxenhope. It must have been quite a sight for any lucky observer of the Queensbury Lines, but did anyone photograph our special train? Our arrival at Keighley allowed 'P' Battery to alight with their gear, then the train, now three-quarters empty, puffed placidly up the Aire valley to its last stop, Skipton. My 'Q' Battery left the train, our lorries taking us to the TA Centre to unpack the gear. We stowed everything away, and after tea and a snack, I was at last on the Ribble bus to Earby on the final stage of the long journey home.

Amid the enormous shrinkage of the rail network—and the demise of the coal-traffic—even the electrified Sheffield-Manchester line via Woodhead has gone (though the goods shed and coal-chutes at Penistone were still extant in 1995), and electric cables have been laid through one of the tunnels; however, the trackbed is conserved. Will trains run again one day? Even the Penistone-Huddersfield branch is partially singled, reducing it to a tenuous link between South and West Yorkshire. The Queensbury Lines were closed to passenger-trains soon after our passage, allowing Halifax station, like many others, to be reduced in size after the end of steam-trains in 1968 to cater simply for the Leeds/Bradford-Lancashire diesel-trains operated by the WYPTE. Three decades later, the disused part of the station with its 1855 frontage and the Great Northern engine-shed, both listed buildings, became part of a big conservation scheme carried out along with the construction of the nine-acre *Eureka! Children's Museum of Discovery*. Unique in Britain, with the Prince Charles and Princess Diana as patrons, *Eureka!* includes the whole area of former sidings, now grassed over, between the station and the Church Street retaining-wall However, the large goods-depot at Shaw Syke is mothballed for conservation. Following the closure of the huge Crossley carpet-mills in 1983, the town's biggest employer at the time, the *Eureka!* project is another new attraction to draw visitors in to Halifax's growing tourist-industry.

Other locomotives noted around Halifax and the Calder valley during 1949-50: 2-6-4T 42110, Black Five 44737, Super 'D' 48942, 2-8-0 LMS 8395 and Austerities 77271, 90171 and 90266.

A Day-Trip to London: The Plant Centenarian

Trains Illustrated had alerted us about this, a day-trip from Leeds to London, organised by Mr Alan Pegler, a director of BR. The power would be provided by two preserved GNR locomotives, the small Atlantic 251, an 1898 prototype and the first in Britain of this wheel-arrangement, and the large Atlantic 990 *Henry Oakley* of 1902. The trip included a conducted tour of the locomotive works at Doncaster in celebration of its centenary. I sent for two tickets.

In father's car, I picked John up from his home in Halifax and drove to Leeds. The low level of road-traffic is revealed by the fact that I was able to park all day on the Central Station's small forecourt—and free. However, it was a Sunday. This station would be closed and demolished more than a decade later—routing all trains into the City station, and high time too, avoiding that irritating change of stations involving carrying luggage along Wellington Street. However, in 1953 the old order still prevailed, and Central remained the terminus of the King's Cross trains.

Once the crowd of photographers had been persuaded off the tracks by the marshals, we set off from Leeds, the two old express engines making rather a slow start and heavy weather of the gradient up to Ardsley, using 35% cut-off. At Doncaster, we found that the famous Stirling No.1 had been brought up from the NRM at York specially and parked in the adjoining bay platform. After studying his racing lines and taking photographs, we walked into the Doncaster Locomotive Works.

In the first erecting-shop, we saw the Standard Class 4MT 2-6-0s being constructed: standing outside in works-grey was 76026 newly finished, pictured. It was one of this class that became the last steam-locomotive to be constructed at Doncaster Works, 76114. Also on shed for the day was ex-NER 4-4-0 1483, also brought from the York museum, and restored to the livery of that company. The 'innards' of a K.3 and a B1 undergoing repairs were points of interest before we passed into the carriage-building shops, where considerable construction-work was still done by hand. Despite the introduction of plastic interior panelling, much fine carpentry was still evident. Our observations confirmed that railway-carriages were built with the strength of tanks. This was especially true of the Gresley teak-bodied East Coast stock of the LNER, mounted on heavy underframes. Accidents have proved this: their bodies usually remained rigid, protecting their passengers. But the foundry and general engineering shops were just as interesting to me, since I was employed at a similar establishment, where only the details differed, and in the shops I was glad to see many machines bearing the names of Churchill-Redman, Swift-Summerskill, Stirk, Butler, Ajax, Asquith and others, representing our big machine-tool industry in Halifax.

Back on the train and now with the engines warmed up, we had a smooth, steady run to King's Cross, where we had only a short turn-round time—just enough to poke our heads out of the station, to claim that we had at least seen London. For the return trip, Gresley's beaver-tail observation-car was coupled on to the rear of the train and the streamlined A.4 pacific locomotive 60014 *Silver Link* was backing on to the front, ready to haul us back to Leeds. I did not record details of the run, simply to note that it was very fast, the 'icing on the cake' to end another splendid railway day out.

1958: I restart serious railway photography

News of BR's sudden reversal of policy in 1955 reached me through *The Yorkshire Post* and *Trains Illustrated*. In 1953, BR had recognized it was losing passengers to the private car, and so the British Transport Commission enlisted the skills of General Sir Brian Robertson to address the problem. He had organized the supplies to Montgomery's Eighth Army in the Egyptian desert during WW2 ready for their attack at El Alamein which would drive the Germans out of North Africa. Steam would be phased out in favour of diesel-power, but it took some time to convert my disillusion with nationalization into enthusiasm for recording myself some of the last years of steam-trains. I took an odd photograph now and again, Derby 2-6-2T 40064 on Hellifield shed in 1952, ready for a duty to Clapham and Low Gill, 8F 48616 trundling the daily BP tanker-train ex-Heysham Harbour through the loop on 14 September 1957 and fellow 48454 slogging up through Gargrave on 28 December. Both 2-8-0s were fitted with under-bufferbeam snow-ploughs, usual on the Leeds-Carlisle line. Earlier, on 24 October 1951, a Saturday-evening call at Skipton sheds had produced ex-LNER (ex-NER) B.16 61443 turning on the table ready for the return-working of the morning Blackpool-excursion from York and the North-east 'over the top' through Bolton Abbey, Ilkley and Harrogate. This showed a practice that operated before Mr Everyman had his car. A consequence of increased private-motoring was the closure of this line, apart from a preserved stretch from Embsay to Bolton Abbey, operated by the 'The Yorkshire Dales Railway', YDR. A proposal to reconnect it to the mineral-only branch at Embsay Junction was reported in the March 2011 issue of *The Railway Magazine*. It would allow the YDR trains to run into the disused branch-platforms at Skipton. In 1952, Skipton shed revealed Ivatt 4MT mogul 43112 and inside, Britannia pacific 70036 *Boadicea,* stored behind the breakdown-crane after a mishap. The BR standard-classes are listed below. On the store-road outside was 0-4-4T 58090 (ex-MR/LMS 1428), superseded by an Ivatt 2-6-2T, and no doubt condemned.

It was at Gargrave, a favourite viewpoint of mine, that I had a singular stroke of good fortune in 1956. While convalescing after influenza, I drove the few miles there on a bright, warm, 7 September, as *Trains Illustrated* had reported a test that BR was carrying out on the Leeds-Carlisle line. Indeed I saw it, the prototype *Deltic* diesel-electric locomotive, a Co-Co machine built in collaboration with English Electric/Napier, hauling the test-train including dynamometer-car, heading for The Long Drag, that arduous testing-ground so much used over the years. The engine, weighing 106 tons, had emerged from English Electric's Dick Kerr Works at Preston in December 1955 as DP1 (diesel-prototype 1), though it never bore that identity, called simply *Deltic,* the name it bore on English Electric's smart finish, grey-green with 'streamline' markings. The Greek letter 'Delta' described the shape of the new diesel-engine, the 'V' developed by completing the third side of the triangle. The dynamometer-car, the LMS post-war vehicle, appears to be painted in plum-and-spilt-milk. Here was clear evidence of the modernization-policy announced by BR in the January of the previous year. Difficulties at EE's Vulcan Foundry works at Newton-le-Willows, Lancashire, delayed the delivery of the twenty-two Type 5 (later Class 55) production-locomotives until February 1961, when they superseded the LNER pacifics on the East Coast main line. Numbered D9000-21, and rated at 3,300hp, the Deltic was the most powerful single-unit diesel-locomotive in the world. The writing was on the wall for steam.

The BR Standard steam locomotives

The BR modernization-plans of 1955 had come as a shock, as some of the standard steam-classes had only recently been launched, evidenced on my visit to the Doncaster locomotive-works only two years earlier, described above. However, construction continued to complete orders for the twelve classes. For reference, they are listed here, with the quantity built shown in brackets.

Britannia pacific for top-link express passenger-trains, also for freight 70000-54 (55)
Clan light pacific for lighter passenger-trains, 72000-10 (10)
Pacific *Duke of Gloucester* 71000 (1)
Class 5 4-6-0, a development of the LMS Black Five, 73000-171 (172)
Class 4 4-6-0 for use on lines requiring lighter axle-loadings 75000-79 (80)
Class 4 2-6-0 replacing various 0-6-0 freight-engines, based on LMS '3000' class, 76000-114 (115)
Class 3 2-6-0 for lighter freight-work, 77000-19 (20)
Class 2 2-6-0 for cross-country lines, based on the LMS '6400' class, 78000-64 (65)
Class 4 2-6-4 tank-engine for heavy suburban trains, based on the LMS 2-6-4, 80000-154 (155)
Class 3 2-6-2 tank-engine for local passenger-work, 82000-44 (45)

Class 2 2-6-2 tank-engine for branch-lines, based on the LMS '1200' class, 84000-29 (30)
Class 9 2-10-0 for heavy freight 92000-250 (251)

Four classes were introduced in 1951, the Britannia pacifics, the class 5 4-6-0s, the 2-6-4 tanks and the light 4-6-0s. As mentioned, the latter had been schemed out by the LMS in 1933, based on the 2-6-4T, itself derived from the Horwich mogul of 1926.

1952-4 saw the introduction of the last three types:
1952 'Clan' pacifics and the 2-6-2 tanks
1953 class 4 and class 3 2-6-0s;
1954 class 9 2-10-0s.

The 9F 92250 was the last steam-locomotive built in Britain. Constructed at Swindon in 1960, it was named *Evening Star*, to recall early GWR engines named after stars. It was also the last engine to be evaluated on the Rugby Testing Station. The unique pacific 71000 was allowed to be added to the planned eleven classes in order to fill the gap created by the loss of 46202 *Princess Anne* (the rebuilt Turbomotive) in the Harrow disaster of 1952. The standards totalled 999 locomotives.

With the benefit of hindsight it is easy to criticize now, but I felt at the time that they—or many of them—were an unnecessary expense, since the traffic was being efficiently hauled by the four railways' own standard-classes. These included substantial builds by BR from 1948-51, and this construction could have been continued to finish the standardization planned by the LMS for example, with more Black Fives and 2-6-4 tanks. These—plus more LNER B.1s and Southern pacifics—would surely have filled the bill. The capital saved could have been put towards further modernization, for example, electrification. But Britain still had a coal-based economy and especially the existing railway-works, therefore to carry out out anything different would have required a firmer and more farsighted approach than the the BR board had at that time. So it was yet another case of 'continue as before.' Furthermore, Britain had barely recovered from WW2 and its shortages; and Riddles, the CME of BR, did not favour electrification—possibly because he wanted to make his mark with new steam locomotives, following his mentor, Sir William Stanier.

However, the official objective was no doubt to use the standard engines to make a policy-statement, signposting the new regime, an important gesture, especially to the railway trade-unions. But the standards, based largely on LMS designs—mainly because of their up-to-date designs and also because of the dominance of ex-LMS staff in senior positions on the new BR—vitiated this aim. The new engines certainly demonstrated to the former Great Western staff that they had to update themselves and conform to the new regime, for example to use more superheat and to become used to left-hand drive locomotives. This was common-sense and safer, with most signals, platforms and other equipment set to the left of the track. It will be recalled that the GWR had sailed almost untouched through the Grouping of 1923, allowing Swindon traditions to continue for a century. Consequently, the new engines were unpopular there at first, just like the front number-plates and the repainting showing the new owners, both resisted for years after 1 January 1948. The high footplating with the inclined front-section resembled late-model American steam locomotives, and also gave useful access for maintenance. It will be recalled that the SC-devices had been borrowed from America and that in 1939 Riddles had taken *Coronation Scot* over there, where he saw their modern steam-engines in action.

Earby

Near my home, I pictured a few trains from time to time. During 1958, two Compounds were 'pensioned off on Manchester-Skipton stopping-trains, 41063 and coincidentally, 41163. I snapped Austerity 2-10-0 90316 on the morning coal-train, taking coal to the mills of East Lancashire. A decade earlier, this train often brought out a LYR 0-8-0, the duty taken over successively by an 'Austin Seven' 0-8-0, and then by one of the many 4F 0-6-0s based at Skipton. At a guess, one of these had failed when rostered for the afternoon up-working and the WD was commandeered from Calder-valley coal at Rose Grove MPD to deputize. But this was to be topped by a lucky shot I got in the following month, August, when two of these 2-10-0s came past, slogging up the gradient one Sunday evening with a rail-train. Permanent-way replacement must have been in progress in East Lancashire, for which this train of eighteen bogey-wagons was bringing supplies. To haul this enormous weight, control had allocated maximum motive-power. Some years later, in February 1963, during that severe winter, 4F 0-6-0 44603 came, a stranger to the area, fitted with a large snow-plough, clearing the line outside our home near Earby Crossing.

Springwood Junction, 1960

Beyond the tunnel from Huddersfield station, West Yorkshire, the lines divide for Manchester and Penistone, the latter sprouting branches to Meltham and Holmfirth. I had just taken a flat nearby and took the opportunity of photographs before closures occurred. I found a spot looking down into the grimy cutting where I saw two trains. The first was Derby 2-6-4 tank-locomotive 42413, a long-time habitué, accelerating his all stations local for Penistone. The second train followed at a slower pace, a goods bound for Holmfirth in the hands of 90322, an Austerity 2-8-0. This service ceased around the following year, but the goods-service to Meltham continued for some time, long trains of flat-wagons carrying farm-tractors and accessories from the David Brown tractor works for export. This ended around 1964 and the track was soon lifted, but before this, in 1958, a serious incident had taken place. One track of the Meltham branch, close by the junction, was used for storing carriages, some of which ran away one afternoon, but the alert signalman prevented a serious accident by switching the runaways into the sidings. In so doing, he had protected the main line at Springwood, but the carriages crashed through the buffer-stops and straddled Swan Lane just below David Brown's gear-works, closing the road and demolishing the roadside booking-office of Lockwood Station beyond. Unfortunately, the rebuilding omitted the LYR keystone, a loss to the historian. Traces of the Holmfirth-branch too have largely disappeared, particularly the long Thongsbridge Viaduct (part of which collapsed during construction). Its site is covered with houses.

The year 1956 saw the attempt by BR to measure the maximum power of the Duchess pacifics, and 46225 *Duchess of Gloucester* was the candidate. Many weeks' testing on the Rugby Testing Station had established an evaporation-rate of about 40,000lbs/hr as the maximum that could be sustained for any length of time. Actually, a maximum of 41,500lbs/hr was attained on the rollers. The Skipton-Carlisle line, still a favourite testing-ground, was chosen for the dynamometer-trial. The train included the special Mobile Test Units, built by the LMS in its last year, 1947. The electrical-braking of the MTUs simulated a load of 900 tons which the Duchess hauled steadily up the 1 in 100 gradient from Settle Junction to Blea Moor at 30 mph with an evaporation-rate of 38,500 lb/hr, using the alternate efforts of two firemen. However, the test was unable to measure the ultimate capabilities of the locomotive, since its boiler continued to produce steam at 250lb-pressure on the climb to Blea Moor without a fall in the water-level, shown on the graph of the dynamometer-car. The trial lasted for 30 minutes and represented *the greatest continuous effort ever put out by a British steam locomotive*. It will stand for all time as the epitaph to Sir William Stanier, FRS. The Duchess must be the greatest of all Stanier's designs—one could almost say immortal.

The 1935 art-deco former Queen's Hotel in Leeds, Yorkshire, renamed 'The Queens', an example of the LMS modernization programme (author).

Chapter 10

1958-62

Many of the Ivatt engines and the Riddles standards had a short service-life, curtailed by the onset of secondary-line closures before, as well as after, BR chairman Lord Beeching's Report of 1963. The Lune Valley, already described, closed to passengers in 1954, the Stainmore line in 1960, the Merthyr to Brecon line in 1962 and the extensive M&GN network back in in 1959, represent examples. Beeching however revealed that thousands of similar route-miles were unprofitable due to bus— and car-competition; mass-closures resulted. These were just the lines for which the Ivatt 2s and 4s and the similar standards were built. The chapter describing the Earby-Barnoldswick branch demonstrates that a convenient, frequent, shuttle-service, put on at the request of local-authorities, attracted little custom and so had to be withdrawn. This made our 2-6-2T 41241 redundant after a life of a decade or so. The year before the 1955-decision to abandon steam had seen the introduction of the diesel multiple-unit trains. They would replace steam on local, cross-country—and branch-lines, and so this fresh aspect of creeping dieselisation was already under way, following the early-1930s pioneer-work of the LMS, explored in Chapter 9.

West Coast Visits

I resolved to restart photographing trains seriously, now with the Zeiss Ikonta camera bought second-hand from Uncle Joseph, so armed with a spare film, I drove out one bright Saturday morning, 14 March 1958, to the famed West Coast Route. I will recount my West Coast visits together for ease of reading. I landed first at Hest Bank, a venue for train-spotters of the crack Scots expresses. This is the place I had wanted to be at before the trains were repainted by BR from 1948, but it was too far from home and too hilly on a bike.

Hest Bank and Bolton-le-Sands, March 1958

I snapped 'The Caledonian', Duchess-hauled, speeding up to Euston, Class Five 45299 on a down milk-train, and Jubilee 45582 *Central Provinces* heading an up semi-fast, probably the through Windermere— or Barrow-Euston. But I needed a better vantage point. Noticing an overbridge down the line, I drove there and found it was Pasture Lane, where I clicked another Black Five, 45371, on fitted-freight. A mile further down the line, I spotted a wayside station and set off to find it. It turned out to be Bolton-le-Sands, down a tiny lane off the Morecambe-Kendal road. It led me to a quiet level crossing beside the wayside-station where walkers and the occasional vehicle crossed to the sand-dunes and beach of Morecambe Bay, north of Bare. It was a superb spot, which I had all to myself. The station was little used, still lit by oil lamps and retained almost its exact appearance when built around 1846, except for an early colour-light signal, the up-starter. Only a few trains stopped here, but I had all the traffic, as the junction for Barrow-in-Furness and West Cumberland (Cumbria) lay to the north at Carnforth, and other junctions were to the south, so it gave me the trunk of the tree, so to speak, having the maximum number of trains.

The traffic varied from the prestigious Royal Scot and Perth afternoon expresses, both up and down, to the humble mixed-goods trains. Almost immediately I saw 46229 *Duchess of Hamilton* heading the up *Royal Scot,* quickly followed by 46203 *Princess Margaret Rose* on an up Birmingham express, both crack trains, hence the top-link motive-power. I was favoured next with a double-header, both namers, 46101 *Royal Scots Grey* piloting Jubilee 45689 *Ajax* on an up Barrow express, the Scot no doubt being worked back this way to avoid light-engine running. I remind you that all the Scots had been converted by this date. Then the newest Duchess flew through on the down Royal Scot, 46257 *City of Salford,* rushing the gentle rise towards Milnthorpe and Oxenholme, the beginning of the arduous climb to Grayrigg. A pause in the traffic enabled me to munch my picnic, sitting on a platform-seat in the sunshine, very pleasant and enjoyable. The up Perth came next,

Royal Scot 46167 *The Hertfordshire Regiment* going all-out, apparently deputising for a failed pacific, the usual motive-power. My first unrebuilt Patriot of the day followed, the aptly-named *Blackpool*, 45524, heading an up-freight, often the role of these engines, now demoted from top-link duties. The lattice-work footbridge framed a second Princess, 46209 *Princess Beatrice*, hauling the down-Perth, and in the pause following, I took a snap of a fire-bucket still showing the impressed initials 'LMS.' Another Scot, 46104 *Scottish Borderer* heading a Glasgow-Blackpool express was soon followed by Fairburn 2-6-4 tank, 42281, running north light-engine, probably to Oxenholme for banking-duties up to Grayrigg. A picture of the LMS level-crossing mechanism completed my pictures for the day as evening was approaching, but I resolved to pay another visit soon.
* *See films 120 and 121.*

Bolton-le-Sands again: 7 April 1958.

This time, the locomotive-range was even better, with a couple of Horwich moguls as bonuses. Again, the weather was fine and sunny and I enjoyed the undisturbed peace. A Jubilee was my first photograph, 45633 *Aden* (formerly *Trans-Jordan*) roaring through on an up-express, soon followed by colleague 45723 *Fearless* heading an up-parcels. Duchess 46250 *City of Lichfield* sped swiftly through on their heels hauling *The Royal Scot* and leaving a delicious aroma of coal-smoke—evidently the result of too little draught down the incline. The first Horwich mogul then arrived, 42776 steadily pulling a down-freight, and in the pause that followed, I took a picture of an LNWR bridge-plate. Then I spotted an unrebuilt Patriot coming up on a special, lucky to see one of these engines on an express again—quite like old times. It was 45518 *Bradshaw*, and making good work of it, possibly bound for Blackpool. *Duchess of Gloucester* 46225 followed in his tracks, heading an up-express, bound for Manchester, followed by 46145 *The Duke of Wellington's Regiment (West Riding)*, also on an express. This engine, one of the early conversions, had earlier been based at Holbeck for *The Thames-Clyde Express*. Another pacific came through next, 46229 *Duchess of Hamilton*, heading the down Royal Scot. I had seen this locomotive on my previous visit to Bolton-le-Sands, and it now represents the class in preservation at the NRM, York, important because of the trip to America in 1939, masquerading as 6220 Coronation. Then my favourite pacific, 46211 *Queen Maud*, ran through with the down-Perth; a favourite because of the trip we had made behind her from Motherwell to Carlisle back in 1945, in LMS days. The up-Perth express was again in the charge of a Royal Scot, today 46126 *Royal Army Service Corps*, then I had to turn round quickly to catch Horwich-mogul 42863 running light-engine down. This locomotive used to be a habitué of the Leeds-Diggle-Manchester line. A down-express soon followed, double-headed by Jubilee 45643 *Rodney* piloting Black Five 44736, probably bound for Barrow-in-Furness, the Jubilee attached to save light-engine running. Coincidentally, I would see this locomotive often on the Leeds-Manchester line near the end of the steam-era. A further Jubilee then ran through on an up-express, 45657 *Tyrwhitt*, then finally 45586 *Mysore* on down ecs. The first, and only, BR Standard then came through, Class 5MT 73061, on a down semi-fast, followed by the Euston-Windermere, graced with Duchess-power, 46241 *City of Edinburgh*. The locomotive would come off just up the line at Carnforth or maybe at Oxenholme. The last train I saw that day was Black Five 45193, heading the Workington-Euston express; surprisingly, I had seen only two of them that day, demonstrating the wide variety of power still available. I took only sixteen shots, finishing the second film near home with a picture of 46109 *Royal Engineer*, the second Scot to be converted, heading a special up the gradient from Skipton approaching Gargrave station.

Charnock Richard, Lancashire, 27 June 1959

At the time, this village was a quiet backwater, but the opening of the M.6 motorway and its eponymous service-area brought it to the notice of people in cars. I had read about the railway there in *Railways*, April 1946 (a short-lived magazine), which described the widening of the route to four tracks. With the intention of building the new pair of tracks alongside the old, the bridge over German Lane was widened, but this plan was altered to an alignment some fifty yards away—perhaps owing to difficulties with land-purchase—leaving the bridge-abutments with empty extensions. We found this to be a really agreeable position for observing trains where a useful metal footbridge spanned the tracks.

We had quite a haul, beginning with Standard 9F 2-10-0 rumbling past on down mineral-empties, followed by Royal Scot 46146 *The Rifle Brigade* speeding by on an up-express. As it was a Saturday, the expected specials began to arrive, first Black Five 45308, down to Blackpool. Jubilee 45653 *Barham* went the other way on another, quickly followed by unrebuilt and unnamed Patriot 45508 hauling a semi-fast. I was pleased to see one of these old engines still employed on express-work at this late date. Another 9F now came past, 90292, this one heading a down special. These large freight-engines were often used on passenger-trains, revealed in many photographs. Another Jubilee brought a further down-special, 45571 *South Africa*, which I had seen only once; now it was almost midday, the time for the pacifics. The down Royal Scot train brought 46234, the unstreamlined *Duchess of Abercorn*, famous for her phenomenal 900-ton test-run of 1939 described earlier, and following her, the down Birmingham-Glasgow hauled by one of my favourites, the Princess Royals, today 46209 *Princess Beatrice*. The unique Scot 46170 *British Legion* was a lucky catch next, on the down Perth again, a pacific roster. However, it *was* a pacific heading the up Royal Scot, 46245 *City of London*, quickly followed by another Jubilee, 45556 *Nova Scotia*, on an Edinburgh-Birmingham. After a short pause, a further Jubilee came along, 45633 *Aden* (formerly *Trans-Jordan*) bringing Londoners to Blackpool, and then we were treated to another pacific. Duchess 46246 *City of Manchester* was taking a Glasgow-Birmingham express, soon followed by Scot 46128 *The Lovat Scouts* speeding the up Caledonian. Next, I was pleased to see another Patriot, 45502 *Royal Naval Division*, also unrebuilt, on an semi-fast express for Workington, seen on the West Coast already and photographed in LMS days at Preston, probably the home depot.

Suddenly, there was a type-change to BR-Standards, then back to Staniers. Britannia 70031 *Byron* was hauling a Euston-Preston express, while Standard 5MT 73126 was heading an up-special. This engine is interesting as one of the batch built with Caprotti valve-gear and later rescued and restored at the Midland Railway Centre, Butterley. An up semi-fast followed, this one with huge power: two Black Fives, 45415 and 45336, I guess the pilot working back in this way to avoid a light-engine movement. Finally an up-freight plodded by in the capable hands of Stanier 8F 2-8-0 48767, nicely framed by the footbridge. Twenty-one locomotives were on film that day, and we drove home well-pleased, particularly as once again we had been blessed with brilliant sunshine.

Milnthorpe, 25 June 1960

One afternoon while taking my parents out, I was driving across from the A65 at Crooklands to the A6, long before the arrival of the M6 motorway, aiming to visit Windermere, when I decided to have a look at Milnthorpe Station. Mother stayed in the car, high on the bridge-approach, to watch some cows grazing, while father and I walked down to the platform. We saw two trains in the space of a few minutes. The first was Britannia 70045 *Lord Rowallan* heading an unidentified down-express, possibly the Perth as it was early-afternoon, quickly followed by Jubilee 45719 *Glorious* taking another down-express, perhaps bound for Windermere. At Oxenholme, a 2-6-4 tank would be substituted for the final stretch down the branch. On the up-side of the line, we were glad to see Libby's Dairy still functioning with a rake of tankers being filled on its private sidings.

South of Lancaster: Garstang

During that autumn of 1960, the weather was kind to me, both for my weekly commuting and for outings. On 26 October, again with my parents, I was lucky enough to see from an overbridge south of Garstang 49191, a Super-D 0-8-0 running light, one of the 7F rebuilds, and in very clean condition. He stopped just up the line, on the water-troughs in the middle of section, perhaps when he saw my camera, enabling me to take two photographs. That was the last LNW 0-8-0 I saw: they had disappeared quite quickly in the 1950s, at least from the northern West Coast line. This little outing gave me the idea of visiting Garstang with John for more railway-photographs. This meant another sally to the West Coast, to the deserted station at Garstang and Catterall, south of Lancaster and at one time the junction for the branch line to Glasson Dock. The main branch had continued to Knott End, the little ferry-stage opposite Fleetwood, from where I had sailed to the Isle of Man during the previous summer. Two Knott End carriages ended up on the Leadhills branch from Elvanfoot, further up the west-coast line in Scotland.

I had read in *Trains Illustrated* that the LMS prototype-diesels 10000 and 10001 were running again, rostered for the Royal Scot train and so I was able to take their photograph to add to the poor one taken at Wishaw South in 1949. By now though, they were painted in BR green. I learned later that occasionally the SR-designed 1-Co-Co-1 diesel-electric locomotives, 10201/2/3, were used to haul expresses such as the Royal Scot past here, though we never saw them. I saw the same wide variety of motive power on the expresses; the majority of the freight was run at night to free the line for the fast traffic. It was a good day and a pleasure to see the two diesels for the last time, as they were soon to be withdrawn (10000 in 1963, 10001 in 1966). However, they had paved the way for the dieselization of the whole of British Railways; I feel the LMS railway did not receive the credit due for their foresight and courage in taking this decisive step forward and for their pioneering-work on forms of diesel-drive. This topic has been extensively covered in Chapter 6, Steam and Diesel Achievements of the LMS. In order to avoid repetition after other wcml accounts, I list the nineteen snapshots with brief details.

Black Five 44678 on up-parcels.
Black Five 44683 on down ecs.
Black Five 45306 on up Workington semi-fast.
Horwich mogul 42842 on down freight.
Black Five 45301 on down-parcels.
Unnamed Patriot 45506 on down stopping-train.
Converted Patriot 45533 *Lord Rathmore* on up fitted-freight.
Diesel-electrics 10000 & 10001 on up Royal Scot.
Black Five 45344 on up through-freight.
46234 *Duchess of Abercorn* on up Glasgow-Birmingham express.
46254 *City of Stoke-on-Trent* on down Royal Scot.
46252 *City of Leicester* on down Perth.
Horwich mogul 42842 again up light-engine (returning from Carnforth).
46255 *City of Hereford* on up-Perth express.
Unrebuilt Patriot 45543 *Home Guard* on up through-freight.
Jubilee 45630 *Swaziland* on down stopping-train.
Royal Scot 46157 *The Royal Artilleryman* on up-express, possibly Carlisle-Manchester or Liverpool

Unnamed, unrebuilt Patriot 45551 (the last of the class) on down through-freight.
Royal Scot 46102 *Black Watch* on up-Manchester express.

I felt this a really good bag, though evidencing more Class Fives than on previous forays to the wcml. However, the Patriots showed up well on this day. The summary of classes seen is:

Horwich moguls: 1 (twice); Class Fives: 5; Patriots: 4; Jubilees: 1; Scots: 2; Duchesses: 4; Prototype diesel-electric Co-Cos: the pair.

Notable for their absence are the Princesses. I discovered later that they tended to be rostered south of Manchester/Liverpool, except on crack-trains such as The Royal Scot, the Perth and Birmingham-Glasgow. *Films 139 & 140 (8-11-58).*

Grayrigg, Westmorland

A fortnight later, in April 1960, John and I went off for the first time in the Ford 'Special' car that I had built on a 1959 *Popular* chassis. It was another visit to the West Coast to savour the scene before the diesels arrived in force to oust steam. This time we chose Grayrigg, a lovely setting with the line levelling off at the summit of the incline and curving away through the fells towards Low Gill, Tebay and Shap. The weather was bright and calm, and the wide down platform of the disused station gave us fine vantage points to see the wide selection of locomotives still passing.

We saw our first mainline diesel-electric locomotive D224, a diesel-electric 1-Co-Co-1 built by Vulcan Foundry, piloting the crack up Perth express. Its role indicated that the diesel crew were probably training and running in the machine, but it was a portent of the future. So we clicked the cameras as much as possible, including at the big Stanier tank engines dropping off the heavy trains as they breasted Grayrigg Summit. A minute after our arrival, unrebuilt Patriot 45502 *Royal Naval Division*, already seen several times, pulled steadily off the bank heading a long parcels-train, shoved at the rear by Stanier 2-6-4 tank 42581. At the platform, the tank's driver snapped his regulator shut, dropping back quickly from the train to stop clear of the crossover outside the signal-cabin. Once crossed over, steam for a few seconds sufficed to send him coasting down the bank back to Oxenholme, ready for the next effort. We had not long to wait for our first Pacific: it was 46231 *Duchess of Atholl* that came speeding through the station on a northbound express. The next train up the incline was Stanier 8F 48297, an ex-War Department engine, steadily hauling a long freight and banked by 42449, another Stanier 2-6-4, built in June 1936. This engine was still here five years later. After he had returned down the hill, we took photographs of the ex-LNWR signal opposite, the loop-to-main starter, a home-and-distant pair, the distant warning of the next box, Mosedale Hall crossing. That day, it was switched out, as evidenced by the raised counterweight of the distant signal. However, no trains used the loop during our visit. LNW-signals had become rare, so we were glad to see this one, unique in this section. A track-plate marked 'LMSR' made another picture.

After this interesting interlude, we had a succession of up trains for a change. Duchess 46240 *City of Coventry* flew past bearing 'The Royal Scot' headboard, followed at a more leisurely pace by unnamed Patriot 45508, pensioned-off on freight. He remained in original condition, except for a horrid stovepipe-chimney. At a guess, he had been held in loop at Tebay to clear the line for 'The Royal Scot'. We had a long interval to wait now, before gaining a bonus in the shape of the first rebuilt Jubilee on an up semi-fast. Coasting easily through Grayrigg, 45736 *Phoenix* was blowing off steam, evidence of efficient steaming, a good fire and probably a full boiler after miles of downhill-running from Shap and on the level through Dillicar in the Lune Gorge. I believe his shed was Crewe North (5A). A double-header quickly followed, Black Five 44761 piloting Jubilee 45702 *Colossus*, Liverpool-bound from Glasgow.

It was nearly lunch-time now, so we walked with our lunch-packets towards the signal-box and, somewhat diffidently climbed the steps, but once again we were welcomed by the signalman, this time into a large ex-LNWR signal cabin, as usual all spick-and-span. We observed the busy scene, watching the track-diagram, but speaking only briefly, so as not to distract the man from his tasks. These included crossing the banking-engines over to the up line for their return light-engine to Oxenholme, fitting them between paths of up-trains. As well as the usual bell-keying, the signalman conferred on the phone with his colleague at Low Gill to the north, and with Lambrigg Xing to the south (the spelling on the cabin nameplate), enquiring on the state of the traffic as far as Tebay and Oxenholme respectively. He let a down-freight out of a siding behind the box, but, judging by the rust on the rails, this group of refuge-sidings was little used, consequently fewer levers in the box were in regular use. The departing freight was headed by a now-rare Horwich mogul, unidentifiable at that distance. However, the siding-provision did demonstrate the weight of traffic in the past. Some of it came over the Stainmore line from the north-east bringing coal to the Barrow area, returning with haematite iron-ore. These NER trains joined the west-coast line at Tebay, then ran through the Lune Gorge and down the Grayrigg bank to Hincaster Junction south of Oxenholme, there turning right along a link to the FR Barrow line. After we had been treated to a cup of tea, we pointed our cameras at another oncoming train, the crack Perth express, in charge of the pioneer Duchess 46220 *Coronation*, the picture framed in the signal-box window. In the pause that followed, I took a snap of the cabin-interior, before Black Five 45293 roared by on a Carlisle freight. We assumed he had been able to build up a healthy fire and steam-pressure on the rising gradients from Hest Bank on Morecambe Bay to Hincaster so as to rush the hill without taking a banker at Oxenholme. The up *Midday Scot* was the last train we saw, another Duchess, late-model 46254 *City of Stoke-on-Trent*, of course coasting easily by, leaving the whole place covered in the smoke that blows down from these locomotives when running under light draught. A good thing we liked that sulphurous smell . . .

To Windermere

That first Saturday in October 1960 was hot like summer and so my parents decided on a short run up to the Lakes, one of our frequent outings. It was while driving along the A.591 between Kendal and Windermere that I received a bonus. Beyond Burneside, where the branch-line to the paper-mill on the river Kent crossed the road, Staveley level crossing-gates were closed to the road and I could see out of the corner of my eye the white steam of the approaching train.

I hastily pulled on to the verge and jumped out with camera at the ready—perfectly safe in those quieter days. I was immediately rewarded with a shot of Derby 2-6-4 tank-engine 42317 heading the afternoon London (Euston)-Windermere train, the last four carriages taken off a Glasgow express at Oxenholme, the main-line junction for Kendal and Windermere. The other duty of this engine would be to bank trains from Oxenholme up to Grayrigg.

Bay Horse, between Preston and Lancaster

This further wayside enclave of the wcml looked so pretty on 22 July 1961, in its tree-clad setting in the summer sunshine. The signal-box was still operating, but the platform-edges had been removed and the rusty sidings appeared disused. The down-platform made an ideal viewpoint, and again I list the locomotives that I photographed, with brief details.

Converted Patriot 45512 *Bunsen* on down Manchester-Glasgow special.
Class 5MT 45070 on up fitted-freight.
Jubilee 45653 *Barham* on up-special express.
Stanier-mogul 42972 running fast on down fitted-freight.
Caprotti 5MT 44745 on up special express, one of the twenty with Ivatt's version of this valve-gear, illustrated earlier.
Duchess 46236 *City of Bradford* on down Lakes Express.
Class 5MT 45286 up light-engine, apparently just out of shops, therefore looking like new.
Converted Scot 46166 *London Rifle Brigade* on down Barrow express.
(Standard) Britannia 70045 *Lord Rowallan* on down-express.
Jubilee 45737 *Atlas* on down-express.
46225 *Duchess of Gloucester* on down Perth-express.
Jubilee 45678 *De Robeck* on down fitted-freight.
Horwich mogul 42942 on down ecs.
Stanier-mogul 42960 on down semi-fast.
Fowler 2-6-4 tank 42376 on up semi-fast, probably ex-Windermere.
It was a good haul, representing a considerable variety across the range of types: more Jubilees this time, also two comparatively-rare Stanier-moguls, but again, no Princesses. The single BR Standard locomotive demonstrated that the former LMS types were holding the fort well.

Noted passing Oxenholme during 1949: 46227 *Duchess of Devonshire,* unnamed Patriot 45513 and Royal Scot 46113 *Cameronian.*

Scotland, Febuary-March 1959

John and I decided to take our 'winter week' holiday touring Scotland, where we would be able to overnight at my Aunt and Uncle's in Wishaw, Lanarkshire. I have described summer holidays spent there, watching the LMS expresses speed through from Glasgow to Euston, but now we would see the Highlands. The 28 February may seem a strange date to depart, but we had no choice, and the weather turned out mild and fine. I will restrict my remarks mainly to spots of railway-interest that we came across in our travels to Oban, Kyle of Lochalsh, Dingwall, and the depots at Perth, Motherwell and Carlisle Kingmoor.

On 1 March we set off from Wishaw for the Highlands. Our first encounter with the railway, Crianlarich, was devoid of trains, so we photographed ex-CR signals and LMS signs. Oban sheltered us for the first night, its shed revealing two ex-CR engines, 0-4-4T 55263, no doubt provided to work the Ballachulish branch-line and 57571, a 3F 0-6-0 goods; also two Class Fives, including 45084. On leaving, we had to wait at the Connel Ferry rail/road bridge for the Ballachulish branch-train to pass, another ex-CR 0-4-4T, 55215. Then, on the way to Fort William, we had the luck to see the daily goods plodding along the glen at Kintallen, Loch Linnhe, in the capable hands of superheated 3F 0-6-0 57667.

From a turning near Garve, a long drive led us across country on single-track roads through Achnasheen to the famous Kyle of Lochalsh, where ex-CR 0-4-4T 55216 was on view, shunting in the yard. This engine had brought in the daily goods, apparently only a few wagons, and so easily handled. During our day on the Isle of Skye, it rained continuously, but the following morning was glorious as we left Kyle, with the sun shining on the coppery Cuillin Mountains. We struck out north, then north-west, passing the new hydro-dam at Aultguish in the Wester Ross. Before leaving Loch Connell at Achnasheen, we watched two Class Fives manoeuvring in the distance as their trains crossed on the Kyle line. They were transferring the restaurant-car from the down-train to the up for its return to Dingwall. At quiet Ullapool, we rose early to watch the fishing-boats unloading their catches in the dim light of early morning, before we set off, curving across to the busier east coast, passing Invershin Castle to arrive at Dingwall, where 0-4-4T 55199 was shunting.

We pushed on to Inverness, where colleague 55226 posed for the camera. This shed was otherwise deserted too, its motive-power evidently out. Down the Great Glen, I can tell you that we did *not* spot the Loch Ness Monster, though a few people were about, fishing and hiking. A long drive south through the Highlands, the Ben Nevis range and by Spean Bridge, the Loch Moy hydro-scheme and Loch Laggan brought us to Perth, which had a splendid array of locomotives. 'Caley bogeys' 54469 and 54499, ex-LNER V2 60959, 4F 44314, 0-4-4T 55209, 2F Jumbos 57276/345, 3F 0-6-0T 56290 and a NBR axlebox on an old carriage, pensioned-off on the breakdown-train, made a varied haul of photographs. We were allowed inside for a look at the engines, a rare collection by that date. The Scots railwaymen called the Dunalastair 4-4-0s 'Caley bogeys', a name I have adopted here. These two were Pickersgill's 1916 successors to the Dunalastair IVs, the second one of the batch having larger cylinders.

We had left the wilds of the Highlands behind now and were on the last leg of the journey back to Auntie Vic's at Wishaw. A few miles short, we stopped off in Motherwell, where I already had an acquaintance with the sheds, and were again rewarded with a super variety of ex-Caley classes on show. 3F 0-6-0Ts 56269/85/338; 3F 0-6-0s 57595/666/88; Pickersgill bogies 54462/4/5 (Dunalastair IIIs, rare by then, and almost certainly condemned), 2F Jumbos 57267/70/363/461/2/ 435/6. An LNE axlebox on an engineers' coach finished the film. The cheery driver of 57462 posed for me to snap him and the crew on the footplate of the 3F tank 56285. One of the drivers, appreciating our interest in the scene, led us along to a row of diesel-shunters parked ominously on the shed, let us on to the footplate of 13351, started it and drove up the yard for two hundred yards. Then he let me drive it back. I was so fascinated with my driving-experience however, that I did not record the builder of the machine, probably Armstrong-Whitworth or Vulcan Foundry. After the usual warm welcome from the Scots folks at Wishaw, we set off the following morning for home, pausing only at Kingmoor sheds, Carlisle. Photographs resulted of ex-CR 4-6-2 tank 55350 (seen here before and almost certainly condemned), Royal Scots, Patriots, a Jubilee, a few Standards, a couple of ex-CR Jumbos and of course several Class Fives.

Visits to the Eastern Region (ex-LNER lines)

York, 18 April 1959

I drove my parents through Skipton, over the Greenhow Moors, down through Harrogate and along to York to see the daffodils in bloom on the slopes of the city-walls. They make a lovely picture, their swathes of yellow on the grassy-slopes a contrast against a background of the ancient grey stonework and gateways. Then we went along to the Railway Museum. "Ah! This was why he wanted to come!" Well yes, actually—but I *had* mentioned it to my parents before we set out. I will list what we saw there, then tell you about my exploits at the station afterwards, when they left to visit the Castle Museum. At this time, many of the exhibits available were displayed at the Clapham Museum, London, the former bus-garage, which I did see much later, with a replica *Rocket* standing on a plinth outside. This explains why we did not see *Mallard*, MR Compound 1000 nor some others, but on view were LNWR 2-2-2 *Columbine*, NER 2-2-4T *Aerolite*, NER 2-4-0 '910', GNR 'Single' No.1, NER '1463', LB&SCR *Gladstone*, NER '1621' and a sign from the Jersey Railway.

Next, I went to see the real action at the big station, another curved example. My vantage-point was beside the well-known Holgate Road bridge. I was lucky with a varied selection of locomotives still in service. The first I saw was a carriage-pilot, one of William Worsdell's venerable North Eastern J72s, 68687. The A4 'streaks' would be running for a year or two yet, and 60030 *Golden Fleece* gave me a chime on his whistle as he left on an up Newcastle express. Unnamed V2 60803 ran through light-engine to the sheds, before 61454, an old NER B16 4-6-0 chuffed by on ecs, clearing just in time to allow me to see another A4, 60016 *Silver King*, gliding into the platforms with a down Edinburgh/Glasgow express. Another light-engine ran past, A1 pacific 60137 *Redgauntlet*. Finally came the sole A3 pacific of the afternoon, 60107 *Royal Lancer*, heading a down Newcastle express into the station. Now my time was up, but I was pleased to have seen some older engines as well as crack express-locomotives. It is convenient to add here a visit five years later to Nether Poppleton, north of York, though this date belongs more properly to 'the last enclave' the era when steam was shrinking almost to invisibility. It was Saturday 24 October 1964 when I saw A4 No.60009 *Union of South Africa* heading a down-special, probably taking football-fans to Newcastle or Sunderland. One of several A4s in preservation, this one lives in Scotland in the care of the SRPS.

The Woodhead Line

Only a few weeks later, on 24 January 1959, I set out for the day in the A.30 *Countryman* from my digs in Huddersfield, West Yorkshire. A fellow-lodger was a Swiss graduate-trainee, so I took him for a ride, as he was at a loose end in a strange town. I drove five miles to Meltham and up into the Pennines, the Peak District National Park, where snow was lying in the gullies and, aiming for Glossop, passed the meeting-point of Yorkshire, Cheshire and Derbyshire. It was new country to both of us, so that when I saw the level-crossing in front, I had to guess where we were: it was Torside Crossing, and luckily the gates were closed. I got a nice shot of Bo-Bo electric locomotive 26037 holding back his mineral-empties on the steep incline down to Penistone. A minute later, I had the luck to snap a train coming up, a similar loco, 26033, steadily hauling his load of south Yorkshire coal up from Wath yard to be burned in Lancashire.

The East Coast Route in Northumberland

These are observations while we were driving on 16 May 1959 to a Whitsuntide-break at Seahouses, Northumberland. My parents liked watching trains too, so I was able to stop here and there. My first stop was the station at Little Mill, which still boasted a clock bearing the initials 'NER'. I photographed this, as well as A1 60143 *Sir Walter Scott* heading an up Newcastle special—possibly bringing football-fans, as it was a Saturday. We drove on, and shortly before Christon Bank, I managed to get a distant picture of a K3/K5 mogul 61844, struggling north on a long through-goods. I drove up to the station, but saw only one train, 61985 of the same class, travelling south light-engine.

A similar NER clock made another picture, also an LNER sign. We continued on to Seahouses, arriving at the hotel in time for tea and a little look at the small resort and its thriving fishing-harbour. From here, trips were offered to the Farne Islands to see the seabirds and the lighthouse, the scene of Grace Darling's heroic rescue of the crew of the *Forfarshire* all those years ago. Taking advantage of the calm weather, we made a trip on the first morning. We had only the long weekend, as father and I had to return to work on the Wednesday, but we managed an afternoon at Chat Hill station as well. This had been the exchange-point with the former LNE light-railway down to Seahouses, operated with ex-NE 0-4-2 tank-engines such as 68089 until closure on 29 October 1951. It was a hot afternoon, so mother was able to take a stroll to watch some cows grazing near the railway, leaving father and me on the station.

The first train was A1 pacific 60126 *Sir Vincent Raven*, on an up-express, quickly followed by A4 streamliner 60004 *William Whitelaw* heading the 'Heart of Midlothian'. A locomotive that we had seen at Christon Bank came next, 61985, a K3/K5 running in the up direction, again light-engine, apparently his service-role. A3 pacific 60060 *The Tetrarch* ran through on a Newcastle-Edinburgh semi-fast, then we had two up trains. Unnamed V2 60942 sped swiftly through hauling a class 'A' goods, followed by a stopping-train, the first we had seen. By now the wayside-stations would receive only one or two stoppers each way per day. However, this one was very welcome for the interest it brought. First, the locomotive was an A3 with a double-chimney, 60078 *Night Hawk*, and second, he uncoupled to pick up refrigerated fish-vans from the goods-yard. Evidently these had been shunted in by the pick-up goods early in the morning ready for the lorry from Seahouses to offload his fish-boxes at tea-time, and now that fish was on its way to the populous cities of the south. We watched, fascinated, as the pacific set back gently over the points, coupled up and drew the vans out of the siding. Once connected up again, *Night Hawk* pulled away smoothly with his light load, and that was our ration, for it was time to return to our hotel for dinner. We had all enjoyed our afternoon in the hot sunshine and fresh air—leavened with a little train-smoke! Another K3/K5, 61900 manfully pulling his up-freight, was the last photograph I took on the line, as we passed Little Mill on our way home on the following morning. We had visited the Farne Islands and the scene of the battle at Flodden Field, as well as Holy Island and Dunstanburgh Castle, so we felt we had done plenty during the long week-end. Our final calls were at the fish-curing house at Craster for freshly-smoked kippers and a brief tour of the excavated Roman town of Corstopitum before driving through Durham to Yorkshire and home.

Heck

That summer, 1959, I decided I needed another photographic session beside the East Coast main line. I had only a few snaps of the former LNER engines, taken at York and Leeds on odd occasions, and I knew that wholesale dieselization was coming soon of the Eastern and North Eastern Regions, geographically the old LNER in England before nationalisation in 1948. But where should I go within easy reach of Halifax? Perusal of the map suggested the stretch between Doncaster and York, so I drove out there and found this village north of Selby—yes, I agree, an incredible name.

Almost all the wayside stations had been closed on the East Coast line, some demolished, including Heck, though here the few up-sidings still remained, rusty but available for the odd 'hot box.' They included the turnout of the former colliery-branch, curving back from the sidings. The road overbridge had recently been rebuilt to a higher level over the tracks. The clearance, I guessed, would be for the overhead wires that were planned—but I expected they would be erected long before the twenty-odd years that actually elapsed. Scheduled to be introduced were the diesel-electric locomotives, the Deltics, to hold the fort in the interim, which is why I was there—to take pictures before the end of steam. In fact, the diesel holding-operation lasted until the summer of 1991.

From the lineside, I took several useful pictures. A4 60013 *Dominion of New Zealand* came first, hurrying his Newcastle-express towards King's Cross, quickly followed, appropriately, by A3 60048 *Doncaster* heading an up special. Neighbour 60047 *Donovan* passed next, but going north on a special, followed by another special, headed by V2 60803, the engine I had seen at York four months earlier. These specials seemed to signify a big football-match somewhere in the north-east, probably at Newcastle or Sunderland, confirmed by the empty-stock train that now passed going south in the hands of B1 61377. It was really busy that Saturday, for I had hardly turned round when another down-express hove in sight. It was the 'Flying Scotsman' in charge of A4 60034 *Lord Finden*, formerly *Peregrine*. The up 'Elizabethan' was next, flying past behind another A4, 60031 *Golden Plover*, and the balancing-working, headed by A1 60116 *Hal o' the Wynd*. I was standing approximately halfway between King's Cross and Edinburgh. Now four up-expresses followed each other in quick succession. The famous A4 60014 *Silver Link* flew past with the up 'Flying Scotsman', another A1, 60126 *Sir Vincent Raven* on the 'Northumbrian', A2 60524 *Herringbone* headed an express and finally V2 60922 on another special. Next, I was lucky to see a comparative rarity, one of the old ex-NER B16s, 61463, running well on a semi-fast bound for York. You will recall that I had seen 61454 at York, but their days were numbered.

Then I strolled along to the signal-box and asked if I might go in. The country signalmen usually welcomed a little company, and again this proved to be the case. He had seen me, of course, standing at the lineside, so we had a chat about the reorganizations of the railway—and his inevitable grumbles about the government. I kept quietly out of the way, eating my sandwiches in the cabin, while the man went about his work on the instruments and levers. It was then that a little incident occurred. The signalman had been complaining that his colleague down the line did not always follow the rule to 'bell' up-trains into his Heck block-section. The line was quiet for a spell, then something made me look round. Alarmed, I saw the streamlined front of an A.4 nosing gently through the overbridge north of the box, gliding quietly towards our tall home signal, which of course was 'on'. I called the signalman's attention to it. "Crikey" he exclaimed, "He's forgotten to bell him through!" He pulled off the signal to avoid bringing the London express to a stand, and it rolled slowly past, the crew staring up at the cabin, no doubt wondering at the cause of the delay. "I'm not pulling off the 'starter' straightaway" said my man, "Otherwise he'll know he's been forgotten. Let him think that I am clearing the line ahead". By reading the semaphore signals in this way, the drivers learned about the precise state of the line ahead and adjusted their speed accordingly. There is more to pulling off signals than the layman imagines—though, of course, this does not apply to colour-lights. Another trick was to pull signals off slowly to warn the driver to proceed cautiously. In this way, our signalman was protecting his colleague from being reported at Doncaster or King's Cross by the train crew as the cause of their late running. Our starting signal swung up in front of the rolling train, which then accelerated on its way south. Our man rang his colleague on the telephone and reprimanded him severely. The incident was interesting to me as a student of railways and, although not inherently dangerous in itself, proved that adherence to the well-proven rules virtually guarantees safety. The incident could have held the train standing on the main line, when a further breach of the same rule by the other signalman could have allowed a second train to collide with it in the rear. I passed the afternoon pleasantly until tea-time, reflecting that I had seen no freight-trains. Evidently Saturday was kept free for expresses and specials for the various events. It had been another very enjoyable interlude, with a number of decent monochrome photographs.

When I passed the spot on an InterCity express years later, in April 1991, the signal-box and sidings had gone, but the name *Heck* remained, painted on a lineside retaining-wall to recall them. The overhead wires had been erected and were almost ready for switching on; I had travelled the line occasionally behind the earlier Deltic locos and now I was taking my one chance to travel it by the diesel InterCity-125, before it was replaced in its turn by the electric service soon afterwards in July.

Wakefield (Westgate)

I drove to this station, used as a railhead for the south-west of the West Riding, to meet a guy I had made while skiing in Austria. He was coming from Beckenham in Kent for a long week-end on 20 May 1961, and I took the opportunity of going early so as to spend an hour or two photographing trains on this main-line from King's Cross to Leeds, just before the impending dieselization of the line. After a B1 4-6-0 had run through the far centre-road behind a standing mineral on the nearer one, A1 pacific 60133 *Pommern* rumbled in with his London-express. Two more followed in quick succession, another A1 60120 *Kittiwake* and A2 60520 *Owen Tudor,* a late-build by the LNER, and I believe based at Doncaster. Additional interest was furnished here, because the Bradford portion was shunted on by the carriage-pilot, an ex-LNER 0-6-0 J.39 goods-engine, from the loop west of the station, a practice that was soon to end. An O4 2-8-0 freight-locomotive ran through the centre-road light-engine just before a London-express, headed by A1 60157 *Great Eastern*, drew in on the other side, making his last stop before Leeds. As usual, he left the Bradford-portion in the platform, which soon departed behind unidentified motive-power—hidden by stock standing on the centre-road—but probably an LMS-type 2-6-4 tank. Another light-engine then ran through the centre-road, A3 pacific 60108 *Gay Crusader*, at a guess bound for Leeds (Neville Hill depot). The last train I saw before Brian arrived was a long coal-train hauled by an Austerity 2-10-0, slowly gaining speed after slogging up the bank from Kirkgate Station on the low-level ex-L & Y Calder Valley line. It was 90329, probably based locally and one of many Austerities of both the 2-8-0 and 2-10-0 varieties handling coal-traffic in the West Riding, including on the old LMS network. A visit to Auntie Flora at Peterborough on 3 December 1962 gave me a final brief opportunity to see the last vestige of steam on the old LNER ecml. It was A3 pacific 60062 *Minoru*, one of the class fitted with high smoke-deflectors, starting a semi-fast for Grantham.

Observations on former Great Western lines: to Guernsey, 6 September 1958

John and I set off on the first leg, overnight Leeds-St Pancras, but the darkness precluded observations. The 'lawn' at Paddington was clean in the cool morning air, with the various signs still announcing 'GWR', a decade after nationalization, evidence of the company's resentment at losing its identity after more than a century. Then we took the *Channel Islands Boat Express*, as the roof-boards grandly announced. My only observation as we pulled out of the platform was 4-6-0 'modified Hall' 6960 *Raveningham Hall* (now preserved) awaiting the next working, then we ran fast to the West Country. Through Yetminster, it was over the Dorset Downs up the punishing Eversholt Bank on the incredible gradients of 1:73/65/53/51, before coasting down, thankfully for the footplate-crew, through Upwey Wishing Well Halt, that favourite spot of photographers, to Weymouth. Here, the train-engine was taken off and a pannier-tank substituted to lead the train down to the harbour along the Weymouth Quay Tramway, where the pedestrians and cars pressed back to the walls to allow the train to pass. This held a great novelty, leaning out and watching our big train rumble at a snail's pace through the old streets to emerge at the harbour. From the deck of the ferry *St Helier*, we watched the pannier-tank uncouple to run round the empty stock, ready to haul it back to the town-station. This quaint link has since been closed—another victim, I expect, of the omnipotent and ever-increasing motor-traffic. On the return train-journey, I recorded nothing save the Jubilee that took us from St Pancras to Leeds, taking a photograph as 45675 *Hardy* swung on to the junction at Trent, against that familiar forest of ex-MR signals.

Torquay

John and I spent a delightful holiday at Torquay in August 1960 where the sun, sand and sea tempted us so much that we made only a couple of forays to see trains. On the 14th, we spent a day at Dartmouth and Kingswear station. The first train to arrive was 4939 *Littleton Hall* heading a local train, and we watched the manoeuvres as he crossed over to run round the train for the return-trip. Then, Prairie tank 5158 arrived with a Dart Valley local. After exploring Dartmouth's narrow streets, we returned to Kingswear station to see the flagship of the day arrive from Paddington, 'The Torbay Express.' The King 4-6-0s had recently been superseded by diesel-hydraulic power, and it was one of these Class 42 'Warships', D.820 *Grenville* that day, in charge of the train. Again we watched the locomotive easing gently over the crossover, ready to haul the long train over the single-line past Goodrington Sands back to Paignton.

Ten days later, we went up the line to Newton Abbot for a little look. It had appeared a hive of activity when we drove past on the way down, and this would be one of our few opportunities to see the old Great Western before more changes occurred. Indeed, the station-awning still bore the name GREAT WESTERN, cut out like fretwork in the metal fascia, therefore hard to erase or change to 'British Railways'. Many of the ex-GW artifacts retained the old name, such as the large goods-depot sign, showing the strong traditions of Swindon persisting. But, it was time for locomotives now, and we made our way across to the engine-sheds, which revealed Prairie tank 4174, 6921 *Borwick Hall*, 5992 *Horton Hall* and 1024 *County of Pembroke*. Three 'namers' were a good haul, but we were soon provided with more, in the shape of 5976 *Ashwicke Hall* on a Birmingham-Dartmouth through-working, followed by 5084 *Reading Abbey* heading a down Penzance express. Apart from an unidentified shunter in the distance, possibly a 2-8-0 tank, this was the sum-total of our observations as we drove out for Torquay and dinner at the Ashley Court Hotel.

Midland lines: Earby

In July, I got two good photographs of trains passing my home at Earby. The first was again a Compound pensioned-off on the 4 o'clock stopping-train from Manchester to Skipton, 41163, clean, showing off the lining-out to advantage, and a few days later Austerity 2-10-0 90316 on the evening coal-train from Skipton to Colne, Nelson and Burnley, the fuel destined for the cotton weaving-mills in East Lancashire. A decade earlier, this train might have brought out a L&Y 0-8-0, the roster taken over successively by an 'Austin Seven' of the same wheel-arrangement, then by one of the many 4F 0-6-0s based at Skipton. I guess one of these had failed when rostered for the afternoon up-working and the Austerity was commandeered from Calder Valley coal at Rose Grove to deputize.

The Midland Line: Bell Busk, north of Skipton

In the spring of 1959, our local newspaper *Craven Herald & Pioneer* publicized the impending closure of Bell Busk station, and it was important to me to cover it. It came as a shock until we realized that several of the Leeds-Carlisle stations had already been closed. Owing to the rapid rise in car ownership, it was simply a matter of time for the rest. It recalled holidays in the Dales and cycling with father to Mrs Bell's farm at Otterburn, a mile beyond Bell Busk, and watching the loading of milk churns on many a sunny war-time evening. I remembered the tall MR signal guarding the station from the north being replaced around 1945 with a shorter one, a standard LMS upper-quadrant on a steel post, and the quaint, quiet goods-yard, tucked into the Craven knoll at the back of the down-line.

So, armed with the trusty Zeiss, I arrived on a sunny 2 May 1959 to watch the trains for the afternoon, culminating with the last train to stop, about 4.50 pm down. Luckily, I got talking to the signalman, who invited me into his cabin, typically spick and span, and smelling of polish. I took a picture of the interior of the box, also several trains. The up 'Waverley' coasted through first, hauled by Jubilee 45568 *Western Australia*. The train was destined for St Pancras, after a change of engine at Leeds (City). His colleague 45564 *New South Wales* then roared through with the balancing-working, blasting up to the Otterburn IB signals atop the low watershed that divides upper Airedale from Ribblesdale, with the stop at Hellifield just beyond. My picture frames him in the cabin-window. Horwich-mogul 42720 was welcome, rolling down the gradient with a mixed-goods. Old faithful 4F 44222 also drifted down the hill with his up pick-up goods, not however calling at Bell Busk, where the sidings appeared disused. Black Five 45017 coasted by with an up Morecambe-Leeds, leaving the station covered in a fog of acrid smoke. He evidently had not turned on enough enforced-draught after breasting the summit at Otterburn. Another Jubilee roared up the incline, heading the down 'Thames-Clyde Express', 45639 *Raleigh*, closely followed by another Horwich-mogul 42851 hauling a long parcels-train composed of the usual miscellany of vehicles. This class rapidly became rare, and all were gone within a few years. An up-Carnforth semi-fast then coasted through, in the hands of Ivatt 4MT 2-6-0 43113. He was followed by another of the Skipton old-faithful 4Fs, 44277, heading a long through-goods, I believe the daily Carlisle-Stourton. This was quite a sight, since this class, old stagers on the Settle-Carlisle, was by now demoted from regular through-traffic on account of the wide availability of bigger motive-power, such as Stanier 8Fs and Standard 9Fs. Perhaps the larger, rostered, locomotive had failed. But, to crown all, one of his colleagues, 44119, then came slogging up the incline with the daily BP tanker-train bound for Heysham Harbour. Leeds control must have been short of modern motive-power that day—but all a bonus for me. Finally, beyond the end of the down platform, I snapped the Black Stanier 45186 pulling out of the station, framed by the bracket upper-quadrant signal beckoning him out, the all-stations Bradford (Forster Square) to Carlisle and the last train to stop at Bell Busk. This was the balancing-working of the train I had often caught from Carlisle in my Army days some seven years before, already described. It was the end of an era for me—and no other visitor was there. In fairness though, Bell Busk was never a busy spot, for the population was sparse, and one cannot expect services to be run on the basis of sentiment. I drove home in a reverie.

As a footnote, the Lord Bishop Eric Treacy, the famous railway photographer (and a former Archdeacon of Halifax; his vicarage in Stafford Avenue was near my home), echoed my feelings when, in his foreword to *Rails In The Fells*, he specifically mentioned Bell Busk as a typical, welcoming, wayside station in the Midland Railway style, and unchanged from those days. I was glad I had gone to see it once more.

Gargrave, 23 May 1959

This pretty village lies five miles north of Skipton a couple of miles short of Bell Busk, with a similar, delightful station, still open, though unstaffed. That day, the weather was hot and sunny, often the case around Whitsuntide, and a variety of locomotives was on offer, so I passed a most pleasant afternoon on the station and in the signal-box for monochrome pictures—colour-photography was still a luxury. Britannia 70044 *Earl Haig* came first, heading the down 'Waverley', the successor to the 'Thames-Forth.' My next shot was of old faithful 4F 44222 heading a down pick-up goods, bursting through his cloud of smoke under the arched bridge. This 4F and several others with weatherboard-cab tenders had their home at Skipton or Hellifield for years. The up-'Waverley' then sped swiftly through, headed by another Britannia, 70053 *Moray Firth*, leaving the station covered in black smoke—evidently through low-draught. Shortly afterwards, 8F 2-8-0 48160 rumbled downhill on mineral-empties, probably having been held in loop at Hellifield, five miles to the north. A sign of the times was a standard Ivatt 4MT, 43070 at the head of a Morecambe-Leeds semi-fast express, a former turn of a Compound. One of the Holbeck Scots, appropriately 46145 *The Duke of Wellington's Regt (West Riding)*, and one of the early conversions to taper-boiler and double-chimney, sped powerfully north on the 'Thames-Clyde' express. I was glad to see a Horwich mogul next, 42835, rolling steadily down-grade with a Carlisle-Skipton goods. He would be destined for the exchange-sidings, leaving his load to be marshalled while he went to the shed for servicing to be ready for a return-trip that evening. A second 4F *habitué* of Skipton now passed through, 44007, pulling steadily up the gradient out of the Aire Valley to the Ribble watershed. His mineral-wagons, labelled LOCO COAL were destined for the sheds at Hellifield. Lastly arrived the sole Black Five of the afternoon, 45083 with the 4.30 Bradford-Morecambe stopping-train. The majority of the wayside-stations remained open at that date, so he would be giving many country folks a service, such as the inhabitants of Giggleswick and Wennington.

Only a month later, father and I happened to be passing Gargrave station and parked to look over the bridge. Ivatt 4MT 43070 was just arriving light-engine from the north. This locomotive was mentioned above on my previous visit, bringing the Morecambe semi-fast. From the Broughton Road overbridge, we watched, fascinated, wondering what was afoot as the mogul stopped opposite the signal-box. Surprisingly, he set back, easing into the rusty sidings, rarely used by that date. At the far end of the siding stood a van, probably dropped with a 'hot box', but the engine did not go thus far. A few yards into the siding, he stopped before moving out again onto the main line. With a whistle, he puffed quickly towards Skipton. We could only conclude that the signalman had wanted him to test the points, either after adjustment or in preparation for the van to be picked up.

Beauchief, south of Sheffield

This intriguing name was my reason for visiting this small country station on 21 June 1961. It lay on the four-track main line beyond Millhouses on the south side of Sheffield, a remarkable little enclave of rural peace so close to the steel city, simply the station in a cutting with its overbridge and signal-box, playing host to few stopping trains, and witnessing the Midland-line expresses to St Pancras and Bristol southbound, and to Leeds and Carlisle northbound. In fact, the line and station were almost exactly as they were when built more than a century before, save for the widening to four-tracks in the Edwardian period. Immediately, Jubilee 45602 *British Honduras* coasted through on a Leeds express and shortly afterwards, another, 45565 *Victoria* headed the up 'Devonian', blasting up the incline from Millhouses down in Sheffield. This train was followed by Royal Scot 46140 *The King's Royal*

Rifle Corps, powering smoothly off the incline with an up special to St Pancras and then another Jubilee, 45576 *Bombay*, heading the down Cardiff-Newcastle express. Finally, Fairburn 2-6-4 tank-engine 42054 ran in on the western-side with a local bound for the Edale-branch. I had obtained a good selection of pictures, before leaving in mid-afternoon to return home via Wakefield to try out my new Grundig tape-recorder, which I had brought with me.

Hellifield, 29 December 1963

As it was too cold for mother to venture out, father and I took a short drive through West Marton to Hellifield. He was always game for a ride. The locomotive-depot had closed that year, so there was not much doing, very sad, since that shed was so visible from the north end of the single island-platform. Two Class 5s, 44904 and 45332 departed in opposite directions, the northern train bound for Carnforth, since the Lancaster (Green Ayre) station and its branch from Wennington Junction had also been closed. From the station approach, I took a picture of a northbound freight, headed by Horwich-mogul 42844, coming off the Blackburn-branch. His neighbour, 2845, had also been a regular performer on this line in LMS days, both possibly shedded here or at Blackburn. He passed along the goods-lines in front of the station, but here, track-lifting had begun. I was fortunate in catching this mogul, as the class was despatched to the scrapyard within the following two years.

Horwich mogul 2769 awaits duty on Skipton MPD in 1947. The first of this class, 13000, later renumbered 2700, appears on the cover of this book (author).

Chapter 11

STEAM WITHDRAWS TO ITS LAST REDOUBT: THE LMS TRIANGLE

This chapter covers approximately the last four years of steam on Britain's railways, the spell that ended in August 1968 north-west of Leeds, a region I have named 'The LMS Triangle.' Later in the chapter, I give further short accounts of my visits to different locations for photographs and sound-recordings. Some locations appear twice to retain chronological order.

Summary of diesel developments

The earlier chapter, *Steam and Diesel Achievements of the LMS,* described some LMS developments which unwittingly presaged the end of steam on Britain's railways, although of course this outcome could not be perceived at the time. The early pioneering designs of steam-railcars and rail-motors were attempts to meet the competition from road-transport beginning before the 1914-18 war. These designs evolved into the LMS Leyland diesel-railcars of 1934, 29950/1/2, and the GWR's AEC diesel-cars. Paralleling the Leylands were the LMS experiments with diesel-shunters, culminating in the excellent 350 hp diesel-electric machine built in collaboration with the English-Electric Company Ltd., also introduced in 1934. These two experimental strands came together in the diesel-hydraulic three-car train introduced by the LMS in 1938, numbered 80000-2. Unfortunately, the outbreak of war in 1939 curtailed its development, and after the end of hostilities with the day of the mainline multiple-unit train still to dawn, the experiment was not continued; however, the concept and its research remained, dormant in the company's archives.

In the short period from the end of WW2 in 1945 to nationalization in 1948, the LMS continued its research and testing of diesels under C.E. Fairburn as the CME and, after his sudden death, under H.G. Ivatt. Fairburn's training as an electrical engineer at The English Electric Company, which built diesel-locomotives at its Vulcan Foundry works, had naturally fitted him to take personal charge of these projects. The culmination was an improved design of diesel-electric shunter, with double frames and a twin-engine drive, the 7120-class. It was adopted by BR as its standard shunter from 1948. The final pioneering-attempt by the LMS took the rails only days before the company lost its identity in nationalization. On the 7 December 1947, Mr H.G. Ivatt drove the 1,600 hp express diesel-electric locomotive *LMS 10000* out of the paint-shop at Derby. With this short ride, he made history. The 12 December saw its first public run from St Pancras down the Midland main-line past its birthplace at Derby on a trial-run to Manchester. Later, 10001 emerged from the works, but without the LMS insignia, as it was now 1948, with BR in charge. The two locomotives in tandem ran exhaustive trials to Manchester and afterwards on the West Coast main-line. I saw them several times with 10000 still bearing the LMS insignia—the only diesel express-passenger locomotive in Britain to carry a private-company's colours; it was unique. Equally important, it presaged the replacement of the large steam passenger-locomotives with diesel-electric traction, although a decade was to pass before this came about. However, a glance across the Atlantic Ocean told us that both the USA and Canada were well embarked on the conversion to diesel-haulage, begun before the second war—but they had oil, while Britain's North Sea field was as yet only suspected, and therefore the British economy remained geared to coal. However, significantly BR dieselized many local services, beginning with the Craven units in 1954. In the 1930s, Stanier and the LMS Executive had foreseen this change: the long development of the steam-locomotive had reached its ultimate stage with the boiler-diameter now at the limit of the loading-gauge, and therefore an alternative source of power had to be found.

BILL HORSFALL

Now we are going to see how creeping dieselization pushed steam eventually into 'The LMS Triangle.' As the first candidate for dieselization, BR had several reasons to select the Great Western network, now its Western Region (WR). Geography was a prime factor: the tracks radiated out like a fan to the north-west and west from a single terminus, Paddington—without any complications of electric suburban-services. The change-over began in 1958 with two pioneer diesel-hydraulics, the A1A *Warships*, D600-1, built by the North British Locomotive Company in Glasgow. A conflict of interests between managements, the WR at Swindon and BR HQ at Marylebone, resulted in a promising idea being aborted: the six A1As as constructed under BR-direction were too heavy, vitiating the designed advantages of a 'monocoque' construction. They were relegated to the Plymouth-Penzance line for a short operating-life.

However, their successors, the D800-series *Warships*, also with hydraulic-drive, with the intended stressed-skin construction to save weight, were excellent machines weighing in at only 78 tons. They took over the heaviest, prestige, trains to the west. I have described how in 1960 I watched D820 *Grenville* arriving at Kingswear with the *Torbay Express*. In the same year, Cecil J. Allen made an excellent recording broadcast by the BBC, on the footplate of D808 *Benbow* from Exeter up to London. His comparisons with the previous King-timing showed the clear advance that diesel-hydraulic power had made, while his crisp, animated descriptions of events on the footplate made exciting listening. The Warships' successors, the '1000s', or *Westerns*, gave even more drawbar horse-power from a machine much lighter than a conventional diesel-electric Type 4. The early, disappointing, failures of some components on these hydraulic-locomotives were largely overcome to make the class extremely successful and they attracted a huge following. Unfortunately, their numerical minority—seventy-four only—indicated they had to give way to BR-standardization—but, with their problems solved, was that a wise or logical decision?

The conversion to diesel of the ex-GWR-network in the late-1950s was swiftly followed by a similar move on the former LMS wcml, Euston to Glasgow and branches. I have mentioned my first evidence, the sighting of 'Peak' D.224 piloting, as a crew-training exercise, an up express at Grayrigg, Westmorland (now Cumbria), in April 1960, while simultaneously the electrification of the routes from Manchester and Liverpool to Watford Junction, and later into Euston, was gradually completed. I rode the line from Manchester to Crewe and back on the first Saturday of its operation, 17 September 1960, by emu up to Crewe, returning on a locomotive-hauled express, but several years were needed for the upgrading of the whole wcml, an enormous task. In 1961 came the dieselization of the of the former LNER East Coast line, using twenty-two 'Deltics', followed by the Scottish Region, ending the swansong of some ex-LNER V.2s and A4 streamliners hauling Glasgow-Perth expresses after their demotion from the East Coast. One of them was 60009 *Union of South Africa,* which remains in Scotland, preserved by the SRPS. It was as if the octopus was withdrawing his tentacles, leaving very little steam-operation remaining across Britain, since the feeder-routes too were by then either closed, many before the Beeching-report as well as afterwards, or operated by dmus. The shrinkage of steam encouraged enthusiasts to organize special-trains, which gradually became more numerous.

A Special Comes through Earby

We did not always have to drive miles to see one of the steam-specials in the sixties: that on 4 May 1963 was routed past my family home at Earby. It was the East Lancashire Railtour, organised by the RCTS and powered by the locomotive owned by Lord Garnock, then a director of Crossley's Carpets in Halifax, the preserved K4, 3442 *The Great Marquess.* The little engine was resplendent in its LNER apple-green, with counter-shaded gilt lettering, all very correct, reminding the older observers of pre-war days, though the engine had actually been built by British Railways in 1949. It had to run round the train at Barnoldswick, followed by a similar manoeuvre at Earby, ready to continue to Great Harwood, near Blackburn, Lancashire.

Beattock, 19 October 1963

After visiting my cousin Heather and husband Ken at Bearsden, Dunbartonshire, west of Glasgow, I was driving home to Yorkshire and planning to call in at Beattock to watch the West Coast trains for an hour or two, including the assisting-engines on their push up the ten-mile Beattock Bank. I was lucky, for there was plenty of steam activity—and this only about four years before it ended on the railways. I began on the up station-platform with microphone in hand. The first engine was Standard 2-6-4 tank 80073 crossing to the shed after a banking-duty—the only locomotive of this type that I saw—followed by the regular Stanier/Fairburn 42170. A colleague, 42192, then banked a long freight up the incline. A further down freight followed, hauled by 'Clan' Light Pacific 72007 *Clan Mackintosh*, a rare sighting of this class of only ten locomotives. Yet another down freight followed, hauled by late-model Black Five 44692. Two up-expresses ran through in quick succession, Type 4s D.371 and D.334, the latter heading the 'Royal Scot.' I gained permission to look around the shed, where I watched the coaling, carried out with a crane made at nearby Annan. It lifted its bucket of coal to the engine-bunker, where the fireman tipped it. I think the system was a stop-gap measure after the original mechanism had expired, as it was not worth the cost of installing large new equipment for the few years of steam that remained. Behind the shed, an unexpected visitor was ex-LNER A2 pacific 60522 *Straight Deal*, buffered up to a former regular, Pickersgill superheated 0-6-0 3F 57658, the last ex-Caledonian engine that I saw. Both were in store and almost certainly condemned.

A G&SWR axle-box on a carriage relegated to an engineers' mess-coach on the breakdown train provided another archive-picture. Then I spotted a Class Five starting his up-freight from a signal-check. Nice and clean, late-model 44674 gave me a good picture and recording. But the principal activity was provided by the big 2-6-4 tank-engines coming and going on their banking duties. I had just snapped another of them, 42200, leaving the coaler and drifting onto the banking-spur, when I caught the eye of the driver, whom I shall call Tom. We began chatting, and then I got my big break: he invited me on to the footplate. We were standing on the spur south of the station ready to bank a train, and I realized he was letting me accompany them.

"Aye, but keep out o' sight as we pass the box" instructed Tom good-naturedly—the same request I had had ten years earlier, when riding the Black Five out of Sheffield (Victoria). I was thrilled, and almost before

I was ready with camera and microphone, we were off, squealing over the points up to the rear of a long express hauled by a Peak 1-Co-Co-1 diesel-electric. We buffered up and whistled the banking code, the guard waved his green flag, and dramatically we all rolled forward. The bunker was piled high with its three-and-a-half tons of coal, the steam pressure was up to the 200lbs mark and the fireman had prepared a hot fire. He would need that for the ten-mile slog.

The din was tremendous, like on the Class Five footplate trip in 1953, but this time it was a tank engine, so at least I had a flat floor to stand on. The cab was cosy and surprisingly roomy, so I was able to stay out of the way of the workers. In fact, I sat on the fireman's seat on the right all the way up the incline—you will guess that he had no need of it—holding the microphone in what I hoped would be a suitable position, near the roof-vent. I was also taking photographs through my cab glass, as we rumbled up the 1:88/74 incline past the landmarks I knew so well, Auchencastle IB signals, Greskine box and Harthope IBs.

We slogged up the bank at about thirty miles per hour, on half-regulator and cut-off of 30-35%. After the viaduct over the river Annan and the Harthope signals, Summit Box came into view on the right. As the train went over the crest, Tom snapped the regulator shut and we dropped back, stopping when the fireman shouted that we had cleared the crossover. The points changed immediately, the ground-signal and advance-starter came off, and we reversed over the crossover, but stopped briefly to give a platelayer a lift down to Greskine. After a few revolutions, Tom closed the regulator and we drifted down the incline, still accelerating. I stood up to allow the fireman to take a well-earned rest; he needed that after shovelling three hundredweight of coal for the ascent. At the Greskine signal-box, we stopped to let the platelayer off, then coasted down the rest of the way through the Auchencastle signals to Beattock station.

I could see what a fine design Stanier had created in terms of efficiency, as well as comfort for the crew. This sub-class was actually one of an even larger number of machines credited to Mr Fairburn for his modifications incorporated to reduce weight and maintenance costs, detailed in chapter 3. My 2-6-4T 42200 was a great engine and I really did like him—even coated with the grime of the late steam-era—but then, I had always adored these big tank-engines. In the following year, 1964, I was to obtain another recording of a similar machine, 42084, though this time from the train, rather than the footplate, a trip described later. Not one shovelful was put into the firebox of 42200 on the downhill run but steam had still begun to blow off before we came in sight of Beattock station, where vestiges of the former branch to the little hydro of Moffat were visible on our left. We reversed across the main-lines onto the shed and the coaler. Here, I took some action-shots of Tom and his fireman re-coaling and taking on water, ready for another push up the famous incline. It was a splendid experience, one I shall always remember, apart from the noisy recording that I obtained. It was only an office dictating-machine that I had, a makeshift job, before I obtained the Grundig portable tape-recorder in the following year. However, the monochrome photographs taken from the footplate of 42200 recorded the scene through the drifting smoke.

The last Southern Region steam operations

The Isle of Wight, August 1961

We go back two years now to another holiday that I spent, driving to the Isle of Wight this time. We arrived on the island on 13 August for a week's holiday at Sandown. The following morning, we took the train back to Ryde, so as to cover this interesting line. The railways on the Wight had by then shrunk to one line only, from Ryde Pierhead to Ventnor, most trains however turning back at Sandown. The motive-power remained the venerable M7 0-4-4Ts, retained in service here far longer than their peers elsewhere on account of their suitability for the short-radius curve coming off Ryde Pier. We were hauled by W18 and returned with W29 on a Ventnor train. W33 had been left at the pierhead evidently awaiting duty, and on our way down the line, two more engines posed for my camera on Ryde shed. Another useful photograph was one of those cast-iron signs announcing the former owners of the line: SOUTHERN RAILWAY. To avoid conflict with other numbers, the Wight engines bore the prefix 'W' to their number on the engine-bunker. The eventual solution to modernising the Wight railway was the introduction of former London Transport electric-stock phased out from the Central Line. If only trains could speak, these carriages would have wondered at their translation to a new home in the green countryside by the sea, far from Epping, Bank or Ealing Broadway. To replace the Central Line stock later, a further cascade took place with stock from the Underground's Northern Line when it was upgraded.

Lymington-Brockenhurst-Bournemouth

One steam-operated line prominent in this era was the ex-SR mainline from Waterloo to Bournemouth—a full-status express-route too, plus its steam-hauled freight-operations, the last remaining enclave of steam in southern England. The rest of the former SR-network had, of course, long been converted to third-rail-electric operation, mainly for commuters. Clearly, change was coming, so we took the opportunity while on the Isle of Wight, to cross on the ferry from Yarmouth to watch the main-line trains. The branch-train from Lymington Harbour up to the junction at Brockenhurst was a delight, an M7 0-4-4 tankengine, 30029, hauling dusty old Maunsell carriages, a scene hardly changed for decades, save for the BR-renumbering of the locomotive from plain 29.

Brockenhurst was a splendid place to watch trains. The O3 0-6-0 30541 shunting carriages was witnessing an apparently-endless stream of trains hauled by several locomotive-types even at that late stage in steam-haulage. Urie S.15 4-6-0 30511 was shunting in the yard as H15 30474 passed on mixed freight, then West Country light-pacific 34047 *Callington* flew through on an up express. A trip to Bournemouth was equally rewarding, the shed well-populated with several types—and visible from the platform too. I identified the leader of the 'Battle of Britain' sub-class, 34049 *Anti-Aircraft Command*, and N15 'King Arthur' 4-6-0 30782 *Sir Brian*. While returning, I noted light-pacific 34089 *602 Squadron* heading the down 'Bournemouth Belle' through Pokesdown, and a short wait on Brockenhurst platform gave me two more, 34029 *Lundy* on a Bournemouth express and 34022 *Exmoor* on an up Waterloo, as well as another Urie S.15, 30509, hauling a down semi-fast passenger, a change from his usual freight-haulage.

Basingstoke

This is further up the line towards London, so three years later, in 1964, having learned that this last outpost of steam in southern England was finally scheduled for conversion to third-rail electrification (which took place only in 1967), I left my holiday-chalet at Sinah Warren on Hayling Island to drive up to Basingstoke for an afternoon's train-watching, where I relished another procession of Merchant Navy and West Country/Battle of Britain pacifics. I photographed 34086 *219 Squadron* as well as 'N' and 'S' 4-6-0s and 'U' class 2-6-0s. N.15 4-6-0 30834 passed through on up freight, MN 35025 *Brocklebank Line* on a down Bournemouth express, WC 34005 *Barnstaple* on up semi-fast and 34108 *Wincanton* arrived on a down all-stations train. S.15 4-6-0 30837 ran through on a down freight and another light-pacific, 34015 *Exmouth*, headed a down semi-fast. A bonus was ex-GW 6952 *Kimberley Hall*, on a down semi-fast to Didcot. Such connecting-services were the role of the remaining ex-GWR locomotives, since the Western Region had already been dieselized. The Basingstoke down home-signals were still represented with a splendid pre-grouping (LSWR) lower-quadrant signal-gantry, making an excellent picture. Clearly, all improvements had been held back for years while the future of the line-equipment was decided.

The twilight of steam and BR's last redoubt: steam shrinks into 'The LMS triangle'

By the 1960s, the railway-map of the Britain comprised largely diesel or electric services. The only area still ruled by steam, save the Waterloo-Bournemouth line just described, was the triangle to the north and west of Leeds, approximately Leeds-Carlisle-Liverpool. It became the theatre where its audience, the fans of steam, witnessed its swansong on the West Coast route, with the expresses and specials following the night-freights, almost all banked over the hills. On the Settle-Carlisle road too we saw it, from the heavy-haul of the Long Meg mineral-trains to the Saturdays-only Nottingham/Birmingham-Glasgow Thames-Clyde relief-expresses. These virtually became excursions for enthusiasts. Some visited the remaining sheds, such as Rose Grove, Bank Hall and others in Lancashire, as well as Leeds (Holbeck), and began to take part in the action, volunteering to clean the last few engines in service, mostly

LONDON MIDLAND & SCOTTISH

Black Fives and 8F 2-8-0s, including the many specials. Hellifield had closed in 1963, sending its engines to Skipton, but it closed too in 1967. However, Leeds Holbeck remained home to a few Jubilees, such as 45573 *Newfoundland* and 45647 *Sturdee*. The last three were 45562 *Alberta*, 45593 *Kolhapur* and 45697 *Achilles*. After *Achilles* was withdrawn early in 1967, the remaining pair, beautifully polished by enthusiasts and bearing the diagonal yellow cabside-stripe denoting exclusion from working 'under the wires' (south of Crewe) and an emblem of the last year or two of steam-operation, were rostered on the SO expresses, working back on freight over Ais Gill—usually on quiet Monday mornings when few were watching. More on the SO expresses comes later.

Leeds (Holbeck) & (Farnley), 25 January 1964

A good variety was standing on Holbeck shed that day, only three years before the end of main-line steam. Jubilee 45568 *Western Australia* shedded there, 55A (LMS 20A), was the first in the line, probably off the up Thames-Clyde express. I could hardly believe it when I saw 45736 *Phoenix*, the first of the two Jubilees rebuilt with the 2A taper-boiler in 1942, and normally resident on the Western Division 'A', then a similarly-converted Patriot, 45527 *Southport*. I had been fortunate in making my visit on this Saturday, for I learned from one of the drivers that these last two had brought football-specials over the Pennines from Manchester. Leeds had long been a Division 1 club, and so attracted the crowds to Elland Road. Farnley, to the west of the city, was the shed that serviced the 'New Line' built by the LNWR through Dewsbury to converge beyond Heaton Lodge Junction with the existing line. Jubilees were shedded at Farnley too, for example 45581 *Bihar and Orissa* and 45643 *Rodney*, but all I saw today were two 0-6-0 shunting-tanks, 47419 and 47589. They were condemned, so it was as well to take a picture.

Leeds (Holbeck & Neville Hill), 8 February 1964

A fortnight later, I was back at Holbeck, and I actually took two colour-shots (what a luxury!) of two Britannia pacifics standing on the shed, 70006 *Robert Burns* and 70007 *Coeur de Lion*, coaled up for their next tasks, possibly the Scots expresses, and Jubilee 45739 *Ulster*, not forgetting a late-model Black Five, 44758, all quite clean and looking fine. This Black Five was the last-built of the class to carry the LMS insignia as 4758. I was lucky also to see a rare 'Clan' pacific, 72006 *Clan Mackenzie* and my 'own' Jubilee 45573 *Newfoundland*, both inside the roundhouse. During the next two years, many engines would look woebegone, streaked with dirt and rust, with steam leaking from glands, but at least here we had not reached that stage yet.

I drove over to the eastern side of the city, to see what was happening at the large, ex-LNER shed, Neville Hill. The roundhouses had gone, leaving their foundations as evidence. Jubilee 45698 *Mars* had brought in a football-special and was standing ready to return. The other locomotives standing on shed were ex-MR 4F 0-6-0 43987, Stanier 2-6-2Ts 40193 and 40148, and Thompson B1 61033. In LMS-days, I had seen 193 as carriage-pilot at the City Station, but 40148 was new to me, and, interestingly, one of the five rebuilt with a larger boiler in an attempt to improve poor performance—which it signally failed to do. Inside the shed were three Q6 0-8-0s, 63417, 63370 and 63348, while on a spur at the back of the building, the restored ex-GNR N7 0-6-2T 69621 was hiding. Again, this collection revealed a surprising variety so late in the steam-era.

Kirkby Stephen, 5 September 1964

After a quick, final, look at Scout Green, recounted later, I took father over to Kirkby Stephen. I had neglected the northern section of the Settle-Carlisle line, so now maybe I could remedy this omission a little. Indeed I did and was lucky again, although we saw only three trains. The first was a down-freight, headed incredibly at this late date by a 4F 0-6-0, 44044, one of the old faithfuls of Skipton. I was amazed at this, because the 4Fs had long been superseded on the through-freights by bigger engines as they had become available in the post-war years. This fellow was coasting down the steepest section from Ais Gill, after having managed to slog up The Long Drag to Blea Moor on the other side.

Father and I were in the signal-box when, shortly afterwards, a mixed-freight arrived from Carlisle, and I mean arrived, for oil-burning Black Five 44677 stopped opposite the signal-box and a conversation ensued.

I nearly said altercation, because the bobby shouted, "Goo in," that is, put the whole train in the sidings, since a fast freight was due shortly, the daily Long Meg anhydrite block-train for ICI Widnes. Evidently a wagon had to be picked up, dropped off with a 'hot box' by an earlier train. During this interchange, the guard had walked up from his van. "We're no'aan gooin' in", (I render the Cumbrian dialect as best I can). Apparently, he wanted to 'be finished' as soon as possible. And they refused to 'goo in', simply leaving the freight standing on the main-line, something that always makes me anxious. Father was examining the instruments and levers, while I, microphone in hand, had migrated to the front balcony, a feature of the Midland timber cabins. The engine rumbled down the neck of the three sidings passing directly below me, coupled up to the unfortunate wagon which he then swiftly pulled out onto the main-line. The signalman was anxious too, his hand resting on the point-lever ready to reverse it the instant he heard the locomotive hoot that they had cleared. They drifted back, buffered up gently, coupled up and 44677 gave a final blast on his LMS hooter. During this time, the signalman had kept glancing nervously at his line-instruments and listening for the expected bell-code from Crosby Garrett offering the fast-freight. I could feel the tension too, but swift and powerful shunting had saved the day. The advanced starting-signal was pointing up now, and the late-model Class Five pulled away strongly, accelerating his twenty-wagon train up the 1:100 gradient, giving me a super recording. In fact, the engine remained clearly audible for some time, the exhaust-sound carried back on the prevailing wind. It had been a splendid interlude, for shunting in the wayside yards was long a thing of the past, even then. We had been lucky to call at just the right time.

Shortly afterwards, the expected through-freight came through, the daily anhydrite-train, headed powerfully by 9F 92009, which made another splendid photograph and recording, again particularly the 'fading sound' as he slogged up the incline towards Mallerstang. We reckoned that the Black Five had just made it and stayed ahead, so that the 9F was not delayed with signal-checks on the steep grade to Ais Gill. But it had been a close call; shunting on the main-line is not to be recommended.

The former GWR around Wrexham & the Ffestiniog special 25 April 1964

The conversion to diesel-haulage in the north and west had left only a few enclaves of steam dotted about the country, discoverable only through magazines or platform chat. A colleague of mine, Derek Phillips, had such connections and came up with suggestions for excursions. You could say that he had the information, while I had the transport. We drove first to Wrexham, where we photographed a 'Hall' passing on freight and several locomotives on Croes Newydd shed; in the roundhouse were 0-6-2T 6611, Pannier-tanks 1628, 1660 and other members of each class, plus a 2-6-0. But our main aim was to be up the line at Ruabon to see the Ffestiniog Special arrive from Paddington. It rolled in majestically, headed by the gleaming 4079 *Pendennis Castle*, bringing the members of the Ffestiniog Society on the first leg of their trip to the Society's AGM. I realized what a bustling place Ruabon had been, typical of many such junctions up and down the country, before the great slimming-down process from the 1950s broke up the network. After snapping Modified Hall 6994 on an InterCity express, we shot off into the wilds of North Wales chasing the special, now hauled by Standard 4MT light 4-6-0s 75009 and 75023 due to weight-restrictions on the Bala line. At Mynffordd, the branch met the higher-level Ffestiniog narrow-gauge line, the subway still equipped with the traditional GWR black-and-white signs. Later, we saw standard 2-6-4 tank 80098 (since rescued and restored) arrive at the station on a regular-service. We finished the day on the FR, gaining further splendid snapshots.

The Solway Ranger, 13 June 1964

It was again Derek who told me about this proposed railtour, advertised in the railway press while I was swotting German for exams. It sounded unusual, so we reserved our seats. Sure enough, the newly-restored former Southern Railway Merchant Navy class Pacific locomotive 35012 *United States Lines* was standing there in Leeds City station at the head of the long train. Some carriages were ex-LNER teak-panelled East Coast stock. I will mention the principal places that we passed through, as the route is of some geographical and historical interest.

Taking the Midland line, we shortly passed my old school, and then Skipton and Hellifield for Carnforth. The engine had some difficulty in starting off from rest, as this class was 'light on its feet' giving much slipping on starting. It also had a very soft exhaust, not good for my microphone—but more on this further on. We crossed the bridge over the West Coast Route at Carnforth's Midland & Furness Junction box, reversing with a pilot-engine on the tail through the former Furness Railways' curved platforms so that *United State Lines* faced north. We glided out on to the main line, and set out to attack the two inclines of Grayrigg and Shap. The SR crew set off determinedly, working up a good lick into Westmorland (now Cumbria), up the rising gradients through Milnthorpe and Hincaster to devour the first incline, to Grayrigg. We swept through the station at quite a clip. But, as we raced over Dillicar troughs in the Lune Gorge towards Tebay at the foot of Shap, I spotted steam ahead: we were following another train. Where was it, Greenholme, or Scout Green? And would it clear in time, or would we catch it up and be stopped? It was the latter: we were brought to a dead stand at Shap Wells down IB signal, where 35012 had the devil of a job restarting on the steep bank. While disappointing for the lineside cameras, it was nectar for my tape-recorder, for I really heard the engine for the first time.

After another severe signal-check at Shap Station, where apparently the goods train ahead was switching into the loop, we really got away and flew down the bank through Clifton & Lowther to Penrith. Here our big engine was uncoupled to run light to Carlisle Kingmoor for servicing, and two Ivatt Class 2MT 2-6-0s, 46425/7, hooked on the back to take us on a scenic ride through Keswick and past pretty Bassenthwaite Lake, to arrive on the grimy West Cumberland coast at Workington (Main). From here, a Craven four-car dmu (our carriage was M79017) took us down the coast to delightfully-named Corkickle, where we branched up into the hills along old colliery lines, first to Frizington, where a railman operated the Birkbridge ground-frame for our passage. We passed the site of the ex-FR engine-shed at Moor Row (12E) and stubs of several former colliery branches to arrive at Rowrah, in the foothills of Lakeland. The end of the circle back to the main Maryport & Carlisle line at Bullgill had been chopped off here, but the lower-quadrant hanging-bracket starting-signal was still connected and was operated enthusiastically from the cabin by enthusiasts.

Reversing down the other leg of the triangle we landed at Sellafield (then named the Windscale Works) within sight of the famous nuclear-factory and power-station at Calder Hall. An Ivatt 4MT mogul was shunting the sidings beyond the station. Forward to Carlisle prepared us for our last foray into the wildernesses of Cumberland.

Much organisation must have gone into the provision of two engines from the Glasgow Transport Museum to haul us along the branch to Silloth and back. CR 123 and GNSR 49 were gleaming, the former in its Caledonian blue, the latter in engine green. I had visited this small seaside resort with army-pal Smudger and his family over a decade before, never imagining I would arrive there in a big train. Much whistling accompanied our progress through the bridges, constructed with very close clearances due to shortage of funds. Woe betide any who put their head out! We arrived in the dilapidated terminus, where the two engines were turned separately on the turntable, itself lost in weeds feet high. Soon afterwards, the branch was closed completely.

Back in Carlisle, the ex-Southern Railway pacific was ready for us on the train, smoking with a full head of steam in the evening sunshine on Platform 5. The crew, Southerners in the North, having been thwarted from showing their mettle on the Shap incline, were evidently determined to put the record straight. I discovered this on putting my head out of the window, when I felt lumps of unburnt coal thrown out of the chimney as we raced up the Eden Valley towards Ais Gill. The Merchant Navy engines were noted for their high coal-consumption— evidently burnt and otherwise . . . It was the fastest run over that route I had ever experienced, but it nearly ended in disaster, for the crew had driven at such a rate that they almost exhausted their water, forcing them to crawl from Settle Junction through Skir Beck and Long Preston to make an unscheduled stop in Hellifield station for a long drink at its water-crane. This triangular route has since become a regular routine for steam specials, while the West Cumbria coastal line is the route of the *Cumbrian Mountain Express* during the summer tourist season. So our trip was something of a pioneer and greatly appreciated by all takers. Some years later, I met some of them, who shared their vivid recollections of that day. The collieries had been closed earlier like the Moor Row depot serving them, and their lines over which we had travelled that day were soon lifted as well, closing another chapter in the life of West Cumbria.

The last train of the day from London to Halifax

Businessmen in the big towns amid the Pennine Hills away from the crack trunk north-south routes had constantly pleaded for a fast daily service to London, so that they could complete a day's work there and be back at home in the evening. Different schemes were tried.

A service in the 1950s operated through-carriages from Halifax to Kings Cross via the Spen Valley line from Low Moor to link up with a Leeds-London express at Wakefield (Westgate). Later in the decade, the authorities put on what became *The South Yorkshireman*, running from Bradford (Exchange) via Halifax, Huddersfield and Penistone, continuing through Sheffield on the old Great Central line to Marylebone. After the closure of the GC in the 1960s, a different through-carriage scheme was introduced. The train itself was unimpressive, simply the last three carriages uncoupled from a Kings Cross-Leeds express at Wakefield and hauled onward by a tank-engine, but it was the manner of its going that was fascinating. Readers living on the North Kent Coast will identify with this, since a similar splitting operation takes place at Faversham, where most trains from London are divided into two parts, one for Ramsgate, the other for Canterbury and Dover. This, however, is straightforward, since an electric train requires no separate locomotive.

In 1964, the West Riding passenger-services had long been operated with diesel multiple-units, but this portion of the business-train required a locomotive for the last stretch. One of the LMS-designed 2-6-4 tank-engines was provided. As they are favourites of mine, I watched with pleasure as the train ran in to Huddersfield bunker-first, because of the reversal there. The locomotive was Brghton-built 42084, allocated to Low Moor MPD. As the engine ran round his train, I took the first compartment, luckily vacant. This, next to the engine, was as good as the footplate—and with less clatter from the recording point of view—and so we set off down the tail of the Colne Valley under light steam, easy work for the engine, heading only a short train on a falling gradient. However, once returned to the Calder valley for Brighouse in the Halifax outskirts, the engine's voice can be heard as we restart from there. But the collar-work was still to come, the climb at 1:48 from the Calder valley at Greetland Junction up into the centre of Halifax. Steam was already blowing off, evidence that the fireman had prepared a good fire in readiness. At the site of Greetland station, the scene of countless hours spent watching trains as a schoolboy, I was looking out for the familiar signal-gantry, and sure enough the right-hand arm was up and shining green. After slowing for the sharp turnout, the engine was really opened out, accelerating over the River Calder, the Rochdale canal and Wakefield Road. As we climbed the bank, our speed fell away gradually. The parallel A.629 Salterhebble Hill rises steeply and crosses the line, but as the train neared the bridge, its speed had fallen to little more than walking-pace, excellent to hear the characteristic 'puff-clank' of the engine with its Walschaerts gear. The locomotive slogged up determinedly, then the lights of Dryclough Junction signal-cabin hove into view. The signalman was peering out at the train, his thoughts no doubt with the footplatemen. Outsiders do not realize that these jobs too had their stresses. Would the engine make it? And so on. But these 2-6-4s were very reliable. We clattered and squealed over the points onto the upper line and, with the controls evidently left unaltered, the train seemed to leap forward through the sandstone-cutting to Simmonds Lane and Holdsworth Bridge before shutting off steam to coast past the Shaw Syke goods-yards and Halifax West signal-cabin. We swept into the curved station and stopped with the familiar screech of brakes, to hear a porter call out, 'Halifax, 'alifax' in his warm Yorkshire voice. All this is different nowadays. I walked up the wooden stairs well pleased. It was only a short journey, but of great interest—and one that would be impossible next year.

Two Nights at Scout Green, Shap Incline, September 1964

The West Coast line north of Warrington, the left leg of *The Triangle*, was a splendid arena for the final flurry of steam-activity in the mid-1960s, where the freights ran mainly at night. The Princesses having been withdrawn, this was the swansong too of the remaining Duchesses until the end of the summer time-table of 1964. Fortunately, Billy Butlin, the holiday-camp magnate, had bought 46201 *Princess Elizabeth,* 46203 *Princess Margaret Rose* and 46229 *Duchess of Hamilton,* which he had cosmetically restored for display at his camps. These locomotives were thus rescued for posterity. In those last few weeks of the Duchesses, I spent two nights at Scout Green, that lonely signal-box in the middle of Shap bank, recording operations on tape and film. I also helped the busy signalman by pulling the levers. By then, the principal companions of the Duchesses were Britannia pacifics and Class Fives, but some Jubilees and Converted Patriots ran through too, some on parcels or freight. Many of the trains were still banked by the faithful Stanier/Fairburn 2-6-4 tanks, such as 42110 and coincidentally 42210, which had superseded the Derby 2-6-4 and weak 2-6-2 tanks. The second visit gave me Britannia 70040 *Clive of India* racing up the bank without assistance. Other trains that day, observed further up the bank near the Shap Wells down IB signal, were 45276 hauling a Manchester-Glasgow special, 9F 92206, lifting another heavy freight Hercules-like, and Britannia 70039 *Sir Christopher Wren* heading a long parcels-train, assisted by 2-6-4T 42251. The assisting-duties lasted until the closure of Tebay shed in 1966, when the powerful Type 4 BR/Sulzer diesel-electrics had taken over completely as train-engines. An unidentified Class Five was pulling an express strongly up the incline unaided, and, coming out on to the open moorland, he made a super silhouette, the exhaust-steam billowing up into the cool morning air. Other photographers have attempted this picture. I list the trains I saw on the two visits of September 1964.

Jubilee 45703 *Thunderer* on Warrington-Carlisle express, unassisted
    "   45629 *Straits Settlements* on down parcels, banker 2-6-4T 42110
42110 returning down the bank (signal-stand at Scout Green: apparently line occupied at Tebay)
Converted Patriot 45526 *Morecambe and Heysham* on freight, banker 42110
Duchess 46236 *City of Bradford* on short down-parcels, unassisted
Jubilee 45588 *Kashmir* on London express (signal stand at Scout Green; evidently banker 42110 was crossing to the shed at Tebay)
Duchess 46228 *Duchess of Rutland* on down-parcels, unassisted
    "   46243 *City of Lancaster*   "   "
Jubilee 45580 *Burma* on down-freight, banked by 42210

8F 2-8-0 48513 on down-freight, banked by 42110
Jubilee 45689 *Ajax*   "   "   4MT mogul 43035
Black Five 44901   "   "   "
   "   45120   "   "   "

Converted Patriot 45531 *Sir Frederick Harrison* on down-parcels, unassisted Black Five 45276 hauling a Manchester-Glasgow special Standard 2-10-0 9F 92206, lifting another heavy freight Britannia pacific 70039 *Sir Christopher Wren* heading a long parcels-train, assisted by 42251. After the end of the summer-timetable, the Duchesses were withdrawn from service and placed into store pending scrapping. The 2-6-4T 42110 I had noted at Halifax in 1950 when new.

An Unusual Railway Line: Staveley Ironworks, 18 August 1965

My destination was this amazing works in Derbyshire, on my way back from Worksop, Notts., where I had attended a job-interview. Staveley was an enormous, sprawling place: it could not properly be called a factory, since it comprised many establishments scattered over an extensive site—and what connected them all together and enabled the departments to work as one coherent whole was a railway line. But this is to underestimate it, for it was a series of lines and branches, with sidings at strategic points—an internal network. Built by the Midland Railway, it even had its own engine shed, Barrow Hill, coded 18D, and operated by their successors the LMS (from 1923) and BR (from 1948).

On entering the ungated site, I parked near a level crossing as one of the ancient tank engines, 0-6-0 1F 41734 of 1878 vintage, came puffing across with a rake of wagons. Quickly I made ready and took a recording. When the shunting brought the engine back to the crossing, the driver stopped to talk to me, culminating with an invitation onto the footplate. The shunter hopped on and off, coupling and uncoupling wagons, and we all had a good natter. Needless to say, it was fantastic—and that I was properly dressed for the occasion—in my new white raincoat.

I spent over an hour with them altogether, puffing up one line and down another, picking up and dropping off wagons as required. I was recording most of the way. We even passed two steam cranes at work, though they ran so quietly that they are barely audible on the tape. The high interest continued when we arrived on the shed, the end of my crew's shift, because they passed me on to colleagues who had a smaller locomotive, 0-4-0 tank 0F 41528, one of ten engines designed by Deeley in 1907 for the Midland Railway—so actually quite modern compared with the 1F 0-6-0 on which I had been riding. This engine carried out the same sort of routine, working its way back through the network, eventually dropping me off where I had started, beside my car. My ears were ringing with the banging and clanking, and once the train had puffed away, I could hear the silence. That hour seemed much longer: it was a journey back in time.

I had been led here by an article in *The Railway Magazine* describing this amazing works, which I felt at the time was an anachronism left over from the Victorian age. I am not aware of how efficient the works itself was, but as described in the magazine, certainly neither the railway network nor its operation had changed much since the original contract had been signed with the Midland Railway in 1866 to run for a hundred years. The locomotives and wagons had hardly changed either—though the contract did not specify that the railway would continue the operation with the same engines! But the LMS, like the other three railways, had hundreds of engines of this age—a few even older. Super for train-spotters to see these antiques, but what does it say about British industry? It was this contract which compelled BR, as the successor of the two preceding signatories, to continue the marshalling of wagons at the Staveley Ironworks in the same way, cocooning the old engines in their working-environment for well over a decade after most of their compatriots had gone to the scrapyard. This made the line a living museum.

But it all ended in 1966, only a year after my visit, so I was just in time. The staff were telling me about it, as they wondered what would become of the system—and of their jobs too, no doubt, but they loyally supported the old steam tank-engines: "They'll goo on fu' yers yet!" I agreed that a modern diesel-shunter would do no better job, besides incurring a huge capital outlay, so it was more cost-effective to keep the old engines. Luckily one of them has been preserved for us to see, LMS

1708. BR were glad to be rid of the commitment as they developed a dislike for shunting in general—after the fortune (of taxpayers' money) spent on new marshalling-yards, too. Peter Walker must have been the worst head of the railways ever. No doubt his attitude at the top contributed to the general decline in rail-borne traffic and its transfer to the road. We had to wait years before the enlightened industrialist Sir Peter Parker was appointed to that top job. He brought in designer Kenneth Green from Kenwood (kitchen tools) to produce an attractive, aerodynamic train, bearing the new slogan 'The Age of the Train' on its carriages. This, the 'HS.125 InterCity', would lift the railways out of the doldrums of media unpopularity, would influence foreign railways, launch an export business and become BR's biggest success. The Age of the Train became a reality, regaining some of the iconic appeal of former days. I had enjoyed another fascinating experience, and a moving one too, in both senses. It is odd, isn't it, that when I describe this outing for a job-interview, the importance of the day was a railway experience! (Actually, I did not get the job—which was unsuitable anyway.)

Another Railway Adventure: Earby to Barnoldswick

I spent the year 1965 chasing round my area to gather what wisps of steam I could. Now it was Saturday, 14 August 1965. I was home at Earby for the week-end and was now driving father along to the station, as we had read in the newspapers that the branch-line to Barnoldswick was to close in October. Sure enough, the poster at the station confirmed the sad news. I was well-prepared with camera and tape-recorder, and had come to watch the morning train leave the branch platform for its two-mile journey. However, once at the station, I decided to travel and booked a return-ticket, then stood with father beside the engine, BR 2-6-2 standard-tank 84015 that day, based on the LMS Ivatt design, and built only a decade earlier especially for this sort of service. My camera recorded the event, with the driver, fireman and guard leaning out of the cab.

We struck up a conversation and I must have made a favourable impression, for the driver asked me if I wanted to come up for a footplate-ride. Well, can a duck swim! I left my astonished father to drive home alone, while we clanked out on to the main line, accelerating our three-coach train past Sough Bridge to Barnoldswick Junction near Kelbrook. I felt the engine rode more smoothly than those I had travelled on earlier. We swung sharply to the right with wheel-flanges squealing on the guard-rails, as the fireman leaned out to take the ringless tablet from the signalman standing on the ballast of the V-junction. We rumbled over the points narrowing the two roads into the single-line branch, echoed over the iron road-bridge at Salterforth, then over the Leeds-and-Liverpool Canal girder-bridge, the only engineering-work of any consequence. Once over the watershed, we drifted down into the single-platform terminus at Barnoldswick. The last time I had seen it was the day of *The Great Marquess* special train two years earlier, but the occasion before that was the Rolls-Royce ten-coach special-train to the Farnborough Air-show in 1955. Now it was 1965 and almost the end for the line, after nearly a century.

The engine eased over the level-crossing into the coal yard, now much depleted. The reduced demand for house-coal following the Clean Air Act had greatly cut the coal-traffic, the mainstay of goods-trains, and the demise of the steam-engines in the cotton mills over the next few years would leave the coal-yard almost redundant. Having cleared the points, the engine reversed over the crossing and through the run-round loop, reversing again beyond the ground-frame to back on to the carriages. For some reason beyond my comprehension, these were now empty stock and so no bookings were accepted. Surely the train could have taken even one or two passengers; after all, some revenue is surely better than none. And, it struck me afterwards, the clerk at Earby had booked me a return-ticket without question. How was I to come back?

After an initial acceleration up to Rainhall Road bridge, the train coasted down to the junction, then, with another burst of energy, the hearty little engine roared along the last mile to Earby Station. As the train was running through to Skipton non-stop, it was double-pegged at Earby Station and over Earby crossing, but it had to stop to let me off. The signalman was staring out, wondering what they were up to, as there were no passengers to alight—officially. He continued staring as I stepped down—not from a carriage either, but from the footplate. I briefly took my leave of the cheery crew, who puffed off, figuratively into the sunset, and the branch closed soon afterwards. It was a super experience, though the tremendous banging swamped the locomotive sounds at the microphone, vitiating a quality recording, as I knew from experience.

The Barnoldswick terminus and coal yard have since been obliterated and the site landscaped, partly as the usual car-park and partly as a children's playground. Along Wellhouse Road from the site of the station, the eponymous cotton-mill has gone too like its contemporaries, only a whitewashed rear wall remaining as a reminder. After the Rainhall Road arch, the trackbed remains as far as the gap where the girder-bridge spanned the Leeds and Liverpool Canal. After another gap at Salterforth caused by the removal of the cast-iron underbridge, the embankments and cutting of the branch-line remain as far as the junction. But here too, the former main line from Skipton to Colne is in the same state, closed five years later, a sad ending to the Leeds and Bradford Railway's Colne Extension of 1848.

A Sequel on 21 August 1965

There was to be a surprising sequel to this short trip—and very soon, too. Time was running out for steam-train enthusiasts, with the mainline-steam already gone, apart from on 'The LMS Triangle.' This arena was to be steam's last fling in the three years remaining before the final excursions in 1968, described later. I therefore planned to travel to Carlisle and back on the following Saturday. The summer time-table Saturdays-Only Nottingham/Birmingham-Leeds-Glasgow 'Thames-Clyde relief-express' left Skipton in mid-morning, and father drove me there. I was smartly dressed in my white raincoat, newly washed by dear mama after the footplate episode at the Staveley Ironworks.

With tremendous pleasure, I watched the Jubilee run in, leaning into Skipton's curved platform 3. I had no prior knowledge of the motive-power provided for the train, but one of the much-loved Jubilees was always a treat—and this locomotive had a particular significance. While still newish in 1937, BR 45660 *Rooke* (then LMS 5660) had hauled a non-stop test-train from Bristol through Leeds to Glasgow and back on this very line, via The Long Drag. The aim of the LMS Executive had been to initiate a major acceleration of journey-times on the Midland Division using the new Jubilees. Rooke ran well and powerfully, described earlier, the dynamometer-car providing the information the management wanted, and the speeded-up timetables were introduced immediately. Now I was to have my own ride behind *Rooke*, my last steam-hauled trip over the line I knew so well.

The weather was poor, typically dull and overcast, but I watched the familiar scenes with pleasure, as *Rooke* slogged up The Long Drag from Settle Junction to Blea Moor. I took a few photographs nevertheless, one a dramatic offside shot of the engine across the curve at Dent station with the smoke blowing down in the drizzle. The fast run down the Eden Valley was as pleasurable as ever, but sadly most of the wayside stations were closed now with sidings and signals removed. From the booked stop at Appleby, the engine made a spirited restart, giving me an excellent recording as he accelerated strongly under the arch towards Long Marton and the Eden Gorge. I was glad to see the Long Meg mineral sidings near Lazonby still open and busy, as another anhydrite train was marshalled ready for its run to the ICI Widnes Works (later demerged by ICI as the United Sulphuric Acid Corporation).

In Carlisle, I spent the afternoon taking pictures and recordings of what was left, 70003 *John Bunyan* heading the down Perth, two Ivatt 2-6-2 tanks acting as carriage-pilots, 41217 and 41229, and Jubilee 45573 *Newfoundland* running through light-engine to Kingmoor sheds, as well as shots of some old artefacts still in use, such as the ex-LNWR water-crane and ground-signals at the Victoria Viaduct overbridge, the Glasgow end of the middle platform. Planning to return to Skipton by my old faithful the 6.50pm Glasgow-Leeds express, of course diesel-hauled for several years by now, at tea-time I was still on the middle platform when the 'CTAC Tours' train ran in from the north also bound for Leeds. The engine came off and 45573 *Newfoundland* came backing down to take the train, the loco I had seen after arriving in Carlisle that morning, home-depot Leeds Holbeck. The train facing me was a summer Saturdays-only special chartered by the CWS (the Co-operative), which consequently did not pick up passengers. It stopped here in Carlisle merely to change engine and crews. But when the relief crew appeared along the platform, who should it be but the driver and young fireman who had welcomed me on to their footplate at Earby the previous week. You can guess what happened next: it was now or never, so I screwed up courage and boldly asked the driver if I could accompany them, and showed him my return-ticket. He was cautious and not too keen, but let me up just before departure. It was to be the pinnacle of my total railway experience: a ride on one of my favourite Jubilees, and up the Settle-Carlisle line too.

Banging and clanking, 45573 *Newfoundland* rumbled to the left over the junctions from Carlisle Number 4 signal-box to Number 5 in order to gain the ex-LMS/LNE joint-line past London Road Junction to Petteril Bridge Junction, there to take the Midland line to Durranhill Junction and open country. This junction was a shadow of its size when I was in Carlisle with the army fifteen years before, with the sheds and the acres of sidings gone. Near the end of the steam era, our locomotive was not in top form either, leaking steam from glands, but we slogged up the long incline through Cumwhinton into the Eden Valley and on towards Armathwaite.

Through the fireman's hard work shovelling coal, the steam-pressure was maintained with a good, even fire, ready for the stiffer climb ahead, so that 45573 was blowing off at the safety-valves as we stood in Appleby. For detailed accounts of trains on the line, giving speeds and mileages, you can refer to back-numbers of *The Railway Magazine* or the former *Trains Illustrated*, where Cecil J. Allen, O.S. Nock *et al* have logged trips on the Settle-Carlisle mile-by-mile. Apart from the railway interest, this is very good for geography. Having passed Kirkby Stephen, where father and I had watched the Black Five shunting the previous year, *Newfoundland* embarked on the last ten—and steepest—miles of the climb, the really hard slog up 1:100 past Mallerstang to the summit at Ais Gill signal-box, the fireman working like a Trojan and his driver co-operating with him, trying to conserve steam, so that the speed fell gradually to about 30mph at the summit. Then the crew were over the worst, the engine accelerated to Garsdale and Dent, the fireman cleared the excess coal back into the tender and hosed down the footplate, before washing his hands and face for arrival at Skipton.

All this time, I had been privileged to sit on his seat on the right of the footplate looking ahead through his cab-glass; I shall never forget the sight of the line unfolding before me as we traversed the many curves, cuttings, viaducts and tunnels, but aware too of the driver on my left, his hand on the regulator, ready too for the brake as he stared ahead for the signals. No more firing was needed now as we flashed down steep Ribblesdale through Horton and Helwith Bridge. Expresses have exceeded 90mph here; we had no speedometer—but we were certainly 'shifting'. Without a stop in Ribblesdale at Hellifield, we rushed the short ascent over the low Otterburn ridge into Airedale, before coasting through the now-closed Bell Busk station, then Gargrave, still open though unstaffed. Trundling over the junctions into Skipton, I stared at the well-known landmarks, including the North Junction signal-box where father and I had been welcomed one dark evening years before.

Leaning out from the high footplate, one feels to be the King of the Road. This can be observed in the drivers' expressions, captured by the cameras of yesteryear all over the world: a confident, relaxed look, but alert; briefly, in command. These thoughts were flashing through my mind as we ran under the signal-gantry and swept triumphantly into Skipton's curved platform 2, where some passengers would be leaving for connections to Bradford, Earby, Barnoldswick and further points in Lancashire. A happy summer-crowd was there including photographers and enthusiasts, in a moment all left behind as the locomotive ran past to the head of the platform. All three of us stepped down from the footplate, a relief-crew took over, and we walked back to the barrier. Then, in the crowd, I spotted my parents, wearing amazed, incredulous expressions.

I had not realized what I looked like: you may imagine, after seventy miles of coal dust, soot and all those tunnels—and in my precious white raincoat too. The crew had washed, but I had not—too busy with camera and recorder, as well as absorbing the passing scene even to think about it. To some of the crowd, it was obvious I had just come off the engine; were they envious? And the passengers sitting at their tables looking out of the carriage-windows: did they think I was an inspector? It had been another splendid day out, a day to remember always. It is notable that my parents were there: after all, I was almost two hours earlier than my intended train; was it telepathy? No, they had come early to watch trains too; it ran in the family. They were astonished to hear about my latest exploit—and mother scolded me over my appearance. Later, before he retired, the driver invited me to afternoon-tea in his quiet bay-windowed house, where we talked 'railways'—and his allotment.

Coal around Wakefield, 28 September 1965

I paid several visits to collieries in this area with the aim of recording the trains pulling out with their loads bound for power-stations. Over the years, I had watched some of them slogging up the Calder Valley to Lancashire, so now I wanted to see them begin their journeys. One occasion was at the Allerton Bywater Colliery, where I arrived just in time to record 2-10-0 Austerity 90132 leaving with a brake-van—and he gave me a good whistle for the microphone. But the memorable part was when K1/4 62007, a 2-6-0, was making valiant attempts to bring his load out. I was standing on the grass bank at the neck of the sidings, unfortunately for the train-crew also the crest of an incline. This engine, after almost breasting the summit twice, incredibly had to roll his train back as far as possible for another attempt, a fast 'run at it'. The engine was most unsuitable for this sort of work—and running tender-first too; the task says something about British industry—particularly as this engine had been built by BR to a recent LNER design.

As mentioned, we had to glean information of isolated steam-workings from anyone we could, and one snippet I received was the place to spot one of the remaining ex-LNER (originally NER) 0-8-0s classed Q6. You have read how I saw three of these great beasts 'sleeping' in Neville Hill sheds, Leeds, a couple of years earlier, but now I wanted to record one. So on the way back from Leeds on 7 July 1966, I drove to a spot between Wakefield and Ardsley, where, after a long wait, I indeed did see one, but only light-engine—and he was coasting down the bank. It was 63387, apparently returning to the depot at Ardsley. I did however see and record him a little later on at Normanton sheds, only a year or so before most of the steam-workings would be dieselized. As I was recording a Q6 entering the yard, actually 63387 again, the driver, interested on seeing my microphone, offered to help. "If yer like, ah'll drive up t' yard wit' 'andbrake on, t' mek it louder?" It was certainly "yes" to this. The brake would, of course, necessitate a wide regulator and consequently a louder exhaust, especially on the rising gradient.

He did this, driving up the full length of the yard, with the result that I made a super recording of an engine that would soon follow his colleagues to the scrapyard. Drivers often obliged enthusiasts by blowing their whistles, but this offer was a real sporting gesture.

An Unusual GW Railway Enclave

At work, Derek came up with another idea, once again involving a drive to Wrexham in North Wales. We were to visit the steel-works at Brymbo, a strange little place up the hill, actually not the steel-works, but the adjacent railway-yards where the wagons were marshalled. Derek had heard that changes were due to take place, in particular the ending of steam-power in that area, so time was of the essence.

That Saturday, 22 June 1965, we started off at the engine-shed in Wrexham, Croes-Newydd, where we had called the previous year to see the London-special arrive in the station on its way to the Ffestiniog line. After recording '5600' class 0-6-2 tank 5667 shunting on the incline, we followed him to the shed and took pictures, mainly of pannier-tanks, 3789 and 1628 (the latter seen on our previous visit) on the ash-pits, plus others of the class, and another 0-6-2T. The railway up to Brymbo ran parallel with the road, giving us a splendid shot of '2800/2884' class 2-8-0 3817 descending with mineral empties. Then we continued up the gentle rise to this strange place called Brymbo.

Briefly, it was a village and steelworks on a hill in the middle of a valley. You can visualise how complex this rendered the railway, with tracks, junctions and inclines everywhere. First, we stopped to watch at East Crossing, then went up to Middle Crossing. Just above it, we found a splendid vantage-point on a wall facing the sidings, the arrival—and departure-point of the trains. West Crossing was less favourable, too far from the action. These junctions demonstrate the volume of traffic: incredibly, *three* big signal-boxes.

It was brilliantly sunny with no wind, and therefore splendid for recordings as well as snapshots, as the engines, mostly the 2-8-0s, puffed up the bank with their trains of coal and steel-scrap in-bound for the works, later braking the balancing empties rolling out and down the incline to Wrexham and the main line. Splendid recordings resulted from 2-8-0 3850 and pannier-tank 3789. On our way down, we paused at a level-crossing on one of the branches bringing limestone down from a quarry, flux for the smelting-furnaces and, luckily, after only a few minutes, pannier-tank 9630 coasted down with a rake of limestone-wagons.

Sadly, this is another factory long closed, way back around 1987. Begun and developed on the strength of local ore with coal nearby, it was too small to compete in the big-league scene of the seventies. Evidently, a company must be large nowadays, though some surveys of industry suggest that 'small is beautiful.' Whom does one believe? It seems to depend on the particular industry, though clearly one cannot have a *small* steelworks. This reflection reminds me of the Staveley Ironworks, and it does suggest that Brymbo was another of Britain's antiquated industries, where little had changed for generations.[2] But we had seen it and spent a really fascinating day. We had also been so smiled on by the gods of weather that we resembled returning holidaymakers.

Another Ffestiniog Special

Only three months later, on 18 September 1965, Derek and I drove again to the GWR, this time to Shrewsbury, but again to see another special full of Ffestiniog devotees. In a bay, we snapped a 'Manor' 4-6-0 awaiting his starting-signal to fall to 'off' and then the special came in. Again, it was *Pendennis Castle*, absolutely resplendent, looking as if he had just rolled out of the erecting-shop. A trip to the engine-shed, however, proved disappointing, revealing only a Standard light 4-6-0, Class 4MT 75053, at rest between trips, so I clicked the camera at old GWR/LMS Joint cast-iron signs for an additional record. On the way home, we stopped at Rossett, Flintshire, and saw this same engine 75053 race through on a semi-fast from Wrexham to Chester. But the message from this trip was that the sands of time were running out for steam-workings in Britain. It was also sadly our last trip out together, for Derek would shortly leave us to work in Rochdale, where he had

---

[2] My memoirs await publication, but I also explore this subject in my MPhil thesis 'Joseph Horsfall & Sons Ltd., Halifax, Cotton and Worsted Manufacturer, 1857 to 1950'. A copy is available for reference in the Central Library, Halifax.

secured a sales-position with Holroyd's, incidentally a competitor to David Brown in the world of gears and transmission-systems. Several of us went over to the couple's house-warming at Farnworth. In the new year, I would move to a fresh job too, helping to export David Brown Tractors from Meltham.

Leeds Central

In March 1967, *The Yorkshire Post* announced that Leeds Central station was to be closed, so I decided to go and take some pictures on the Saturday preceding the sad event. *Trains Illustrated* had informed me that junctions had been laid in to bring the trains from the Central approaches down to join those in the Leeds (City) Station, so that the closure of Central was expected. The new services began on 1 May 1967. All the same, it was a significant milestone, a large station opened at the very beginning of railways in the 1830s, suddenly disappearing—especially in that railway city with several locomotive-builders down at Hunslet. I parked in the small forecourt where John and I had left the Austin A.40 back in 1953 for our trip on *The Plant Centenarian*; today I walked in for a last look.

The closure was a good long-term investment, combining all the services in one station, City—and long overdue. You may recall reading my account of our family's traipsing along Wellington Street from one station to the other on our Scottish trips. It was an inconvenience that, in the context of road competition, people were no longer prepared to tolerate. Thus fewer were travelling by train: by the sixties, the car had really and truly taken the market for travel, not to mention long-distance coaches offering comparable journeys at half the cost, and coincidentally departing from that same street. Competition was the spur to modernization, and this particular piece was decades overdue, but unachievable earlier due to various factors, principally two different ownerships, the 1930s slump in trade and the 1939 war.

In the middle of a spring Saturday afternoon, the station was quiet and I was able to take some pictures of the interior, in dappled-sunlight under the glass roof. The station was clean and airy, a few passengers going to their trains for Bradford or Wakefield. The London trains had departed in the morning and it would be evening when they returned, though I did snap one early Bradford portion departing on the last leg of its journey and the 'Peak' diesel-electric locomotive, escaping light-engine afterwards. Other pictures were of light-engines, one inevitably a Black Five, late-model 44662, but they were favourites of mine anyway; a Craven diesel multiple-unit, and some parcel-vans. I ended my visit with pictures of the station-frontage and railway signs, one of them attached to the sooty retaining-wall in Wellington Street. That was it, the end for the Yorkshire terminus of the Kings Cross Line, but I think no one regretted it—no more hiking up Wellington Street carrying luggage when making connections. It was the end of an era which began with the Great Northern Railway's crack expresses of the nineteenth-century to King's Cross and the Lancashire and Yorkshire Railway's cross-country services to Halifax and Manchester, with local-services to Bradford Exchange. The *Yorkshire Evening Post* photographer did a splendid job, recording the last day of operations for posterity in a special issue of the paper and a photograph-album. Central faded away, and a few years later, having quit Yorkshire to teach in Kent, I saw the new GPO (later 'Royal Mail'/'Post Office') Sorting Office built on the site, close to the city-centre. So, at least, parcels were still being handled at Wellington Street. The new *Yorkshire Post* building was also constructed nearby, its clock-tower useful to me coming off the new M.1 Motorway.

A Last Look at Scout Green

I took father with me. It was 25 June 1966 a typical June day in Britain, unseasonably chilly and overcast. The railway matched the weather, uninspiring, with very few steam trains. It was near the end of steam-haulage on the line, but we did see one steam passenger-train, a Black Five on a Blackpool-Carlisle special. A bonus was that it was no ordinary Five either, but the unique example fitted with the outside Stephenson's link motion, 44767—quite a catch. This locomotive was one of the last to be built by the LMS in 1947 as 4767, and is now safe in preservation, on the North York Moors Railway.

Lambrigg Xing, 1966-67

Close to the end of steam, I made several forays to another lonely signal-box, *Lambrigg Xing*, the spelling of which I confirmed to you earlier. Lambrigg lay on the Grayrigg bank, only Mosedale Hall Crossing intervening before Grayrigg station. It was an interesting spot, the tiny cabin guarding an equally-tiny level-crossing, where, during several visits, the only vehicle I ever saw pass over it was a dustcart. The signal-box controlled its four signals: the down semaphore home was an upper-quadrant arm on the tall teak post still with its front ladder, a distinctive feature of LNWR signals. The up-home was a standard LMS upper-quadrant on a steel post, a colour-light distant each way and a crossover—without a ground-signal incidentally, but used only by engineers' trains. Extra interest was added by no less than two sets of intermediate signals to the south, at Peat Lane and Hay Fell, in the order they come when travelling north from Oxenholme, where the boxes had been removed for economy and colour-light signals substituted as down IBs to retain the short blocks on the incline. We watched their repeater-lights glow and buzz when we pulled the levers. The tiny cabin was therefore a busy little place, controlling three block-sections of line with their associated instruments. To allow the signalman more time to operate them, we pulled off the signals, and when I was out on the line, friend John continued. As for locomotives though, the variety had almost gone, including sadly, most of the big tank-engines, latterly leaving banking in the hands of Ivatt 4MTs 43029 and 43035, evidently posted from closed Tebay, as we had noted these two up at Scout Green in 1964. The train-engines comprised Britannias and Black Fives: 70017 *Arrow* swished downhill with a fitted van-train and 45170 puffed up the incline manfully unaided with his through-freight. The last Horwich moguls had gone for scrap earlier, the pacifics, Royal Scots and Patriots earlier still, while the few remaining Jubilees were stabled at Leeds Holbeck on the Midland line.

My last visit to Lambrigg in the steam-era, on 22 April 1967, was remarkable however for the variety of classes indeed still represented. 8F 2-8-0 48699 coasted through on an up fast freight, Standard Class 4MT 4-6-0 75026 ran up the incline light-engine, probably to assist on the Shap bank from closed Tebay, a further up-freight was headed by Class Five 44832 while colleague 44836 crossed with a northbound freight, banked by Fairburn 2-6-4T 42210. This engine, you will recall, had been a banker at Tebay for years, now transferred to Oxenholme for the last year of that shed's operations. This confirmed that at least a few of my favourite tank-engines were still with us. Sulzer type 4 (later Class 47) D.1835 roared up the bank with an express, headcode 1P18, a sign of things to come. A further down fitted-freight passed in the charge of another Black Five, 45236. I felt this to be a reasonable range of motive-power represented in the very last months of steam on BR.

The West Riding Railtour, August 1967

That summer saw a spate of special-trains. We were in the throes of a frantic 'end-of-steam' craze among railfans, almost a mania, resulting in specials all over the place. But I wanted to see this one, in particular the train slogging up the Greetland Bank into central Halifax. Perched on the wall opposite Dryclough Junction signal-box with camera and tape-recorder, I heard the LMS hooter as the train coasted through the closed Greetland Station, slowed for the sharp junction-turnout, then the crisp six-beat exhaust as the Jubilee was really opened out to blast up the 1-in-48 bank 'all-out.' It was 45562 *Alberta*, splendid in gleaming black with diagonal cabside yellow stripe—and sounded in fine form. With no banking-engine to assist him, he pulled powerfully off the incline past the cabin then, with controls apparently left unaltered, accelerated smartly through the sandstone cutting to Holdsworth Bridge box and Shaw Syke before shutting off steam before Halifax West box—a tremendous recording. It reminded me of the evening three years before when I had travelled on the late down London-portion to gain another excellent recording on the same stretch of line from the train itself, and of the dramatic scene not long before that when another Jubilee, 45593 *Kolhapur*, had restarted the Saturdays-only express for Carlisle at Settle. I saw these two engines several times that year, usually reserved for specials or the Saturdays-Only 'Thames-Clyde' relief-trains, patronized largely by railfans, described next. He was one of the last Jubilees to go to the scrapyard, later that year.

The SO expresses

In the meantime, I had made a few excursions closer to home for train recordings and photographs, to Settle, Gargrave and Skipton. One afternoon at Settle station was particularly rewarding. During the period 1965-68, the twilight of the steam-era, when 'the octopus' had withdrawn his tentacles to leave only *The LMS Triangle*, BR was running Saturdays-only expresses twice daily from Nottingham/Birmingham-Leeds-Carlisle as reliefs to the timetabled Peak-hauled 'Thames-Clyde Express.' Indeed, I had travelled from Skipton to Carlisle on the morning-train hauled by the famous Jubilee *Rooke* two years before. These SO trains had now become virtually enthusiasts' specials, crowded with fans of all ages holding cameras, movie-cameras (before the now-ubiquitous camcorders) and microphones, eager to get a look, or one last look, at the line hauled by steam.

My session with the camera at Settle was memorable that sunny summer afternoon, 26 August 1967, through the dramatic restart of the down relief afternoon-express and an introduction to Mr O.S. Nock, the well-known railway author, who had also come to see it. He had spent his working-life with the Westinghouse Railway & Signal Co Ltd at Chippenham, Wiltshire, and had just paid a return visit to nearby Giggleswick School, his *alma mater* of many years before. I complimented him on his splendid books and articles, written in his precise, rather racy style, telling him what intense pleasure they had given me over the years. His death was reported in the railway-press in November 1994.

Settle: Preparing for Action

The Thames-Clyde relief-express for Carlisle rolled in smoothly and stopped at the water-column. You may know the routine. The fireman climbs onto the tender carrying the pipe, which he inserts into the tank while the driver steps down to the water-valve. This was another moment when I felt the drama and excitement building, which I will attempt to share with you. The fireman is standing on top of the tender, watching the water-level, ready to heave out the heavy pipe when the tank overflows; his mate the driver is looking up with hand on stop-cock, ready to screw it shut. Their actions in the foreground heightened the tension against the background of gleaming 45593 Jubilee 4-6-0 *Kolhapur* blowing off steam with a roar and pushing a column of black smoke into the blue. We hardly noticed a Black Five drifting down with a through-freight. I call the scene 'Preparing for Action', because these men, proud of their calling, were preparing their locomotive for the stiff climb up north Ribblesdale to Blea Moor, 'The Long Drag', and wanted to make a good job of it. The tension in the air was palpable. Now the signal was pointing up, and then came their dramatic departure: a wave of the green flag and a blast on the LMS hooter, followed by a crisp exhaust that developed into the familiar six-beat rhythm; the carriages glided out of the platform, dum-dumming past with excited faces at the windows, the scene and its exhaust-sound fading as the train accelerated up and away towards Stainforth.

A later shot of the train saw *Kolhapur* again, happily now preserved. John and I snapped the train racing past the Ingber IB signals north of Gargrave, giving us only a glimpse of the train this time. At Skipton soon afterwards, I saw the morning train again, hauled by *Alberta*, with time to watch and appreciate the details from my vantage point on the Carleton Road bridge between the station and Engine Shed Lane.

Skipton Station and Sheds, 1966-67

On number 2 platform, I took a recording of Black Five 45014 restarting his Carnforth-Leeds semi-fast, an excellent spot for this, as the exhaust-sound continued audibly for half-a-mile over the curve to the branch-overbridge at Skipton South Junction. Britannia 70036 *Boadicea* came slinking through the goods-loop behind platform 4, another Black Five 45295 drifted through light-engine on the up main-line, followed by 8F 48399, a habitué of 55C (Farnley, Leeds) accelerating his fitted van-train after a signal-check at North Junction.

One summer Saturday that year, while waiting to see the morning SO express, I caught Black Five 44831 (shed 8F, Springs Branch,) crawling along the goods-loop with a class B freight at Skipton Station South Junction cabin and colleague 45273 running through the station with an up-parcels. He was soon followed by a further Five, 44879 of 55A

(Holbeck) on a through-goods. Opposite the cabin, just before the express was due, yet another Black Stanier, 44872, had taken refuge on the turntable. I had not seen an engine so far 'down the back' for years; the tracks were rusty and overgrown. Perhaps he was testing them for the signalman opposite. Then the SO express ran in carrying railfans, again with Jubilee 45562 *Alberta*, gleaming black in the sunshine after enthusiasts' polishing at Holbeck, the name on a red ground, a fashion of that time, and the yellow diagonal stripe on the cab prohibiting running 'under the wires' south of Crewe, betraying the last years of steam. As I was absorbing this dazzling scene, 44872 had sidled light-engine along the goods-loop to stand head-to-head with the Jubilee; perhaps he wanted a look or a word with the crew before drifting along the loop to the sheds. The crowds on the island-platform had a field-day with cameras and recorders. Then the Jubilee set off, steadily and majestically accelerating his train, the six-beat of the exhaust carried back on the breeze as the carriages glided away with their excited enthusiasts and masses of equipment.

North of the station, from Engine Shed Lane opposite the Skipton Station North Junction signalbox, I spent many hours taking further recordings and photographs in the last years of the shed's operation. On 23 April 1966, with a couple of schoolboys I had often met on the station, I even had a footplate-ride, although only up the shed-yard to the coaler and back to the turntable, but it was a pleasure. The engine was Standard 4MT light 4-6-0 75019 which I had just pictured with driver Donald Palmer oiling round. These locomotives had taken over from the long-serving Fowler 4Fs and became the last stud based at Skipton. Class Five 45054 turned on the table, an unidentified colleague passed on a down-freight and 9F 92086 eased his freight along the up-loop towards the signal-gantry before Skipton Station North junction. Inside the shed, beyond the breakdown train, was regular visitor 70036 *Boadicea*, hiding after a mishap. On calling in at Skipton station one evening in August, I was even invited up for a ride, on Class Five 44853 manoeuvring and crossing from platform 3 to the bay after bringing in a parcels. This engine had been a regular in the district from new as 4853 in 1944. It was the only occasion when I tried to place a shovelful of coal on the fire. Those who have tried this will appreciate the difficulty of attempting it on the shaking, swaying, footplate. Usually, most of the coal ends up on the floor. It was also the sole occasion when I drove a steam-engine, albeit only for a short distance. On my recording, the driver's voice can be clearly heard, telling me to "goo on!" and "Whoa!" Wonderful.

On 14 May 1966, an unidentified Black Five was accelerating his 'conflats' up towards the station after a signal-check at North Junction, while 0-6-0 shunter 47427, resident there for some years, was busy in the adjacent exchange-sidings. Standard 4 light 4-6-0 75049 and 8F 48157 were standing beside the turntable, and inside were two Class Fives. We never used to see such big engines on this shed; the usuals would include a 2P 4-4-0, perhaps a compound, 4F and 3F 0-6-0s, even the earlier 2F and 1F tank, of 1878 vintage. Later, on 26 May 1966, two locomotives only stood there, Class 4 mogul 43096 and Standard 4 light 4-6-0 75048. On my last visit, 4 March 1967, all I saw was Standard 4MT 75041 and colleague 75059 buffered-up to Ivatt 4MT 43098. It was almost the end. Significantly, a notice-board warned 'Watch That Smoke!' A decade earlier, the Clean Air Act had made a cleaner environment a government policy, rendering smoky, dirty, steam-locomotives unfashionable. Coal itself would soon follow. The writing was on the wall for steam, and that year, 1967, witnessed a wholesale closure at Skipton: the exchange sidings on both sides of the line, as well as the adjoining locomotive depot, leaving only a goods loop each way. To the south of the station, the local yard beside the Keighley Road (opposite Whinfield Hospital where mother was kept awake in the 1950s with all-night shunting) was also swept away, to become the site of a Tesco superstore. All were further signs of the shrinkage in the movement of goods by rail—and the anti-shunting policy already mentioned. The smaller quantities could be more profitably handled with road-feeders to fewer, centralized, depots, in this case the new marshalling-yard, Healey Mills at Horbury, near Wakefield, opened three years earlier.

In fact, the branch, running off the Carlisle line at North Junction (in MR/LMS days 'Engine Shed Junction'), to Earby, Barnoldswick and Colne—the 1848 Colne Extension of the Leeds & Bradford Railway—was also closed three years later, following the closure of the Barnoldswick-branch in August 1965, reducing further the traffic that used to congregate at Skipton. The network was disappearing, and without a network, you have no need of concentration-points. Much of the line's goods had consisted of coal, hauled to Earby, Barnoldswick and the East Lancashire towns, both for the cotton-mills and domestic grates. The burning of coal was diminishing, owing to two principal factors emanating from the Clean Air Acts: the conversion of the remaining mills to electric-drive, while domestic gas central-heating was coming into vogue. BR was planning to close everything north of Skipton—or even north of Leeds—to concentrate north-south traffic on the East coast main-line, but the Settle & Carlisle preservation-movement put paid to this, with the restoration of the Ribblehead viaduct, and so we still have the S&C and the branch to Carnforth.

The ending of steam on the railway in December 1967 also ended 'The Triangle', its final enclave. It left a strange hiatus until the 'last day' excursion, the so-called champagne-special—or 15-guinea-special—hauled by 70013 *Oliver Cromwell* on 11 August 1968, described below. It outflanked the RCTS 'end of steam' excursion on the previous Saturday, to the chagrin of its members who had booked tickets in order to ride the very last trip.

The Last Day of Steam on BR

The first episode of this little saga was the special organised by the West Riding branch of the RCTS to run on 4 August 1968 as the last steam-train on the line. As mentioned, my immediate boss in David Brown Tractors, Arthur Kinder the export manager, was a leading-light in this august body, and became its chairman, a post he held for over fifteen years. You will have read two of his anecdotes earlier. Well, of course AK was chuffed, to say the least, to be on this special on his beloved Settle-Carlisle line, and I heard all about it on arriving at Meltham Mills on the Monday morning. I do not have the motive-power details, but perhaps you do. Arthur told me about the dirty trick played by British Railways on the RCTS, by organising on 11 August 1968 their own "cosy, champagne-special", as AK dubbed it—all first-class, of course, at fifteen-guineas per seat, "for the hobnobs" retorted AK. The RCTS quite naturally resented this; they had organized *their* special train to run a week earlier, believing it to be the last steam passenger train on the line, or on *any* line—a typically devious BR trick, according to Arthur. Their intention was not revealed all those months earlier when the RCTS was chartering its train. But you will probably know of tricks employed by BR, including those to have a line closed.

The Prequel at Garsdale

Commitments at work had prevented us from watching the RCTS special, so we were determined to remedy this by seeing *the very last* steam excursion-train. John came over from Halifax to Earby on the Friday evening, in order to be ready for an early start on the great day, 11 August 1968. The train was due to arrive at Ais Gill, that lonely outpost on top of the Pennines, at 1pm, but we still went early—and just as well, as things turned out. Having decided to pause for old time's sake at Garsdale, the station before Ais Gill box, we had only just arrived there when the northbound signals swung up. Soon we heard the train approaching, a steam one too, but what could it be? No time to switch on the tape-recorder, nor to set the camera, before the train came, running fast.

It comprised simply two engines coupled together, Black Fives, racing like greyhounds to Carlisle ahead of the special. We deduced they were rostered for the return trip, an assumption that turned out to be correct. Strangely enough, their numbers were 44781 and 44871. The latter is now gleaming in preservation, but they were both gleaming that day, cleaned and polished largely by enthusiasts at their Lancashire depot. They raced through Garsdale station and flew around the curve to Moorcock; their white exhaust evaporated in the warm air, the signals fell back to danger and quiet reigned again. Had they really been there—or was it a dream?

Ais Gill

We drove along the narrow lane to Ais Gill and parked past the railway cottages. Other fans were already there, setting up sophisticated equipment, cameras on tripods, ciné-cameras, and tape-recorders with special wind-proof microphones. Coils of cable covered the fields. I had never seen so much expensive equipment gathered in one place. The newspapers reported that eventually the parked cars stretched for three miles. We walked down the sheep-track past the cottages to the overbridge a hundred yards north of the signal-box and waited. It was a gorgeous day, so fortunate when even summer weather up there can be a reminder of winter in milder climes. The time passed, and now there were people everywhere: the whole of Ais Gill Moor was dotted with colourful groups of people picnicking with their equipment—or rather, to quote their priorities correctly, they were there with their equipment and also picnicking. At the appointed hour, a chime-whistle up the line warned us of the approach of special 1T57. It coasted gently round the bend to stop at Ais Gill signal-box. The signals remained at danger for the photographic stop. Cameras sprouted everywhere; one bold spirit even climbed the up-home signal-post for a shot of the engine.

The locomotive was 70013 *Oliver Cromwell*, the last pacific to undergo heavy repairs in Crewe works, gleaming in Brunswick green. We took pictures from the bridge, before I scrambled down into the cutting below and switched on the tape-recorder. I was making an introduction to the recording and had just described the scene, " . . . as the end of the Ais Gill photographic stop nears," when the engine chimed and rolled forward puffing softly, continuing my recording perfectly. He made a dramatic sight, looming over me larger and larger, filling the arch of the bridge, then clanked by veiled in a cloud of smoke and steam. In a moment he was past, accelerating down the steep gradient towards Carlisle as the blue-grey and crimson carriages dum-dum, dum-dummed past us. The train shrank to toy-size in the mighty landscape of Wild Boar Fell as it disappeared towards Mallerstang. The dramatic moment had passed, but later the train would return non-stop. We would wait.

John and I scrambled through the tussocky grass along the boundary-wall of the line on the down side nearly as far as the warning up distant-signal. When this swung up, the squeak of its wire through the pulleys at our feet would alert us to the approach of an up train. We did see several and thank goodness I did take four snaps—against my will really, because they were diesels. But these pictures are well worth having now, the Class 45s having passed into history too as the diesel age moved on to new models, and even some of them have been preserved. In between, we munched mother's picnic.

The sun was sinking but it was still hot when we heard the whistles of the returning special. With memories of my footplate trip past this very spot only three years earlier, when the out-of-condition Jubilee *Newfoundland* had struggled to hold thirty miles per hour, I saw with astonishment that the returning express speeding towards us was travelling at twice that speed—which was only to be expected with double the normal motive-power. The two black engines were racing towards us, hooting excitedly at and for the bystanders—and probably because the drivers saw microphones held out to catch every sound; they often obliged us in this way. We managed two hasty photographs as well before the train was past in a flurry of smoke and dust, and that really was the end. We packed up and drove slowly home with many more impressions on our memory than we had recorded on film or tape, and realizing that we had just witnessed a milestone of history.

Steam working had officially ended on 31 December 1967, so that the specials of 4 and 11 August 1968 were bright stars in a diesel firmament. However, we were not aware that one more goods train had run, a stone-special three months previously on 31 May 1968. The Standard 4MT 4-6-0 75019, on which I had ridden at Skipton sheds, had hauled limestone-ballast from the Swinden Quarry on the Grassington Branch through Skipton to Appleby.

Woodham's Scrapyard and Preservation

Finally, a word on this unique place. The collapse of the coal-exporting trade during the 1950s had left a fan of sidings empty at Barry Docks, Glamorgan, South Wales, where Dai Woodham, an astute entrepreneur, had been recovering metals and old rope from ships. The British Railways 1955 modernization-plan had made thousands of steel four-wheeled coal-wagons redundant, no longer appropriate to the new, high-speed, clean-air, age. Dai contracted to scrap them at Barry. He followed this initiative by bidding for locomotive-tenders in 1959, and shortly these began to arrive from Swindon. They were followed by locomotives for scrapping, but it was the large and continual contracts for wagons that kept the yard busy, so that Woodhams actually scrapped very few locomotives.

The engines and tenders arriving from Swindon would, over the next eleven years, be joined by over 300 from other places. The lists reveal they represented mainly the former Great Western Railway and the Southern Railway, reflecting Barry's catchment-area of the south-west of England and Wales. This explains why only one ex-LNER engine, a B1 4-6-0, and few ex-LMS types arrived at the yard. The LMS engines comprised two 7F 2-8-0s, 53808/9, and a 4F 0-6-0, 44422, from the Somerset & Dorset Joint Railway at Bath Green Park, and two Jubilee 4-6-0s, 45690 *Leander* and 45699 *Galatea*, withdrawn from Bristol Bath Road shed in 1964, all great catches for the preservationists. The two 7F 2-8-0s have been restored. The author saw 53809 (LMS 13809) at Butterley on 30 June 1993; the 4F 44422 is restored and operating at Cheddleton, Staffordshire. Jubilee 5690 *Leander* is also restored, splendid in LMS red, and has hauled special excursions, while colleague *Galatea* is at Carnforth in the hands of West Coast Railways Ltd. Some of the motion to complete this restoration came from 45562 *Alberta*, the surplus parts then passed on to the LMS-Patriot Project, described below.

At first glance, Barry seems an unlikely spot for this activity, until one notices its docks, through which much of the scrap was exported, just as coal had been. A high proportion was shipped to Japan, some of it as dismantled, for example, wheel-sets and cylinders loaded straight into ships. I imagined them smelted into ingots and rolled into plate, to reappear in Britain in the form of Japanese cars. A 1960s cinema-newsreel poignantly depicted ex-GWR Pannier tank-engines being cut up by the man with the torch, representing the engines that were actually scrapped. However, Woodham Bros held their huge stock of engines in their yard more or less intact, the sole redeeming feature of the accelerated replacement of steam with diesel by British Railways after 1955.

Barry was the key to locomotive-preservation in Britain and was unique. How so many engines escaped the gas-axes for so long has been recounted by Dai Woodham, who resisted the temptation to cut up most of the hundreds of engines that were rusting in his yard, many for over twenty years. Rows and rows of steam-locomotives stood there forlornly among the weeds. He scrapped only a few, leaving the majority to linger on into the mid-1960s as the preservation-movement gathered pace, allowing time for the various railway-groups urgently to raise funds for the purchase of their heart's desire.

Earlier, during the 1960s, a few locomotives that had arrived intact were rescued through ardent fund-raising of the several thousand pounds needed for purchase, and were able to leave under their own steam. But now, the remainder had to await additional fund-raising for transport by heavy road-transporter such as Wynn's of Newport to the railway-centre where the restoration was to be put in hand. Most of these projects needed a great deal of work, often taking years to complete, and some are ongoing. One project, the unique pacific 71000 *Duke of Gloucester*, was declared impossible at first owing to the lack of so many key-parts, but 'the impossible' was eventually achieved, and this magnificent locomotive has hauled special trains.

Unfortunately, most of the older, and historically more valuable, engines had gone for scrap by the early 1960s. One was an 0-4-4 tank-engine, 58086 (MR/LMS 1423), the last representative of these branch-line locomotives, and stored at Bath Green Park, ex-S&DJR, in 1960. As time went on, preservationists strove to preserve every locomotive remaining in Woodham's yard. However, after seven years of scrapping only wagons, suddenly in 1980 two locomotives were cut up, ex-GWR 'Prairie' tank 4156 and 92085, a Standard 9F 2-10-0, in order to keep Woodham's men employed, owing to the lack of further wagons for scrapping. This fresh turn of events stirred the preservation-movement to react vigorously. Rail-enthusiast MP Robert Adley asked questions in parliament concerning the preservation of the remaining engines at Barry. Action followed: the 1975-formed ASLOA immediately set up the Barry Rescue Project, a scheme to rescue the last sixteen locomotives, which it purchased *en bloc*.[3] Therefore, most of the 213 restored engines were BR Standards, many of them identical types, leaving older classes unrepresented. In order to redress the imbalance,

---

[3] 'Sixteen and two-thirds', actually! Southern Railway S.15 30825 had lost its boiler to friends at Alresford, Hampshire, since this type of boiler was also fitted to their S.15s and therefore useful as a spare. Both of their S.15s, 506 and 499, came from Barry too.

schemes are afoot to construct locomotives to represent lost classes. One scheme has come to fruition, the A.1 pacific 60163 *Tornado*, completed in the Darlington works in 2009. Unfortunately, faults discovered in its welded firebox during routine maintenance during 2011 at the NRM caused withdrawal for its boiler/firebox to be returned for repair to the makers, Deutsche Bahn, at Meiningen, Germany.

Further projects are afoot, including the construction of a GWR Hawksworth-designed 1000 County-class 4-6-0 and an LMS Patriot 4-6-0, the original parallel-boilered version of 1930. This will plug 'the LMS-gap' in preservation and, as such, has been well received by the public, reflected in the funds raised so far. The LMS-Patriot Project Ltd. launched a competition in the railway press to choose a name for the new-build locomotive, which culminated in a vote by the public in favour of *The Unknown Warrior*, and the number 45551, replicating the last of the fifty-two engines. Because the Jubilee-class immediately followed the Patriots—as an 'improved taper-boiler version'—the next number (45552) was unavailable. The first Patriot was dismissed, 45500 *Patriot,* since it was officially a rebuilt LNW Claughton, but 5551 was a new LMS locomotive. Since *Patriot* was the LNWR, afterwards the LMS, memorial-engine, commemorating those who died during the Great War, the new-build engine will recall those lost in the second world war and in conflicts since. In this context, the LMS-Patriot Project directors approached the Royal British Legion, an organization that looks after ex-servicemen and their families. The Legion welcomed their association with the project, and gave its blessing for the RBL crest to surmount the name-plates. These have already been cast, and additional funds raised has enabled construction of the frames, by Corus Steel and the Boro' Foundry, Lyle, Worcs. They were delivered to Llangollen Works in March 2009, where the locomotive is to be assembled. This date is the official birth of *The Unknown Warrior.*

Woodham's Yard became a living legend as 'the graveyard of steam', one of the most important and influential aspects of British locomotive-preservation. It contributed around half of the preserved standard-gauge steam-locomotives in the country and in fact created the preservation boom of the 1970s-80s by retaining the ultimate stock of locomotives which could have been summarily scrapped. *The Barry Story* (paper) pictures the unique story, many photographs showing the engine-number and its preservation-society's name painted in white on the locomotive to reserve it. An eponymous book (published in 2010, GBP 6.95), shows Woodham's archive photographs. Both are available from the Urie Locomotive Society at Alresford, Hampshire, whom the author gratefully acknowledges for some of the above information and for permission to reproduce the photograph.

3944, an ex-MR 4F 0-6-0, awaits next duty beside Skipton shed turntable.

This 1936 Morris Commercial parcel-van awaits loading on the station-bridge, Halifax in 1946 (author).

Chapter 12

WHAT MIGHT HAVE BEEN

The Company Policy from 1948

The LMS will continue to enhance its services across the board, rather than concentrating on one high-speed prestige-line. The company foresees increased competition from the road, once the current austerity period is over and will take appropriate measures to compete. Policies have been formulated for the short, medium and long terms.

In the short term, steam-locomotives of five standard classes, including new construction, will be used to haul main-line traffic, allowing older, non-standard locomotives to be withdrawn. The five classes will comprise an improved 'Coronation' pacific, a 4-6-4, along with a 2-8-2 heavy-freight version using common parts, both already schemed out; the Class Five 4-6-0; the new freight 4F 2-6-0; and the 2-6-4 passenger-tank. For the medium-term, the company is continuing its development of the diesel-electric locomotive for express passenger-trains, based on the successful 10000/1. New carriages of the latest type will enable the last of the old stock to be replaced. The diesels are an interim plan, pending the finalization of a scheme to electrify the west coast from Lancaster to Carlisle with 25KVa overhead catenary. The Carlisle to Glasgow and the Euston to Lancaster/Manchester/Liverpool sections will follow. The high capital-cost of these schemes will be partially offset by the ending of investment in banking-engines and maintenance of their associated depots, no longer needed on the three inclines involved. The staff will be redeployed, avoiding redundancies. The new electric-trains will provide a faster service, their express diesels cascaded to the non-electrified lines, which will be upgraded to electric-haulage themselves when finance permits, for example, Derby-Birmingham-Bristol. Diesel multiple-units (DMUs) will operate the cross-country and branch-line services, based on the 1938 diesel-hydraulic three-car set 80000-2, designed for sets to be coupled together to form longer trains.

Shipping-services will be continued from the existing ports, with construction of new ships as required, including the replacement of wartime losses. The mechanization of facilities at the harbours will be extended and developed to handle the varied merchandise and luggage. Our hotel-business will be developed to cater for evolving needs, such as conferences and the launch of new products to meet a changing market.

Goods-depot mechanization will also be continued to reduce handling and to ensure a quicker turn-round of wagons, requiring fewer wagons altogether; older types will then be withdrawn. Additional specialist-wagons will be built as necessary to cater for customers' requirements, and private-siding facilities at their sites will be provided or developed. In this way, the company will encourage manufacturers to receive and send their goods by rail, for bulk-haulage in particular. Larger containers with their carrying-wagons will be introduced, particularly for transport to and from ports, where close liaison with other shipping-companies will be developed. With the aim of accelerating freight-movement, high-capacity bogey-wagons will be introduced, on the lines of those carrying coal to Harlesden power-station and on foreign railways. Faster, continuously-braked, freight-trains will need bogey-stock, rendering the traditional four-wheel wagon obsolete. A further initiative towards competing with the road will be to extend our joint bus-services, coupled with a move into coach-transit: an integrated transport-service is our goal.

Marshalling is being concentrated on regional depots (railheads), from which additional express freight-services will be run, offering overnight deliveries. Their road feeder-services will be updated. Publicity is being employed to advertise what we are offering, to show how this improved service will compete with road-transport. Marshalling-yards are being extended or constructed to serve this objective, in particular the overdue rationalization of facilities at key centres such as Carlisle. The marshalling will be carried out with the improved model of our diesel-electric shunter, the 7120-class. To encourage further business, through-carriages, joint-services and running-powers with other railways will be continued or extended where necessary, all giving through services across the country. Low-interest funding has been obtained under the government scheme. *LMS Magazine, Spring 1948*

Ivatt 2-6-0 power-class 4F 3002 departs from Bletchley, wcml, in 1947 (H.C. Casserley collection).

In early BR days, uBlack Five 45211 stands on Low Moor MPD (H.C. Casserley collection).

(Colour Rail permission, but ack to T.K. Chambers required).

'Pensioned-off' on a local-train, 4-4-0 Compound 41063 departs Earby for Skipton in 1959. One of the last six to survive, this engine was withdrawn in the following year, leaving the final two Compounds to be scrapped in 1961 (author).

LMS turbine-steamer *Queen Mary* (internet, copyright-free)

A new design of LMS high-capacity goods-wagon (RealPhotos/ H.C. Casserley collection)

'Turbomotive', the LMS experimental turbine-driven locomotive of 1935, leaving Liverpool for London (H.C. Casserley collection). No other railway in Britain built a turbine engine.

The LMS diesel-hydraulic experimental 3-car train 80000-2 of 1938 at Bletchley, is preparing for the run across country to Oxford (H.C. Casserley collection).

LMS experimental flat-bottomed rail, a pioneering-development of 1936 (National Rail Museum).

One of the experimental diesel shunters of the 1930s, Hunslet 7050, stands in the National Rail Museum (author).

In May 1964, rebuilt 'Jubilee' 45736 Phoenix & standard 'Jubilee' 45568 *Western Australia* on Leeds Holbeck MPD. They have brought football-fans from Manchester United over the Pennine Hills for a cup-game at Elland Road, the home of Leeds, a longtime First Division club, and will work back home after the match. *Phoenix* and neighbour *Comet* were rebuilt in 1942 in an attempt to cure persistent bad steaming of some Jubilees. The rebuilds were immediately a great success and formed the blueprint for the 'converted' Royal Scots (author).

Ivatt '2' 2-6-2 tank-engine 41241 in store on Skipton MPD in April 1966. Redundant upon the closure of the Barnoldswick branch, he stood here for ages 'awaiting instructions', after a working-life of only a decade or so. Such a fate awaited many of these small, modern engines constructed for secondary duties – uniquely by the LMS Railway. However, 41241 was saved for posterity and can be seen working on the nearby Keighley & Worth Valley Railway, Yorkshire, a preserved Midland Railway branch-line (author).

A result of the LMS pioneering-work on diesel-traction during the 1930s: 0-6-0 diesel-electric shunter 7114 works in the Durran Hill South Sidings, Carlisle (author).

Black Five 44745, one of the twenty fitted with Caprotti valve-gear, heading a Windermere express up to London through Burton-and-Holme, Lancashire, wcml (author).

The 'Ro-railer', the LMS experimental railbus which connected its hotel at Stratford-upon-Avon, Warwickshire, with the wcml at Blisworth, Northamptonshire. (H.C. Casserley collection).

Ex-LYR 0-6-0 saddle-tank 11484 is shunting Skipton South sidings in 1947 (author).

The LMS Sports Club for the Skipton staff retains its old name (author).

Ivatt 2-6-2 tank-engine 1205 on Hellifield MPD awaits a branch duty to Low Gill, wcml (author).

Newly-installed ash-tipping plant adjoining a new coaling-tower, examples of the LMS 1930s-modernizations (courtesy NRM/SSPL)

Near the end of his life in 1960, ex-LNW 0-8-0 'Super-D' coal-engine 49191 runs north over the water-pickup troughs south of Garstang, Lancashire, wcml (author).

LMS holiday poster of Morecambe & Heysham from the 1930s (National Rail Museum).

Stanier pacific 6201 *Princess Elizabeth*, as restored at Butterley, Derbyshire, 1993 (author).

A 4-4-0 of the CR '139' class, 54449, rather similar to a 'Dunalastair', runs from Motherwell MPD to the station for a duty in 1949.

The last of the Furness Railways' 3F 0-6-0 'Jumbo' goods-engines, 12499, on Upperby yard, Carlisle (author).

The prototype 'Deltic' running north on trial in 1956 is approaching Gargrave, Leeds-Carlisle line, a favourite route for testing (author).

During the locomotive-exchanges of 1948, several LMS engines worked on the other three railway networks. Here, Royal Scot class 46162 *Queen Victoria's Rifleman* is seen departing Paddington station, London, on a run to the West Country of Devon and Cornwall, before one including the dynamometer-car to measure performance.

Woodham's scrapyard at Barry, South Wales, stored many condemned engines, rusting for twenty years or more. Here two ex-LMS Stanier engines await their fate. (R. Hardingham, Chairman of the Urie Locomotive Society, Alresford, Hampshire).

On Motherwell MPD in March 1959, ex-CR 0-6-0s in store, probably condemned.

During the 'Plant Centenarian' tour of Doncaster Works, Yorkshire, in 1953, the author found 76026, a brand-new BR Standard '4' 2-6-0 standing outside the paint-shop (author).

Ex-CR 0-6-0 3F 'Jumbo' 57666 stands in store at Motherwell in March 1959, (author).

Two ex-CR 'Dunalastair' III 4-4-0s stand condemned on Motherwell MPD in 1959 (author).

On a sunny July afternoon in 1959, BR Standard pacific 70044 *Earl Haig* speeds *The Waverley* through Gargrave, Leeds-Carlisle line, destined for Edinburgh, (author).

Ex-CR 0-6-0 shunter 16285 works on the sidings of the Bridge Engineering Co. Ltd. at Motherwell, near Glasgow, Scotland, 1947 (author).

On 'the last day of steam' on 11 August 1968, Standard pacific 70013 *Oliver Cromwell* puffs away gently from the Ais Gill signal-box downhill to Carlisle with 1T57, the so-called '15 guinea champagne special' (author). This locomotive is preserved.

Driver Donald Palmer is oiling his Standard '4' light 4-6-0 75019 at Skipton in 1966. Several of these engines replaced the long-lived 4F 0-6-0s here. With his oiling finished, Donald gave the author a short ride along the depot (author).

After taking on water at Settle, Yorkshire in 1966, Leeds-Carlisle line, Jubilee 45593 *Kolhapur* awaits the 'right-away' before making a dramatic departure with the SO Nottingham-Glasgow 'Thames-Clyde relief-express' (author). This engine survives in preservation.

The LMS experimental Ivatt/English Electric diesel-electric express-locomotive departs St Pancras station, London, for its first run to Manchester (Getty images).